HOWARD KEEL

Howard Keel circa 1950. Photograph courtesy of Milton Moore, Jr.

HOWARD KEEL

A Bio-Bibliography

Bruce R. Leiby

Bio-Bibliographies in the Performing Arts, *Number 67*
James Robert Parish, Series Adviser

GREENWOOD PRESS
Westport, Connecticut • London

Library of Congress Cataloging-in-Publication Data

Leiby, Bruce R.
    Howard Keel : a bio-bibliography / Bruce R. Leiby.
       p.   cm.—(Bio-bibliographies in the performing arts, ISSN
  0892–5550 ; no. 67)
    Includes bibliographical references and index.
    ISBN 0–313–28456–3 (alk. paper)
    1. Keel, Howard, 1917– . 2. Keel, Howard, 1917– —
Bibliography. 3. Actors—United States—Biography. 4. Singers—
United States—Biography. I. Title. II. Series.
PN2287.K46L45 1995
792′.028′092—dc20
  [B]   95–22407

British Library Cataloguing in Publication Data is available.

Library of Congress Catalog Card Number: 95–22407
ISBN: 0–313–28456–3
ISSN: 0892–5550

First published in 1995

Greenwood Press, 88 Post Road West, Westport, CT 06881
An imprint of Greenwood Publishing Group, Inc.

Printed in the United States of America

The paper used in this book complies with the
Permanent Paper Standard issued by the National
Information Standards Organization (Z39.48–1984).

10 9 8 7 6 5 4 3 2 1

I would like to dedicate this book to Howard Keel and his family; to his many fans; to Mrs. Myra Chipman, who inspired me to write; to my beloved wife, Linda and our loving families; and last but not least to the memories of my mother, Margaret and my father-in-law, Clyde.

CONTENTS

Photographs follow page 146

PREFACE

Howard Keel possesses a magnificent, God-given bass voice
that has enabled him to rise out of a childhood of poverty
to become one of Hollywood's greatest musical stars. Many
felt he was better and less wooden than Nelson Eddy who was
popular in the 1930s and 1940s. He was even thought of as
the Clark Gable who could sing. His arrival in Hollywood
was late in comparison to such competitors as Gordon
MacRae, Mario Lanza, and Tony Martin and the change in MGM
leadership did not afford him the guidance his talent
deserved. By the late 1950s, the musical was on a decline
and the demand for the big-voiced singer was disappearing
thus making his tenure as a musical star a short one. He
proved himself a competent actor in dramatic roles in the
1960s and his talents have taken him into every media open
to a singer. At seventy-six, he is still going strong
because of a voice that has withstood the test-of-time and
because of the new-found popularity afforded him as Clayton
Farlow in the TV series "Dallas" (1981-1991). His "Dallas"
popularity has brought him TV and film appearances,
sold-out European concerts and a first-time recording
career. Author Doug McClelland puts things in perspective
when he says of Keel, "He and his delightful films have
brought us all a great deal of pleasure, and he has been
vastly underrated."
     The purpose of this book is to present for the first-
time the only in-depth study to be documented in one place
of the life and career of Howard Keel for the use of fans,
libraries, researchers, and students in such areas as film,
theatre, television, and music.
     Following a biography, which traces the life and career
of Mr. Keel from childhood to the present, is a chronology
that documents important events in his life and career by
year.
     Following the chronology is a separate chapter docu-
menting each of Mr. Keel's media credits. Each credit is
assigned a letter (S) Stage; (F) Filmography; (BC) Broadcast; (D) Discography; (SM) Sheet Music; (V) Videolog; (NC)
Night Clubs and Concerts followed by a number.
     The first media chapter documents, in chronological
order, each of Mr. Keel's Broadway, London, stock and

touring appearances on stage. For those productions with
no precise date available, the show is placed at the start
of the decade in which it was most likely performed. For
each show, the date, theatre and location, credits, cast and
character, synopsis, reviews and comments are given. For
musicals, songs and character, performing them are also
included.

A filmography comes next and is also listed in
chronological order. For each film, the production
company, date of release, whether it was filmed in black
and white or color, length, credits, cast and characters,
synopsis, songs and performers (for musicals), review,
additional review sources, and comments are provided.

The third chapter documents Mr. Keel's broadcast
credits both in the U.S. and Britain. The radio shows are
listed first followed by television, both of which are
arranged chronologically. For each entry, network, air
date, time, length, credits, casts, songs (where
applicable), comments, and a review (where available) are
given. Most shows from the mid-1960s were filmed in color.
Cross references are given for shows available on video or
recordings.

A discography follows documenting Mr. Keel's
recordings. The 45s are listed first followed by albums in
LP, cassette, and CD formats. Both sections are listed
alphabetically. The various sizes and versions are given
under the same entry. For each entry, label and number,
year, conductor, songs by side (for albums), and others
performing with Mr. Keel are given. Charted and gold
recordings are noted. For charted recordings, the date of
charting, length of charting, and highest position reached
are also noted. Cross references are given for film,
stage, broadcast, and concert recordings.

Following the discography is a chapter listing sheet
music associated with Mr. Keel. If the sheet music deals
with a film, the year of the film is given and not
necessarily the publication date. Each entry also provides
who is pictured on the cover and what company published it.

A videolog comes next and documents, alphabetically,
Mr. Keel's video releases as of this writing. The format
(VHS, Laserdisc, Beta, RCA CED) is given with releasing
company and date of release.

A chapter on Mr. Keel's night club and concert
appearances (U.S. and Europe) follows the videolog and is
listed chronologically providing place, date, others on the
bill, songs performed by Keel, and a review and comment.

An annotated bibliography is next and is broken down
into two parts. The first part documents newspaper and
magazine articles and the second books providing
information on Mr. Keel.

Song, title, and general indexes complete the book
reflecting the letter and number system and are arranged in
a letter-by-letter format.

There are eleven photographs included which illustrate
highlights from Mr. Keel's career.

Hopefully, the reader will find this work informative
and useful and for the researcher a good foundation is
provided on which to build further research.

The author welcomes any corrections or additions to be incorporated in any future editions of this work.

ACKNOWLEDGMENTS

A work of this kind could not have been possible without the help of others so I would like to express my thanks to the following for their invaluable assistance in the preparation of this book.

Series adviser James Robert Parish and editors Dr. George Butler and Desiree Bermani for their guidance and support.

Judith Kass for her research assistance in supplying articles and clippings.

The New York Public Library (Billy Rose Theatre Collection), Museum of the City of New York (Theatre Collection), the Philadelphia Free Library, the University of California, and the Media-Upper Providence Library for their assistance in finding articles, clippings and other research materials.

Milton Moore, Jr.; Howard and Ron Mandelbaum of Photofest; and The Harvard Theatre Collection (Jean T. Newlin, curator) for supplying the photographs used in this book.

Larry Billman, Margie Shultz, Laura Wagner, Joan M. Caro (Muny Theatre), Michael Pitts, Doug McClelland, Mrs. Pat Robinson (Founder of the International Friends of Gordon MacRae), and my wife, Linda for their various invaluable contributions.

HOWARD KEEL

1

BIOGRAPHY

The possessor of a natural, untrained, and God-given
talent, Howard Keel, with a magnificent bass voice,
developed into one of the best leading men in film
musicals during the 1950s. Although Nelson Eddy was popular
during the 1930s and 1940s, especially when teamed with
Jeanette MacDonald, Keel was considered by many to be better
than the more wooden Eddy. He possessed Douglas Fairbanks,
Jr.'s sophistication along with Clark Gable's masculinity.
Keel's arrival in Hollywood was late in coming in comparison
to that of his competitors. Although MGM was still churning
out the big-budget musical, the frequent change in leadership at MGM did not give his career the proper guidance it
deserved. Because of this, he would be assigned one good
picture then two bad ones. At this point, audiences would
go see the films of his competitors, Gordon MacRae, Mario
Lanza, and Tony Martin. In the late 1950s musicals began a
period of decline thus making his tenure as a musical star a
short one. By the end of the 1950s, the demand for the
big-voiced singer in film musicals had all but disappeared.
Rock and roll became popular and such stars as Elvis Presley
and the Beatles became prominent in musical pictures. Keel
would go on to make some low-budget dramas and westerns in
the 1960s, but nothing to equal his better musicals. His
career would continue to prosper when he turned his talents
to other media.
      Howard Clifford Keel never dreamed he would go from a
life of poverty in the coal-mining town of Gillespie,
Illinois, where he was born Harold Clifford Leek (Leek
reversed is Keel) on April 13, 1919, to stardom on stage,
screen, night clubs and concerts, television, and records.
      Life was not easy for young Howard, who was born of
English ancestry. His father, Homer, worked in the coal
mines. "My Pa was a coal miner at depression time when coal
miners didn't bring home the bacon," Keel would later re-
call, "They brought home a little flour and some lard."[1]
His mother, Grace, earned additional money by hanging paper
for $3 a day. "My mother worked hard as a cook, a maid,"
Keel said, "whatever she could get."[2] Keel was a shy,
skinny kid and was not very popular with the other boys.
When it came time to choose teams for a game of baseball,

he was picked last. Even when his older brother, Bill, (by
six years) and he would get into a fight, Bill would beat
him up. When the circus came to town, Howard's dad let him
bring a few friends. This made him a hero for the day.
However the next day, he would be treated the same as
before. Young Keel enjoyed going to the movies and shined
shoes to earn the money to buy the tickets.

In 1930, Howard's dad died tragically. Although Howard
Keel never really discussed the details, he once revealed
that Homer had become a heavy drinker and was responsible
for taking his own life. Grace would never remarry. The
eleven-year-old boy deeply felt the loss of his father.
He missed their fishing trips together as well as the
stories his dad would tell about his Navy days aboard the
flagship <u>Tennessee</u>. His father had a love of music. Howard
remembered, "He would come home, scrub and drive us boys
miles to hear any kind of a band concert. He tried to teach
me and my brother, Bill, to play valve trombones."[3]
Before the depression hit, the family purchased a player
piano, paying for it on time.

With the death of Howard's dad, Grace was forced to
take on more of the responsibilities for the support of her
family. In addition to paper hanging, she baked, washed
and ironed for the more affluent members of Gillespie. As
odd jobs were not easy to come by in the town of 3,000,
Grandma Osterkamp provided them with what food she could
spare from her struggling farm.

The family was not accepted socially, and young Howard
had no real friends. As a boy, he was rebellious and
unhappy. When Grace developed asthma, Howard went to the
relief office to get them rolled oats and gravy to eat.
Bill joined the Civilian Conservation Corp and moved away to
California.

Howard Keel went out for his high school football team
but ended up not playing. When the coach played everybody
on the team except him, he quit. "If he'd let me just walk
through and make one scrimmage," Keel once remarked, "I'd
have jumped through hoops for him."[4]

Bill kept after his mother and brother to join him in
California. Grace's doctor thought the move would be a
good one as the climate there might help her asthma. Grace
decided to take her doctor's advice, and in 1934 she sold
most of their things and fixed up their old car. At 5 a.m.,
she and her son left on their journey to California.
However, they only got as far as Fallbrook, near the
Palomar Mountains, when their car broke down. They planned
to stay there until they could afford to move on. Grace
got a job as a hotel cook while Howard entered his senior
year of high school. His new classmates were more
accepting of him. Because of this, Keel's self-confidence
grew. He played end on the football team, center on the
basketball team, and first base on the baseball team.

After graduation from high school, Howard took a job
weeding under and around orange trees for which he earned
three cents a tree. His dream, however, was medicine.
One day he took a bus to Glendale where he planned to enroll
in the community college. When some students laughed at
him, he felt self-conscious and fled, thus ending his

college plans.

Grace and Howard moved to Los Angeles and Keel stayed, temporarily, with his Uncle George while Grace worked a short time for a family. Although Uncle George was a hard worker, he only had a four-room house. With two children of his own, he finally asked his nephew to find a place of his own. In later years, he apologized to Howard who told his uncle "take it off your conscience, Uncle George. You did me a favor."[5]

Keel saw a help wanted sign in the window of the White Log Tavern advertising for a waiter and dishwasher. After passing the window several times, he finally got up the courage and went inside and applied for the job. His efforts were rewarded. Next, he took a room with a Mrs. Kellogg. Three months later, Howard was getting ready for a date when he got a call saying he was needed at work. When he explained he could not come in, he was told he had to work. Losing his temper, he quit. Mrs. Kellogg was understanding and did not press him for the rent. She would even save him left-overs to eat.

Keel's next job (in 1937) was a parking lot attendant behind a gas station located across the street from Paramount Studios. He parked the cars of such celebrities as Cary Grant and Fred MacMurray. Ironically, MacMurray and Keel would later star together in the 1951 film CALLAWAY WENT THATAWAY. His work day ran from 7 a.m. to 7 p.m. and he was paid $9 a week minus meals. He also paid $3.50 for his room.

Grace got a job at a UCLA sorority house and became well liked by the girls. Through her connections at the sorority, Grace helped Howard get a job at Douglas Aircraft in 1937. After only seven months with the company, he became a skinfitter (one who installs aluminum sheathing on an airplane). Because Keel worked too fast, he had a tendency to make mistakes and he ended up quitting out of frustration. The foreman tried in vain to reason with him about reconsidering his decision to resign. Because of his youth and stubbornness, he declined the foreman's advice. He went to North American (a competing aircraft company) to find a job. While at North American, he met and made friends with Art Shields and Walter Young. His friends persuaded Keel to sing "That Old Feeling" at the Casino Garden's Amateur Night. He did not make much of an impression, although Amy Parnell, a member of the Tommy Tucker Band, thought enough of his performance to suggest, "you shouldn't be singing popular stuff. Your voice is good enough for light opera."[6]

Keel went to a USC-UCLA football game with Art and Walter. Kenny Washington, a UCLA player, missed a touchdown on the one-yard line costing his team the game. The guys, feeling down about the loss, went back to Art and Walter's rooming house. After a few drinks, Howard loosened up and felt less self-conscious when his friends asked him to sing for their landlady, Mom Rider. She was impressed and felt that Howard should take lessons. She got Burt Roverie to give Keel a job at his Paris Inn as a singing waiter for $15 a week. Part of the deal for working at the inn was music lessons with a famous teacher,

although one was never assigned him because of his short
tenure on the job. Howard quit his job at North American
and went to work for Roverie. One day the head bus boy
yelled at him to speed things up. Keel got mad, threw
three pitchers of water on the floor, and walked out.

Howard returned to Douglas to ask for his old job back.
Keel then moved in with Mom Rider and his friends. Mom
Rider got him to enroll at Boyle Heights Music School where
each lesson cost twenty-five cents. When his voice became
hoarse trying to be heard over mixed voices, he walked out,
deciding that maybe singing was not for him after all.

Mom did not give up. She got him to sign up for night
classes with Ralph Bloom at Los Angeles High School. When
Bloom heard him sing "Without a Song," he was impressed.
Ironically, Howard had failed to make his high school glee
club. Bloom insisted on hard work and discipline, causing
Keel to take a dislike to his instructor. However, Bloom
recognized Keel's talent. When ex-singer Richard Lert and
actor-singer George Huston needed talent for the operas
they were staging, in English, for the American Music
Theatre at the Pasadena Auditorium, they went to Bloom.
Huston, who was founder and director of the theatre, acted
in films during the day in order to be able to put on the
operas at night. He was responsible for helping such
singers as George London, Norwood Smith, Brian Sullivan, and
John Raitt. He sent Keel over to audition. Howard won the
George Huston Scholarship and was permitted to watch the
rehearsals of MARTHA for which he would later study the part
of Plunkett. He would also appear in the productions of
THE BARBER OF SEVILLE, THE MYSTERY OF THE HOLY GRAIL, and
THE MARRIAGE OF FIGORO.

When the singer who was to sing Prophet in Handel's
SAUL AND DAVID left for Texas, Lert needed a replacement and
called Mom Rider asking for Keel. Howard agreed to fill
in but felt that nothing would come of the opportunity.
After learning the role in two days, he rehearsed for the
first time before the Pasadena Symphony which was conducted
by Lert himself. He enjoyed George London and Brian
Sullivan's performances. The two soloists would later
achieve fame in both concerts and opera. In 1939, Mom
Rider took Keel to a Lawrence Tibbett concert at the
Hollywood Bowl. It was at this concert, with a crowd of
12,000, that Howard became inspired by Tibbett. He
considered Tibbett and singer John Charles Thomas his
inspirations because of how they interpreted and phrased
songs.

Huston told Howard "you have a lot of talent....I
want nothing out of this but the pleasure of working with
you and trying to help."[7] Because Keel still did not
trust people, he was skeptical of Huston. But after Huston
began working with him and overlooking his moods, Howard
realized that Huston's word was good.

In 1943, Keel had a busy day working at Douglas,
taking lessons and understudying with Huston at Pasadena.
Huston, in his forties, would die in 1943 from overwork.

Douglas wanted Keel to travel around the country as
their sales representative as well as to entertain
employees of its customers and suppliers as part of a

public relations campaign. It was on one of these trips
that he met Rosemary Cooper during her appearance on stage
in Hollywood in KEN MURRAY'S BLACKOUTS OF 1941. They were
married in 1943. The marriage would be short-lived as she
would later divorce him in Las Vegas in October 1948.
Howard, who had started at age 17 as a mechanic in the
fuselage department and by the age of 20 had 350 men under
him, was on the way up and would now travel the United
States.

Howard was in San Francisco on business when he
decided to go to a movie. In the theatre's lobby was a
psychic who invited people to drop questions into a bowl.
Keel dropped in a question asking, "will I ever have a
career in music, and when will it start?" After the film,
the psychic called out the initials H.C.K. The psychic
told Keel that, "In the middle of 1944, you'll meet with
some success. All of a sudden, things will stop. In the
middle of 1945 you'll start again, and from there you'll go
right on."[8]

On the day of a concert, the Pasadena Civic Symphony's
featured singer took sick and Keel filled in for him. The
audience's response to his performance was so zealous it
got him thinking seriously about a professional singing
career. When Douglas offered him the position of
production supervisor at their Oklahoma City plant, he had
some serious thinking to do as to what direction to follow.
After serious thought, he decided that show business was the
choice for him.

In the middle of 1944, while in Moline, Mississippi,
Howard entered and won first prize at the Mississippi Valley
Festival Contest. Lawrence Tibbett was guest artist at the
contest. Tibbett was not in good voice because of problems
that had caused him to begin drinking heavily. Preceeding
Tibbett, Keel did an aria from MAGIC FLUTE and the "Song of
the Flea" from FAUST. When Tibbett was performing, he told
the audience that he had planned to do the "Song of the
Flea" but because Keel had done it so well he did not need
to perform it. Keel was impressed and after the contest
was introduced to Tibbett and they spoke for over an hour.
In August 1944, he won second prize at the Chicago Music
Festival. The judges chose him for his big, natural voice
rather than his musicianship. After that, he sang at a few
concerts in college towns or for women's clubs in Los
Angeles. One night, Keel got a call from his mother
informing him that his Uncle George had died suddenly that
day. The news came as a shock to him and he did not feel
much like singing for awhile.

Upon Keel's return to California in 1945, the National
Concert Agency asked him to audition for them. Lotte
Lehman, president of the agency, thought Howard should try
getting into films. Howard thought Lehman was crazy to make
such a suggestion and returned to Douglas at $45 a week.
The agency did not give up and called him again to let him
know that Oscar Hammerstein was waiting at the Beverly Hills
Hotel to hear him sing. It was Oscar's brother, Reggie, who
first brought Keel to Oscar's attention. Howard went to the
hotel where he sang "Oh What a Beautiful Morning" and a bass
aria from SIMEON BOCANEGRA for the famous lyricist.

Hammerstein was impressed and told Keel "we need replacements for the leads in OKLAHOMA! (1943) and CAROUSEL (1945).
I'd like you to go to New York and tryout."[9]   Unfortunately, Keel's draft board would not let him leave his
defense job until V-J day as he was needed for the war
effort.   Three months had gone by when Howard got a letter
from Oscar Hammerstein.   In the letter, Oscar told Keel that
he had spoken to the Theatre Guild about him and that an
audition had been arranged for him upon the guild's arrival
in Los Angeles.   Howard met with the guild and they liked
what they heard.   In 1945, the singer quit Douglas and went
to New York to see CAROUSEL and John Raitt.   Raitt was
planning a three week vacation in August 1945, and they
wanted Keel to fill in for him.   Howard purchased the record
and was on a rehearsal stage at 9:30 the following morning.
John Fearnly, one of Rodger and Hammerstein's directors,
took Howard to Westchester County and within four days had
taught Keel the lead.   The part called for a high baritone
which was lowered for Keel.   Within two and one half weeks,
Howard was on the Broadway stage at the St. James Theatre.
    When Raitt returned from vacation in September 1945,
Keel learned the role of Curly in OKLAHOMA! and spent his
time going back and forth playing both parts.   For nearly
two years CAROUSEL played across the street from OKLAHOMA!
Sometimes he would play Billy in CAROUSEL in the afternoon
and Curly in OKLAHOMA! at night.   "Looking back it seems
like a frightening baptism for a young singer," Keel
recollected, "but I wouldn't have missed the experience for
the world."[10]   Howard brought Grace to New York to see
the shows.   He earned $250 a week while playing in CAROUSEL.
While doing the show, he got bronchitis and had trouble
singing over the orchestra.   He asked Joseph Liban, the
show's conductor, to play a little softer.   Instead, Liban
increased the volume.   Keel nearly got into a fight with the
conductor but fortunately some stage hands intervened.   Not
long afterwards, he switched over to OKLAHOMA! permanently.
    In 1947, Howard opened in the London production of
OKLAHOMA!   After the show, he did 14 encores.   After one of
the performances, Queen Mary came back stage to express how
much she had enjoyed both him and the show.   "It was the
smash of the country," Keel later stated.   "I was the toast
of the West End.   And English people are very faithful
fans.   Once they like you, they don't forget."[11]   During
the run of the show, he was entertained by Sir Laurence
Olivier (Keel was a fan of Olivier) and asked to tea by
Noel Coward.   While in the 1947 production of OKLAHOMA!, he
met dancer Helen Anderson (who was of Swedish descent) and
they became friends.   When she left for the United States
for a brief vacation with her family in Florida before
beginning a U.S. tour in OKLAHOMA!, Keel began to miss her.
After two weeks, he realized he was in love and called
Helen and proposed to her over the phone.   However,
commitments kept them apart until finally they were married
at the Mission Inn in Riverside, California on January 3,
1949.
    After doing the show for eighteen months, Howard began
to feel his performance as Curly was getting stale and felt
he needed a vacation.   The producers refused his request

for time off because they believed he was going to use that
time to make a screen test. When his Theatre Guild contract
ran out in 1947, he quit the show and went to California.
While there, he made a screen test in CROSSFIRE (1947) for
Warner Bros. The studio chose not to pick up his option as
they already had Gordon MacRae and Dennis Morgan under
contract. He also tested for Paramount producer Hal Wallis
but received no offers. Keel, who felt that the tests had
gone poorly, returned to London to look for work.

Anthony Havelock-Allen was the producer of the film
SMALL VOICE (1948) starring his wife, Valerie Hobson. The
previous year, 1947, the couple had seen Howard in
OKLAHOMA! and noted a quality in him they felt would make
him right for a part in their upcoming movie. The part was
offered him and he accepted. Keel went through a lot of red
tape in order to work in the film. He needed approval from
the Ministry of Labor, those who dealt with foreign
exchange, and the British Equity who granted working permits
to work in England. In the film, Howard played an escapee
from a military prison. The film was released in the United
States in 1948, under the title HIDEOUT and Keel was billed
under the name of Harold Keel.

After the filming of THE SMALL VOICE was completed,
Howard returned to New York. Because of his success in
London in both theatre and film, Keel felt that agents would
be readily willing to hire him. However, he soon learned
that he still had to audition for parts, which he felt was
degrading. He turned down a part in the play INSIDE U.S.A.
(1948) which became a hit. Rodgers and Hammerstein wanted
Howard for a dual purpose--to play Cable in SOUTH PACIFIC
(1949) as well as an understudy for the show's lead, Ezio
Pinza. However, in 1949, MGM was planning to film a musical
based on the characters in ANNIE OAKLEY (1935) entitled
ANNIE GET YOUR GUN, for which they paid $650,000 for the
rights.

MGM was formed in 1924, when Metro Pictures joined
forces with Goldwyn Pictures and Louis B. Mayer
Productions. MGM developed into one of the biggest and
finest of the Hollywood studios. It distributed over 1,000
of the best films in Hollywood history. The studio became
home to many of Hollywood's greatest stars. Before the
star-contract system collapsed, sometime about 1959, MGM
got much coverage in the movie magazines, influenced how
the world dressed, and what makeup and hair styles were
worn by the world's moviegoers. It was also responsible
for a lot of war bond sales.

Arthur Freed was looking for someone to play the Frank
Butler role. John Raitt was tested but Freed decided not to
use him because despite his beautiful delivery of the songs,
he was not photogenic enough and his personality and
physical appearance did not come across strongly enough.
Warner Bros. casting directors told talent scout Al
Trascony, and casting director Bill Gray about Keel's screen
test in CROSSFIRE. Warner Bros. loaned Gray a copy and he
showed it to Freed. Although Freed did not think it was
good, he still did not rule Keel out. He obtained and
viewed a print of SMALL VOICE. But it was only after
receiving a recommendation from Oscar Hammerstein that he

told Bill Gray he wanted Howard for the part that would earn him $850 a week.

The producers felt that Ethel Merman and Mary Martin, who had played Annie on Broadway, were too old and would not be a big enough box office draw to be considered for the film.   They hired Judy Garland to play Annie Oakley.   Judy had wanted to do the role and did not object when Busby Berkeley was assigned as director, although they had proved incompatible during the filming of FOR ME AND MY GAL (1942) and GIRL CRAZY (1943).   When Keel came on the set, he was nervous but did not feel so bad after he learned that Judy Garland was more nervous than he was.   Judy and Howard rehearsed several scenes and recorded the songs which would be released years later as a collector's album.   The excitement Garland created while singing was lacking.   Keel was a fan of Garland's and thought very highly of her.

Troubles soon beset the picture.   On April 4, 1949, a horse fell on Keel's right ankle and broke it.   His ankle was put into a cast and he was unable to walk which caused director Busby Berkeley to film around him for six weeks. Freed felt that Berkeley's concept of the film was all wrong and let him go on May 3, 1949, bringing in Charles Walters to replace him.   Judy Garland began calling in sick frequently and would request to leave early.   As time went on, she felt insecure about playing a character as opposed to herself.   She was also going through a period of emotional and drug-addiction problems.   So on May 10, 1949, she was released from the movie.   "Judy would have been wonderful in the part," said Keel.   "She would have been incredible."[12]

MGM studio head Louis B. Mayer did not think a lot of Garland until Denna Durbin went to Universal and he needed someone to take Shirley Temple's place in THE WIZARD OF OZ (1939).   It was Ida Koveman, Mayer's secretary, who through Garland's mother, Ethel Gumm, brought Judy to Mayer's attention.   Mayer soon realized he had gold in Garland and kept her constantly busy.   The studio gave Garland pep pills to keep her going for long hours of shooting and then needed to give her sleeping pills to bring her down so she could get some sleep.   When she developed emotional and psychological problems, the studio labeled her a prima donna and would not release her for medical help because of contracts and the millions at stake at the box office.

A replacement for Garland was needed.   The studio considered Judy Canova, Doris Day, and Betty Garrett. After Freed viewed Paramount's THE PERILS OF PAULINE starring Betty Hutton, a $150,000 deal was made in which she was loaned to MGM.   Hutton, however, felt ill-at-ease at first being the outsider at the studio and replacing one of MGM's biggest stars—Garland.   However, she soon gained the respect of her colleagues.   When Charles Walters's contract expired in August of 1949, George Sidney persuaded Louis B. Mayer and Dore Schary to let him take over as director. Walters learned of the change after reading about it in Hedda Hopper's column in The Los Angeles Times.   Frank Morgan (Buffalo Bill) died of a heart attack on September 18, 1949, and was replaced by Louis Calhern.   Geraldine Wall no longer was available for her role as Dolly Tate and the

studio brought in Benay Venuta to take her place. Six
months had passed since the shooting had begun and the
children hired for the film had grown up and needed to be
recast.

During ANNIE GET YOUR GUN'S problem period in 1949,
Keel went to the Santa Monica Gun Club where he learned to
shoot. He would do his own shooting in the film. Also,
during this time, he was considered for the role Robert
Young played in THAT FORSYTE WOMAN (1949) and David Brian's
part in INTRUDER IN THE DUST (1949) but Mayer insisted
Keel's first movie role would be in a musical.

ANNIE GET YOUR GUN was finally released in April 1950
and opened to favorable reviews. It would become one of the
year's top moneymakers and would win an Academy Award for
best scoring of a musical. Moviegoers particularly liked
Keel's songs, especially those he sang with Hutton. Howard
did not find working with Hutton especially enjoyable.

When MGM's publicity department spoke to Hedda Hopper,
one of them got his name wrong and it appeared in print as
Howard. Keel liked it and changed it from his real name
Harold.

Helen's dancing career ended when the couple were
blessed, on January 14, 1950, with the birth of a daughter,
Kaija Liane. Howard felt that at least one parent should
stay at home with the children. They rented a home in
Brentwood until they could find the ranch-style home they
wanted. Keel was careful with his money, probably because
of the hard times he had experienced while growing up.
Howard was married for three years before he met Helen's
relatives in Florida.

While at MGM, Keel reported daily to the studio's
vocal coach, Leon Ceppan, for three hour sessions. He
developed a range of low D to F sharp. His natural voice
was bass but for films a high baritone was needed. The key
was lowered to enable him to handle the baritone range.

His next motion picture was the 1950 MGM production of
PAGAN LOVE SONG co-starring Esther Williams. In the film,
Howard goes to Tahiti to take over a plantation left him by
his uncle. In the process, he falls for Williams. Williams
refused to make the film if Stanley Donen directed because
of a statement he had made declaring that Williams possessed
no talent. Unable to reconcile the situation, Freed brought
in choreographer Robert Alton to direct. The movie was to
be shot in Tahiti but travel proved too complicated so the
location was changed to the Hawaiian Island of Kauai.
However, the time chosen for filming turned out to be the
island's rainy season. A special bicycle had to be built
for "The Singing in the Sun" sequence to accommodate Keel's
long legs and a broken arm that had to be camouflaged by a
towel. Alton, fearing the ire of Freed and the studio
brass, pushed ahead in order to keep on schedule despite the
heavy wind during the filming of a love scene between
Williams and Keel in which her hair was blown. In his rush
to keep to the schedule, Alton also neglected to realize
Miss Williams was not wearing her contacts thus not focusing
on Keel but past his face.

During breaks in the filming, Keel would go golfing.
He hired two young boys as caddies. One was John, and the

other Abraham Nelson Lopez. Nelson was the smaller of the
two and had trouble carrying the golf bags. He tried to
play hookie from school so he could run errands on the set
for Howard. Keel made sure he went to school. When
filming was over, both boys begged Howard to take them with
him back to the mainland. The film was released in December
of 1950. Co-star Esther Williams would later give Keel's
daughter, Kaija, swimming lessons.

Esther Williams was MGM's answer to Twentieth Century-
Fox's Sonja Henie. She made $80,000,000 for the studio in
the 18 films she did for them. She was not an actress or
singer but her swimming routines were as interesting as
Astaire's dances and brought the fans to the theatre. To
keep the public interested in her films, MGM used color and
beautiful locales as well as guest performers.

Keel's first picture of 1951 was MGM's THREE GUYS NAMED
MIKE which co-starred Jane Wyman, Van Johnson, and Barry
Sullivan. In the film, which was released in March 1951,
he played a pilot who tries to beat out the competition
for the affections of stewardess Wyman. While making the
movie, Howard received a 3x5 foot post card expressing
messages of good luck from the folks in Gillespie, Illinois.

Except for Frank Sinatra, Van Johnson was the only
star during World War II to get female fans to the
theatres. In 1945, he was the second top money maker and
ranked third in 1946. He would receive 8,000 letters weekly
from female fans requesting he not marry. He was a fan
of other stars himself. His tenure with MGM ran from
1942-1956. He never requested a change in his contract or
a raise, just that his contract be renewed. When he left
MGM, he was making a weekly salary of $8,000.

Howard's next project, in 1951, was the motion picture
SHOW BOAT. Producer Arthur Freed and Roger Edens (unbilled
associate producer) wanted to make a few changes in Oscar
Hammerstein's book so that Magnolia and Gaylord would be
reunited sooner and as a younger couple rather than twenty
years later and elderly as had been done in Hammerstein's
book. Also, they wanted to enlarge Julie's part. Freed
wanted Judy Garland to play Julie, but because of her
previous problems, the studio released her from her
contract. The studio's new boss, Dore Schary, suggested
Dinah Shore for the part, but Freed was able to persuade her
not to take the role by telling her the part was that of a
whore. He gave the role to Ava Gardner. Gardner had her
mind set on singing her own songs and asked to be tested.
Frank Sinatra used his influence with arranger-conductor
Axel Stordahl and Manny Sacks (an executive at Columbia
Records) to get Ava her chance to prove she could handle
her own songs. During her tryout, she sang to a recording
by Lena Horne. Roger Edens tried in vain to help Ava
prepare for her audition. Because the studio was not
thrilled by Miss Gardner's performance, they tested Marni
Nixon, Anita Ellis, Carol Richards, and Annette Warren as
possible choices to dub Gardner's songs. It was decided
to use Warren as she came closest to Ava's speaking voice.
When Gardner learned the studio had still decided to dub
her, she walked off the picture and it took Sinatra and
Louis B. Mayer three days to convince her to return to the

film. William Warfield was discovered after a review of
his Town Hall recital was seen in <u>Time</u>. His rendition of
"Ol' Man River" (one of Keel's favorite songs) was
magnificent. For his leads, Freed chose Kathryn Grayson and
Howard Keel. Edna Ferber had Joe E. Brown in mind when she
created the character of Captain Andy.

Freed had originally thought of shooting SHOW BOAT on
location on the Mississippi River, but because the costs
were too high, he was forced to use the Tarzan Jungle Lake
on the back lot. The film had its problems. One was
keeping the fog consistent as it was the time of year in
which fog drifted in from the Pacific. Another was when
the show boat (called the <u>Cotton Blossom</u>) caught fire and
nearly burned entirely. After all the expense of repairing
the <u>Cotton Blossom</u>, (except for Keel's film DESPERATE
SEARCH) it was left to rot on the lake. Roger Edens temporarily took over for ailing director George Sidney.

While filming SHOW BOAT, Howard Keel and Kathryn
Grayson became friends. "To know Katie was to love her,"
Keel said. "She was a gorgeous, delightful creature."[13]
He also felt that Ava Gardner was fun to work with. MGM
did not permit drinking alcohol at the studio. If anyone
broke the rule, they faced Mayer's ire and the possibility
of suspension. At the end of shooting for the day,
Grayson, Keel, and Gardner would sneak tequilas into their
dressing rooms and end up drunk. No one seemed to find
out or notice they had strayed from the clean-cut image MGM
tried to create for their stars. Howard's Grandma Osterkamp
and his mother, Grace, visited the set during production.
After the film was completed, the cast celebrated at
Mocambo's. SHOW BOAT was one of the top moneymakers that
year and was nominated for Academy Awards for best scoring
of a musical picture and for cinematography. Howard would
later appear in a stock version of SHOW BOAT.

Kathryn Grayson had desired a career in opera
especially at the Metropolitan Opera. Her dream never
materialized. She was popular with the public but MGM kept
her in light, less important films and never advertised her
as the lot's big female singing star. Her professional
goals were never quite fulfilled. When her best pictures
SHOW BOAT(1951) and KISS ME, KATE (1953) came about, her
film career and movie musicals were on the decline.

Ava Gardner was an MGM contract star of distinction
and beauty, perhaps the last (with the possible exception
of Grace Kelly). Ava never liked Mayer but felt before he
lost control of MGM you knew where you stood. With him gone
and Dore Schary in control, she felt MGM was going downhill.

Mayer's style of leadership was free-wheeling and he
allowed the budget for films to be high (often they went
over budget) as long as money was made on the film. He
cared about his stars. For many years, he made more money
than any other American executive. When films began to
fail, MGM began having problems. Mayer was not able to
come up with a remedy to fix things. They considered
bringing in Dore Schary to help solve the problems.

Dore Schary, who had left MGM, went to RKO where he
planned to stay until Howard Hughes bought out RKO in
1948. Schary was unhappy no longer controlling the

reigns, and decided to accept an offer to go back to MGM
on July 1, 1948, as production chief. Officially Schary was
responsible to Mayer who now became honorary Vice-President
of the studio. Mayer and Schary were constantly in
conflict, primarily over a film's subject matter. Mayer
liked small-town America stories whereas Schary preferred
films with realism and a message. Schary was also more
concerned with the content of the pictures than with the
stars. Schary took his problems over Mayer's head to studio
chief Nicholas Schenck who usually sided with Schary.
        Schary brought a temporary prosperity to MGM, at least
until TV began to draw audiences from film theatres. In
1951, Schenck decided to let some of the key executives have
stock options. Mayer made a list of his idea of who should
receive the options and for how much. Schenck did not pay
much attention to Mayer's list. Without consulting Mayer,
Schenck gave Schary 100,000 shares. Mayer was angered and
gave Schenck an ultimatum either Schary go or he would.
Schenck used this opportunity to force Mayer out by telling
him Schary was needed if MGM was to flourish. Mayer had no
choice but to resign on June 22, 1951. While Schary ran the
studio, it was felt by many that the players and technicians
began to stagnate. He ruled with a heavy hand and many of
his message pictures lacked entertainment value and
inspiration.
        Howard Keel was voted Television & Screen Guide's 1951
eighth-place male star and fourth-place newcomer. He was
named number-one star of tomorrow by Motion Picture Herald's
annual exhibitor's poll. Runners up included: Thelma
Ritter, Shelly Winters, Frank Lovejoy, Debra Paget, David
Brian, Piper Laurie, Gene Nelson, Dale Robertson, and
Corinne Calivet. Keel was considered, by some, the Clark
Gable who could sing. At one time during his film career
there had been talk of teaming him with Gable in TWO IF BY
SEA.
        In 1951, Keel went to U.S. Air Force bases during the
Korean War to entertain soldiers. The 1951 Warner Bros.
film STARLIFT, starring Gordon MacRae, Doris Day, Gene
Nelson, and most of the studio's contract players, was based
on this idea. He also made a rare radio appearance on
"Hedda Hopper" (NBC, 1951) along with Tony Curtis and Jan
Sterling.
        TEXAS CARNIVAL was released by MGM in 1951 and
co-starred Esther Williams, Red Skelton, and Ann Miller.
Keel also did the narration (as Gable's son) for ACROSS THE
WIDE MISSOURI, also released that year. Gable's fourth wife,
Sylvia, joined him on location in rugged Colorado and tried
to make things cozy but never really fit in.
        MGM released CALLAWAY WENT THATAWAY in 1951. Howard
played a dual role. The first one was an old western star
who became a drunk and whose popularity grows when his
films are released for television. The second was a look-a
-like who is hired to assume the identity of the real
Callaway. The film was released in London under the title
THE STAR SAID NO. Keel trained for three weeks with fight
trainer Johnny Indrisano for the fight scene. Indrisano was
cast as a trainer in the film. Howard also introduced
"Where the Tumbleweed is Blue" in the otherwise non-

musical. Keel's character was based on the careers of
western stars Gene Autry, Roy Rogers, and William Boyd.
     On February 11, 1952, Howard teamed with his film
co-stars Kathryn Grayson, Ava Gardner, William Warfield,
and Marge and Gower Champion on the CBS radio show "Lux
Radio Theatre" in a broadcast of SHOW BOAT. On March 20,
1952, Keel appeared on the "1951 Academy Awards" broadcast
from RKO's Pantages Theatre on which he sang the nominated
song "Wonder Why." Howard and Helen became the proud
parents of Kristine on June 21, 1952.
     Howard Keel had originally been considered for the
1952 film version of SINGING IN THE RAIN but because Betty
Comden and Adolph Green had problems writing about a
singing movie cowboy, they changed the idea of the picture
and rewrote it with Gene Kelly as their star. Keel only
filmed twice in 1952. The first time in the motion picture
LOVELY TO LOOK AT (released in July), a remake of ROBERTA
(1935), starring Kathryn Grayson, Red Skelton, Ann Miller,
and Marge and Gower Champion. Shortly before its release,
Keel and Grayson were sent on a promotional tour for all
curent MGM films to the major cities in South America where
their performances were well received. The second movie was
DESPERATE SEARCH in which he played a pilot in search of his
children lost in a plane crash in the Canadian wilderness.
     Keel made five motion pictures for MGM in 1953. In the
first, he had a guest shot in I LOVE MELVIN but his scenes
eventually were cut from the film. In FAST COMPANY, he
co-starred with Polly Bergan in a movie about race horses
who raced to music. RIDE VAQUERO starred Robert Taylor,
Ava Gardner, and Anthony Quinn. It was MGM's first
wide-screen production. In the picture, Keel tries to
build a cattle empire but is opposed by a gang of outlaws
led by Quinn.
     Robert Taylor was with MGM for twenty-five years which
ranked him as having the second longest contract only
surpassed by Lewis Stone who was with MGM for twenty-nine
years. Taylor had pleasant memories of Mayer and his days
with MGM. He had a more masculine image than Tyrone Powers
and was more perplexing than Errol Flynn. He was cast as a
ladies man until after World War II service. It was felt
he had a limited acting ability. After the war, he played
heroes with strength, modesty, and honor.
     For his next film, Keel was loaned to Warner Bros. as
Doris Day's co-star in CALAMITY JANE (1953). Day played
the title role and eventually marries Wild Bill Hickock
played by Keel. CALAMITY JANE was released in November of
1953, and the song "Secret Love" sung by Doris Day won an
Academy Award for best song. It would also become one of
Doris Day's big hits, selling over a million copies.
     Doris Day was cast in girl-next-door roles and became
Warner Bros. top female singing star, often playing
opposite Gordon MacRae. Her image stuck with her
throughout her career, although her real life was full of
tragedies. She became a top recording artist. She was
versatile and could play drama as well as comedy. It was
for her late 1950s sex-comedies, in which she kept her
wholesome image, that she became number one at America's
box office.

Arthur Freed had other commitments, so Jack Cummings became the producer for the 1953 motion picture KISS ME, KATE. George Sidney was chosen to be his director. In his unpublished oral history at the Director's Guild of America, George Sidney mentioned that Keel was not a good dancer and that he had to work around him. They would frequently go skeet shooting together. Howard Keel wanted to play the lead, but Cummings thought that he was overweight and out of voice so he turned him down. "But I've got to have the part. I'll be a reformed character," Keel promised. "I'll even quit smoking. I'll shed beef."[14] Keel proceeded to loose weight and vocalize. He even permanently stopped smoking. Kathryn Grayson had been loaned to Warner Bros. for a four-picture deal but she only made two pictures: SO THIS IS LOVE (1953) playing Grace Moore opposite Merv Griffin and DESERT SONG (1953) with Gordon MacRae. After completing DESERT SONG, she returned to MGM to film KISS ME, KATE. Cummings choice for the dual role of Fred Graham and Petrichio had been Laurence Olivier. He planned to dub Olivier's voice. "Mr. Olivier is a great actor," said Miss Grayson, "but Mr. Keel is a great singer and that is what we need."[15] Keel was ultimately cast in the part.

Cummings was impressed by the new 3-D process and used the process in KISS ME, KATE. By the time KISS ME, KATE opened at Radio City Music Hall in November 1953, the 3-D craze was declining and the film was shown in 2-D. However at the West Coast premiere at Loew's State Theatre in Los Angeles, the 3-D version was shown. KISS ME, KATE was the only musical filmed in 3-D.

Unlike the play, the location of the story was entirely in New York rather than Baltimore. Because of censorship, several of the songs had lyric changes. The studio wanted to build up Ann Miller's part so the first scene opened with her doing "Too Darn Hot" which had originally been intended to open the second act and be performed by a minor male character. The film was nominated for an Academy Award for best scoring of a musical film. Keel would later play the male lead in a stock version of KISS ME, KATE.

Ann Miller's tap dances (on screen) were the most vigorous of any female dancer. By the time she arrived at MGM, the big musical was on a decline.

James Whitemore was given character parts because he was not handsome enough to play romantic leads. MGM tried to mold him in the image of Spencer Tracy but it did not work.

At MGM, stars were assigned to a unit. Keel belonged to the Arthur Freed unit which meant he worked in Freed projects. Arthur Freed came to MGM with a theatre background and for ten years was paired with Nacio Herb Brown as one of the studio's best song writing teams. This was only the beginning for Freed, who was destined to become a producer with his own unit. The Freed Unit was completely established by mid 1942 and would last for more than twenty years turning out many classic film musicals. It was also the first to do on-location shooting and the dream ballet. Freed surrounded himself with creative talent from the theatre including his longest partner, Roger

Edens, who was a composer, arranger, and musical director. Together they invented the unit. MGM was pleased with the unit and did not interfere with them. Freed continued to be left primarily alone after Dore Schary became head of the studio but had received more support under Mayer.

The Freed Unit earned MGM money (even when many other films failed) and when musicals were mentioned in the 1940s and 1950s, audiences immediately thought of MGM. The demise of the unit in 1963 was due to the advent of television as a permanent fixture in American homes.

In 1954, MGM wanted to remake ROSE MARIE. Howard Keel was assigned to the picture. He disliked both the part and the script. Although he was one who never complained about the assignments given him by the studio, he refused to make the movie. The studio responded by placing him on suspension. He finally agreed to do the film only after the script had been rewritten. The picture was released in April 1954, and was the first musical shot (but not the first released) in CinemaScope and co-starred Ann Blyth, Fernando Lamas, Bert Lahr, and Marjorie Main. Keel played a mountie who falls for Blyth but in the end gives her up and she rides off with Lamas. One day during filming, Jack Benny dropped by the set. Keel got Benny to dress up in a mountie uniform, get on a gentle horse, and ride into camera range. Howard always had a good sense of humor. Director Mervyn LeRoy simply laughed at his practical joke and cut the footage. Four caravans of buses, actors, and trucks were needed to transport the cast and equipment to Mammoth Lake, California for some shooting. Most of the filming, however, took place in the Canadian Rockies.

Co-star Fernando Lamas sang well and was often cast as a romantic leading man because of his charisma. MGM even threatened overweight Mario Lanza that they would use Lamas as his replacement. After the completion of ROSE MARIE, Lamas' contract expired. He did not feel he had advanced any because in the six or seven films he had done at MGM, he had played the same type of role.

The trend in Hollywood musicals, in 1954, was to film stage successes. SEVEN BRIDES FOR SEVEN BROTHERS broke the trend in that it was an original piece. The studio was more interested in financing BRIGADOON (1954), and SEVEN BRIDES FOR SEVEN BROTHERS was almost never made. Producer Jack Cummings luckily was able to persuade MGM to take a chance on the project, even offering to take a cut in the budget. Cummings wanted Keel to play Adam, the oldest brother, and Jane Powell to play his leading lady. MGM had wanted to make the film five years earlier, but director Joshua Logan held the option, planning to use the property for a Broadway musical. Ironically, in 1978-1979, Keel and Powell co-starred in a musical stage version of SEVEN BRIDES FOR SEVEN BROTHERS which flopped when it went to Broadway starring Debbie Boone. The Keel-Powell tour of the show broke all box office records. Despite their being married in the film, Jane Powell and Keel had few scenes together and their friendship really grew later on after costarring in the stage version as well as versions of other stock productions.

Two drawbacks to the picture were the use of Ansco

color and soundstages as settings. Keel enjoyed making the
film, which took 34 days to shoot and earned him $10,000.
This kind of money was unusual because during the 1940s and
1950s most of the big stars at MGM were earning between
$5,000-$6,000 weekly for a 40-week period. When Keel
negotiated a new contract, MGM raised his weekly salary to
$3,000. British film writer David Shipman said, "Howard
Keel is recognized as one of the cornerstones of the MGM
musical."[16]

SEVEN BRIDES FOR SEVEN BROTHERS won an Academy Award
that year for best scoring of a musical film. It was also
one of the year's top moneymakers. SEVEN BRIDES FOR SEVEN
BROTHERS served as the inspiration for the ABC-TV show "Here
Come the Brides" which ran from 1968-1970.

MGM had never let Jane Powell play anything but
someone's daughter or adolescent roles and she was not
permitted to mature on screen. When she finally became a
star, musicals were on the way out.

Keel made a guest appearance, singing "Your Land is My
Land," in his last 1954 film DEEP IN MY HEART, a biography
of composer Sigmund Romberg (played by José Ferrer). Also in
the film were opera singer Helen Traubel, whose night club
career began with the help of producer Roger Edens, and
dancer Gene Kelly and his brother, Fred (also a dancer) who
appeared together only this one time.

Gene Kelly was often compared to Fred Astaire, even
though their styles were different. Kelly was known for
his athletic dances and seemed to have an instinct on how
the dance should be done in films.

Howard Keel earned a star on the Hollywood Walk of
Fame for his work in films. The star is located on block
fourteen at 6253 Hollywood. Also, Helen and Howard moved
into a big home in Beverly Hills.

JUPITER'S DARLING opened on February 18, 1955, and
co-starred Esther Williams. The MGM film concerned an
attempt to take over Rome and Keel's seduction by Williams
in an attempt to keep him from his goal. One hot day during
filming, Keel was riding a tall elephant while singing
"Hannibal's Victory March" and because of the heat and the
swaying and rocking motion made by the elephant, he became
violently seasick. The picture did not do well and as a
result, MGM released several of its stars from their contracts including Esther Williams, George Sidney, and the
Champions.

Marge and Gower Champion were a popular husband and
wife team and were often compared to Irene and Vernon
Castle. Light, imaginative, meticulous, and exuberant
were often used to describe their dancing. They not only
performed specialty numbers but also routines that told a
story. They made few movies together and, although they
were not as big as Ginger Rogers and Fred Astaire, were
still quite popular.

Helen and Howard became parents again with the birth
of a son, Gunnar Lewis, on June 3, 1955. Howard's second
motion picture that year was KISMET, which was released in
December 1955 and co-starred Ann Blyth, Dolores Gray, and
Vic Damone. Vincent Minnelli did not want to direct the
film but Schary persuaded him to take the assignment. He

did not pursue the project enthusiastically as his interest leaned toward a film he wanted to do entitled LUST FOR LIFE. Because Howard Keel was not a great dancer, he tried to enhance his dancing by spending time at a gym working out and by rehearsing for four hours daily with choreographer Jack Cole.

Ann Blyth was mostly cast in nice girl roles and had a pleasant voice. It was felt by many that had she come to Hollywood earlier she might have been a bigger star than Kathryn Grayson and Jane Powell because in addition to her singing, she had a good dramatic range.

After KISMET failed at the box office, Keel tried in vain for months to get out of his MGM contract. Had he been successful, he might have been able to film SOUTH PACIFIC (1958). However, he later did the show in stock in 1957 with Martha Wright and again in 1965 and 1977 with Jane Powell. The 1977 tour was a record-breaking National Theatre tour of SOUTH PACIFIC.

After his December 1955 Copacabana appearance, he was to report to MGM to film HIGH SOCIETY (1956) as well as a musical version of ANNA CHRISTIE (1930), but he did neither project.

Although KISMET (1955) did not do well, MGM (because of the success of 1954s SEVEN BRIDES FOR SEVEN BROTHERS) planned to star Keel in a musical version of ROBIN HOOD (1922) but because musicals were on a decline, MGM never followed through. The studio decided to release Howard and their other musical stars from their contracts in 1957. Keel felt bitter about the way the studio informed him of their decision. "I was notified that I would be released from the studio the next week," Keel recalled. "You think after seven years, at least one of the bosses would say he was sorry to see me go."[17] Instead, it was publicity chief Howard Strickley who notified him of the termination of his contract.

Howard Keel did not let his family be used in publicity shots until later in his career because he believed in keeping his personal life private. For relaxation, he enjoyed going to the golf course including the Riviera Club. He kept his golf balls in a red canvas bag bearing his name. He also found painting a form of relaxation. His likes included horses, early American furniture, fresh bread with lots of butter, poker games, and men pals. Among his dislikes were formal clothes, cocktail parties, and people who were late. When asked for advice by would-be-actors, he told them to believe in their luck, be ready for any break and never moan over bad luck. Over the years, his childhood shyness turned into outspokeness.

During Howard's four-year absence from the screen, he worked in stock, concerts and night clubs, with some rare television spots including the "Dinah Shore Show" (1957), "General Motor's Fiftieth Anniversary Show" (1957), "Zane Grey" (1957), "Bing Crosby & Friends" (1958), and "Bob Hope Show" on which he did the play ROBERTA (1958). In 1957, Keel was contacted by the American National Theatre and Academy about going to the Far East on a good will tour in a program of classical music. The venture was in connection with the U.S. government and was planned for 1958, depending on Keel's availability.

Howard Keel was to play the part of Franklin D.
Roosevelt in the 1958 Broadway production of SUNRISE AT
CAMPOBELLO. He was not happy with the first draft of the
script. A second draft was sent to him while he was
appearing on Broadway in a revival of CAROUSEL (1959).
Unfortunately, he was coming down with a cold which turned
into bronchitis. He eventually ended up in the hospital
when it developed into double pneumonia. By the time he
got out of the hospital, Ralph Bellamy had replaced him.
Keel did get a chance to play Roosevelt in a 1960 stock
version of the show. David Rothenberg was the press agent
for such clients as Sir John Gielgrid, Richard Burton, and
Howard Keel. He decided to give it up to help ex-convicts
go straight.

On December 7, 1959, Howard (in his first original
role) opened on Broadway with Carol Lawrence in the short-
lived musical SARATOGA which was based on Edna Ferber's
Saratoga Trunk. Edna Ferber was not happy with Morton Da
Costa's script and was ignored when she wrote her own
version. The production was so greatly anticipated that
its advanced ticket sales reached $1.5 million. It was felt
that the show's short life was due, in part, to the
audiences lack of interest in both leads seeking revenge and
that during the streamlining of the show (because of length)
much of the best material was cut.

Howard Keel had always wanted to be in an action or
western film. His wish came true, for the rest of his film
career was spent in low-budget dramas and westerns.

Keel returned to London to make the film FLOODS OF
FEAR released in the U.S. by Universal in April 1959. In
the film, he played an escaped prisoner who becomes a hero
during a flood and assumes the life of the man whose
testimony was responsible for his conviction. Although not
his most rewarding film, it was probably Keel's most
powerful performance.

Producer Rowland Lee almost did not cast Keel in the
$4,000,000 Walt Disney motion picture THE BIG FISHERMAN
because he felt that Howard was too sophisticated.
Fortunately, Lee's family had seen Keel in SEVEN BRIDES FOR
SEVEN BROTHERS and convinced Lee to give him a screen test.
Howard was signed to play Simon Peter. The movie was
filmed in the San Fernando valley and the California desert
and took liberties with the facts. THE BIG FISHERMAN
premiered in 1959 at the Rivoli Theatre and was based on
the best-seller by Lloyd C. Douglas.

In 1960, Howard Keel became the president of the
Screen Actor's Guild. Howard's next film, ARMORED COMMAND,
was made in West Germany and released by Allied Artists in
1961. In the movie, he played an Army Colonel during the
Battle of the Bulge.

For his next picture, Howard Keel returned to London
to make the 1963 film DAY OF THE TRIFFIDS, a science
fiction piece in which he regains his sight enabling him to
help fight off plant-like creatures. He was unhappy with
the script so he rewrote most of his own dialogue. In July
1963, Keel was in New York doing the Broadway version of NO
STRINGS with Barbara McNair and attended a reunion of the

Richard Rodgers Alumni Club before he and McNair started on an 18 month tour of NO STRINGS that would begin on August 5, 1963. NO STINGS was Richard Rodger's first show since Oscar Hammerstein's death. He not only wrote the music but also the lyrics. It was innovative in that the orchestra was backstage while musicians were on stage to accompany the singers. Also stars and chorus helped move scenery while the audience watched. Also in 1963, Howard flew to London to star in the BBC-TV version of KISS ME, KATE with co-star Patricia Morison.

Feeling that some of his touring directors were incompetent, Howard Keel not only starred in but directed CAMELOT (1964), SOUTH PACIFIC (1965), and CAROUSEL (1966). In 1965, Keel sang the theme song for the United Screen Arts film THE MAN FROM BUTTON WILLOW. This was the first motion picture released by Dale Robertson's distribution company. The picture was billed as the first full-length color animated western film. Robertson invested $1,000,000 in the film because he wanted to see more family oriented movies. He served as the voice and model for the lead character. The idea for the picture was Robertson's as was the original story and some of the songs.

Keel had a private pilot's license and frequently flew up the California coast on weekends. His wife Helen also became a pilot. By 1966, he had 100 hours of flying time to his credit.

Producer A. C. Lyles signed Keel for three low-budget westerns filmed at Paramount. The first was WACO (1966) in which actor Lorne Greene, best known as Ben Cartwright in the hit TV series "Bonanza," performed the title song. This was followed by RED TOMAHAWK (1967), and ARIZONA BUSHWHACKER (1968). Roy Rogers, Jr. made his film debut in the 1968 film. Howard was able to fit in Universal's WAR WAGON (released in May 1967) co-starring John Wayne and Kirk Douglas. In the film, which cast him in his best role in several years, he played an indian by the name of Levi Walking Bear. During this time, Ronald Reagan was running for governor of California. Kirk Douglas, who was anti-Reagan, took time off to make an ad opposing Reagan. Wayne got even with Douglas when he closed down shooting to make an ad supporting Reagan but did not tell Douglas, who reported to the desert for filming.

John Wayne was an American Legend and institution. He was the only actor to be a top ten box office star for 25 years. He represented what was America--strength, rugged individualism, reassurance, and patriotism. He remained a leading man long after many of his peers turned to character acting.

Kirk Douglas is one of Hollywood's most respected stars who is readily identified with the cocky, forceful roles that he first played as a boxer in the 1949 film CHAMPION that made him a star. He is an ambitious man of many talents who has had many hit films. His career has survived and he has continued to be popular with audiences.

While appearing in the play ON A CLEAR DAY YOU CAN SEE FOREVER in Chicago on August 10, 1967, Keel attended a party at the Ambassador West Hotel after attending the premiere of THOROUGHLY MODERN MILLIE at the United Artists Theatre.

The party honored the film's stars Carol Channing, and Mary Tyler Moore. Elliott Reid, starring in THE ODD COUPLE and the picture's producer Ross Hunter, were also in attendance.

Howard's twenty-one year marriage to Helen ended in 1970. Keel felt that "after so many years it took a lot of courage but neither of us was happy and it seemed ridiculous to go on."[18] Later that year, he met Judith Ann Magamoll on a blind date. She was a stewardess for National Airlines. When Howard found out that Judy was 30 years younger than he was, he felt that the relationship would not work because of the big difference in their ages. Judy felt that if they were to marry, the relationship would work in spite of the age difference. Keel resisted seeing her until she mentioned Robert Frost's poem "What Fifty Said" which was about age learning from youth. After he read the poem, Howard realized that age did not really matter after all. The couple were married on December 21, 1970. "My wife," he said, "is the best thing that ever happened to me."[19]

Ralph Edwards Productions offered Howard Keel a long-term TV contract in 1970. In the first year of the variety-talk show, Howard would receive $425,000 and another $1,700,000 over the next four-year period. Tom Nand, who worked for the production company, was to film a 90-minute pilot in January 1971. However for no reason made known to the public, negotiations broke off.

Tired of being concerned about neighbors, taxes, and mortgages, Howard Keel sold his 12-room, $150,000, two-acre Beverly Hills home which cost him $6,000 in property taxes alone. He then bought a 41-foot cabin-cruiser named Hojudo at Marina Del Rey in Los Angeles. The boat cost $49,000 and took an additional $10,000 to fix it up to Howard's liking. He paid a monthly charge of $160 to rent a slip. He was now free to set sail whenever he wanted. When he did sail, his crew consisted of Judy, his brother-in-law, Pete Magamoll, and Pete's wife, Cookie.

In 1971, Keel was offered a role in the production FOLLIES but turned it down because he did not like any of the male parts. He opened in London on October 19, 1971, in AMBASSADOR at Her Majesty's Theatre. The show was not a hit and ran for 89 performances. The backers, however, were not discouraged and brought the musical to the Lunt-Fontanne Theatre on Broadway in 1972, where it closed after 9 performances. One hundred American investors were in London on opening night. Before reaching Broadway, AMBASSADOR went through rewrites including the elimination of the opening scene that sets up Strether's character. With the failure of the show, composer Don Gohman committed suicide.

With the end of his film career in the late 1960s, Howard Keel remained quite active by appearing in stock productions, night clubs, and on occasional television shows. "The actual making of movies I didn't enjoy," Keel once said. "I'm a little restless and there was too much sitting around and waiting."[20] Among his numerous stock appearances was a ten-month tour with Betty Garrett in PLAZA SUITE in 1969 and MAN OF LA MANCHA in 1972 with Lainie Kazan. It was after an appearance by Keel in MAN OF LA MANCHA at

the Wesbury Music Fair on September 16, 1972, that Roddy and
Maxine Richman filed a suit with the Manhattan Supreme
Court asking for $1,000,000, claiming that they were
injured after a sword slipped from Keel's hand during the
performance. Howard had wanted to play the lead in the
1972 film version of MAN OF LA MANCHA but the role went to
Peter O'Toole who co-starred with Sophia Loren. One of
Keel's pet peeves was that non-singing actors were now
being cast in theatre and film musicals. The modern day
musical no longer needed the big-voiced singers, thus
making roles hard to come by.

In 1973, Howard toured in THE UNSINKABLE MOLLY BROWN
with Tammy Grimes who had created the role on Broadway. He
would also often tour with former co-star Jane Powell in
such shows as the 1974 and 1980 productions of I DO! I DO!
Howard felt that Jane Powell was totally professional and
was always prepared when she stepped on stage. Jane Powell
said of Keel, "I really like Howard, and I understand he
couldn't be more complimentary about me. I think Howard
always thought that he should have been a bigger star than
he was and felt frustration and disappointment."[21] After
the show, they seldom socialized. Keel often got discouraged after a long run and thought of retirement because he
felt today's new critics did not understand the modern
musical which no longer had a lot of songs you hummed after
leaving the theatre. Also, he grew tired of the grind of
traveling for such long periods of time. However, the
anticipation of a new project would help him bounce back.
Keel wanted to do some concerts from a Broadway theatre but
unless something special came along, he had doubts about
doing another Broadway show because the shows he had done,
against his better judgement, were flops. He had even
considered a one-man show that, in part, would reflect his
own life through songs he had done in previous shows.
"I prefer the theatre to making pictures," he once
remarked. "I think 75 percent of Hollywood actors would
rather be on Broadway."[22] In doing theatre, he was
able to experience the reactions of a live audience and it
enabled him to keep in touch with the country. Live
productions also enabled him to vocalize on a daily basis.
He once recalled doing an Eastern city tour. It was a
humid summer and they played over a tire factory. The
piano player was not familiar with the score and Keel was
not fitted by wardrobe until 15 minutes before show time.

In 1974, United Artists released MGM's THAT'S
ENTERTAINMENT! which was written, produced, and directed by
Jack Haley, Jr. The film was a compilation of great moments
from MGM musicals and was narrated by a number of the
studio's stars. Keel was featured in a clip from SHOW BOAT
in which he sang "Make Believe" with Kathryn Grayson. The
picture became one of the year's top moneymakers and was
followed by a less successful sequel in 1976 called THAT'S
ENTERTAINMENT PART 2 narrated, by Fred Astaire and Gene
Kelly. This time, Keel was featured in a clip singing
"There's No Business Like Show Business" from ANNIE GET YOUR
GUN with Betty Hutton, Keenan Wynn, and Louis Calhern.

Howard and Judy became parents with the birth of a
daughter, Leslie Grace, on September 1, 1974. His

daughter Kaija made Keel a grandfather in 1975.

Howard Keel's night club act played most of the big clubs around the country and in London. He oftened teamed with former MGM co-star Kathryn Grayson at such places as the Fremont in Vegas, LA's Cocoanut Grove, and Harrah's in Reno. He has stayed particularly popular in London, along-side Danny Kaye and Judy Garland, and has played the London Palladium, Talk of the Town, among others. Among his fans are Queen Elizabeth. "Sobbin' Women," "When You're in Love," and "Bless Your Beautiful Hide" are requested by audiences wherever his club act plays. He went to Australia in a July-August 1975 tour and played the Greek Theatre, in Los Angeles in 1989. On November 26, 1978, he set sail on a Caribbean cruise sponsored by the American Film Institute and featuring actress Olivia de Havilland, and director King Vidor. On the cruise, the stars discussed their Hollywood careers and there were screenings of some of their best films.

With the death of Jim Davis, who played Jock Ewing on the CBS-TV night-time soap, "Dallas," the producers needed someone to fill the void, [left by the death of Davis] that of a strong older character. In 1980, Keel learned that the producers were interested in testing him. "We required an actor who had to be larger than life for the role," said producer Leonard Katzman. "I immediately put out feelers to find Howard."[23] Judy was a "Dallas" fan and urged her husband to read for the part of rancher Clayton Farlow. "I was ready to get out of the business. Things weren't clicking," Keel said. "Then "Dallas" came along and started the whole thing over again. It's been wonderful."[24] After spending eight or nine months a year on the road, Keel was tired of the grind of the stock, concert, and night club life and believed that the public had lost interest in him. "As a commercial proposition," Keel said in 1987, "my type of singing fell by the wayside during the days of Elvis and the Beatles...a lot of people thought I was dead."[25] He was about to quit show business and move to Oklahoma to take a job with an oil company until the Clayton Farlow role on "Dallas" came along. Because of the exposure given him by the show, his popularity soared and fan letters from around the world convinced him to sing again. On a tour in England to promote his album AND I LOVE YOU SO, he realized how popular he had become. Ironically, the series was shot on MGM's stage 25 where Keel had filmed many of his studio musicals, including ANNIE GET YOUR GUN. His role as a widowed oil man who owned a ranch The Southern Cross, was to start as a two-shot guest appearance in which he befriends Sue Ellen (Linda Gray) who would eventually fall in love with Clayton's son, Dusty Farlow (Jared Martin). Keel described Miss Gray as being "so warm and generous--and a very fine actress."[26] Upon accepting the role on "Dallas," Keel was concerned about how he would be accepted by the rest of the cast. "Sometimes the cast will accept you and sometimes they won't," Keel remarked, "but the people were so warm to me on 'Dallas' that was no problem."[27] He was also concerned about his work and how his character would be accepted as he had been away from the camera for a long time. He also wondered about how to

develope a character he did not know anything about. In a
movie or play you get to see the story and characters from
the start. His character clicked and he became a regular in
the 1981-1982 season. He patterned Clayton Farlow after a
Texas friend. He often received letters from viewers asking
him to hit J.R. After joining "Dallas," he started an oil
investment company in Oklahoma City along with two other
partners.

Although Howard Keel had made occasional TV
appearances including "Bell Telephone Hour" (1960), "Tales
of Wells Fargo" (1961), "Death Valley Days" (1963), "Run
For Your Life" (1965), "Here's Lucy" (1968), and "The
Quest" (1976), "Dallas" was his first TV series. During
the 1984-1985 season, Donna Reed replaced Barbara Bel
Geddes as Keel's TV wife, Miss Ellie, as Bel Geddes had
left the show to undergo heart surgery. Miss Reed could
not overcome the fan's strong identification of Barbara Bel
Geddes as Miss Ellie. Bel Geddes was persuaded to return
to the show the following season and Donna Reed sued for
breach of contract. She reportedly received an unrevealed
seven-figure amount.

While taking part in the 1985 Steve Kanaly Celebrity
Ski Tournament, Keel fell. He thought he had sprained his
elbow but x-rays showed he had fractured his collarbone and
two ribs. In December of 1985, Howard Keel was playing
golf with his doctors when he experienced chest pains.
After running tests, the doctors discovered two blockages
and wanted to operate before Keel had a heart attack.
Howard was afraid if he had the operation, he would be
written out of "Dallas." "I could have waited until
'Dallas' was finished shooting before having surgery," he
said in 1986, "but Judy put her foot down and said, 'No
way. Not if your life is at stake.'" Keel gave in
realizing Judy was right. He checked into the hospital and
had the operation on January 8, 1986. Donna Reed phoned
Keel to wish him well shortly before her death from
cancer on January 14, 1986. Keel got his inspiration from
friend and co-star Barbara Bel Geddes, who returned to
"Dallas" after recovering from heart surgery. "Seeing her
since her return has been a real inspiration," he said.
"It just shows how you can come back from heart
surgery."[29] Howard not only planned to return to
"Dallas" but to go ahead with plans to do a 20-city
European tour after the show's season was over, sooner
than the two-month rehabilitation period suggested for
such surgery.

In March 1986, Keel appeared on the "1985 Academy
Awards" with fellow MGM stars in a tribute to MGM musicals.
Howard exercises by running in place, and by taking long
walks. He watches his diet and plays golf (handicap of
11). In 1987, Willie Morgan, a former Manchester United
and Scotland soccer great, asked Keel if he would agree to
the use of his name to form the HOWARD KEEL GOLF CLASSIC.
Howard readily consented. Every September, the classic
takes place at the Mere Golf Country Club in Cheshire with
proceeds going to the NSPCC. In 1989, he had been a member
of the Bel-Air Country Club for 37 years. He was in New
York in June 1989 to do a radio interview from Sardi's

restaurant, located at West 44th Street, the same street
where he had played in OKLAHOMA! (1945). After the Sardi's
interview he was scheduled to do another back at his hotel.
On June 10, 1989, he appeared on his own PBS special "Howard
Keel at the Royal Albert Hall." The concert was filmed in
London in 1987. PBS rebroadcast it on December 2, 1990.

Keel's popularity on "Dallas" has resulted in standing
room only tours in England, where he remains popular.
Although he had recorded soundtrack albums of his films and
plays, Howard had not had a recording career until "Dallas."
He recorded "J.R.! Who Do You Think You Are?" for the
Warner/Lorimar album DALLAS THE MUSIC STORY. In London, he
recorded AND I LOVE YOU SO, which ended in the top three
selling LPs there, coming right behind Michael Jackson's
THRILLER and Lionel Richie's CAN'T SLOW DOWN. It sold more
than 100,000 copies in a week. In the U.S., the album was
released as WITH LOVE, HOWARD KEEL. It was so popular that
REMINISCING WITH HOWARD KEEL soon followed. He also
recorded an album YOU NEEDED ME for Capitol Records as well
as a LIVE IN CONCERT album in 1989, recorded at the
Theatre Royal in Norwich, England. Four of his albums have
sold nearly 1,000,000 copies and it was reported on August
27, 1990, that a fifth album was to be released shortly and
was to feature the song "Music of the Night" from THE
PHANTOM OF THE OPERA.

The last season for "Dallas" was during 1990-1991 and
Keel was limited to only a few appearances, as Barbara Bel
Geddes had left the show and the writers had him traveling
with Miss Ellie.

Howard appeared as Farrah Fawcett's father on the CBS
series "Good Sports" in 1991. Howard Keel continues to tour
the U.S. and London. His special, "Howard Keel: Close to My
Heart," aired on PBS on August 9, 1991. The show was
filmed at his Sherman Oaks ranch in California and resulted
in a video and album under the same title. He had moved to
the ranch from Oklahoma in 1981 with his wife, Judy. He
also made an appearance on CBS's "Murder he Wrote" on
November 24, 1991. He appeared at the Muny in St. Louis in
June 1992, in the show SOUTH PACIFIC. Howard continues to
play golf and enjoy flying and his dogs. He completed plans
to open the $10,000,000, 2,100-seat, HOWARD KEEL SHOW BOAT
THEATRE in Branson, Missouri scheduled for completion in
April 1994. He will perform there six months annually on a
stage large enough to handle Broadway shows. In addition to
the theatre, there are plans for a hotel. On May 1, 1993
Keel hosted a portion of the film THAT'S ENTERTAINMENT! III,
in which never-before-seen footage from his films (as well
as others) is featured. Others sharing the hosting duties
include Gene Kelly, June Allyson, Cyd Charisse, Debbie
Reynolds, Mickey Rooney, and Esther Williams. Keel was a
guest, on May 24, 1993, on the BBC1-TV show "Bruce's Guest
Night." On February 18, 1994, Howard played the villain,
Captain Jack, on "Hart to Hart," a segment of "NBC's Friday
Night Mystery Movie."

In 1993, Keel performed in what was to be his farewell
British concert tour, but popular demand has caused him to
change his mind and return to Britain for a 32-date
comeback tour (April 23-May 29, 1994) much to the delight

of his many fans. Keel was interviewed on British radio,
in April 1994, to promote the concert series. During the
interview, he mentioned that his theatre deal in Branson,
Missouri had fallen through because the backer had changed
his mind. He said hopefully something might develope to
make the theatre a reality.

THAT'S ENTERTAINMENT! III opened in New York and
California on May 6, 1994 with first-night earnings being
donated to the American Film Institute.

In October 1994, Howard and Judy Keel put their
Sherman Oaks home, located off Mulholland Drive, up for
sale listing it for $895,000. The home had been built in
1958 and had been remodeled in 1989, with a 180-degree
view of the San Fernando Valley. The couple, who own a
vacation home in Telluride, Colorado, decided to sell their
Sherman Oaks place so they could buy a home in Palm Desert,
a place Keel loves, and play his favorite sport--golf.

Keel attributes, in retrospect, the ups and downs of
his Hollywood career to not playing studio politics. "As
long as I can sing halfway decent, I'd rather sing [than
act]," he said in 1989. "There's nothing like being in
good voice, feeling good, having good numbers to do and
having a fine orchestra."[30]

Howard Keel has come a long way from his boyhood days
of poverty in Gillespie, Illinois to stardom in a
multi-media career. His career has had many highs and some
lows but has survived the changes in music and the
entertainment world because of a still great talent able
to be showcased in various media and because of a new-found
popularity brought about by playing Clayton Farlow in
"Dallas." He continues to work and record and we are
reminded of his great talent when his films are shown on
TV. Author Doug McClelland puts things in perspective when
he says of Keel, "He and his delightful films have brought
us all a great deal of pleasure, and he has been vastly
underrated."[31] Howard Keel has had a long and varied
career crossing the boundaries of all areas open to a
singer, making him truly a man for all media.

NOTES

1. _Philadelphia Inquirer_. January 14, 1960.
2. Flett, Scarth. _London Sunday Express_. June 30, 1974.
3. Ship, Cameron. _Saturday Evening Post_. October 15, 1955.
4. Zeitlin, Ida. _Photoplay_. October 1951.
5. _Ibid_.
6. _Ibid_.
7. _Ibid_.
8. _Ibid_.
9. _Ibid_.
10. Graver, Jack. _Newark Evening News_. July 26, 1963.
11. Everett, Todd. _Los Angeles Herald Examiner_. July 14, 1989.
12. _Ibid_.
13. Flett, Scarth. _London Sunday Express_. June 30, 1974.
14. Ship, Cameron. _Saturday Evening Post_. October 15, 1955.
15. _1991 Arnold Talking Yellow Pages_.
16. _Ibid_.
17. Thomas, Bob. _Newark News_. July 17, 1958.
18. Flett, Scarth. _London Sunday Express_. June 30, 1974.
19. _The National Enquirer_. February 18, 1982.
20. Flett, Scarth. _London Sunday Express_. June 30, 1974.
21. Powell, Jane. _The Girl Next Door...And How She Grew_. (Morrow, 1988).
22. Cleaves, Henderson. _New York World Telegram_.
23. _1991 Arnold Talking Yellow Pages_.
24. Everett, Todd. _Los Angeles Herald Examiner_. July 14, 1989.
25. _Examiner_. February 3, 1987.
26. _The National Enquirer_. October 2, 1984.
27. _Newark (N.J.) Star Ledger_. May 25, 1982.
28. _The National Enquirer_. 1986.
29. _Ibid_.
30. Hawn, Jack. _Los Angeles Times_. July 15, 1989.
31. Mr. McClelland's response to author's letter on July 2, 1992.

2

CHRONOLOGY

The following is a chronological listing of significant
events in the life and career of Mr. Keel.

1919   April 13-Harold Clifford Leek is born in Gillespie,
        Illinois.

1930   Keel's father, Homer, dies.

1934   Leaves Gillespie with mother for California.

1937   Parks cars across from Paramount Studios for stars
        Cary Grant, Fred MacMurray, among others.

        Takes job at Douglas Aircraft.

1939   Sees Lawrence Tibbett (his inspiration) in concert.

1943   Studies under voice coach George Huston.

        Marries Rosemary Cooper.

1944   Wins first prize at Mississippi Valley Festival
        Contest in Moline, Mississippi.

        August-wins second prize at Chicago Music Festival.

1945   Auditions for the National Concert Agency, Oscar
        Hammerstein II at Beverly Hills Hotel, and for the
        Theatre Guild.

        Quits Douglas Aircraft to go to New York.

        August 26-fills in for vacationing John Raitt in
        Broadway's CAROUSEL at St. James Theatre.

        September-learns role of Curly in Broadway's
        OKLAHOMA! and fills in for both CAROUSEL and
        OKLAHOMA!.

1947   April 29-opens in London production of OKLAHOMA! at

Theatre Royal.

Meets dancer, Helen Anderson, in cast of OKLAHOMA! and later proposes.

Theatre Guild contract expires.

Screen tests in CROSSFIRE for Warner Bros. and later for producer Hal Wallis.

1948   October-Rosemary Cooper gets Vegas divorce.

November-film SMALL VOICE is released.

1949   January 3-marries Helen Anderson in Riverside, California.

Offered Cable role and understudy for lead in Broadway production SOUTH PACIFIC.

Signs with MGM in Frank Butler role in movie ANNIE GET YOUR GUN.

April 4-breaks leg when horse falls on it during filming.

October 10-production of ANNIE GET YOUR GUN resumes.

December 16-ANNIE GET YOUR GUN is completed.

1950   January 14-Daughter Kaija Liane is born.

Rents Brentwood home.

April-ANNIE GET YOUR GUN is released.

June 2-soundtrack for ANNIE GET YOUR GUN (MGM E-509) reaches music charts.

July 8-PAGAN LOVE SONG concludes production.

November 17-SHOW BOAT starts filming.

December-PAGAN LOVE SONG is released.

1951   January 9-motion picture SHOW BOAT concludes production.

February and March-SHOW BOAT retakes are taken.

March-THREE GUYS NAMED MIKE is released.

July 13-SHOW BOAT is released and soundtrack (MGM E 559) hits charts.

Voted Television & Screen Guide's 8th place male star and fourth place newcomer.

Voted <u>Motion Picture Herald's</u> number one star of tomorrow.

Entertains U.S. Air Force soldiers.

October 1-ACROSS THE WIDE MISSOURI is released.

October 5-TEXAS CARNIVAL premieres.

November 15-CALLAWAY WENT THATAWAY hits theatres.

Appears on radio's "Hedda Hopper Show."

1952   February 11-appears on "Lux Radio Theatre" in SHOW BOAT.

March 20-sings nominated song "Wonder Why" on the radio broadcast of the "1951 Academy Awards."

June 21-daughter Kristine is born.

July 4-films LOVELY TO LOOK AT and DESPERATE SEARCH are released.

July 4-soundtrack of LOVELY TO LOOK AT (MGM E 150) hits charts.

1953   March 20-I LOVE MELVIN released with Keel's scenes cut from final print.

May 12-FAST COMPANY comes out.

July 17-RIDE VAQUERO premieres.

November 14-CALAMITY JANE comes to theatres.

November 26-KISS ME, KATE is issued.

1954   February 14-guests on TV's "Toast of the Town."

March-plays the Last Frontier in Las Vegas, Nevada.

Royal Command Performance at the Palladium in London, England.

Receives star on Hollywood Walk of Fame.

Moves to Beverly Hills, California home.

Earns $10,000 for role in SEVEN BRIDES FOR SEVEN BROTHERS.

Renews MGM contract at $3,000 a week.

January 23-the soundtrack of CALAMITY JANE (Columbia 6273) hits the music charts.

April-ROSE MARIE is released.

April 17-ROSE MARIE (MGM E-229) appears on the charts.

August-SEVEN BRIDES FOR SEVEN BROTHERS premieres.

September 4-SEVEN BRIDES FOR SEVEN BROTHERS (MGM E-244) reaches the charts.

December 26-DEEP IN MY HEART comes to theatres.

1955   January 22-soundtrack of DEEP IN MY HEART (MGM-3153) reaches the charts.

February 18-JUPITER'S DARLING is released.

June 3-son Gunnar Lewis is born.

September 27-plays at Dunes in Las Vegas, Nevada.

November-appears at Town Casino in Buffalo, New New York.

December-KISMET premieres.

December-headlines at Copacabana in New York City, New York.

1956   April 2-plays at Empire in Glasgow, Scotland.

April 9-appears at the Palladium in London, England.

October 13-guests on "President Eisenhower: Sixty-Sixth Birthday."

1957   January 13-plays at the Sands in Las Vegas, Nevada.

May 19-appears on British TV's "Sunday Night at the London Palladium."

May 22-appears at Empire in Glasgow, Scotland.

Stars in CAROUSEL at Dayton Memorial Hall in Dayton, Ohio.

June 24-begins tour in SOUTH PACIFIC.

November 3-guests on TV's "Dinah Shore Chevy Show."

November 17-appears on "General Motors Fiftieth Anniversary Show."

December 7-guests on the "Polly Bergen Show."

December 13-stars on "Zane Grey Theatre."

1958   Illness prevents Keel from doing Broadway's SUNRISE AT CAMPOBELLO.

January 12-guests on TV's "Bing Crosby and Friends."

March 12-appears on "The Big Record."

March 29-tours in KISMET at Valley Forge Music Fair in Devon, Pennsylvania.

April 27-appears on British TV's "Sunday Night at the London Palladium."

September 19-co-stars in TV version of ROBERTA.

1959   March 4-appears on "Bell Telephone Hour."

April 6-appears on "1958 Academy Awards".

April-film FLOODS OF FEAR (made in London) is released.

April-Disney film THE BIG FISHERMAN is made.

September 22-guests on TV's "A Toast to Jerome Kern."

October 26-tryout of SARATOGA at the Shubert Theatre in Philadelphia, Pennsylvania.

December 7-opens on Broadway in SARATOGA.

1960   President of Screen Actor's Guild.

March 11-guests on TV's "Bell Telephone Hour."

July 11-tours in SUNRISE AT CAMPEBELLO at Playhouse in the Park in Philadelphia, Pennsylvania.

August 29-tours in SOUTH PACIFIC at Oakdale Musical Theatre in Wallingford, Connecticut.

September 30-hosts "Bell Telephone Hour."

October 8-appears on British TV's "Saturday Spectacular."

1961   Films ARMORED COMMAND in West Germany.

September 3-appears on British TV's "Bernard Delfont's Sunday Show."

September 30-guests on TV's "Tales of Wells Fargo."

Appears on "Here's Hollywood."

November 10-guests on "Bell Telephone Hour."

December 31-appears on "Let Freedom Ring."

1962   March 19-guests on "Hollywood Melody."

April 9-appears on "1961 Academy Awards."

May 27-plays in THE CROSSING at Bucks County Playhouse in New Hope, Pennsylvania.

December 16-guests on TV's "Voice Of Firestone."

1963   Appears on BBC-TV version of KISS ME, KATE.

April 4-stars on TV's "Death Valley Days."

Films DAY OF THE TRIFFIDS.

May 27-opens in THE CROSSING at Bucks County Playhouse in New Hope, Pennsylvania.

June 3-Broadway replacement in NO STRINGS at Broadhurst Theatre in New York City, New York.

August 5-begins 18 month tour of NO STRINGS.

1964   July 20-opens in CAMELOT at the Carousel Theatre in Farningham, Massachusetts.

August 5-appears in and directs stock version of CAMELOT at Westbury Music Fair in Long Island, New York.

August 11-CAMELOT opens at Camden County Music Fair in Camden, New Jersey.

August 30-CAMELOT plays at Valley Forge Music Fair in Devon, Pennsylvania.

Guests on TV's "Match Game."

1965   March-appears in CAMELOT at Mineola Playhouse in Long Island, New York.

June 21-appears in and directs stock version of SOUTH PACIFIC.

Makes animated film MAN FROM BUTTON WILLOW.

December 6-guests on TV's "Run For Your Life."

1966   Appears in and directs stock version of CAROUSEL.

Reaches 100 hours of flying time.

Makes film WACO.

1967   Makes film RED TOMAHAWK.

May 23-WAR WAGON is released

August 10-while in Chicago in tour of ON A CLEAR DAY YOU CAN SEE FOREVER, attends premiere of THOROUGHLY

MODERN MILLIE at United Artists Theatre.

1968   January 22-does play THE FANTASTICKS at Parker Playhouse, Ft. Lauderdale, Florida.

Makes film ARIZONA BUSHWHACKERS.

September-plays at Fremont in Las Vegas, Nevada.

November 29-headlines at Harrah's in Reno, Nevada.

1969   April 23-plays Cocoanut Grove in Los Angeles,
California.

August 4-does stock version of PLAZA SUITE in
Chicago, Illinois.

Guests on TV's "Here's Lucy."

December 24-plays Fremont in Las Vegas, Nevada.

Tours in ON A CLEAR DAY YOU CAN SEE FOREVER at
Parker Playhouse in Ft. Lauderdale, Florida.

1970   Divorces Helen after twenty-one years of marriage.

January 19-stars in PLAZA SUITE at Locust Theatre
in Philadelphia, Pennsylvania.

July 13-stars in MAN OF LA MANCHA at Valley Forge
Music Fair in Devon, Pennsylvania.

September 14-MAN OF LA MANCHA retutrns to Valley
Forge Music Fair.

Offered TV contract by Ralph Edwards Productions.

December 21-marries Judith Ann Magamoll. The couple
had met on a blind date earlier that year.

Sells home and moves onto a cabin cruiser.

1971   March 25-plays London's Talk of the Town in London,
England.

Turns down role in Broadway's FOLLIES.

July 6-plays in stock version of THE MOST HAPPY FELLA
at Dayton Memorial Hall in Dayton, Ohio.

October 19-opens in London, England in musical
AMBASSADOR at Her Majesty's Theatre.

1972   February 25-plays Fremont in Las Vegas, Nevada.

Tours in DARK OF THE MOON at Westbury Music Fair
in Long Island, New York.

June 11-plays in MAN OF LA MANCHA at Meadowbrook Dinner Theatre in Cedar Grove, New Jersey.

September 11-begins tour of MAN OF LA MANCHA at Westbury Music Fair in Long Island, New York.

September 15-guests on TV's "Sonny & Cher Comedy Hour."

September 16-Roddy and Maxine Richman file $1,000,000 suite against Keel for injuries they claimed were received during performance of MAN OF LA MANCHA at Westbury Music Fair in Long Island, New York.

November 19-opens on Broadway in AMBASSADOR at the Lunt-Fontaine Theatre in New York City, New York.

November 25-AMBASSADOR closes.

1973   August 14-does stock production of THE UNSINKABLE MOLLY BROWN at the Valley Forge Music Fair in Devon, Pennsylvania.

September 15-soundtrack of ANNIE GET YOUR GUN (MGM 2 SES-42) hits charts.

November 1-is guest on "Merv Griffin Show."

1974   Does stock production of I DO! I DO!.

June 18-plays Palladium in London, England.

September 1-daughter Leslie Grace is born.

MGM/UA releases film THAT'S ENTERTAINMENT! Keel is featured in SHOW BOAT clip.

1975   Daughter Kaija makes Keel grandfather.

July/August-Australia tour.

September 16-appears at Civic Center in St. Paul, Minnesota in GENE KELLY'S SALUTE TO BROADWAY.

1976   MGM/UA releases THAT'S ENTERTAINMENT PART 2. Keel featured in sequence from ANNIE GET YOUR GUN.

May 31-does stock version of MUSICAL JUBILEE in Toronto, Canada.

November 3-guests on TV's "The Quest."

1977   July 11-begins tour in SOUTH PACIFIC at O'Keefe Center in Toronto, Canada.

1978   August 27-begins tour in stage version of SEVEN BRIDES FOR SEVEN BROTHERS at Fair Park Music Hall in Dallas, Texas.

November 26-appears on AFI Caribbean Cruise.

1980   October 22-does stock version of I DO! I DO! at
        Valley Forge Music Fair in Devon, Pennsylvania, then
        plays at the Pantages Theatre in Los Angeles,
        California.

        Begins 26-U.K. concert tour.

1981   February 20-joins cast of TV's "Dallas."

        Moves from Oklahoma to Sherman Oaks, California.

        May 9-guests on TV's "Love Boat."

1982   Tours in SLEUTH (4 weeks).

        May 1-guests on TV's "Fantasy Island."

1983   Guests on TV's "Love Boat."

        June 25-guests on "Song By Song By Irving Berlin."

        November 12-guests on "Love Boat."

        December 11-appears on "All-Star Party For Frank
        Sinatra."

        Begins 15-date U.K. tour.

1984   April 14-album AND I LOVE YOU SO (Warwick WW-45137)
        hits British charts for nineteen weeks, peaking at
        number six. It had sold over 100,000 copies in one
        week.

        April 16-begins 30-date tour.

1985   Breaks collarbone and ribs during Steve Kanaly
        Celebrity Ski Tournament.

        November 19-album REMINISCING-THE HOWARD KEEL
        COLLECTION hits the British charts for twelve weeks
        climbing to position 20.

        December-experiences chest pains while playing
        golf.

1986   January 8-has Bypass operation.

        March 24-appears on "1985 Academy Awards."

        Guests on "Irving Berlin's America."

1987   February 23-guests on TV's "From Tahiti Bob Hope's
        Tropical Comedy Special."

July 11-appears at South Shore Music Circus in Cohasset, Massachusetts.

Appears at Royal Albert Hall in London, England.

The HOWARD KEEL GOLF CLASSIC is formed and is played in September each year at the Mere Golf Country Club in Cheshire.

1988   March 28-album JUST FOR YOU (Telstar Star 2318) reaches British charts for five weeks, climbing to spot 51.

April-plays at Barbican in London, England.

July-plays in I DO! I DO! at Pantages Theatre in Los Angeles, California.

1989   June-does radio interview from Sardi's in New York City, New York.

July 15-plays Greek Theatre in Los Angeles, California.

Member Bel-Air Country Club for 37 years.

LIVE IN CONCERT album is recorded at Theatre Royal Concert in Norwich, England.

October-appears at Dominion Theatre in London, England.

1990   June 10-PBS broadcasts "Howard Keel at the Royal Albert Hall."

Album HOWARD KEEL: CLOSE TO MY HEART is released.

1991   June 22-guested as Farrah Fawcett's father on TV's "Good Sports."

August 9-PBS broadcast of "Howard Keel: Close to My Heart" (filmed at Keel's California ranch).

November 24-guests on TV's "Murder She Wrote."

Plays in golf tournament and performs at show afterwards in Manchester, England.

1992   June 22-stars in stock version of SOUTH PACIFIC at Muny in St. Louis, Missouri

1993   April 12 & 13-farewell U.K. tour ends at Barbican.

May 1-shoots hosting segment in THAT'S ENTERTAINMENT! III.

May 24-appears on BBC1 TV's "Bruce's Guest Night."

1994   February 18-appears on NBC-TV in "Hart to Hart."

April-HOWARD KEEL SHOW BOAT THEATRE scheduled to
open in Branson, Missouri but deal falls through.

April-is interviewed on British radio's "Gloria
Hunniford."

April 23-a 32-date United Kingdom tour begins.

May 6-THAT'S ENTERTAINMENT! III openes in New York
and California.

October-Keel sells Sherman Oaks home and buys one
in Palm Desert.

3

STAGE

This chapter documents, chronologically, Mr. Keel's
Broadway, London, stock and touring appearances on stage.
Where possible, the date, theatre and location, credits,
cast (with characters played), synopsis, songs (where
applicable) with characters singing them, reviews, and
comments are given for each play. When no precise date is
available, the production is listed at the beginning of the
decade where it most likely was performed.

S 1. CAROUSEL

Broadway. August 26, 1945. Majestic Theatre in New
York City, New York. 3 Weeks.

Broadway. June-September 1946. Majestic Theatre in New
York City, New York.

CREDITS: Book & Lyrics by Oscar Hammerstein II. Music
by Richard Rodgers. Based on Ferenc Molnar's LILIOM.
Adapted by Benjamin Glazer. Produced by The Theatre
Guild. Director: Rouben Mamoulian. Choreographer:
Agnes de Mille. Set Designer: Jo Mielziner. Costume
Designer: Miles White. Dance Arranger: Trude Rittmann.
Musical Director: Joseph Littau. Orchestrator: Don
Walker. Production Supervisors: Theresa Helburn,
Lawrence Lagner.

CAST: Jeane Darling (Carrie Pipperidge); Jan Clayton
(Julie Jordan); Jean Casto (Mrs. Mullin); **Harold Keel**
(Billy Bigelow); Mimi Strongin (Bessie); Jimsie
Somers (Jessie); Lew Foldes (Juggler); Robert Byrn
(1st Policeman); Franklyn Fox (David Bascombe);
Christine Johnson (Nettie Fowler); Pearl Lang (June
Girl); Eric Mattson (Enoch Snow); Murvyn Vye (Jigger
Craigin); Annabelle Lyon (Hannah); Peter Birch
(Boatswain); Connie Baxter (Arminy); Marilyn Merkt
(Penny); Joan Keenan (Jennie); Genna Moise (Virginia);
Suzanne Tabel (Susan); Richard Gordon (Jonathan); Larry
Evers (2nd Policeman); Blaker Ritter (Captain); Velie
(1st Heavenly Friend); Tom McDuffie (2nd Heavenly
Friend); Russell Collins (Starkeeper); Bambi Linn

(Louise); Robert Pagent (Carnival Boy); Ralph Linn
(Enoch Snow, Jr.); Lester Freedman (Principal).

SYNOPSIS: The story takes place between 1873-1888 and
concerns Billy Bigelow, a carousel barker, who is fired when
he pays attention to Julie Jordan, a mill worker. Against
Bascombe's (owner of the mill) advice, Julie decides to
stay with Billy and she loses her job. Billy and Julie are
married and live with her Aunt Nettie.
     When Billy learns he is to be a father, he agrees to
join his unsavory friend, Jigger, in a robbery. Billy is
killed and goes to heaven. He is given a chance to go back
to earth to help his unhappy daughter, Louise.
     At her graduation, he convinces her to listen to the
advice of the speaker and not live by her parents deeds.
He returns to heaven knowing he has done some good.

SONGS: "Carousel Waltz"; "Mr. Snow" (Carrie); "If I Loved
You" (Billy, Julie); "June is Busting Out All Over" (Nettie,
Carrie); "When the Children Are Asleep" (Enoch, Carrie);
"Soliloquy" (Billy); "A Real Nice Clambake" (Carrie, Nettie,
Enoch, Jigger); "What's the Use of Wondering" (Julie);
"Highest Judge of All" (Billy).

REVIEWS: The New Yorker, Wolcott Gibbs, (April 28, 1945)
Gibbs thought that there were "some very fine songs" and he
especially liked "If I Loved You." He felt the show was "one
of the delights of the season."

New York Journal-America, George Jean Nathan, (April 30,
1945) Nathan felt that CAROUSEL was a "very good show."

ADDITIONAL REVIEWS: The Nation (May 5, 1945); New Republic
(May 7, 1945); Time (April 30, 1945).

COMMENTS: The musical was based on Ferenc Molnar's
LILOM in 1921. For the musical, the location was changed
from Budapest to New England. For nearly two years,
CAROUSEL played across the street from OKLAHOMA! In the
original run, Keel replaced John Raitt on Broadway during
Raitt's vacation in September 1945 and again from June to
September 1946. Jan Clayton played Julie on Broadway.
CAROUSEL ran on Broadway from April 19, 1945 to May 24,
1947 for a total of 890 performances. Iva Withers replaced
Miss Clayton in December 1945. CAROUSEL won the New York
Drama Critics Circle Award for Best Musical (1944-1945);
Donaldson Awards (1944-1945) for Best Musical; Best
Performance in a Musical (Male), John Raitt; Best Direction,
Rouben Mamoulian; Best Dancer (Male), Peter Birch; Best
Dance Direction, Agnes de Mille; Best Book and Lyrics, Oscar
Hammerstein II; and Best Score, Richard Rodgers.
     Raitt (some twenty years later) reprised his role at
Lincoln Center.
     The London version opened at the Theatre Royal on
June 7, 1950, and closed on October 13, 1951, playing for
566 performances with stars Stephen Douglas and Iva Withers.
     CAROUSEL was filmed by Twentieth Century-Fox and was
originally to have teamed Frank Sinatra and Shirley Jones.

Sinatra left the picture after learning it was to be shot twice, once in 35mm and again in 55mm CinemaScope. Gordon MacRae, who badly wanted to be cast in the role of Billy, was chosen to replace Sinatra. Most of the film was shot on location in Boothbay Harbor, Maine. It premiered at the Roxy in New York on February 16, 1956.

S 2. OKLAHOMA!

Broadway. September 1945-June 1946. St. James Theatre in New York City, New York.

Broadway. September 1946-April 1947. St, James Theatre in New York City, New York.

CREDITS: Book & Lyrics by Oscar Hammerstein II. Music by Richard Rodgers. Based on Lynn Rigg's GREEN GROW THE LILACS. Produced by the Theatre Guild. Director: Rouben Mamoulian. Choreographer: Agnes de Mille. Set Designer: Lemuel Ayers. Music Directors: Jacob Swartzdorf, Jay Blackton. Conductor: Robert Russell Bennett. Production Supervisors: Theresa Helburn, Lawrence Langner.

CAST: Ruth Weston (Aunt Eller Murphy); **Harold Keel** (Curly Mclain); Iva Withers (Laurey Williams); Barry Kelley (Ike Skidmore); Edwin Clay (Fred); Herbert Rissman (Slim); Tom Avera (Will Parker); Richard Rober (Jud Fry); Bonita Primrose (Ado Annie Carnes); Joseph Buloff (Ali Hakim); Vivienne Allen (Gertie Cummings); Dania Krupska (Ellen); Vladimir Kostenko (Jess); Scott Merrill (Chalmers); Ellen Love (Kate); Joan McCracken (Sylvie); Kate Friedlich (Armina); Bambi Linn (Aggie); Ralph Riggs (Andrew Carnes); Owen Martin (Cord Elam); Paul Shiers (Mike); George Irving (Joe); Hayes Gordon (Sam).

SYNOPSIS: The story takes place about the turn of the century in indian territory just before Oklahoma becomes a state.

The play concerns the love story between Curly Mclain, a cowman, and Laurey Williams, who lives with her Aunt Eller on a farm. When Curly waits to ask Laurey to the box social, she tells hired hand Jud Fry she will go with him just to spite Curly.

When Curly bids for Laurey's food hamper, it proves he loves her. They are married. After the ceremony, Jud picks a fight with Curly but falls on his own knife and is killed. Curly is tried for murder but is acquitted right away, thus enabling the couple to go on their honeymoon.

SONGS: "Oh What a Beautiful Morning" (Curly); "The Surrey With the Fringe on Top" (Curly, Eller, Laurey); "Kansas City" (Will, Eller); "I Can't Say No" (Ado Annie); "Many a New Day" (Laurey); "It's a Scandal, It's an Outrage" (Ali); "People Will Say We're in Love" (Curly, Laurey); "Poor Jud is Dead" (Curly, Jud); "Lonely Room" (Jud); "Out of My Dreams" (Laurey); "Farmer and the Cowman" (Andrew, Eller, Curly, Laurey, Ado Annie); "All or Nothing" (Will, Ado

Annie); "People Will Say We're in Love"-Reprise, (Curly,
Laurey); "Oklahoma" (Curly, Laurey, Eller, Ike, Fred); "Oh
What a Beautiful Morning"-Reprise (Curly, Laurey).

REVIEWS: The Nation, Joesph Wood Krutch, (April 17, 1943)
Mr. Krutch said that OKLAHOMA! was "one of the most lively,
entertaining and colorful musicals it has been my privilege
to see."

New York Times, Olin Downes, (June 6, 1943) Olin Downes
felt that OKLAHOMA! was a "delightful show."

Variety, Jack Pulaski, (April 7, 1943) Mr. Pulaski thought
OKLAHOMA! had a "superlative score" and "clever players
to provide a diverting evening."

ADDITIONAL REVIEWS: The New Republic (April 19, 1943); The
New Yorker (April 10, 1943); Time (April 12, 1943).

COMMENTS: OKLAHOMA! was the first show by the team of
Rodgers and Hammerstein II. It was also the first book
musical for choreographer Agnes de Mille. The show was
based on the 1931 play GREEN GROW THE LILACS by Lynn Riggs.
By the time it reached Broadway, the original title AWAY WE
GO! was changed to OKLAHOMA!. It opened at the St. James
Theatre on March 31, 1943, and closed May 29, 1948, (5
years, 9 weeks) running for 2,212 performances of which 44
were done as matinees especially for the Armed Forces.
March 31, 1993, marked the 50th anniversary of the Broadway
opening of OKLAHOMA! and of the partnership of Rodgers and
Hammerstein. Several books and recordings marked the
celebration as well as a U.S. postage stamp. From July 1,
1946-July 11, 1961, OKLAHOMA! was the longest running
Broadway musical until MY FAIR LADY surpassed it.
     The original cast members that had been replaced when
Keel appeared in the show included: Betty Garde (Aunt
Eller); Alfred Drake (Curly); Joan Roberts (Laurey); Lee
Dixon (Will Parker); Howard de Silva (Jud Fry); Celeste
Holm (Ado Annie); Jane Lawrence (Gertie Cummings);
Katharine Sergava (Ellen); George Church (Jess); Marc Platt
(Chalmers). Cast replacements during Keel's appearance
included: Iva Withers (Laurey) by Jane Watson October 1945-
February 1946; Miss Watson by Ann Crowley until March 1946,
when Miss Watson returned until December 1946 when she was
replaced by Mary Hatcher. James Parnell replaced Mr. Avera
(as Will Parker) in October 1945. Bruce Hamilton took over
the part of Jud (replacing Mr. Rober) from May 1946-August
1946, and again in September 1946. Dorothea MacFarland
replaced Miss Primrose (as Ado Annie) from December 1946,
until Vivienne Allen took over in April 1947. David Burns
replaced Mr. Buloff (as Ali Hakim) in August 1946.
Patricia Englund replaced Miss Allen (as Gertie Cummings)
in July 1946. Gemze de Lappe replaced Dania Krupska (as
Ellen) in July 1946. John Butler replaced Mr. Merrill (as
Jess) in October 1945, until he was replaced by Erik
Kristen in September 1946. Boris Runanin replaced Kristen
in April 1947.
     Bruce Yarnell (Curly) and Leigh Beery (Laurey)

starred in OKLAHOMA! in a 1969 revival at the Music Theatre
of Lincoln Center.

On December 13, 1969, William Hammerstein (Oscar's
son) directed a New York production which ran for eight
months and a total of 293 performances.

Rodgers and Hammerstein II waited until the Broadway
and touring companies were over before filming OKLAHOMA!
It was released in Todd-AO process by Magna and became the
first film to be released in the new process. Twentieth
Century-Fox re-released the film in CinemaScope. Dancers
Bambi Linn and Marc Platt were in the original Broadway
cast. Choreographer Agnes de Mille, and musical director
Jay Blackston also did the film. The songs "It's a
Scandal, It's an Outrage," and "Lonely Room" were not used
in the film. OKLAHOMA! marked director Fred Zinnemann's
first musical.

Paul Newman and James Dean were among the many actors
who tested for the role of Curly. The part eventually went
to Gordon MacRae. Joanne Woodward was considered, among
others, for Laurey. Shirley Jones got the part which
marked her film debut. She was the only person who was put
under exclusive contract by Rodgers and Hammerstein II.
Eli Wallach tried out for Jud but Rod Steiger was cast in
the role. Charlotte Greenwood, who had been unable to play
Aunt Eller on Broadway, got her chance in the film version.

The film began shooting on July 7, 1954, and had a
$6,000,000 budget. They spent seven weeks at MGM
rehearsing on mock sets. Exterior shooting was done in the
San Rafael valley at the Greene Cattle Company Ranch which
was located some thirty-six miles northeast of San Nogales,
Arizona. Arizona was chosen instead of Oklahoma because of
fewer signs of progress.

The film premiered at the Rivoli Theatre in New York
on October 11, 1955. At the opening ceremonies, Raymond
Gary (Oklahoma's governor) rode a white horse down the
streets of New York. OKLAHOMA! won an Academy Award for
best scoring of a musical and one for best sound recording.
It had also been nominated for best cinematography and film
editing. (See D36, D37)

S 3. OKLAHOMA!
London. April 29, 1947. Theatre Royal, Drury Lane in
London, England. 18 Months.

CREDITS: Book & Lyrics by Oscar Hammerstein II. Music
by Richard Rodgers. Based on Lynn Rigg's GREEN GROW THE
LILACS. Produced by H.M. Tennent Ltd. with restaging by
Jerome Whyte. Choreographer: Miss de Mille's dances
reproduced by Gemze de Lappe. Set Designer: Lemuel
Ayers. Costume Designer: Miles White. Musical Director:
Salvatore Dell'Isola. Conductor: Robert Russell
Bennett.

CAST: Mary Marlo (Aunt Eller Murphy); **Harold Keel**
(Curly Mclain); Betty Jane Watson (Laurey Williams);
Thomas Spencer (Ike Skidmore); Walter Donahue (Will
Parker); Henry Clarke (Jud Fry); Dorothea MacFarland
(Ado Annie Carnes); Marek Windheim (Ali Hakim);

Jacqueline Daniels (Gertie Cummings); William S.
McCarthy (Andrew Carnes); Leonard Mence (Cord Elam).

REVIEWS: London Daily Express, Leonard Mosly, (May 1, 1947)
Mr. Mosly said that OKLAHOMA! "is a gem...It is one of those
musical plays that I believe will carve a niche in the
memories of all who see and hear its songs."

London Daily Mail, Lionel Hale, (May 1, 1947) Mr. Hale
described OKLAHOMA! as a "piece of such frolic and freshness." He lauded the performances.

London Daily Telegraph, W. A. Darlington, (May 1, 1947) Mr.
Darlinton said that OKLAHOMA! was "a terrific show. For
drive and vitality I don't remember having seen anything
like it."

London Observer, J. C. Trewin, (May 4, 1947) Mr. Trewin said
that "Rodgers has managed to make an expert, exciting, (and
how singable!) pastiche."

London Sunday Times, James Agate, (May 4, 1947) Mr. Agate
stated that the "production sizzles with slickness."

Times of London (May 1, 1947) said of OKLAHOMA!, "It is
quite true--as we had been most persistently and skillfully
led to expect--that this musical comedy has some things to
teach the English stage."

COMMENTS: When OKLAHOMA! reached 1,380 performances, it
became the Drury Lane's longest-running show since its
opening in 1663. Keel, who had replaced Alfred Drake in
the Broadway production, opened the show in London at the
Theatre Royal, Drury Lane, on April 29, 1947, where it ran
until May 27, 1950, before moving to the Stoll Theatre from
May 29, 1950-October 21, 1950, for a total of 1,548
performances. It grossed $4,300,000. On opening night,
the audience gave the show a standing ovation and insisted
on hearing more of the songs before it would leave the
theatre. During the run of the show, Keel was replaced by
Chris Robinson. (See S2 for synopsis and songs)

S 4. CAROUSEL
Stock. 1957. Dayton Memorial Hall, Dayton, Ohio.

CREDITS: Book & Lyrics by Oscar Hammerstein II. Music
by Richard Rodgers. Based on Ferenc Molnar's LILIOM as
adapted by Benjamin Glazer. Musical Director: Julian
Stein. Choreographer: Tao Strong. Musical Staging by
Tao Strong. Set Designer: Don Jensen. Lighting by G. E.
Naselius. Production Stage Manager: Leonard Patrick.

CAST: Betty Oakes (Carrie Pipperidge); Gloria Hamilton
(Julie Jordan); Mildred Germanson (Mrs. Mullin);
Howard Keel (Billy Bigelow); Lispet Nelson (Bessie);
Barbara Miller (Jessie); Don Strong (Juggler); Bill
McIntyre (1st Policeman); Edward Dwyer (David
Bascombe); Elizabeth Mannion (Nettie Fowler); Judy

Weber (June Girl); Robert Lenn (Enoch Snow); Roy
Hausen (Jigger Gragin); Deborah Choate (Hannah); Don
Strong (Boatswain); Del Nelson (Arminy); Anne Perillo
(Penny); Charlotte Small (Jennie); Ann Woodward
(Virginia); Rachel Martin (Susan); Dick Moll
(Jonathan); Don Strong (2nd Policeman); Ray Morrissey
(Captain); Heinz Neuman (1st Heavenly Friend-Brother
Joshua); Richard Mathey (2nd Heavenly Friend); Richard
Dayna (Starkeeper); Tao Strong (Louise); Jose Falcion
(Carnival Boy); Bill McIntyre (Principal); Richard
Dayna (Dr. Seldon).

COMMENT: (See S1 for synopsis and songs)

S 5. SOUTH PACIFIC
Stock. June 24, 1957-July 7, 1957. Starlight Theatre,
Kansas City, Kansas.

CREDITS: Book by Oscar Hammerstein II, Joshua Logan.
Lyrics by Oscar Hammerstein II. Music by Richard
Rodgers. Based on James Michener's Tales of the South
Pacific.

CAST: Martha Wright (Ensign Nellie Forbush); **Howard
Keel** (Emile de Becque); Gloria Lane (Bloody Mary);
Benny Baker (Luther Billis); Jim Hawthorne (Lt.
Cable); George S. Irving (Harbison).

SYNOPSIS: American sailors and Marines are stationed on a
South Pacific island during World War II. Emile de Becque,
a planter, came to the island from France. He met and
married a native girl with whom he had two children.
    After his wife died, he meets Ensign Nellie Forbush,
a nurse, and they fall in love. When she finds out about
his marriage and children, she has second thoughts about
him. When Emile puts himself in danger to help the American
cause, Nellie overcomes her doubts about him. She realizes
how much she loves Emile and returns to him.

SONGS: "Dites-mois Pourquois" (Ngana, Jerome); "A Cockeyed
Optimist" (Nellie); "Twin Soliloquis" (Nellie, Emile);
"Some Enchanted Evening" (Emile); "Bloody Mary" (Sailors,
Seabees, Marines); "There is Nothing Like a Dame" (Luther,
Professor, Sailors, Seabees, Marines); "Bali Hai" (Bloody
Mary); "I'm Gonna Wash That Man Right Outa My Hair"
(Nellie, Nurses); "Younger Than Springtime" (Lt. Cable);
"The Thanksgiving Follies" (Nurses, Seabees); "Happy Talk"
(Bloody Mary, Liat, Cable); "Honey Bun" (Nellie, Luther);
"You've Got to Be Carefully Taught" (Lt. Cable); "This
Nearly Was Mine" (Emile).

COMMENTS: The show was based on James Michener's 1947
Pulitzer Prize-winning novel. SOUTH PACIFIC opened on
Broadway on April 7, 1949, at the Majestic Theatre where it
ran 1,925 performances. It was director Joshua Logan who
brought the idea to the attention of Rodgers and Hammerstein. Mary Martin starred as Nellie Forbush. It was Enzio
Pinza's (star of the Metropolitan Opera) Broadway debut.

SOUTH PACIFIC was the second musical to receive the Pulitzer Prize in Drama and became the decade's second longest running musical.

A 1967 revival at the Music Theatre of Lincoln Center starred Florence Henderson and Giorgio Tozzi. Tozzi would provide the singing voice for Rossano Brazzi who starred in the 1958 Twentieth Century-Fox film co-starring Mitzi Gaynor. Elizabeth Taylor and Doris Day were also considered for the film. Joshua Logan directed the film. Juanita Moore recreated her Broadway role of Bloody Mary but Muriel Smith dubbed her voice in the film and Bill Lee dubbed for John Kerr who played Lt. Cable. SOUTH PACIFIC was filmed primarily on the Hawaiian Island of Kauai and became the fourth highest fifties musical to be rented to domestic theatres.

S 6. CAROUSEL

Revival. September 11, 1957-September 29, 1957. New City Center Light Opera in New York City, New York. 24 Performances.

CREDITS: Book & Lyrics by Oscar Hammerstein II. Music by Richard Rodgers. Based on Ferenc Molnar's LILIOM. Adapted by Benjamin Glazer. Produced by the New York City Center Light Opera Company directed by Jean Dalrymple. Directors: John Fearnley, Robert Pagent. Choreographer: Agnes de Mille, restaged by Robert Pagent. Set Designer: Oliver Smith. Costume Designer: Florence Klotz. Hair Stylist: Ernest Adler. Lighting by Peggy Clark. Musical Director: Julius Rudel. Choral Director: Charles Smith. Associate Conductor: Samuel Matlovski. Production Assistant: Alan Green. Production Stage Manager: Herman Shapiro. Stage Manager: Kermit Kegley. Press by Shelly Secunda.

CAST: **Howard Keel** (Billy Bigelow); Barbara Cook (Julie Jordan); Pat Stanley (Carrie Pipperidge); Russell Nype (Enoch Snow); James Mitchell (Jigger Craigin); Marie Powers (Nettie Fowler); Bambi Linn (Louise); Kay Medford (Mrs. Mullin); Victor Moore (Starkeeper); Robert Echles (David Bascombe); Evans Thornton (First Policeman); Elisa Monte (Girl with Bear); Evelyn Taylor (June Girl); Joan Eheman (Hannah); Robert Pagent (Boatswain); James Gannon (Second Policeman); Sam Kirkham (Captain); Leo Lucker (Heavenly Friend Joshua); Robert Pagent (Carnival Boy); Larry Fuller (Enoch Snow, Jr.); Bruce Baggett (Principal).

REVIEWS: <u>New York Journal-American</u>, John McClain, (September 12, 1957) Mr. McClain felt that this version of CAROUSEL was "the best version of this timeless musical I have ever seen." He thought that Keel played Billy Bigelow "with suitable strength, stature, and an amiable set of pipes."

<u>New York Times</u>, Brooks Atkinson, (September 12, 1957) Mr. Atkinson felt Keel was "obtuse" about some of his character but had a "splendid baritone" and handled the music with

"authority."

<u>Show Business</u>, Ira J. Bilowit, (September 16, 1957) Mr.
Bilowit said that the present production was "an
entertaining and wholly satisfying venture." He felt that
Keel was "an impressive Billy Bigelow, and his total effect
makes up for his stiffness and lack of power."

COMMENTS: Evan Thornton was Keel's understudy. Janet Blair
had originally been cast as Julie but left the show because
it was centered so much around Keel. Barbara Cook was
chosen to replace Miss Blair. (See S1 for synopsis and
songs)

S 7. **KISMET**

Stock. March 29, 1958. Valley Forge Music Fair, Devon,
Pennsylvania.

CREDITS: Book by Charles Lederer and Luther Davis.
Lyrics & Music by Robert Wright and George Forrest.

CAST: **Howard Keel** (Haji).

SYNOPSIS: Haji plans to marry off daughter, Marsinah to
Caliph. When the police Wazir kidnaps Marsinah, Caliph
rescues her and they are married. Meanwhile, Haji weds
LaLume, widow of the police Wazir, and competes with Omar
the tent maker in writing poetry.

SONGS: "Sands of Time" (Haji); "Rhymes Have I" (Haji); "Not
Since Nineveh" (LaLume); "Baubles, Bangles, and Beads"
(Marsinah); "Stranger in Paradise" (Marsinah, Caliph);
"Night of My Nights" (Caliph); "And This is My Beloved"
(Haji, Marsinah, Caliph); "The Olive Tree" (Haji);
"Gesticulate" (Haji); "Fate" (Haji); "He's in Love;"
"Bored" (Haji); "Was I Wazir"; "Rahadlakum" (Haji);
"Zubhediya."

COMMENTS: The play was written by Edward Knoblock, who was
an Englishman, and it became a hit for Otis Skinner in
1911. Oscar Asche did the London version in 1911. Before
its Broadway debut, KISMET had been performed, in the
summer of 1953, by Edwin Lester's Los Angeles and San
Francisco Civic Light Opera Association. The adaptations
for KISMET were taken from the works of 19th-Century
Russian composer Alexander Porfiryevich Borodin.

KISMET opened on Broadway at the Ziegfeld Theatre on
December 3, 1953, and ran for 583 performances. It was
written by Charles Lederer and Luther Davis, and was
financed by Lederer's aunt, Marion Davies. It starred
Doretta Morrow, Joan Diener, and Alfred Drake, who created
the role of Haji and revived it in a 1965 Music Theatre of
Lincoln Center production. KISMET was done on ABC-TV on
october 24, 1967, starring Jose Ferrer (in the Keel role),
Anna Maria Alberghetti, George Chakiris, Hans Conreid, and
Barbara Eden. Howard Keel portrayed Haji in the 1955 MGM
film. (See F20)

S 8. SARATOGA

October 26, 1959-November 28, 1959. Shubert Theatre,
Philadelphia, Pennsylvania. (Pre-Broadway tryout).

Broadway. December 7, 1959-February 13, 1960. Winter
Garden in New York City, New York. 80 performances.

CREDITS: Lyrics by Johnny Mercer. Music by Harold
Arlen. Lybrettist: Morton Da Costa. Based on Edna
Ferber's novel Saratoga Trunk. Produced by Robert
Fryer. Director: Morton Da Costa. Choreographer: Ralph
Beaumont. Set Designer: Cecil Beaton. Costume
Designer: Cecil Beaton. Lighting by Jean Rosenthal.
Dance Arranger: Genevieve Pitot. Musical Director:
Jerry Arlen. Vocal Arranger: Herbert Greene. Conductor:
Philip J. Lang. Production Supervisor: Morton Da Costa.
Production Stage Manager: Edward Padula. Stage Manager:
Duane Camp. Press by Arthur Cantor.

CAST: **Howard Keel** (Clint Maroon); Carol Lawrence
(Clio); Carol Brice (Kakou); Warde Donavan (Bart Van
Steed); Truman Gaige (M. Begue); Richard Graham
(Austin Haussy); Edith King (Mrs. Bellop); James
Millhollin (Mr. Bean); Odette Myrtil (Belle Piquery);
Augie Rios (Shorty); Tun Tun (Cupide); Albert Popwell
(Carpenter); Brenda Long (Maudey); Virginia Capers
(Charwoman); Martha King (Mrs. Le Clerc); Beatrice
Bushkin (Madame Dulaine); Jeannine Masterson
(Charlotte Therese); Frank Green (Haberdashery Clerk);
Barney Johnston (Fabric Salesman); Lanier Davis (M.
La Fosse); Gerrianne Raphael (Daisy Porcelain);
Isabella Hoopes (Clarissa Van Steed); Janyce Wagner
(Miss Diggs); Natalie Core (Grandmother Dulaine/Mrs.
Porcelain); Mark Zeller (Drapery Man/Leon, a Waiter);
Truman Gaige (Editor/Mr. Gould).

SYNOPSIS: In 1880, Clio returns from her Paris exile to
the Dulaine Family mansion on Rampart Street in New Orleans
to avenge the Dulaine Family's rejection of her mother as
well as to seek fortune, status, and a husband. A representative of the family tries to persuade Clio to leave the
city but Clio scoffs at the idea. Although westerner Clint
Maroon does not appear to be the right man for a husband,
Clio is attracted to him. Clint wants to get back at the
railroad owners who forced his family from their Montana
ranch. Clint and Clio join forces. The two eventually win
their battle with the Dulaines.
     Clio and Clint try to get into society by masquerading
as a widowed French countess and a rich rancher. Railroad
heir Bart Van Steed falls for Clio. Clint wants out of the
masquerade but Clio can not give up her quest for wealth
and status.
     Clint defends Van Steed's railroad against gangs and
is injured. When a fight takes place, Clio hears of it
and decides all she wants is Clint and is rejected by
society when she dresses as a wash woman.
     Clint returns owning a big part of the railroad and
his and Clio's love grows stronger. Clio does not need to

worry about wealth and status anymore.

SONGS: "One Step, Two Step" (Belle); "I'll Be Respectable"
(Clio); "Gettin' a Man" (Kakou, Belle); "Why Fight This"
(Clint, Clio); "Petticoat High" (Clio); "A Game of Poker"
(Belle); "Saratoga Duet" (Clint, Clio); "Countin' Our
Chickens" (Clint, Clio); "You or Noone" (Clint); "The
Cure"; "The Man in My Life" (Clio); "The Men Who Run the
Country" (Clint); "Goose Never Be a Peacock" (Kakou); "Dog
Eat Dog"/"The Railroad Fight" (Clint, Cupide); "The
Gamblers" (Clio); "The Gossip Song" (Mrs. Bellop); "The
Poka" (Clio); Love Held Lightly"-Reprise (Clio);
"Petticoat High"-Reprise (Clio); "Game of Poker"-Reprise
(Clint, Clio, Belle).

REVIEWS: New York Morning Telegraph, Whitney Bolton,
(December 9, 1959) Whitney Bolton felt that the book "is
old-fashioned, heavy-footed, and contains some of the lamest
jokes since 1920." It was also stated by Bolton that "here
is Howard Keel busting out with the voice and striding man-
fully through the occasion and once more nothing vibrant
readily happens."

New York Journal-American, John McClain, (December 8, 1959)
Mr. McClain felt that SARATOGA "is no block buster,...but
it has grace and class and--above all--a highly popular
score." He said, "Mr. Keel is a towering and personable
gentleman, with voice to match, and he wins you at once."

New York Times, Brook Atkinson, (December 8, 1959) Mr.
Atkinson thought that SARATOGA was "dull" and despite the
number of professionals connected with the show, that one
way or another they were "off their form." Despite Miss
Lawrence's "lovely supple" singing and the fact that Howard
Keel had "one of the finest" voices on the Broadway stage,
the songs became "increasingly innocuous" the further along
the show went.

The Philadelphia Inquirer, Henry Murdock, (October 27,
1959) Mr. Murdock felt that SARATOGA "is rich in
production, fortunate in its leads, thin in story and
sometimes slow in action." He thought that Keel was
"convincing" and that he had a "bass-baritone" that was
rarely used in today's musicals.

Variety (December 9, 1959) felt that SARATOGA was an
"extravagantly beautiful and paralyzingly tedious
operetta." It was stated that Keel's "playing is rather
inflexible, and although his baritone voice is properly
resonant, he doesn't enunciate the lyrics clearly."

ADDITIONAL REVIEWS: Newark Evening News (December 8, 1959);
Newsday (December 16, 1959); Newsweek (December 21, 1959);
New York Daily News (December 8, 1959); The New Yorker
(December 19, 1959); New York Herald Tribune (December 8,
1959); New York Mirror (December 8, 1959); New York Morning
Telegraph (December 23, 1959); New York Post (December 8,
1959); New York World Telegram & Sun (December 8, 1959);

Saturday Review (December 26, 1959); Time (December 21, 1959); Women's Wear Daily (December 8, 1959).

COMMENTS: After reading Morton Da Costa's script, Edna Ferber (whose 1941 novel the show was based on) made a rewrite of her own but left the show after being ignored. While SARATOGA was on the road, Harold Arlen (in what would be his last musical) became ill as well as discouraged with the show. While Arlen was ill, Johnny Mercer wrote the words and music to three songs "Gettin' a Man," "The Men Who Run the Country," and "Why Fight This." Several songs were dropped from the show before it opened on Broadway. They included "Al Fresco," "Bon Appetit," "Here Goes Nothing," "I'm Headed For Big Things," "Lessons in Love," "The Parks of Paris," "Readin' the News," "Work Songs," and "You For Me." The anticipation of the show, which started rehearsals on September 21, 1959, was so great that it caused advanced ticket sales to reach $1,500,000. It grossed $345,000 during its pre-Broadway run in Philadelphia. Gerrianne Raphael filled in occasionally for Miss Lawrence while the show played in Philadelphia. Cecil Beaton won a Tony for his costume designs.
  Rock Hudson and Jeanmarie had been mentioned for the leads that eventually went to Carol Lawrence and Howard Keel. SARATOGA was Keel's first original role. NBC and RCA Victor Records absorbed the show's $400,000 cost. During the show's tryouts, Jane Darwell quit the show and her role of Mrs. Bellop went to Edith King.
  It was thought that some of the show's problems might have been that the audience was not interested in a show where both leads were out for revenge. Due to the show's length, much of the better material was dropped during tryouts. Da Costa was not able to bring life to the romance between the two leads. (See D41)

S 9. MISTER ROBERTS
  Stock. 1960s. Dayton Memorial Hall, Dayton, Ohio.

  CREDITS: Play by Thomas Heggen, Joshua Logan. Based on the book Mister Roberts by Thomas Heggen. Produced by John Kenley. Set Designer: Paul Kimpel. Carpenter: Ralph Bailey. Lighting by Carl Phillips. Spotlight by Mike Uhler. Props by Conrad Button. Staged by Ray Parker. Stage Manager: Joseph Chestnut.

  CAST: Jack Darrow (Chief Johnson); **Howard Keel** (Lt. J. G. Roberts); Robert Cromwell (Doc); David Doyle (Dowdy); Jack Goode (Captain); Richard Sakal (Insignia); Charles Cagle (Mannion); Robert Murray (Lindstrom); Peter Held (Strefanowski); George Salisbury (Wiley); Ken Noetzel (Schlemmer); Hazen Gifford (Ensign Pulver); Jimmy Reuff (Reber); Wendell Gray (Dolan); Jerry Meehan (Gerhart); Ruthanne Myers (Lt. Ann Girard); Ron Riegler (Shore Patrolman); George Yarrick (Military Policeman); Richard Olson (Shore Patrol Officer).

  SYNOPSIS: MISTER ROBERTS is about a bored crew who are on

the back waters of the Pacific during World War II.
Lieutenant Douglas Roberts throws the captain's scrawny palm
tree overboard to help relieve boredom. Captain Morton is
furious and gets Roberts to stop asking for a transfer to
active duty in exchange for liberty for the crew.
    Ensign Pulver designs a firecracker he plans to use to
blow up the captain's bunk but while testing it it blows up
the laundry. After a contest to forge the captain's
signature, to show appreciation to Roberts for getting them
shore leave, Roberts is transferred to active duty where he
is killed.

COMMENTS: Thomas Heggen wrote a series of articles on his
World War II experiences. Atlantic Monthly published the
first story Night Watch in August 1946. Heggen's entire
series was published in book form and titled Mister
Roberts (1946). The book had ten editions and sold more
than 75,000 copies. Producer Leland Hayward purchased the
rights to the book. He persuaded Heggen to team up with
Max Shulman to write a play. The script was not good so
Hayward took Joshua Logan up on his offer to work with
Heggen on a new script. MISTER ROBERTS won a Tony in
1948 for the year's Best Dramatic Play. Logan won the New
York Drama Critics Poll as Best Director. Henry Fonda
shared a Tony for Best Actor for his portrayal of Mr.
Roberts with Paul Kelly and Basil Rathbone.
    Tyrone Powers played the title role in the London
production which opened on July 19, 1950, at the Coliseum
Theatre with Jackie Cooper as Ensign Pulver. The London
production played for six months.
    Charlton Heston revived the title role in 1956 at
the New York City Center. William Harrigan was the
captain, and Orson Bean played Pulver.
    Warner Bros. had planned to cast either William Holden
or Marlon Brando as Mr. Roberts in the film, but Henry
Fonda signed to recreate his original role. John Ford was
hired to direct. Filming began on the Island of Midway
aboard the U.S.S. Hewell. Ford left the project and was
replaced by Mervyn LeRoy who moved the filming location to
Hawaii. William Powell, in what would be his last film,
played Doc, James Cagney was the captain, and Jack Lemmon
played Ensign Pulver. Lemmon received an Oscar for best
supporting actor.
    MISTER ROBERTS debuted on NBC-TV on September 17,
1965, but was not successful.

S10. KISS ME, KATE
    Stock. 1960s.

    CREDITS: Book by Samuel and Bella Spewack. Lyrics and
    Music by Cole Porter.

    CAST: **Howard Keel** (Fred Graham/Petrichio).

SYNOPSIS: Lilli Vaneswsi and Fred Graham have been
divorced. When Lilli announces she is going to marry Tex
Callaway, Fred says he is engaged to Lois. They both
become jealous, thus realizing they still love each other.

Fred tells Lilli he plans to let Lois play the female lead
in the musical version of THE TAMING OF THE SHREW in order
to get Lilli to take the role.
They begin to rekindle their love until some misunder-
standings concerning Fred and Lois cause Lilli to walk out
on opening night. Two gangsters, Lippy and Slug, have been
sent to collect an I.O.U. that Fred owes their boss. They
keep Lilli from leaving in order to protect their boss'
interest.
Things are eventually straightened out and Fred and
Lilli remain together.

SONGS: "Another Opening, Another Show"; "Why Can't You
Behave?" (Lois, Dancer); "Wunderbar" (Graham, Lilli); "So
in Love" (Graham, Lilli); "We Open in Venice" (Graham,
Lilli, Lois, Dancers); "I Hate Men" (Lilli); "I've Come to
Wive It Wealthily in Padua" (Graham); "Tom, Dick, or
Harry" (Lois, Dancers); "Were Thine That Special Face"
(Graham); "Too Darn Hot" (Lois); "So Kiss Me, Kate"
(Graham, Lilli); "Where is the Life That Late I Led?"
(Graham); "Always True to You in My Fashion" (Lois, Dancer);
"So in Love"-Reprise (Graham); "Brush Up Your Shakespeare"
(Gangsters); "I Am Ashamed That Women Are So Simple."

COMMENTS: KISS ME, KATE was based on the Alfred Lunt-Lynn
Fontanne production of THE TAMING OF THE SHREW. Stage
manager Saint Subber thought of a musical version of the
show after taking note of the on and off stage bickering of
Lunt and Fontanne. Subber and his co-producer, Lemuel
Ayers, got Bella and Spewack to write the script. Subber
and Ayers approached Burton Lane to compose the music but
he turned down the project. They then went to Cole Porter.
Porter felt that Shakespeare (who wrote THE TAMING OF THE
SHREW circa 1596) was too highbrow for Broadway but Spewack
was able to change his mind.
The show premiered in the fall of 1948 with Alfred
Drake, Lilli Vanessi, Patricia Morison, and Lisa Kirk. It
opened on Broadway at the New Century Theatre on December
30, 1948. It ran for 1,070 performances and was Porter's
biggest hit and won a Tony for Best Musical. Porter had
teamed with Samuel and Bella Spewack some ten years earlier
in LEAVE IT TO ME. KISS ME, KATE was the fourth longest
running musical of the forties. Before the role was given
to Patricia Morison, it had been offered to Jarmila
Novotna, Mary Martin, Lily Pons, and Jeanette MacDonald.
Keith Andes and Ted Scott were replacements for Drake
during the shows run.
KISS ME, KATE was done twice on TV. The first time
was on NBC's "Hallmark Hall of Fame" on November 20, 1958,
starring Alfred Drake (as Graham/Petrichio), Patricia
Morison (as Lilli/Katherine), Bill Hayes, and Jack Klugman.
The second time was on ABC's "Armstrong Circle Theatre" on
March 25, 1968, starring Robert Goulet (as Graham/
Petrichio), Carol Lawrence (as Lilli/Katherine), Jessica
Walters, and Marty Ingels. Howard Keel played
Graham/Petrichio in the 1953 MGM film. (See F15)

S11. SHOW BOAT
Stock. 1960s.

CREDITS: Book & Lyrics by Oscar Hammerstein II. Music by Jerome Kern. Based on Edna Ferber's novel.

CAST: **Howard Keel** (Gaylord Ravenal).

SYNOPSIS: The story takes place between the mid 1880s and 1927 and concerns Gaylord Ravenal (a gambler) who joins Captain Andy Hawks and his wife Parthy on the Cotton Blossom as an actor. Aboard the Mississippi show boat, he meets and falls in love with the Captain's daughter, Magnolia, and they are married.
     When there is marital trouble, Gaylord leaves Magnolia, not knowing she is expecting a child. When he learns he is the father of a girl, he goes back to see her and Gaylord and Magnolia are reunited.

SONGS: "Make Believe" (Gaylord, Magnolia); "Ol' Man River" (Joe); "Can't Help Lovin' Dat Man" (Julie); "Life Upon the Wicked Stage" (Ellie, Frank); "You Are Love" (Gaylord, Magnolia); "Why Do I Love You?" (Magnolia, Gaylord, Andy, Parthy); "Bill" (Julie); "After the Ball" (Magnolia); "Nobody Else But Me"; "I Might Fall Back on You" (Ellie, Frank).

COMMENTS: SHOW BOAT (based on Edna Ferber's 1926 novel) appeared on Broadway from December 27, 1927 to May 4, 1927, at the Ziegfield Theatre and ran 572 performances. It starred Norma Terris (Magnolia) and Howard Marsh (Ravenal). It had a return engagement at the Casino Theatre from May 19, 1932-October 22, 1932, and played 180 performances. This time Gaylord was played by Dennis King. Its London run was at the Theatre Royal, Drury Lane from May 3, 1928-March 2, 1929 for a total of 350 performances. Julie was played by Marie Burke and Gaylord by Howett Worster. SHOW BOAT was revived again from January 5, 1946-January 4, 1947, starring Jan Clayton (Magnolia) and Charles Fredericks (Ravenal) and ran for 418 performances.
     Howard Keel and Kathryn Grayson played Gaylord and Magnolia in the 1951 MGM Film. (See F5)

S12. THE RAINMAKER
Stock. 1960s.

CREDITS: N. Richard Nash wrote the three act play.

CAST: **Howard Keel** (Bill Starbuck).

SYNOPSIS: A long summer drought in Kansas has H. C. Curry and his sons Noah and Jim worried about what will happen if it does not rain. Con man Bill Starbuck arrives and claims he can make it rain in twenty-four hours for $100. He gets Jim to beat a bass drum to bring storm clouds while he romances Lizzie (Curry's daughter).
     Deputy Sheriff File wants to arrest Starbuck for fraud but is convinced not to. File realizes he loves

Lizzie and when Starbuck asks her to go away with him, she realizes life would be better with File. As Starbuck leaves, it storms--thus he no longer is a fraud.

COMMENTS: After the initial appearance of the RAINMAKER on TV's "Philco Playhouse" in 1953, Richard Nash changed it into a three act play. The Broadway production opened at the Cort Theatre on October 28, 1954, and ran for 125 performances.
     The London production, which opened on May 31, 1956, at the St. Martin's Theatre, was more successful than the Broadway version. The London production ran 228 performances. Geraldine Page appeared in both the Broadway and London productions. On Broadway, Darren McGavin played Bill Starbuck while Sam Wanamaker played the part in London.
     A musical production entitled 110 IN THE SHADE was produced by David Merrick and opened on Broadway on October 24, 1963, at the Broadhurst Theatre. Harvey Schmidt composed the music and Tom Jones wrote the lyrics. The musical starred Inga Swenson, Stephen Douglas, Robert Horton, and Will Geer. 110 IN THE SHADE ran longer than the original play with 330 performances.
     THE RAINMAKER was filmed by Paramount and was released in December 1956. It starred Katharine Hepburn as Lizzie Curry, Burt Lancaster as Starbuck, and Wendell Corey as File.

S13. SUNRISE AT CAMPOBELLO
     Stock. July 11, 1960-July 16, 1960. Playhouse in the Park, Philadelphia, Pennsylvania.

     CREDITS: Play by Dore Schary. Produced by Ethelyn R. Thrasher in association with The Theatre Guild and Dore Schary. Director: Jean Barrere. Advance Director: Dick Robbins. Set Designer: Charles Evans. Lighting by Bruce McMullen.

     CAST: Pat Snyder (Anna Roosevelt); Michaele Myers (Eleanor Roosevelt); Lester Lockwood, Jr. (Franklin D. Roosevelt, Jr.); Charles Murphy (James Roosevelt); John Nangle (Elliott Roosevelt); Wally Peterson (Edward); **Howard Keel** (Franklin Delano Roosevelt); Guy Lee Lockwood (John Roosevelt); Russell Collins (Louis McHenry Howe); Nancy Cushman (Mrs. Sara Delano Roosevelt); Vera Lockwood (Miss Marguerite, [Missy] LeHand); William Fort (Doctor Bennet); Beau Tilden (Mr. Brimmer); Wally Peterson (Mr. Lassiter); John Cecil Holm (Governor Alfred E. Smith); William Fort (Senator Walsh); Wally Peterson (A Speaker).

SYNOPSIS: The play traces the period when Franklin D. Roosevelt comes down with polio, in 1921, while at his summer home in Campobello, Canada. It also relates the struggle of his wife and friend Louis Howe to get him back to health and into public life against his mother's wishes to keep him a wealthy country squire. The play concludes at Madison Square Garden in 1924, when Roosevelt nominates

Al Smith for president.

REVIEWS: Philadelphia Evening Bulletin, Ernie Schier,
(July 12, 1960) Mr. Schier felt that Howard Keel "makes a
superb F.D.R....Keel turns in a winning, modulated and
completely relaxed performance." He also said of the show
that "It is an entertaining and moving evening."

Philadelphia Inquirer, Clark Larrabee, (July 12, 1960) Mr.
Larrabee felt that SUNRISE AT CAMPOBELLO "is not a great
play. Often it is even rather superficial in its treatment
of matters that are profoundly important. But it remains a
heart-warming evening in the theatre...Howard Keel as
F.D.R. and Michaele Myers as Eleanor Roosevelt are both
excellent."

COMMENTS: Mr. Schary was screen-writer/producer and MGM
production head. Ralph Bellamy created the role on
Broadway, in 1958, and again in the 1960 Warner Bros. film.
Howard Keel was scheduled to do the Broadway version but
hospitalization with double pneumonia prevented him from
doing the show.
    The playhouse production played during the week of the
Democratic Convention.

S14. SOUTH PACIFIC
Stock. August 29, 1960-September 3, 1960. Oakdale
Musical Theatre, Wallingford, Connecticut.

Stock. September 5, 1960-September 18, 1960. Carousel
Theatre, Framingham, Massachusetts.

COMMENT: (See S5 for synopsis and songs)

S15. THE CROSSING
Stock. May 27, 1963-June 8, 1963. Bucks County Playhouse, New Hope, Pennsylvania.

CREDITS: Play by Howard Fast. Director: Edmon Ryan.
Set Designer: Clarke Dunham. Costume Designer:
Georgene. Lighting by Robert Brand.

CAST: Edward Shambaugh (Adam Haynes); Ann Williams
(Annie Anderson); James Pritchett (Thaddeus Brown);
Claude Harz (Alexander Hamilton); **Howard Keel** (General
George Washington); William Hughes (Colonel Knox);
Paul Larson (Colonel Glover); Dillon Evans (Sergeant
Hasbrook); Mark Mensch (The Fisherman); Carl Rayborn
(Colonel Mifflin); Bob Hosbach (General Greene);
George Ives (General Gates); Robert Glaesman, Robert
Lawton, Russell Stagg, David Vine (Continental
Soldiers).

SYNOPSIS: THE CROSSING is a drama centering around General
George Washington's crossing of the Delaware.

S16. NO STRINGS
Broadway. June 3, 1963-August 3, 1963. Broadhurst

Theatre in New York City, New York.

CREDITS: Book by Samuel Taylor. Lyrics & Music by
Richard Rodgers. Produced by Richard Rodgers in asso-
ciation with Samuel Taylor. Director: Joe Layton.
Choreographer: Joe Layton. Associate Choreographer:
Buddy Schwab. Set Designer: David Hays. Lighting by
David Hays. Costume Designers: Fred Voelpe, Donald
Brooks. Dance Arranger: Peter Matz. Musical Director:
Peter Matz. Conductor: Ralph Burns.

CAST: Barbara McNair (Barbara Woodruff); **Howard Keel**
(David Jordan); Yvonne Constant (Jeanette Valmy);
Alvin Epstein (Luc Delbert); Polly Rowles (Mollie
Plummer); Don Chastain (Mike Robinson); Mitchell Gregg
(Louis De Pourtal); Bernice Massi (Comfort O'Connell);
Ann Hidges (Gabrielle Bertin); Paul Cambeilh
(Marcello Agnolotti).

SYNOPSIS: Barbara Woodruff, who is a model, meets Pulitzer
Prize-winning novelist David Jordan in Paris where he has
decided to forgo writing for the life of living off wealthy
American tourists. They fall in love and Barbara tries to
make him go back to writing. He realizes if he is going to
succeed, he will have to return home to Maine, thus the two
must separate.

SONGS: "The Sweetest Sounds" (Barbara, David); "How Sad"
(David); "Loads of Love" (Barbara); "The Man Who Has
Everything" (Louis); "Be My Host" (David, Comfort, Mike,
Luc, Gabrielle); "La, La, La" (Jeanette, Luc); "You Don't
Tell Me" (Barbara); "Love Makes the World Go" (Mollie,
Comfort); "Nobody Told Me" (Barbara, David); "Look No
Further" (Barbara, David); "Maine" (David, Barbara); "An
Orthodox Fool" (Barbara).

REVIEWS: The New Yorker, Edith Oliver, (March 31, 1962)
Edith Oliver felt the show's weakness was in the "book and
the characters....Aurally and visually, it is a delightful
show."

Variety, Hobe Morrison, (March 21, 1962) Morrison felt that
the songs were "generally good" but were not up to Rodgers'
"incomparable best." The book was "at best adequate."

ADDITIONAL REVIEWS: The Nation (April 14, 1962); Saturday
Review (March 31, 1962); Time (March 31, 1962).

COMMENTS: In his first project following the death of
lyricist Oscar Hammerstein II, Richard Rodgers handled both
the music and lyrics. The production was unique because
the orchestra was backstage while musicians were on stage
to play for the singers, and because the major players and
chorus moved scenery in front of the audience. "Yankee Go
Home" was cut from the score before the New York
production.
       Keel and McNair replaced Richard Kiley and Diahann
Carroll in the Broadway production. Noelle Adams created

the role of Jeanette Constant. NO STRINGS opened at the
54th Street Theatre on March 15, 1962, where it ran until
September 29, 1962, before moving to the Broadhurst Theatre
on October 1, 1962, until it closed (after 580
performances) on August 3, 1963. NO STRINGS won Tony
Awards in the 1961-1962 season for Best Score, Richard
Rodgers; Best Performance in a Musical (female), Diahann
Carroll; and Best Choreographer, Joe Layton. It also won a
Grammy for Best Original Cast Album in 1962 and an Outer
Circle Award for Best Musical in the 1961-1962 season.

S17. NO STRINGS
Tour. August 5, 1963-August 19, 1963. Shubert Theatre,
Boston,

Tour. October 7, 1963-October 12, 1963. Music Hall,
Kansas City, Missouri.

Tour. November 25, 1963-January 4, 1964. Curran
Theatre, San Francisco.

CREDITS: Book by Samuel Taylor. Lyrics & Music by
Richard Rodgers. Produced by Richard Rodgers in asso-
ciation with Samuel Taylor. Director: Joe Layton.
Choreographer: Joe Layton. Associate Choreographer:
Buddy Schwab. Set Designer: David Hays. Lighting by
David Hays. Costume Designers: Fred Voelpe, Donald
Brooks. Dance Arranger: Peter Matz. Musical Director:
Jack Lee. Conductor: Ralph Burns.

CAST: Barbara McNair (Barbara Woodruff); **Howard Keel**
(David Jordan); Beti Seay (Jeanette Valmy); Juki Arkin
(Luc Delbert); Jane Van Duser (Mollie Plummer); Robert
Goss (Mike Robinson); Ferdinand Hilt (Louis De
Pourtal); Kit Smythe (Comfort O'Connell); Ann Hodges
(Gabrielle Bertin); Marc Scott (Marcello Agnolotti);
Standby for Keel was Robert Goss and for McNair
Beverly Todd.

COMMENT: The touring production played in 7 cities. (See
S16 for synopsis and songs.)

S18. CAMELOT
Stock. July 20, 1964-July 25, 1964. Carousel Theatre,
Franingham, Massachusetts.

Stock. August 5, 1964-August 9, 1964. Westbury Music
Fair, Long Island, New York.

Stock. August 11, 1964-August 18, 1964. Camden County
Music Fair, Camden, New Jersey.

Stock. August 30, 1964-September 5, 1964. Valley Forge
Music Fair, Devon, Pennsylvania.

Stock. March 1965. Mineola Playhouse, Long Island, New
York.

CREDITS: Book & Lyrics by Alan Jay Lerner. Music by
Frederick Loewe. Based on THE ONCE AND FUTURE KING by
T. H. White. Produced by Frank Connelly. Director:
James Hammerstein. Choreographer: Peter Conlow.
Musical Director: Anton Coppola.

CAST: **Howard Keel** (King Arthur); Constance Towers
(Guenevere); Lester James (Lancelot); Laurie Main
(Pellinore); John Voight (Mordred); Sam Kressen
(Knight).

CAST: (Carousel Theatre): **Howard Keel** (King Arthur);
Constance Towers (Guenevere); Bob Holiday (Lancelot);
Laurie Main (Pellinore); Morgan Paull, Richard
Neilson, Kelly McCormick.

SYNOPSIS: CAMELOT concerned the Knights of the Round Table
and the romantic triangle between King Arthur, Queen
Guenevere, and Sir Lancelot. Even though his kingdom is in
ruins and Guenevere has been lost to Lancelot, Arthur tells
a young boy to tell others about the glories that once were
Camelot.

SONGS: "I Wonder What the King is Doing Tonight" (Arthur);
"The Simple Joys of Maidenhood" (Guenevere); "Camelot"
(Arthur); "Follow Me"; "The Lusty Month of May"
(Guenevere); "C'est Moi" (Lancelot); "Then You May Take Me
to the Fair" (Guenevere & Knights); "How to Handle a Woman"
(Arthur); "If Ever I Would Leave You" (Lancelot); "Before I
Gaze At You Again" (Guenevere); "The Seven Deadly Virtues";
"What Do the Simple Folk" (Arthur, Guenevere); "Fie on
Goodness"; "I Loved You Once in Silence" (Guenevere);
"Guenevere"; "Camelot"-Reprise (Arthur).

COMMENTS: Richard Burton, Julie Andrews, and Robert Goulet
appeared in the Broadway production which opened on
December 3, 1960, at the Majestic Theatre and ran for 873
performances. The show was based on THE ONCE AND FUTURE
KING (1939) and had been originally titled JENNY KISSED ME.
During tryouts, director Moss Hart had a heart attack and
Lerner filled in as temporary director. As of that time,
CAMELOT's advance ticket sales were the largest in
Broadway's history.
    Richard Burton reprised his role for a 1980 tour which
had a limited New York run. While on the road, Burton
became ill and was replaced by Richard Harris.
    Ironically, it was Harris who starred in the 1967
Warner Bros. film with co-star Vanessa Redgrave. Lerner
wrote the script for the film which dropped the song
"Before I Gaze At You Again." Exterior shooting was done
in Spain and the production, which opened in October 1967,
cost $15,000,000.

S19. SOUTH PACIFIC
    Stock. Summer 1965. Westbury Music Fair, Long Island.

    Stock. June 21, 1965-June 28, 1965. Valley Forge
    Music Fair, Devon, Pennsylvania.

CREDITS: Book by Oscar Hammerstein II, Joshua Logan. Lyrics by Oscar Hammerstein II. Music by Richard Rodgers. Based on James Michener's Tales of the South Pacific. Director: Wakefield Poole.

CAST: Joanne Lester (Ensign Millie Forbush); **Howard Keel** (Emile de Becque); Sylvia Syms (Bloody Mary); Jim Tushar (Lt. Cable); Bob Wiensko (Stewpot); Roddi & Jodi King (Children).

REVIEW: Philadelphia Evening Bulletin, George Beezer, (June 22, 1965) Mr. Beezer felt that the show was a "responsible, entertaining production" and that Keel's "baritone voice fills the tent, sounding almost unbelievably like the original Emile--even the accent is the same."

COMMENT: (See S5 for synopsis and songs)

S20. CAROUSEL
Stock. 1966. Storrowton Music Fair, Hartford, Connecticut.

COMMENTS: It opened in Baltimore, Maryland, and also played Camden, New Jersey, and Cleveland, Ohio. (See S1 for synopsis and songs)

S21. ON A CLEAR DAY YOU CAN SEE FOREVER
Tour. May 22, 1967. O'Keefe Center, Toronto-October 7, 1967. Shubert Theatre, Chicago.

Tour. June 19, 1967-June 24, 1967. Morris A. Mechanic.

Tour. December 31, 1967. Civic Auditorium, Sacramento, California-May 26, 1968. Music Hall, Seattle.

Tour. 1968. Parker Playhouse, Ft. Lauderdale, Florida.

TORONTO TO CHICAGO PRODUCTIONS

CREDITS: Book & Lyrics by Alan Jay Lerner. Music by Burton Lane. Produced by Zev Bufman in association with Nederlander-Steinbrenner Productions. Director: Milton Katselas. Choreographer: Eddie Roll. Set Designer: Peter Wexler. Costume Designer: Brooks Van Horn. Lighting by James Riley. Dance Arranger: Betty Walberg. Musical Director: Richard Parrenello. Music Continuity by Trude Rittman. Vocal Arranger: Trude Rittman. Conductor: Robert Russell Bennett. General Manager: M. Bufman. Production Associate: Jerry Douglas. Special Coordinator: Diane Krasny.

CAST: **Howard Keel** (Dr. Mark Bruckner); William Coppola (James Preston); Francine Beers (Mrs. Hatch); Jodi Perselle (Muriel Bunson); Barbara Lang (Daisy Gamble); Lester James (Edward Moncrief); Leon Benedict (Samuel Welles); Nancy Wiench (Mrs. Welles); William Coppola (Sir Hubert Isdale); Joseph Pichette (Sir Hubert's Son); George Comtois (Solicitor); Cy Young

(Warren Smith); Harriet Lynn (Patty); Cindy Roberts (Sally); Marjory Edson (Flora); Rowan Tudor (Dr. Conrad Fuller); Leon Benedict (B.C.A. Official); Barbara Lang (Melinda).

CALIFORNIA TO SEATTLE PRODUCTIONS

CREDITS: Book & Lyrics by Alan Jay Lerner. Music by Burton Lane. Produced by Robert Cherin Productions in association with Joseph Weill and Arthur Kellman. Director: Ross Bowman. Choreographer: Luis de Yberrando. Musical Numbers Staged by Luis de Yberrando. Set Designers: Herbert Senn, Helen Pond. Costume Designer: Brooks Van Horn. Lighting by Robert Steele. Musical Director: Gordon Munford. Coordinator: Edward Meyers.

CAST: **Howard Keel** (Dr. Mark Bruckner); Ruth Warshawsky (Mrs Hatch); Linda Michele or Carla Alberghetti (Daisy Gamble); Sandra Nitz (Muriel Bunson); Walter Willison (James Preston); Bert Conway (Samuel Welles); Ruth Warshawsky (Mrs. Welles); Robert Hatton (Sir Hubert Insdale); John Rubinstein (Sir Hubert's Son); Craig Yates (Solicitor); Brian Avery (Edward Moncrief); John Rubinstein (Warren Smith); Carol Carle (Flora); Bert Conway (Dr. Conrad Fuller); R. G. Denison (B.C.A. Official).

SYNOPSIS: Daisy Gamble can see the future and when Dr. Bruckner hypnotized her, Daisy recounts her life as Melinda Wells during London's 18th Century. When Mark becomes interested in Melinda, Daisy runs off. The couple eventually get back together.

SONGS: "Hurry! It's Lovely Up Here" (Mark, Daisy); "First Regression" (Edward); "Solicitor's Song" (Solicitor, Trundle, Hubert Insdale, Welles); "He Wasn't You" (Daisy, Edward); "On a Clear Day You Can See Forever" (Mark); "The Gout" (Muriel, Chorus); "On the S.S. Bernard Cohn" (Daisy, Muriel, Patty, Sally, Chorus); "She Wasn't You" (Edward, Melinda); "Melinda" (Mark); "When I Come Around Again" (Preston & Students); "What Did I Have That I Don't Have" (Daisy); "Wait Till We're 65" (Daisy, Warren); "Come Back to Me" (Mark); "Come Back to Me"-Reprise (Mark); Finale (Mark).

COMMENTS: Alan Jay Lerner was interested in ESP and teamed with Richard Rodgers, in 1962, to write the musical I PICKED A DAY. When the partnership did not work out, Lerner got together with Burton Lane and renamed the show ON A CLEAR DAY YOU CAN SEE FOREVER. Barbara Harris was the only one considered for the female lead. Six actors were considered for the male lead and the role went to Louis Jordan. When the show tried out in Boston, John Cullum replaced Jordan. It was the first Broadway show to have a $11.90 ticket price. The show opened on Broadway at the Mark Hellinger Theatre on October 17, 1965, and ran 280 performances.

In the Toronto to Chicago tour, the show played at
the Parker Playhouse in Ft. Lauderdale, Florida. In that
production Karen Black played Daisy/Melinda, Alfred Toigo
played Edward Moncrief, Marybeth Lahr played Flora, and Erik
Rhoades did Dr. Conrad Fuller. The musical director was
Pembroke Davenport.

John Raitt, Bill Hayes, and John Ericson also played
Bruckner in the California to Seattle tour.

The Paramount film, released in June 1970, starred
Barbara Streisand and Yves Montand. Many of the stage
songs were dropped from the film. Burton Lane added two
songs to the film "Love With All the Trimmings" and "Go to
Sleep." The flashback scenes were filmed at the Royal
Pavilion in Brighton.

S22. THE FANTASTICKS
Stock. January 22, 1968-January 27, 1968. Parker
Playhouse, Ft. Lauderdale, Florida.

CREDITS: Book & Lyrics by Tom Jones. Music by Harvey
Schmidt. Based on the play LES ROMANTIQUES by Edmond
Rostand. Produced by Zev Bufman. Director: William
Francisco. Set Designer: James Riley. Set Builder:
Harry Schmale, Jr. Lighting by James Riley. Musical
Director: Glen Clugston.

CAST: **Howard Keel** (Narrator); Susan Watson (The Girl);
Jack Blackton (The Boy); Dean Dittmann (The Boy's
Father); Gwyllum Evans (The Girl's Father); Lionel
Wilson (The Actor); Edward Garrabrandt (The Man Who
Dies); Don Miller (The Mute).

SYNOPSIS: The narrator (Keel) explains that a boy, Matt
(Blackton) and a girl, Luisa (Warson) are in love but are
kept apart by his father (Dittmann) and her father (Evans)
because they feel that by keeping them apart they will be
drawn closer together.

The fathers hire a bandit, El Gallo (Keel) and an
actor (Wilson) to stage a rape so that Matt can come to
Luisa's rescue. Matt and Luisa are drawn together until
the couple learn that they were manipulated by their
fathers. The couple argue and Matt leaves to travel around
the world while Luisa goes off with El Gallo. The couple
eventually come to their senses and are reunited.

SONGS: "Try to Remember" (The Narrator); "Much More" (The
Girl); "Metaphor" (The Boy, The Girl); "Never say No" (The
Fathers); "It Depends on What You Pay" (The Narrator, The
Fathers); "Soon It's Gonna Rain" (The Boy, The Girl); "The
Rape Ballet" (The Company); "Happy Ending" (The Company);
"This Plum is Too Ripe" (The Boy, The Girl, The Fathers);
"I Can See It" (The Boy, The Narrator); "Plant a Radish"
(The Fathers); "Round and Round" (The Narrator, The Girl,
The Company); "They Were You" (The Boy, The Girl); "Try to
Remember"-Reprise (The Narrator).

COMMENTS: LES ROMANTIQUES (on which the show is based) was
originally done in 1894. THE FANTASTICKS opened

Off-Broadway at the Sullivan Street Playhouse on May 3, 1960 and by its 25th year had played 10,470 performances. There had been 8,228 productions in the United States, 15 national tours, 452 presentations in 66 countries. The show had 57 backers who invested $16,500 each and received 8,000% return on their investment.

The original reviews were not good and producer Lore Noto almost closed the show but an Off-Broadway award for the song "Try to Remember" and word of mouth turned things around for the show.

Originally, Schmidt and Jones had titles the show JOY COMES TO DEAD HORSE with Mexican and Anglo families on neighboring Southwestern ranches. They were not pleased with the concept and turned the show into a one-act production and changed the title to THE FANTASTICKS. On August 3, 1959, the show ran for a week at Barnard College where Lore Noto saw the show and convinced Schmidt and Jones to turn the show into a two-act musical.

The role of the narrator and El Gallo was originated by Jerry Orbach. Others playing the role included Bert Convy, David Cryer and Keith Charles.

THE FANTASTICKS was televised on NBC's "Hallmark Hall of Fame" on October 18, 1964 with Ricardo Montalban as El Gallo, John Davidson as Matt, and Susan Watson as Luisa.

S23. PLAZA SUITE
Tour. 1969. Playhouse, Delaware.

Tour. August 4, 1969-October 12, 1969. Chicago, Illinois.

Tour. January 19, 1970-February 15, 1970. Locust Theatre, Philadelphia, Pennsylvania.

CREDITS: Play by Neil Simon. Director: Mike Nichols. Staged by Robert V. Straus. Set Designer: Oliver Smith. Costume Designer: Patricia Zipprodt. Lighting by Jean Rosenthal.

CAST: **Howard Keel** (Sam Nash); Betty Garrett (Karen Nash); Emil Belasco (Waiter); Paulette Sinclair (Jean McCormick) in VISITOR FROM MAMARONECK.

Howard Keel (Jesse Kiplinger); Betty Garrett (Murial Tate); Emil Belasco (Waiter) in VISITOR FROM HOLLYWOOD.

Howard Keel (Roy Hubley); Betty Garrett (Norma Hubley); Mark Hampton (Borden Eisler); Paulette Sinclair (Mimsey Hubley) in VISITOR FROM FOREST HILLS.

SYNOPSIS: The three one-act plays take place in the present in suite 719 at the Plaza Hotel.

In the first act, VISITOR FROM MAMARONECK, the action takes place on a late winter afternoon in which a couple are celebrating 23 years of marriage. The evening is ruined when the husband declares the marriage is falling apart.

In the second act, VISITOR FROM HOLLYWOOD, the action takes place on an early spring afternoon in which a New Jersey housewife comes to see an old school boyfriend who has become a Hollywood producer. The couple do a mating dance after having Vodka stingers. The idea was that of director Mike Nichols and was a funny part of the sketch.

In the third act, VISITOR FROM FOREST HILLS, the action takes place on a Sunday afternoon in June and concerns a couple from Forest Hills who are at the Plaza, with their daughter, to give her away in marriage. She has locked herself in the bathroom and refuses to come out. At one point, the father climbs up on the window ledge in an attempt to get his daughter to the minister on time.

REVIEW: Philadelphia Evening Bulletin, Wayne Robinson, (January 20, 1970) Mr. Robinson thought the first act was the "weakest" and that the last act "the best." He felt that PLAZA SUITE was "not up to THE ODD COUPLE but good laughs anyway."

COMMENTS: Mr. Keel replaced Forest Tucker who had opened the show on October 14, 1968. Standby for Mr. Keel was Alan North, for Miss Garrett and Miss Sinclair was Kathryn Terwilliger, and for Mr. Hampton and Mr. Belasco was Ronn Cummins. Mr. Tucker replaced Mr. Keel on October 13, 1969. Larry Parks filled in the first week of the Locust production until Mr. Keel returned to the show the second week.

George C. Scott and Maureen Stapleton played in the Broadway production and Walter Matthau and Maureen Stapleton were in the 1971 Paramount film.

S24. PAINT YOUR WAGON
Stock. 1970s.

CREDITS: Book & Lyrics by Alan Jay Lerner. Music by Frederick Loewe.

CAST: **Howard Keel** (Ben Rumson).

SYNOPSIS: The story takes place in 1853 and concerns Ben Rumson, a grizzled prospector, who with his daughter, Jennifer, lives in Rumson, California, a town named for its founder.

While drawing water from a stream, Jennifer finds gold. When word of this gets around, prospectors from all around come to town. Jennifer, the only girl in town, draws attention. Ben sends her back East to school. However, she has already fallen for Mexican prospector, Julio Valveras.

The gold find in Rumson begins to dwindle. Jennifer returns home in time to be with Ben before his death. Her romance with Julio starts again. Irrigation and agriculture give Rumson a chance for survival.

SONGS: "I'm On My Way"; "Rumson"; "What's Going On Here?" (Jennifer); "I Talk to the Trees" (Julio); "They Call the Wind Maria"; "I Still See Elisa" (Ben); "How Can I Wait?"

(Jennifer); "In Between" (Ben); "Whoop-Ti-Ay!" (Chorus);
"Carino Mio" (Jennifer, Julio); "There's a Coach Comin' In"
(Chorus); "Hand Me Down That Can O' Beans"; "Another
Autumn" (Julio); "All of Me" (Jennifer); "Wand'rin Star"
(Ben); "Take the Wheels Off the Wagon" (Ben).

COMMENTS: PAINT YOUR WAGON opened on Broadway at the
Shubert Theatre on November 12, 1951, and ran 289 perform-
ances. Lerner and Loewe included real incidents and background in the show. The Broadway production was produced by
Cheryl Crawford, directed by Daniel Mann, and choreographed
by Agnes de Mille. James Barton played Ben Rumson, Olga San
Juan played Jennifer, and Tony Bavaar played Tony. James
Barton had been away from Broadway for 20 years. Barton was
replaced by Burl Ives and Ives by Eddie Dowling.
     The film version was produced by Alan Jay Lerner for
Paramount and was released in October 1969. The film was
directed by Joshua Logan. Jack Baker handled the
choreography and William Fraker photography. The original
story and more than half of the original songs were
dropped. Lerner did the screenplay using Paddy Chayevsky's
adaptation as a guide. Five new songs were added with
music provided by Andre Previn. It still centers around
the 1849 California gold rush but was filmed in Oregon.
The film starred Lee Marvin, Clint Eastwood, Jean Seberg
(voice dubbed by Anita Gordon), Harve Presnell, Ray
Walston, Alan Baxter, and Tom Ligon.

S25. MAN OF LA MANCHA
     Stock. July 13, 1970-August 4, 1970. Valley Forge
     Music Fair, Devon, Pennsylvania.

S26. THE MOST HAPPY FELLA
     Stock. July 6, 1971-July 11, 1971. Dayton Memorial
     Hall, Dayton, Ohio.

     CREDITS: Book, Lyrics, Music by Frank Loesser. Based on
     Sidney Howard's play THEY KNEW WHAT THEY WANTED.
     Produced by John Kenley. Director: Leslie Cutler.
     Musical numbers Staged by Mario Melodia. Musical
     Director: Gordon Munford. Set Designer: Pat Belew.
     Costumes Designer: Sherry Lynn Morley. Stage Manager:
     Douglas Wallace.

     CAST: Doug Hunt (Cashier); Karren Morrow (Cleo);
     Catherine Christensen (Rosabella); David Baker
     (Postman); **Howard Keel** (Tony); Carol Trigg (Marie);
     Dean Dittmann (Herman); Martin Vidnovic (Clem); Harry
     Fawcett (Jake); Charles Cagle (Al); Terence Monk
     (Joe); Renato Vellutino (Giuseppe); Allan Baker
     (Pasquale); Doug Hunt (Ciccio); Charles Cagle
     (Doctor); John Brigleb (Priest); John Roberts
     (Brakeman); Doug Mullins (Bus Driver).

SYNOPSIS: Tony Esposito, who is growing older, is Italian
and owns a vineyard. He has proposed, by mail, to
Rosabella by sending her a picture of Joe, his handsome
foreman. When Rosabella arrives at the ranch, she is

shocked to find that Tony is old. She becomes pregnant on her wedding night, the father being Joe. Tony becomes enraged when he learns of this but eventually all is forgiven. He agrees to raise the child as his own.

SONGS: "Ooh, My Feet" (Cleo, Cashier, Waitress, Busboy, Rosabella); "Somebody Somewhere" (Rose); "The Most Happy Fella" (Tony, Postmaster, Townspeople, Fransworth, Max, Marie); "Standing on the Corner" (Herman, Clem, Jake, Al, Girl Dancers); "Joey, Joey, Joey" (Joe); "Rosabella" (Tony); "Abbondanza" (Pasquale, Ciccio, Giuseppe, Electrician, Country Girl, City Boy, Townspeople, Tony, Joe); "Sposalizio" (Pasquale, Ciccio, Giuseppe, the players, Doc, City Boy, Country Girl); "Don't Cry" (Joe, Rose); "Fresno Beauties" (Workers, the Players); "Love and Kindness" (Doc, Tony); "Happy to Make Your Acquaintance" (Tony, Rose, Cleo); "Big D" (Cleo, Herman, Workers, the Players); "How Beautiful the Days" (Tony, Rose, Marie, Joe); "Young people Gotta Dance" (Marie, Tony, the Players); "Warm All Over" (Rosabella, Tony); "I Like Everybody" (Herman, Cleo); "My Heart is So Full of Love" (Rosabella, Tony); "Mama" (Mama, Tony); "Goodbye Darlin'" (Herman, Cleo); "I Like Everybody" (Herman, Cleo); "Please Let Me Tell You" (Rosabella, Tony); "She Gonna Come Home With Me" (Tony); "I Made a First" (Herman, Cleo); Finale (Tony, Rosabella, the Players).

COMMENTS: Frank Loesser adapted the 1924 Sidney Howard play THEY KNEW WHAT THEY WANTED as the basis for the show. Among the 30 individual numbers were arias, duets, trios, quartets, choral numbers, and recitatives.
　　The musical opened on Broadway on May 3, 1956, at the Imperial Theatre where it ran for 676 performances. The part of Tony was created by Robert Weede. Giorgio Tozzi played Tony in the 1979 Broadway revival.

S27. AMBASSADOR
London. September 14, 1971. Palace Theater in Manchester, England.

London. October 19, 1971. Her Majesty's Theatre in London, England. 89 Performances.

CREDITS: Book by Don Ettlinger and Anne Marie Barlow. Lyrics by Hal Hackady. Music by Don Gohman. Based on Henry James's novel The Ambassadors. Director: Stone Widney. Set Designer: Peter Rice. Costume Designer: Peter Rice. Lighting by Francis Reed. Dance Arranger: Ray Holder. Musical Director: Gareth Davies. Orchestrator: Philip Lang. Vocal Arranger: Gareth Davies. Dances and Musical numbers staged by Gillian Lynne.

CAST: **Howard Keel** (Lambert Strether); Gerard Hunt (Mailman); Neville Jason (1st Townsman); Wayne McKnight (2nd Townsman); Beverley Martell (1st Townswoman); Margaret Courtenay (Amelia Newsome); Judith Paris (Sarah-her daughter); Nevil Whiting (James-her son-in-law); Dianne Roberts (Maid); Toni-Sue Burley

(Flower Girl); Danielle Darrieux (Countess Marie de
Vionnet); Michael Logan (Waymarsh); Richard Heffer
(Chadwick Newsome); Brian Rowley (Waiter); Ellen
Pollock (Gloriani); Isobel Stuart (Jeanne de Vionnet);
Blain Fairman (Bilham); David Wheldon Williams
(Monsieur Blanc); Penny Everton (Babette); Neville
Jason (French Artist); Brian Rowley (Italian Artist);
David Wheldon Williams (English Artist); Nevil Whiting
(American Artist); John Moore (Guide); Neville Jason
(Artist); David Wheldon Williams (Waiter); Beverley
Martell (Innkeeper); Judith Paris (Solange); Judy
Gridley (2nd Prostitute); Dianne Roberts (3rd Prosti-
tute); Joan Ryan (Germaine); David Wheldon Williams
(Headwaiter); John Moore (1st Friend); Nevil Whiting
(2nd Friend); Neville Jason (Anton); Penny Everton,
Judy Gridley, Lamona Snow (Hatgirls); John Moore
(Hotel Manager).

SYNOPSIS: In 1908, a lawyer from Wooette, Massachusetts,
Lewis Strether, goes to Paris to help a wealthy New England
widow, Amelia Newsome, get her son, Chad, to stop his
relationship with an older woman, Marie de Vionnet and
return to America. He succeeds.
        While in Paris, Lambert becomes enchanted with the
city and with Marie.

SONGS: "A Man You Can Set Your Watch By" (Lambert,
Townspeople); "It's a Woman" (Amelia, Lambert, Sarah,
James); "Lambert's Quandary" (Lambert); "Lilas" (Flower
Girl); "The Right Time the Right Place" (Guests);
"Surprise" (Marie); "Charming" (Lambert, Marie); "All of My
Life" (Lambert); "What Can You Do With a Nude?" (Artists);
"Love Finds the Lonely" (Jeanne); "Surprise"-Reprise
(Marie, Lambert); "La Femme" (Lambert); "La Femme"
(Lambert, Chorus); "Young With Him"/"I Thought I Knew You"
(Marie, Lambert); "Lilas"/"What Happened to Paris?" (Flower
Girl, Lambert); "La Nuit D'Amour" (Prostitutes); "Am I
Wrong?" (Lambert); "Mama" (Jeanne); "That's What I Need
Tonight" (Marie, Lambert, Friends); "You Can Tell a Lady By
Her Hat" (Anton); "This Utterly Ridiculous Affair" (Amelia,
Lambert); "Not Tomorrow" (Marie); "All of My Life"-Reprise
(Lambert); "Thank You No!" (Lambert).

REVIEWS: <u>New York Morning Telegraph</u>, Collie Knox, (November
3, 1971) Mr. Knox felt that despite what other critics were
saying AMBASSADOR "is worth visiting for the two principals
alone, the magnificently voiced and towering Howard Keel and
the enchanting French actress Danielle Darrieux."

<u>Plays and Players</u>, John Russell Taylor, (December 1971) Mr.
Taylor said, "I did enjoy the show as much as any musical I
have seen for quite a long time." He said that Keel
sometimes...is genuinely touching...and he is in as good a
voice as ever." He thought that the show with "whatever
minor reservations one might have, sends the whole audience
out of the theatre in a happy mood."

<u>The Stage & Television Today</u>, R. B. Marriott, (October 28,

1972) R. B. Marriott felt AMBASSADOR "on the whole tends
to be on the tepid side." It was felt that Keel was "in as
good a voice as ever, and he gives his songs more than
their true value. His portrait of Lambert is amusing and
likeable. Together Miss Darrieux and Mr. Keel play their
scenes beautifully."

Variety (November 24, 1971) felt that AMBASSADOR was "a
good show, but perhaps not good enough." It was also felt
that "Keel dominates the proceedings, contributing strongly
in both singing and acting, giving the show its best and
most believable moments."

ADDITIONAL REVIEWS: Christian Science Monitor (October 23,
1971); London Observer (October 24, 1971); London Sunday
Times (October 24, 1971); Punch (October 27, 1971); The
Stage & Television Today (September 30, 1971).

COMMENTS: James's novel, on which the play is based, was
written in 1903. The production in London cost $265,000
while the Broadway version cost $800,000. The producers
were American. Over 100 American investors flew to London
for opening night.

S28. DARK OF THE MOON
> Stock. 1972. Westbury Music Fair, Long Island, New
> York.

SYNOPSIS: A witch-boy gets to take human form in order to
wed Barbara Allen with the stipulation she remain faithful.
When Barbara Allen betrays her husband, she dies and he
goes back to the mountain witches.

COMMENTS: This play was based on the Barbara Allen ballad
(1794). The setting for this show was in the Smokey
Mountains in North Carolina. The original play opened on
Broadway on March 14, 1945, and starred Richard Hart and
Carol Stone.

S29. MAN OF LA MANCHA
> Stock. June 11, 1972-June 25, 1972. Meadowbrook Dinner
> Theatre, Cedar Grove, New Jersey.
>
> Stock. September 1, 1972-September 16, 1972. Westbury
> Music Fair, long Island, New York.
>
> Stock. September 25, 1972-September 30, 1972. Valley
> Forge Music Fair, Devon, Pennsylvania.
>
> CREDITS: Book by Dale Wasserman. Lyrics by Joe Dario.
> Music by Mitch Leigh. Produced by Lee Guber, Shelly
> Gross. Director: Edward Roll. Choreographer: Edward
> Roll. Set Designer: Larry Reehling. Lighting by Larry
> Reehling. Costume Designer: Sara Brooks. Musical
> Director: R. Bennett Benetsky. Production Stage
> Manager: Frank Brit.
>
> CAST: **Howard Keel** (Don Quixote/Cervantes); Edward

Roll (Sancho); Lainie Kazan (Aldonza/Dulcinea); David
Holland (Innkeeper); Louis Monica (Padre); Michael
Amber (Dr. Carrasco); Marcia O' Brien (Antonio); Rick
Podwell (Barber); Dan Merriman (Pedro, Head Muleteer);
David Hall (Anilmo, a Muleteer); Louise Armstrong
(Housekeeper); Gloria Hodes (Maria, the Innkeeper's
wife); Donna Nigro (Fermina, a Slave); John David
Rude (Captain of the Inquisition); Jose Antonio (Jose,
a Muleteer and the Mule); Chet D' Elia (Juan, a Mule-
teer); Robert Yarri (Poco, a Muleteer); Dan Merriman,
Rick Podwell (Horses); Jose Antonio, Robert Yarri
(Dancing Horses); Robin Polseno (Guitarist); John
Hemmer, David Wilkie, George Stelvin (Guards and Men
of the Inquisition).

SYNOPSIS: Novelist Miquel de Cervantes is imprisoned for
debts occurred during the Spanish Inquisition. He tells
his fellow prisoners the story of Don Quixote who sets out
with his servant, Sancho, and his wench, Aldonza, to do
battle to prove he is worthy of his knighthood to Aldonza
whom he worships as Dulcinea. Aldonza thinks he is foolish
but ends up loving him and Don dies believing his dream.

SONGS: "Man of La Mancha" (Quixote, Sancho); "It's All the
Same" (Aldonza); "Dulcinea" (Quixote); "I'm Only Thinking
of Him" (Padre, Antonio, Housekeeper); "I Really Like Him"
(Sancho); "What Does He Want of Me?" (Aldonza); "Little
Bird, Little Bird" (Anselmo, Muleteers); "Barber's Song"
(Barber); "Golden Helmet of Membino" (Quixote, Sancho,
Barber, Muleteer); "To Each His Dulcinea" (Padre); "The
Impossible Dream" (Quixote); "The Combat" (Quixote,
Aldonza, Sancho, Muleteer); "The Dubbing" (Innkeeper,
Aldonza, Sancho); "The Abduction" (Aldonza, Muleteers);
"Aldonza" (Aldonza); "The Kights of Mirrors" (Quixote,
Knight, Attendants); "A little Gossip" (Sancho);
"Dulcinea"-Reprise (Aldonza); "Psalm" (Padre); "Man of La
Mancha"-Reprise (All); "The Quest"-Reprise (All).

REVIEW: Bea Smith (Reviewing Meadowbrook production, June
1972) felt that Keel had "a fine voice." Smith thought that
since his MGM days, he has become "versatile, experienced,
a bit more mature, more handsome" and that he retained his
"familiar operatic voice with as much (if not more)
resonance as ever before. His acting has improved
immensely."

COMMENTS: MAN OF LA MANCHA was based on the TV play I DON
QUIXOTE (1959) by Dale Wasserman. The idea for a musical
was thought of by director Albert Marre. Michael Redgrave
was originally to be cast as Don. The musical show opened
on Broadway on November 22, 1965, at the ANTA Washington
Square Theatre and ran for 2,328 performances. Richard
Kiley created the role of Don Quixote. Jacqueline Alloway
played Keel's Aldonza in the 1970 Valley Forge production.
Roddy and Maxine Richman brought a suit to the Manhattan
Supreme Court, against Keel for $1,000,000, claiming a
sword slipped from his hand during his performance at the
Westbury Music Fair on September 16, 1972.

Jose Ferrer played the lead in the National Touring Company.

Kiley reprised his role in 1972 at the Lincoln Center's vivian Beaumont Theatre. His co-star was Joan Diener. The show ran for 144 performances. Kiley also played the part in New York in 1977, with Emily Yancy and Tony Martinez.

Peter O' Toole, Sophia Loren, and James Coco were in the 1972 United Artists film. Keel had longed to do the film version.

S30. AMBASSADOR

Broadway. November 19, 1972-November 25, 1972. Lunt-Fontanne Theatre in New York City, New York. 9 Performances.

CREDITS: Book by Don Ettlinger and Anne Marie Barlow. Lyrics by Hal Hackady. Music by Don Gohman. Based on Henry James's novel The Ambassadors. Produced by Gene Dingenary, Miranda d'Ancona, Nancy Levering, Dan Rodden. Associate Producer: Dan Rodden. Director: Stone Widney. Choreographer: Joyce Trisher. Set Designer: Peter Rice. Costume Designer: Peter Rice. Costume Supervisor: Sara Brooks. Hair Stylist: Ronald DeMann. Lighting by Martin Aronstein. Dance Arranger: Trude Rittman. Musical Director: Herbert Grossman. Conductor: Herbert Grossman. Production Supervisor: Robert Guerra. Production Stage Manager: Alan Hall. Stage Manager: Mary Porter Hall. Press by Reginald Denenholtz.

CAST: **Howard Keel** (Lambert Strether); Danielle Darrieux (Marie de Vionnet); Adam Petriski (Porter); David Sabin (Waymarsh); Patricia Arnell (Flower Girl & Germaine); Carmen Mathews (Gioriani); Dwight Arno (Waiter); Michael Goodwin (Bilham); Michael Shannon (Chad); Andrea Marcovicci (Jeanne de Vionnet); Larry Giroux (Dancing Master & Artist); Jack Trussel (Guide & Hotel Manager); Robert Hultman (Waiter & Head Waiter); Marsha Tamaroff (Innkeeper's Wife); Nikolas Dante (Bellboy); Dixie Stewart (Lady in Park); M'el Dowd (Amelia Newsome); Steve Arlen (Standby for Mr. Keel); Margot Moser (Standby for Miss Darrieux); Michael Goodwin (Understudy for Chad); Patricia Arnell (Understudy for Jeanne).

SYNOPSIS: During the turn of the century, a lawyer from Massachusetts, Lewis Strether, goes to Paris to help a wealthy New England widow, Amelia Newsome, get her son, Chad, to stop his relationship with an older woman, Marie de Vionnet and return to America. He succeeds. While in Paris, Lambert becomes enchanted with the city and with Marie.

SONGS: "All of My Life" (Lewis); "A Boy Like That" (Lewis); "Gossip" (Ladies of Paris); "Happy Man" (Lewis); "I know the Man" (Marie); "Lambert's Quandary" (Lewis); "Lilas" (Flower Girl); "Love Finds the Lonely" (Jeanne); "Mama"

(Jeanne); "Maxixe" (Habanera); "Not Tomorrow" (Marie);
"The Right Time, The Right Place" (Gioriani's Guests); "She
Passed My Way" (Marie); "Something More" (Lewis);
"Surprise" (Marie, Lewis); "Thank You, No" (Lewis); "That's
What I Need Tonight" (Lewis, Marie); "Too Much to Forgive"
(Lewis); "Valse"; "What Happened to Paris? (Lewis, Flower
Girl); "Why Do Women Have to Call it Love" (Gioriani,
Waymarsh); "Young With Him" (Marie); "Kyrie Eleison."

REVIEWS: The New Yorker (December 2, 1972) felt that
nothing could be done to fix what the authors of the
musical had done wrong and that Danielle Darrieux and
Howard Keel were not to blame for the "poverty of material"
they were asked to perform. It was also stated that the
cast was "over-miked."

New York Post, Richard Watts, (November 20, 1972) Mr. Watts
felt that AMBASSADOR was "by no means terrible, but
unfortunately it never comes to interesting dramatic life."
He thought that "Mr. Keel and Miss Darrieux...are
excellent."

New York Times, Clive Barnes, (November 20, 1972) Mr.
Barnes felt AMBASSADOR was "effete" and "pallid" and
despite the efforts of Miss Darrieux and Mr. Keel the show
was "pernicious." Miss Darrieux sang "deliciously" and she
acted with "grace." Mr. Keel had a "marvelously glistening
baritone voice" and he manages to make his "badly written
part convincing and engaging."

ADDITIONAL REVIEWS: Christian Science Monitor (November 24,
1972); Cue (December 2, 1972); Greater New York Radio
Theatre Review (November 20, 1972); New York Daily News
(November 20, 1972); Variety (November 22, 1972); Women's
Wear Daily (November 21, 1972).

COMMENTS: The show previewed between November 2,
1972-November 17, 1972. Before the show opened on
Broadway, it went through a rewrite. The opening scene,
set in Massachusetts and used to introduce the Lambert
Strether character to the audience was cut. When
AMBASSADOR failed, composer Don Gohman took his own life.
(See S27, D16)

S31. THE UNSINKABLE MOLLY BROWN
   Stock. July 30, 1973-August 19, 1973. Camden County
   Music Fair, Camden, New Jersey.

   Stock. August 14, 1973-August 19, 1973. Valley Forge
   Music Fair, Devon, Pennsylvania.

   Stock. August 20, 1973-August 25, 1973. Musicarnival,
   Cleveland, Ohio.

   Stock. 1973. Westbury Music Fair, Long Island.

   CREDITS: Book by Richard Morris. Lyrics & Music by
   Meredith Wilson. Director: Christopher Hewett.

Choreographer: Richard Corrigan. Set Designer: Larry
Reehling. Costume Designer: Sara Brooks. Lighting by
Larry Reehling. Musical Director: Herbert Hecht.
Production Stage Manager: Frank Birt.

CAST: Tammy Grimes (Molly Tobin); **Howard Keel** (Johnny
Leadville Brown); Jamie Haskins (Michael Tobin); John
Melof (Aloysius Tobin); Daniel Cass (Patrick Tobin);
Victor Gordon (Father Flynn); Skedge Miller (Shamus
Tobin); Edith Meiser (Mrs. McGlown); John LeGrand
(Monsignor Ryan); Grant Walden (Roberts); Llewell
Thomas (Christmas Morgan); Gail Hecht (Princess
Delong); Mitchell Gregg (Prince Delong); Brennan
Roberts (Charlie).

SYNOPSIS: The action takes place between 1900 and 1912 and
concerns Molly, who rises from poverty to Denver society
via the Colorado silver mines. She meets and falls for
Leadville Johnny Brown, who is a prospector, and they are
married.
    Despite Molly's wealth, Denver society does not
accept her so she goes to Europe and is well liked by Monte
Carlo's social leader.
    After nearly losing Johnny, Molly returns to Denver
after becoming a hero on the Titanic. Johnny and Molly
eventually find their place in Denver's society.

SONGS: "I Ain't Down Yet" (Molly, Brothers); "Belly Up to
the Bar Boys" (Molly, Christmas); "I've Already Started In"
(Johnny, Christmas, Charlie, Burt, Gitter); "I'll Never Say
No" (Johnny); "My Own Brass Bed" (Molly); "The Denver
Police" (Three Policeman); "Beautiful People of Denver"
(Molly); "Are You Sure" (Molly, Monsignor); "I Ain't Down
Yet"-Reprise, (Molly, Johnny); "Happy Birthday, Mrs. J. J.
Brown" (Princess Delong); "If I Knew" (Johnny);
"Chick-a-Pen" (Molly, Johnny); "Bon Jour" (Molly, Prince
Delong); "Keep-a-Hoppin" (Johnny); "Leadville Johnny Brown"
(Johnny); "Up Where the People Are" (Monte Carlo Guests);
"Dolce Far Niente" (Prince Delong, Molly); "I Ain't Down
Yet"-Reprise (Johnny, Molly, Leadville Friends).

REVIEW: Philadelphia Inquirer, Jack Lloyd, (August 1, 1973)
Mr. Lloyd stated that THE UNSINKABLE MOLLY BROWN "is
certainly just about everything a musical comedy should be.
It's good-natured and lively." He said the show, Miss
Grimes, and Mr. Keel "have credentials."

COMMENTS: THE UNSINKABLE MOLLY BROWN opened on Broadway on
November 3, 1960, at the Winter Garden and ran for 532
performances. It starred Tammy Grimes (who won a Tony) and
Harve Presnell. Presnell would later star with Debbie
Reynolds in the 1964 MGM film. The film only had five of
Meredith Wilson's 17 songs and the song "He's My Friend"
was added. Peter Gennaro, who was the original
choreographer, did the film. The film was shot at Black
Canyon in Colorado's Gunnison National Monument.

S32. I DO! I DO!
    Stock.

COMMENT: (See S37)

S33. GENE KELLY'S SALUTE TO BROADWAY
    Revue. September 26, 1975–December 6, 1975. Civic
    Center, St. Paul, Minnesota.

    CREDITS: Presented by Rogo. Production by Harry
    Kobrin. Continuity by Alan Jay Lerner. Choreographer:
    Gene Kelly. Staging by Gene Kelly. Set Designer:
    Mischa Petrow. Costume Designer: Frank Thompson. Music
    Arranger: Jack Elliott. Musical Director: Norm Geller.

    CAST: **Howard Keel**, Mimi Hines, Lainie Nelson, Ken
    Berry, John Calvert, William Dance, Barnara Franklin,
    Sara Jane Gould, Larried Montgomery, Carol Perea.

SYNOPSIS: The show was a salute highlighting 50 years of
Broadway with 43 musical numbers from numerous Broadway hit
shows.

SONGS BY KEEL: "Impossible Dream," "September Song."

REVIEW: <u>Variety</u> (October 8, 1975) felt that despite the
talent involved in the show it "fizzles" primarily because
of the script and "stodgy staging...Surprisingly, with the
production strikes against it, 'Salute' does offer moments
of classy entertainment, thanks to the performers." It was
said of Keel that he "still knows his way around a ballad"
and that he was "in fine voice."

COMMENTS: Rogo was Robert Goulet's company. Gene Kelly
left the production early because of illness. The show was
scheduled to run 13 weeks in 60 cities including Chicago,
Pittsburg, Philadelphia, and Atlanta with two-to
three-night stands in each city. After a Christmas break,
it was to continue into 1976.

S34. A MUSICAL JUBILEE
    Stock. May 31, 1976. Toronto, Canada.

    CREDITS: Written by Marilyn Clark, Charles Burr.
    Produced for the Theatre Guild by Philip Langner,
    Armina Marshall, Marilyn Langner. Choreographer:
    Robert Tucker. Set Designers: Herbert Senn, Helen
    Pond. Costume Designer: Donald Brooks. Lighting by
    Leon DiLeone. Dance Arranger: Trude Rittman. Musical
    Continuity by Trude Rittman. Musical Supervisor:
    Lehman Engel. Musical Director: Sherman Frank. Orches-
    trator: John Lesko. Dialogue by Max Wilk.

    CAST: **Howard Keel**, Patrice Munsel, Eartha Kitt, Cyril
    Ritchard, Larry Kert, Joe Masiell, Richard Woods.

SYNOPSIS: The show was given in two acts and showed the
evolution of the Broadway musical with show tunes, folk

songs, songs from vaudeville, war, the frontier, jazz, operetta, and other numbers by various composers and lyricists.

SONGS BY KEEL: "Lorena"; "Battle Hymn of the Republic"; "I'm in Love With Vienna" (Keel, Munsel); "Song of the Vagabonds"; "You Are Love" (Keel, Munsel); "This Song is You"; "We're Blose"; "You Go to My Head"; "Great Day"; "How Jazz Was Born" (with cast); "Hallelujah."

COMMENTS: Howard Keel replaced John Raitt. The idea for the show came from a show THEATRE AT SEA done aboard a ship sailing the Caribbean in April 1974. The performers wanted to continue the idea and did so through the help of the Theatre Guild.

S35. SOUTH PACIFIC

Stock. July 11, 1977–July 16, 1977. O'Keefe Center in Toronto, Canada.

Stock. July 24, 1977–July 30, 1977. Smithville Summer Theatre, Smithville, New Jersey.

Stock. August 22, 1977–August 29, 1977. Wolf Trap Farm Park.

Stock. October 12, 1977–February 1978. Pantages Theatre, Los Angeles, California.

SMITHVILLE PRODUCTION

CREDITS: Book by Oscar Hammerstein II, Joshua Logan. Lyrics by Oscar Hammerstein II. Music by Richard Rodgers. Based on James Michener's Tales of the South Pacific.

CAST: Jane Powell (Ensign Nellie Forbush); **Howard Keel** (Emile de Becque); Queen Yahna (Bloody Mary); Joanna Pang (Liat); Garrett Brown (Lt. Cable); Brandon Maggart (Luther Billis).

REVIEW: The Philadelphia Bulletin, Charles Librizzi, (July 1977) Mr. Librizzi felt that the Smithville Summer Theatre production was good enough to be a Broadway revival. He felt that Miss Powell's performance was "delightfully adept and credibly girlish" and that Keel played the French planter with "forcefulness" and that his singing could not "be faulted."

O'KEEFE CENTER AND WOLF TRAP PRODUCTIONS

CREDITS: Book by Oscar Hammerstein II, Joshua Logan. Lyrics by Oscar Hammerstein II. Music by Richard Rodgers. Based on James Michener's Tales of the South Pacific. Director: Donald Driver. Choreographer: Arthur Faria. Set Designer: Peter Wolf. Costume Designer: Brooks Van Horn. Musical Director: Herbert Hecht.

CAST: Jane Powell (Ensign Nellie Forbush); **Howard Keel** (Emile de Becque); Queen Yahna (Bloody Mary); Brandon Maggart (Luther Billis); James Ferrier (Lt. Cable).

COMMENT: (See S5)

S36. SEVEN BRIDES FOR SEVEN BROTHERS
Tour. June 6, 1978-June 18, 1978. Fair Park Music Hall, Dallas, Texas.

Tour. June 19, 1978-June 25, 1978. Muny, St. Louis, Missouri.

Tour. July 4, 1978-July 9, 1978. Starlight Theatre, Kansas City, Kansas.

Tour. July 17, 1978-July 29, 1978. O'Keefe Center For the Performing Arts, Toronto, Canada.

Tour. August 22, 1978-August 27, 1978. Chrysler Theatre, Norfolk, Virginia.

Tour. Atlantic Civic Center.

Tour. Tulsa Performing Arts Center, Tulsa, Oklahoma.

Tour. 1979. Parker Playhouse, Ft. Lauderdale, Florida.

Tour. January 23, 1979-February 1979. Theatre of the Performing Arts, Miami, Florida.

CREDITS: Book by Lawrence Kasha, David Landay. Lyrics by Johnny Mercer. Music by Gene de Paul. New Songs by Al Kasha, Joel Hirschhorn. Adapted from THE SOBBIN' WOMEN by Stehphen Vincent Benet and the Screenplay by Albert Hackett, Frances Goodrich, Dorothy Kingsley. Produced by Lawrence Kasha, Norman Sedawie, Barry Brown. Director: Lawrence Kasha. Choreographer: Jerry Jackson. Set Designers: Michael Bottari, Ronald Case. Costume Designer: Brooks Van Horn. Lighting by David Gibson. Dance Arranger: Rob Webb. Musical Director: Richard Parrinello. Orchestrator: Irwin Kostal. Assistant Conductor: Rob Webb. Production Stage manager: Jane Newfeld. Company Manager: Jo Rosner. Sound by David Teepe.

CAST: Stuart Carey (Ephraim); John Attle (Daniel); Randy Doney (Benjamin); Craig Peralta (Gideon); Richard Warner (Frank); John Appleton (Caleb); **Howard Keel** (Adam); Al Evans (Mr. Bixby); Jane Powell (Milly); Steve Memel (Joel); John Hart (Matt); Phillip Candler (Luke); Brad Moranz (Zeke); Anthony Christopher (Carl); Jeffrey Reynolds (Jeb); Pepper Clyde (Ruth); Nancy Fox (Alice); Jean Fraser (Sarah); Dorothy Holland (Dorcas); Mary Kilpatrick (Liza); Laurel Van Der Linde (Martha); Gino Gaudio (Mr. Perkins); Don Wyse (Preacher); Understudies for Keel and Powell were Gino Gaudio and Dorothy Holland.

SYNOPSIS: The action takes place in the Oregon backwoods in 1850 and concerns Adam Pontipee who persuades Milly to marry him and take care of his mountain home. He neglects to mention his six brothers are also living there. The six brothers kidnapp six girls and eventually the girls fall in love with them and they are married.

SONGS: "Women's Work*" (Brothers); "Bless Your Beautiful Hide" (Adam); "I'm Jumpin' In*" (Milly); "Wonderful Wonderful Day" (Milly); "I Married Seven Brothers*" (Milly); "Goin' Co'tin'" (Milly, Brothers); "The Challenge Dance" (Company); "Love Never Goes Away" (Adam, Milly, Gideon); "Lonesome Polecat*" (Brothers); "Sobbin' Women" (Adam, Brothers); "When They Grow Up*" (Milly, Girls); "We Gotta Make It Through the Winter" (Brothers); "If I Was a Different Man*" (Adam); "Winter/Spring Dance" (Brothers, Girls); "Glad That You Were Born" (Milly, Brothers, Girls); "Finale" (Company). *Indicates songs dropped before Broadway opening.

REVIEWS: <u>Dallas Morning News</u>, John Neville, (June 7, 1978) Mr. Neville felt the stage production (at Fair Park Music Hall) was a "solid, fun, entertaining piece of theatre." He thought that Powell and Keel were "terrific" and that each were in "great voice. Miss Powell moves on stage like a dream and Keel has the kind of commanding presence that makes him an honest-to-goodness patriarchal figure."

<u>Fort Worth Star-Telegram</u>, Perry Stewart (June 8, 1978) Mr. Stewart felt that Keel was "rich-voiced" and that the Powell-Keel pairing "is magical and the songs--new--and old--compliment the chemistry of the stars."

<u>Kansas City Star</u>, Harry Haskell, (July 4, 1978) Mr. Haskell described the show (at the Starlight Theatre) as "snappy" and "high-spirited." He felt the leads were "splendidly cast." He said that Keel was a "blustery, stenor-toned, he-man" who showed the "tender, likeable" part of Adam's character from beneath the character's outward gruffness.

<u>St. Louis Post-Dispatch</u>, John McGuire, (June 20, 1978) Mr. McGuire felt that the play (at the Muny) is a "fast-paced, old-fashioned, not at all taxing musical comedy, and easy and pleasant way to spend a June night under a full moon." Of Keel's performance, Mr. McGuire said, "His commanding baritone has made the journey into the late 1970s with no sign of weariness. Keel still seems made for the part of Adam."

<u>Toronto Sun</u>, Sylvia Train, (July 19, 1978) Sylvia Train said that "the leads are perfectly cast--Howard Keel as the eldest brother looks the strapping he-man he's supposed to be and his leading lady, Jane Powell, looks just right ever so pert, blonde and tiny beside him." She felt that "it's ideal entertainment for a summer evening."

ADDITIONAL REVIEW: <u>Dallas Times Herald</u> (June 8, 1978).

COMMENTS: This production was a pre-Broadway tour. SEVEN
BRIDES FOR SEVEN BROTHERS opened on Broadway at the Alvin
Theatre on July 8, 1982, and ran for 5 performances.
Debbie Boone played Milly. Also starring were David-James
Carroll, Craig Peralta, and Nancy Fox.
    Howard Keel and Jane Powell were the leads in the 1954
MGM film on which this play is based. The film was based
on Stephen Vincent Benet's The Sobbin' Women written in the
mid-1920s. (See F17)

S37. I DO! I DO!
    Stock. October 22, 1980-November 1, 1980. Valley Forge
    Music Fair, Devon, Pennsylvania.

    Stock. 1980. Pantages Theatre, Los Angeles,
    California.

    CREDITS: Book & Lyrics by Tom Jones. Music by Harvey
    Schmidt. Based on THE FOURPOSTER by Jan de Hartzog.
    Director: Lucia Victor. Choreographer: Bonnie Evans.
    Set Designer: Tom Barnes. Costume Designer: Stanley
    Simmons. Lighting by Ruth Roberts. Musical Director:
    William Cox.

    CAST: Jane Powell (Agnes); **Howard Keel** (Michael).

SYNOPSIS: I DO! I DO! takes place just before the turn of
the century and is a two-character musical about fifty
years of marriage and the ups and downs of that marriage.

SONGS: "All the Dearly Beloved," "Together Forever," "I Do!
I Do!," "Good Night" (Michael, Agnes); Love My Wife"
(Michael); "Something Has Happened" (Agnes); "My Cup
Runneth Over," "Love Isn't Everything," "Nobody's Perfect"
(Michael, Agnes); "A Well Known Fact" (Michael); "Flaming
Agnes" (Agnes); "The Honeymoon is Over," "Where Are the
Snows," "When the Kids Get Married" (Michael, Agnes); "The
Father of the Bride" (Michael); "What is a Woman?,"
"Someone Needs Me" (Agnes); "Roll Up the Ribbons," "This
House" (Michael, Agnes).

REVIEWS: Philadelphia Evening Bulletin, Joe Adcock,
(October 22, 1980) Mr. Adcock said (of the Valley Forge
production) "that as far as singing and dancing were
concerned Miss Powell and Mr. Keel were quite good." He
felt that Keel's hair piece and "mature figure" caused him
to be less convincing in the earlier scenes."

Philadelphia Inquirer, William Collins, (October 1980) Mr.
Collins felt that the stars (of the Valley Forge
production) were "limited." He said that Miss Powell's
singing is "something less than a sheer delight" and Keel
could still sing but his acting was "primitive."

COMMENTS: The show (based on the 1950 play THE FOURPOSTER)
was most likely the first musical on Broadway with only two
characters. Gower Champion directed the Broadway
production which opened at the 46th Street Theatre on

December 5, 1966, and ran for 560 performances before it
closed on June 15, 1968. Mary Martin and Robert Preston
created the roles of Michael and Agnes. Carol Lawrence and
Gordon MacRae began doing matinees on October 18, 1967, and
replaced Martin and Preston on December 4, 1967, while the
latter toured with the show.

Lawrence and MacRae performed an abbreviated version of
the show twice. The first time at the wedding eve dinner
for Lynda Bird Johnson and Marine Captain Charles S. Robb.
The second time was at a White House dinner honoring
Vice-President Hubert Humphrey and Supreme Court Justice
Earl Warren.

S38. SLEUTH
Stock. 1982. 4 weeks.

CREDITS: SLEUTH was a two-act play by Anthony Shaffer.

CAST: **Howard Keel** (Andrew Wyke).

SYNOPSIS: SLEUTH combines spoof and mystery. The story
takes place in the present at the country home of Andrew
Wyke in Whiltshire, England. The story concerns a very
successful writer of detective stories, Andrew Wyke, whose
lead character, John Lord Merridew, easily solves crimes.
Wyke invites travel agent, Milo Tindle, his spoiled wife's
lover, to his home.

After drinks are served, Andrew confronts Milo about
being his wife's lover. Wyke begins games of cat and mouse
including a fake theft, revenge, sex, super sleuthing and
the eventual murder of Milo.

COMMENTS: Anthony Shaffer had a twin brother, Peter, who was
a playwright. SLEUTH opened on Broadway on November 12,
1970, at the Music Box where it ran for 229 performances
before closing on October 13, 1973. Anthony Quayle played
Andrew Wyke and Keith Baxter, Milo Tindle.

SLEUTH originally appeared in London starring Maius
Goring and John Fraser. Quayle repeated his role opposite
Donal Donnelly at the Ashman Theatre on January 11, 1972.

S39. I DO! I DO!
Stock. July 1988. Pantages Theatre in Los Angeles,
California.

COMMENT: (See S37)

S40. SOUTH PACIFIC
Stock. June 22, 1992-June 28, 1992. Muny Theatre, St.
Louis, Missouri.

CREDITS: Book by Oscar Hammerstein II, Joshua Logan.
Lyrics by Oscar Hammerstein II. Music by Richard
Rodgers. Based on James Michener's <u>Tales of the South
Pacific</u>. Director: Paul Blake. Choreographer: Robert
Longbottom. Set Designer: Paul Wonsek. Musical
Director Kevin Farrel. Sound: Bruce Cameron.
Production Stage Manager: Susan Whelan.

CAST: Natalie de Lucia (Ngana); Robert Jason Friedman
(Jerome); **Howard Keel** (Emile de Becque); Leslie
Denniston (Ensign Nellie Forbush); Carmille Saviola
(Bloody Mary); Todd Susman (Luther Billis); Jeb Brown
(Professor); Whit Reichert (Stewpot); Nat Chandler
(Lt. Cable); Grady Smith (Capt. Brackett); Joneal
Joplin (Cmdr. Harbison); Barb Chan (Liat).

COMMENT: (See S5 for synopsis and songs)

4

FILMOGRAPHY

Mr. Keel's feature films listed in this chapter are
arranged chronologically and for each, the production
company, release date, whether color or black and white,
length, credits, cast (with characters played), synopsis,
songs (where applicable) with singer, reviews, sources for
additional reviews, and comments are given.

F 1. **THE SMALL VOICE** [HIDEOUT-U.S.] (British Lion, November
1948) B&W 83 Minutes.

CREDITS: Producer: Anthony Havelock-Allen. Director:
Fergus McDonell. Based on the novel by Robert Westerby.
Screenplay by Derek Neame, Julian Orde. Cinematogra-
pher: Stan Pavery. Editor: Manuel del Campo. Musical
Director: Stanley Black.

CAST: Valerie Hobson (Eleanor Byrne); James Donald
(Murray Byrne); **Harold Keel** (Boke); David Greene (Jim);
Michael Balfour (Frankie); Joan Young (Potter); Angela
Foulds (Jenny); Glyn Dearman (Ken); Norman Claridge
(Police Superintendent); Edward Palmer (Joe Wallis);
Lyn Evans (Ticket Collector); Alan Talvern, Hugh Owens,
Frederir Steger, Godfrey Barrie, Edward Wicks, Kathleen
Michael, Sidney Benson, Edward Judd, Grace Denbigh-
Russell.

SYNOPSIS: Playwright Murray Byrne (Donald), who received an
injury during the war that left him slightly crippled, meets
his wife Eleanor (Hobson) at the Llanbach station. Their
marriage is in trouble. While on the way home, they see a
car that has crashed. They stop to give assistance. The
couple give a lift to Boke (Keel) and Jim (Greene) who have
escaped from a nearby military prison.
Boke takes Murray and Eleanor prisoner, while Jim
rescues Frankie (Balfour) and two children Jimmy (Foulds)
and Ken (Dearman) from the reckage. After they all get
back to the Byrne Cottage, Ken becomes ill. Murray tries
to break Boke's nerve so that he can get Ken a doctor. He
succeeds and all ends well. The ordeal helps draw the
couple closer together and they are reunited.

REVIEW: Variety (November 24, 1948) felt that the film was a "neatly contrived thriller, strong in suspense values." It was felt that Harold Keel, James Donald, David Greene and Michael Balfour "turn in neatly convincing studies." Previewed at the Plaza, in London, on November 10, 1948.

COMMENTS: This was Anthony Havelock-Allen's first independent production since leaving Cineguild. Valerie Hobson was his wife. They had seen Keel in the London production of OKLAHOMA! and knew he was right for their film. After some red tape, Keel was granted permission to work on the film by the Minister of Labor.

F 2. ANNIE GET YOUR GUN (MGM, April 1950) Color. 107 Minutes.

CREDITS: Producer: Arthur Freed. Director: George Sidney. Book by Herbert and Dorothy Fields. Based on musical play produced by Rodgers and Hammerstein. Screenplay by Sidney Sheldon. Cinematographer: Charles Rosher (Technicolor). Editor: James Newcom. Lyrics & Music by Irving Berlin. Musical Director: Aldolph Deutsch. Musical numbers staged by Robert Alton. Art Directors: Cedric Gibbons, Paul Groesse. Set Designer: Edwin B. Willis, Richard A. Pefferle. Women's Costume Designers: Helen Rose and Walter Plunkett. Men's Costume Designer: Walter Plunkett. Makeup Artist: Jack Dawn. Hair Stylist: Sydney Guilaroff. Sound by Douglas Shearer. Special Effects by Arnold Gillespie, Warren Newcombe. Color Consultants: Henri Jaffa, James Gooch. Montage Director: Peter Ballbusch.

CAST: Betty Hutton (Annie Oakley); **Howard Keel** (Frank Butler); Louis Calhern (Buffalo Bill); J. Carrol Naish (Sitting Bull); Edward Arnold (Pawnee Bill); Keenan Wynn (Charlie Davenport); Benay Venuta (Dolly Tate); Clinton Sundberg (Foster Wilson); James Harrison (Mac); Bradley Mora (Little Jake); Diana Dick (Nellie); Susan Idin (Jessie); Eleanor Brown (Minnie); Chief Yowlachie (Little Horse); Robert Malcolm (Conductor); Lee Tung Foo (Waiter); William Tannen (Barker); Anne O' Neal (Miss Wiloughby); Evelyn Beresford (Queen Victoria); John Hamilton (Ship Captain); William Bill Hall (Tall Man); Edward Earle (Footman); Marjorie Wood (Constance); Elizabeth Flourney (Helen); Mae Clarke (Mrs. Adams); Frank Wilcox (Mr. Clay); Andre Charlot (President Loubet of France); Nino Pipitone (King Victor Emmanuel); John Mylong (Kaiser Wilhelm II); Carl Sepulveda, Carol Henry, Fred Gilman (Cowboys).

SYNOPSIS: The action takes place in the mid 1880s when Buffalo Bill's Wild West Show arrives in Cincinnati, Ohio, Annie Oakley (Hutton) joins the show as Frank Butler's (Keel) assistant. Annie and Bill fall in love but both are champion sharpshooters and Bill's pride is hurt when Annie's show supercedes his. Bill leaves the show to join Pawnee Bill's which also represents Sitting Bull. Sitting Bull takes a liking to Annie and takes her as his daughter.

On a European tour, Annie does well, but Buffalo Bill is broke upon his return to America. A merger takes place with Pawnee Bill and the lovers get back together again.

SONGS: "Colonel Buffalo Bill" (Wynn, Venuti, Keel); "Doin' What Comes Naturally" (Hutton); "The Girl That I Marry" (Keel); "You Can't Get a Man With a Gun" (Hutton); "They Say It's Wonderful" (Hutton, Keel); "My Defenses Are Down" (Keel); "I Got the Sun in the Morning" (Hutton); "Anything You Can Do" (Hutton, Keel); "There's No Business Like Show Business" (Hutton, Keel, Calhern, Wynn); "I'm An Indian Too" (Hutton).

REVIEWS: New York Times, Bosley Crowther, (May 18, 1950) Mr. Crowther felt that ANNIE GET YOUR GUN was a "whale" of a film and that Miss Hutton played her role with a "great deal of humor and bounce." He thought that Howard Keel performed "vigorously" and sang in a "full, rich voice." Reviewed at Loew's State in New York on May 17, 1950.

Variety (April 12, 1950) felt that ANNIE GET YOUR GUN was given a "wow" screening that it was "stimulating" and the outlook box office wise was "socko." It was also felt that Keel's baritone voice was "particulary adaptable" to the music and he sings his numbers with "resonance." Previewed at the Tradeshown April 5, 1950.

ADDITIONAL REVIEWS: BFI/Monthly Film Bulletin (July 1950); Christian Century (July 19, 1950); Commonweal (June 2, 1950); Cue (May 20, 1950); Film Daily (April 12, 1950); The Hollywood Reporter (April 12, 1950); Library Journal (May 1, 1950); Life (April 17, 1950); London Times (July 3, 1950); Motion Picture Herald Product Digest (April 15, 1950); The New Republic (May 29, 1950); Newsweek (June 5, 1950); The New Yorker (May 20, 1950); The Spectator (June 30, 1950); Time (April 24, 1950).

COMMENTS: When Jerome Kern died, Rodgers and Hammerstein asked Irving Berlin to score the 1946 Broadway musical (on which the film is based) which would star Ethel Merman and Ray Middleton. Berlin was hesitant about doing the project because he would have to write an entirely new score rather than use his previously published songs. After finishing "Doing What Comes Naturally" and "They Say It's Wonderful" his confidence grew and he auditioned for Rodgers and Hammerstein.

The producers felt that Ethel Merman and Mary Martin were not young enough to play Annie Oakley Mozie. Judy Canova, Betty Garrett and Doris Day (who badly wanted the role) were all considered but the studio chose Judy Garland to play Annie in their musical based on the character created by Barbara Stanwyck in the film ANNIE OAKLY (1935) which co-starred Preston Foster as Frank Butler.

Because Garland wanted the part so much, she did not make any objections when Busby Berkeley became director even though they did not get along during the filming of FOR ME AND MY GAL and GIRL CRAZY. She would have preferred

Charles Walters to direct. Although the recording sessions
went fine, they lacked the usual excitement Garland created
when she sang. She felt more comfortable playing herself
rather than a character.

John Raitt tested for the Frank Butler role but
even though he sang the songs beautifully they felt he was
not photogenic enough or that his personality and physical
appearance were not strong enough to be offered the part.
He did the role with Mary Martin on stage in 1957. The
production was filmed and aired on TV the same year.

The picture became plagued with problems. On April 4,
1949, Keel's right ankle was broken after his horse fell on
it. Arthur Freed did not like Berkeley's concept of the
film and on May 3, 1949, Charles Walters replaced him. Judy
Garland's emotional and drug-addiction problems caused her
release from the film on May 10, 1949.

On June 21, 1949, a contract was signed in which Betty
Hutton was loaned to MGM by Paramount in a $150,000 deal.
Hutton had seen Ethel Merman play Annie on Broadway and
ever since had longed to play the role. Hutton reported to
the studio on September 10, 1949, for pre-recording sessions.
Orchestrations were changed to fit her range. Production
resumed on October 10, 1949. The movie had already cost
$1,877,528 and was forced to increase its budget to
$3,707,481. Most of the costumes designed for Judy Garland
by Walter Plunkett were dropped and Helen Rose became Miss
Hutton's wardrobe designer. Hutton felt uncomfortable, at
first, because she came from another studio and was taking
the place of Judy Garland who had been one of the studio's
biggest stars. It took her only a short time to gain the
respect of he colleagues.

Charles Walters's contract was up in August of 1949,
and George Sidney tried to get Mayer and Schary to give
him the director's job. Walters learned of his dismissal
from the project only by accident whe he saw mention of it
in Hedda Hopper's column in the Los Angeles Times. Louis
Calhern took over the role of Buffalo Bill when Frank Morgan
died of a heart attack on September 18, 1949. Geraldine
Wall had other commitments and was replaced by Benay Venuta.
The children had out-grown their parts and were replaced by
younger ones.

The wild west circus sequence (the most costly)
required 250 feet of a backdrop consisting of a painted
Monument Valley. The sequence intended to provide a few
minutes of atmosphere, required 1,000 spectators and
thousands of painted ones, 175 cowboys and indians, 135
riding horses, 25 wagon horses, hundreds of trick riders
and gunmen. In order to keep ahead of the indians and Miss
Hutton's double, a camera truck containing six
photographers had to drive fifty miles an hour. Other items
needed were 7,000 square feet of backdrop canvas, 25,000 feet
of lumber, 14,000 feet of canvas, 1,940 feet of bleacher
backing, a maypole with 25,000 feathers, 550 painted arrows,
280 bows, and 190 spears. It took two months and $200,000
to construct and less than a week to erect.

Several of the Broadway songs were deleted from the
film including "Moonshine Lullaby," "I Got Lost in His
Arms," "Who Do You Love I Hope." Berlin had written

"Let's Go West Again" for Garland but when she left the film, the song was dropped. Lyrics were changed in "Doing What Comes Naturally," "You Can't Get a Man With a Gun," and "My Defenses Are Down" because of censorship. The songs Keel and Garland recorded are now in a collector's album.

The film, together with its 1956 re-release, would gross more than $8,000,000. ANNIE GET YOUR GUN's production number was 1450. "I'm a Bad Bad Man" was used as a background number. In order to focus on 800 horsemen and stars Hutton and Keel in the finale featuring "There's No Business Like Show Business," two cameras were placed on a newly constructed 500-foot tower an another on a 200-foot tower. Sidney used 1,040 extras, 224 musicians and two mounted bands in the scene. The sequence required only one day to shoot. A beacon was needed for the 500-foot tower so that planes landing at nearby airports would not hit it.

The picture, requiring 46 days to shoot, finished production on December 16, 1949, 4½ days ahead of schedule. It's total cost was $3,768,785 which was $61,304 over budget.

ANNIE GET YOUR GUN received a favorable response at its preview on January 29, 1950, at the United Artist Theatre in Long Beach. In addition to the Academy Award for best scoring of a musical, the picture would also receive nominations for cinematography (color), art direction/set direction (color) as well as film editing.

In May 1976, MGM/United Artists released THAT'S ENTERTAINMENT PART 2 which did not equal the success of the earlier released THAT'S ENTERTAINMENT! (1974). The film was a compilation of more great moments from MGM movies and was narrated by Fred Astaire and Gene Kelly. Keel was pictured in the "There's No Business Like Show Business" sequence from ANNIE GET YOUR GUN in which he sings with Betty Hutton, Keenan Wynn, and Louis Calhern. (See D19, D20)

F 3. PAGAN LOVE SONG (MGM, December 29, 1950) Color. 76 Minutes.

CREDITS: Producer: Arthur Freed. Associate Producer: Ben Feiner, Lela Simone (Uncredited), Roger Edens (Uncredited). Director: Robert Alton. Based on William Stone's Tahiti Landfall. Screenplay by Robert Nathan, Jerry Davis. Cinematographer: Charles Rasher (Technicolor). Editor: Adrienne Frazan. Lyrics and Music by Harry Warren, Arthur Freed. Musical Director: Adolph Deutsch. Choreographer: Robert Alton. Vocal Arranger: Robert Tucker. Conductor: Conrad Salinger. Art Directors: Cedric Gibbons, Randall Duell. Set Designers: Edwin Willis, associate Jack Moore. Costume Designer: Helen Rose. Makeup Artist: William Tuttle. Hair Stylist: Sydney Guilaroff. Recording Supervisor: Douglas Shearer. Special Effects by Arnold Gillespie, Warren Newcombe. Color Consultants: Henri Jaffa, James Gooch. Technical Adviser: William Stone.

CAST: Esther Williams (Mimi Bennett); **Howard Keel**

(Hazard Endicott); Minna Gombell (Kate Bennett);
Charles Mauu (Tavae); Rita Moreno (Teuru); Phillip
Costa (Manu); Dione Leilani (Tani); Charles Freund
(Papera); Marcella Corday (Countess Mariani); Sam
Maikai (Tua); Helen Rapoza (Angele); Birdie De Bolt
(Mama Ruau); Bill Kaliloa (Mata); Carlo Cook (Monsieur
Bouchet).

SYNOPSIS: When his uncle dies, an Ohio school teacher
Hazard Endicott (Keel), arrives in Tahiti to take over the
plantation his uncle left him in his will and ends up
falling in love with Mimi Bennett (Williams) who is an
islander with money.
    Mimi, who went to college in the United States and is
an equal mixture of white and native, defends the natives
when Hazard gets upset when the native workers attend their
wedding during a storm. An argument follows but they are
reunited with the help of the natives.

SONGS: "Pagan Love Song" (Keel); "Tahiti" (Keel); "Singing
in the Sun" (Williams, Keel); "Etiquette"; "Why is Love So
Crazy?" (Keel); "The House of the Singing Bamboo" (Keel);
"The Sea of the Moon" (Williams).

REVIEWS: New York Times, Thomas Pryor, (December 26, 1950)
Mr. Pryor felt that the only thing going for the film was
the scenery. He thought that Miss Williams was "wonderfully
graceful" in her water exercises, and that Howard Keel had
a "mellow baritone" that he used often and "well." Reviewed
at the Capitol Theatre in New York.

Variety (December 20, 1950) felt that PAGAN LOVE SONG was
"one of the weaker" of Freed's musical films and that it
would do "okay" at the box office because of Keel and
Williams. It was also felt that the role did not have Keel
do more than use his "robust baritone" and be "pleasant."
Previewed at the Capitol Theatre in New York on December
12, 1950.

ADDITIONAL REVIEWS: B.F.I./Monthly Film Bulletin (May
1951); Chicago Sun Times (December 26, 1950); Film Daily
(December 26, 1950); The Hollywood Reporter (December 20,
1950); Library Journal (January 15, 1951); Motion Picture
Herald Product Digest (December 23, 1950); Newsweek
(January 8, 1951); Time (January 15, 1951).

COMMENTS: Robert Nathan was asked to write a screenplay by
friend Arthur Freed. After he finished and turned in the
screenplay about Tahiti, he left the studio when his
seven-year contract expired. Freed assigned Stanley Donen
to direct PAGAN LOVE SONG (titled after Freed's song) and
Jerry David to write a script. Esther Williams refused to
work with Donen because he had commented that he thought
she had no talent. When they were unable to change her
mind, Donen was released from the film. Freed chose Robert
Alton (best known as a choreographer) to replace Donen.
    When travel to Tahiti became a problem, the Hawaiian
island of Kauai was chosen as the new location. Before

leaving, pre-recordings were made. The first three weeks in
March 1950, were used for pre-recordings and completion of
the script.

Alton feared flying and he arrived in Honolulu during
a tropical storm which did not help matters. Before going
to Kauai, some first-class non-Polynesian swimmers were
found for Williams' water ballet. Tahitian music needed to
be pre-recorded. They could not find any Tahitian natives
for the job so they hired a trio of Polynesian night club
entertainers to do the pre-recording. They had to use the
run down back room of a music store for the sessions as
they were the only recording facilities available.

The flight to Kauai was a disastor with a plane of
natives, birds, dogs, flowers, and a ride similar to a
roller coaster. They flew up to and veered around a steep
hillside and found themselves suddenly on the ground.

Lihue was the only village on the island and its only
hotel--the Kauai Inn was run down. The studio rented
Esther Williams a modern house and furnished it for her and
infant son Benjy. The crew stayed ten miles away in two
country inns.

April 3, 1950, began the first week of filming but rain
or clouds interfered with shooting, because as it was
learned, this was the island's rainy season.

Alton was so concerned about not upsetting Freed and
the studio, he became indecisive and this feeling was
passed onto the cast and crew.

For the "Singing in the Sun" number, Keel was to ride
a bicycle down a country lane. A large bicycle was built
because of Keel's long legs and his broken arm was hidden
by a towel.

So concerned about not getting behind schedule, Alton
went ahead with a love scene between Williams and Keel even
though the wind was blowing Miss Williams's hair. He
did not even notice that Williams was looking past Keel's
face because she was without her contacts.

Williams told associate producer Lela Simone (Lela and
Roger Edens worked as associate producers without screen
credit) she thought she was pregnant. They persuaded a
Japanese school teacher to let Williams use his ham radio to
talk with her husband Ben Gage. She did not want to come
out over the airways and say she was pregnant so she told
Ben that Lela was pregnant. She said Ben would understand
her message. Simone was upset because her husband would
hear the news and think she was pregnant. The Los Angeles
relay man happened to be an MGM sound mixer and by morning
the news had spread around the studio.

During filming, Keel would go golfing. The two boys
he used as caddies wanted to go back to the mainland after
shooting was over.

The production number was 1489. The song "Coconut
Milk" was used as a background number. The songs "Music on
the Water" and "Here in Tahiti We Make Love" were dropped
from the film.

By May 26, 1950, the cast and crew were back at the
studio for a few interior shots. By July 8, 1950, filming
had been completed at a cost of $1,906,265 surpassing its
budget by $399,749. After its release on December 29,

1950, the film grossed more than $3,205,000.   (See D38, V13).

F 4. THREE GUYS NAMED MIKE (MGM, March 1951) B&W. 90 Minutes.

CREDITS: Producer: Armand Deutsch. Director: Charles Walters. Based on Story by Ruth Brooke Flippen. Screenplay by Sidney Sheldon. Cinematographer: Paul Vogel. Editor: Irvine Warburton. Music by Bronislau Kaper. Art Directors: Cedric Gibbons, William Ferrari. Set Designer: Edwin Willis. Associate Set Designer: Arthur Krams. Makeup Artist: William Tuttle. Hair Stylist: Sydney Guilaroff. Technical Advisers: Gerald Tierney, Ethel "Pug" Wells. Recording Supervisor: Douglas Shearer.

CAST: Jane Wyman (Marcy Lewis); Van Johnson (Michael Lawrence); **Howard Keel** (Mike Jamison); Barry Sullivan (Mike Tracy); Phyllis Kirk (Kathy Hunter); Anne Sargent (Jan Baker); Jeff Donnell (Alice Raymend); Herbert Heyes (Scott Bellemy); Robert Sherwood (Benson); Don McGuire (MacWade Parker); Barbara Billingsley (Anne White); Hugh Sanders (Mr. Williams); John Maxwell (Dr. Matthew Hardy); Lewis Martin (C. R. Smith); Ethel "Pug" Wells (Herself); Sydney Mason (Osgood); Percy Helton (Hawkins); Dan Foster (Rogers); Jack Shea (Nashville Passenger Agent); King Mojave (Passenger Agent); Arthur Space (Clerk); Matt Moore (Mr. Tannen); Mae Clarke (Convair Passenger); Jack Gargan (Mr. Rogers).

SYNOPSIS: Marcy (Wyman) is a stewardess, who has an innocent, sympathetic manner, which makes her attractive to men.   Among those showing interest in Marcy are Michael Lawrence (Johnson) who is a science student and part time bartender, Mike Jamison (Keel) a pilot and Mike Tracy (Sullivan) who works for an ad agency.
      Because of Marcy's overeagerness, she makes many mistakes all adding to the comedy.   When she learns how to handle things, Marcy gets back the respect of both passengers and airline personnel.
      In the end it is Michael Lawrence who ends up with Marcy.

REVIEWS: New York Times, Bosley Crowther, (March 2, 1951) Bosley Crowther felt that the film was a "bird-brained little romance." Reviewed at the Capitol Theatre in New York on March 1, 1951.

Variety (February 14, 1951) felt that the film was a "lightweight" comedy and its middleweight box office appeal would be due, in part, to the names of Van Johnson and Jane Wyman, Armand Deutsch's "impressive" production and Charles Walters's direction. Wyman, Johnson, Keel and Sullivan "show to special advantage." Previewed at Loew's State in New York on January 17, 1951.

ADDITIONAL REVIEWS: B.F.I./Monthly Film Bulletin (March

1951); Christian Century (March 28, 1951); Film Daily
(February 9, 1951); The Hollywood Reporter (February 9,
1951); Motion Picture Herald Product Digest (February 10,
1951); New York Herald Tribune (March 2, 1951); The New
Yorker (March 10, 1951); Senior Scholastic (March 7, 1951);
Time (March 19, 1951).

COMMENTS: American Airlines provided the backdrop for
the film. The people from Gillespie, Illinois remembered
their native son and wished him luck in a 3 x 5-foot post-
card sent to him during filming.

F 5. SHOW BOAT (MGM, July 3, 1951) Color. 108 Minutes.

CREDITS: Producer: Arthur Freed. Associate Producers:
Ben Feiner, Roger Edens (not credited). Director:
George Sidney. Based on Edna Ferber's novel and Jerome
Kern and Oscar Hammerstein's play SHOW BOAT. Screenplay
by John Lee Mahin, George Wells, Jack McGowan (not
credited). Cinematographer: Charles Rosher (Techni-
color). Editor: Albert Akst. Lyrics and Music by Oscar
Hammerstein and Jerome Kern. Musical Director: Adolph
Deutsch. Music Staged and Directed by Robert Alton.
Vocal Arranger: Robert Tucker. Conductor: Conrad
Salinger. Art Directors: Cedric Gibbons, Jack Martin
Smith. Set Designers: Edwin Willis, Alfred Spencer.
Costume Designer: Walter Plunkett. Makeup Artist:
William Tuttle. Hair Stylist: Sydney Guilaroff. Special
Effects by Warren Newcombe. Color Consultants: Henri
Jaffa, James Gooch. Montage Director: Peter Ballbusch.

CAST: Kathryn Grayson (Magnolia Hawks); Ava Gardner
(Julie Laverne); **Howard Keel** (Gaylord Ravenal); Joe E.
Brown (Captain Andy Hawks); Marge Champion (Ellie May
Shipley); Gower Champion (Frank Schultz); Robert
Sterling (Stephen Baker); Agnes Moorehead (Parthy
Hawks); Adele Jergens (Cameo McQueen); William War-
field (Joe); Leif Erickson (Pete); Owen McGiveney
(Windy McClain); Frances Williams (Queenie); Regis
Toomey (Sheriff Ike Vallon); Frank Wilcox (Mark
Hallson); Ian MacDonald (Drunk Sport); Fuzzy Knight
(Troc Piano Player); Emory Parnell (Jake Green);
Chick Chandler (Herman); Joyce Jameson and Lyn Wilde
(Chorus Girls); Annette Warren (Julie's singing voice);
Edward Keene (Hotel Manager); Tom Irish (Bellboy); Jim
Pierce (Doorman); William Tannen (Man with Julie);
Anna Nilsson (Seamstress); Bert Roach (Drunk); Earle
Hodgins (Bartender); Ida Moore (Old Lady); Alphonse
Martell (Headwaiter).

SYNOPSIS: The action takes place between the mid 1880s and
1927, where Julie (Gardner) is an entertainer aboard the
riverboat Cotton Blossom owned by Captain Andy Hawks
(Brown) and his wife Parthy (Moorehead). Julie does not
give in to the sexual advances of laborer Pete (Erickson)
and he charges her with being the offspring of a mixed
couple. Eluding the sheriff (Toomey), she loses her job.
     Andy's daughter Magnolia (Grayson) and gambler

Gaylord (Keel) fall in love and Gaylord gives up his
gambling to become an actor on the Cotton Blossom.
Eventually, Gaylord returns to gambling and the
marriage falls on hard times. He leaves to pursue
gambling. Meeting up with Julie, he learns he has a
daughter. He returns to Magnolia and they are reunited.

SONGS: "Who Cares If the Boat Goes Upstream?" (Keel);
"Cotton Blossom" (Orchestra, Chorus); "Where's the Mate
For Me?" (Keel); "Make Believe" (Grayson, Keel); "Can't Help
Lovin' Dat Man" (Gardner, dubbed by Annette Warren); "I
Might Fall Back On You" (Marge & Gower Champion); "Ol' Man
River" (Warfield); "You Are Love" (Grayson, Keel); "Why Do I
Love You?" (Grayson, Keel); "Bill" (Gardner, dubbed by
Warren); "Life Upon a Wicked Stage" (Marge & Gower
Champion); "After the Ball" (Grayson).

REVIEWS: New York Times, Bosley Crowther, (July 20, 1951)
Mr. Crowther felt that this version of SHOW BOAT was
"brilliant" and was "so magnificent" in many ways. He felt
that Miss Grayson (as Magnolia) was a "doll" playing the
part with a combination of "wholesome spunk and beauty" and
that Howard Keel played Gaylord with "devilish charm and
idyllic manliness." Reviewed at Radio City Music Hall in
New York.

Variety (June 6, 1951) felt that this version "continued the
beguilment" of its predecessors and was a "socko" version
with a box office appeal that was the "best." It was felt
that Kathryn Grayson and Howard Keel had voices with "show-
tune ableness" and their singing would "capture the ears and
tear at the emotions." Reviewed at the Tradeshown in
Hollywood on June 1, 1951.

ADDITIONAL REVIEWS: B.F.I./Monthly Film Bulletin (July
1951); Christian Century (August 1, 1951); Commonweal (June
29, 1951); Cue (July 14, 1951); Film Daily (June 5, 1951);
The Hollywood Reporter (June 5, 1951); Library Journal (June
15, 1951); Life (July 30, 1951); Motion Picture Herald
Product Digest (June 9, 1951); Newsweek (July 2, 1951); The
New Yorker (July 28, 1951); New York Times (July 22, 1951);
Radio City Hall Program (August 30, 1951); Saturday Review
(June 9, 1951); Time (July 2, 1951).

COMMENTS: SHOW BOAT (based on the 1927 Broadway musical) had
been filmed twice before. The first time in 1929, by
Universal starring Laura LaPlante and Joseph Schildkraut and
again in 1936, at Universal this time starring Irene Dunne
and Allan Jones. MGM purchased the rights planning to
remake the film (in the late 1930s) for stars Jeanette Mac-
Donald and Nelson Eddy but the film was never made.
Arthur Freed and Roger Edens wanted to reunite
Magnolia and Gaylord sooner, so they made changes in Oscar
Hammerstein's book. Freed's first choice for the role of
Julie was Judy Garland but she was let go by the studio
because of the problems they had had with her in the past.
Dore Schary wanted Dinah Shore to play the role. Freed told
Shore the part was that of a whore, hoping she would back

out so he could give the part to Ava Gardner. The studio as
well as columnists Hedda Hopper and Louella Parsons were not
sure that Gardner was the right choice for Garland's
replacement.

Gardner felt strongly about doing her own singing.
She insisted she be given a test. Frank Sinatra went to
bat for her and got his friends Axel Stordahl and Columbia
Records executive Manny Sachs to aid him in his cause. She
was granted her test in which she sang to a recording of
Lena Horne's. Because of her nervousness, the lights were
dimmed. Roger Edens attempted to coach her but was not too
successful. Marni Nixon, Anita Ellis, Carol Richards, and
Annette Warren were all tested as possible choices to dub
Gardner's singing voice. Warren, a night club singer, was
chosen to do the dubbing as her voice was the closest to
Gardner's speaking voice. When Gardner learned that the
studio still planned to go ahead and dub her singing voice,
she quit the picture. Frank Sinatra and Louis B. Mayer
tried to convince her to return to the film and after three
days she relented. Ironically, it was decided to leave
Gardner's voice on the soundtrack record as her name would
help record sales.

Freed wanted to use the Mississippi River for the
film's location but because of costs it was decided to use
the Tarzan Jungle Lake located on the back lot. The lake
was drained for the five weeks it took to build the Cotton
Blossom. The Cotton Blossom had a 19½-foot paddle wheel,
and measured 171 feet long, it had 34-foot beams and
measured 57 feet to the top of the stacks. It received its
power from two 225 horse power aircraft engines. Two
retarding cables and three touring winches were used to
steer the boat around the lake which was only ten feet at
one end and four at the other. In order for thirty-seven
men to operate the boat, they needed walky talkies and
ship-to-shore communications. The Cotton Blossom was probably the most expensive prop built as construction ran
$126,468. A camera had to be placed on an outrigger built
by Eddie Stone. One of the tanks, using oil injection, to
make smoke for the stacks caught fire and nearly destroyed
the Cotton Blossom. It cost $67,000 to repaint. Interest-
ingly, it was not used much after that except for such films
as DESPERATE SEARCH also starring Keel. It wound up rotting
on the lake.

It was through a report in Time of his Town Hall
recital in New York, that William Warfield was discovered
by the studio. Warfield auditioned by singing German and
French songs as well as other classical numbers as he had
never performed a popular song. He felt he could easily
make the transition. It took only one take to record "Ol'
Man River" and anyone hearing it agreed unanimously that
it was sensational.

Edna Ferber based the character of Captain Andy on Joe
E. Brown. During the December shooting, a natural fog would
drift in from the Pacific causing delays in shooting.
However, Charles Rosher, who was the director of photography, was able to remember camera and lighting details thus
causing no delays when filming resumed.

SHOW BOAT (production number 1520) started production

on November 17, 1950, and concluded on January 9, 1951.
Because Freed and Roger Edens, who directed during Sidney's
illness, were not happy with the rough cut, they wanted to
tighten and cut scenes. Additional filming was done on
February 5, 1951, and again on March 1, 1951. Songs not
used in the film included "Nobody Else But Me," "I Still
Suits Me," and "I Have the Room Above."
    Kathryn Grayson had played Captain Andy's daughter in
TILL THE CLOUDS ROLL BY in the SHOW BOAT sequence. SHOW
BOAT marked Marge and Gower Champion's first film together.
At the film's preview on March 22, 1951, at Pacific
Palisade's Bay Theatre, it was decided to dub Gardner's
singing voice with that of Annette Warren's because the
Pacific Palisades audiences felt that Gardner's voice
lacked the necessary passion. There was a second preview on
April 3, 1951, at the Picwood Theatre in West Los Angeles.
The New York preview was at Loew's 72nd Street Theatre on
May 21, 1951. SHOW BOAT was generally released in July of
1951, at a cost of $2,295,429. It grossed more than
$8,650,000 making it one of the years top moneymakers. It
received a nomination for an Academy Award for both best
scoring of a musical and for cinematography.
    In May 1974, MGM/United Artists released THAT'S
ENTERTAINMENT! produced and directed by Jack Haley, Jr. It
showcased great moments from MGM musicals. It was narrated
by Fred Astaire, Bing Crosby, Gene Kelly, Peter Lawford,
Liza Minnelli, Donald O'Conner, Debbie Reynolds, Mickey
Rooney, Frank Sinatra, James Stewart, and Elizabeth Taylor.
It became a top moneymaker. Keel appeared in the "Make
Believe" sequence, from SHOW BOAT, with Kathryn Grayson.
(See S11, D43, D44, V16)

F 6. TEXAS CARNIVAL (MGM, October 5, 1951) Color. 77
Minutes.

> CREDITS: Producer: Jack Cummings. Director: Charles
> Walters. Based on story by George Wells and Dorothy
> Kingsley. Screenplay by Dorothy Kingsley. Cinematog-
> rapher: Robert Planek (Technicolor). Editor: Adrienne
> Fazan. Musical Director: David Rose. Choreographer:
> Hermes Pan. Art Directors: Cedric Gibbons, William
> Ferarri. Set Designers: Edwin Willis, Keough Gleason.
> Costume Designer: Helen Rose. Makeup Artist: William
> Tuttle. Hair Stylist: Sydney Guilaroff. Recording
> Supervisor: Douglas Shearer. Special Effects by Arnold
> Gillespie, Warren Newcombe. Color Consultants: Henri
> Jaffa, James Gooch.

> CAST: Esther Williams (Debbie Telford); Red Skelton
> (Cornie Quinell); **Howard Keel** (Slim Shelby); Ann
> Miller (Sunshine Jackson); Paula Raymond (Marilla
> Sabinas); Keenan Wynn (Dan Sabinas); Tom Tully
> (Sheriff Jackson); Glenn Strange (Tex Hodgkins); Dick
> Wessel (Concessionaire); Donald MacBride (Concession-
> aire); Majorie Wood (Mrs. Gaytes); Hans Conried (Hotel
> Clerk); Thurston Hall (Mr. Gaytes); Duke Johnson
> (Juggler); Wilson Wood (Bell Boy); Michael Dugan (Card
> Player); Doug Carter (Cab Driver); Earle Hodgins

(Doorman); Gil Patrick (Assistant Clerk); Rhea
Mitchell (Dealer); Emmett Lynn (Cook); Bess Flowers,
Jack Daley, Fred Stantley (People in the Lobby); Joe
Roach, Manuel Petroff, Robert Fortier, William Lundy,
Alex Goundovitch (Special Dancers); Fog Williams & His
Orchestra; Red Norvo Trio.

SYNOPSIS: Barker Cornelius "Cornie" Quinell (Skelton) and
his assistant Debbie Telford (Williams) are traveling in
Texas with the Belrow Western Carnival. Debbie is tired
of being dunked when customers hit a target with a ball and
wants to go back to her home in Montana.
    Two carnival men try to cheat cattle baron Dan Sabinas
(Wynn) but are thwarted by Cornie. To show his gratitude,
Sabinas tries to get Cornie to accept a Cadillac. Cornie
turns it down but he and Debbie end up using it to escape
from the two carnival men.
    When they go to Sabinas's hotel to return the car,
Cornie and Debbie are thought to be Sabinas and his sister
Marilla (Raymond). The real Sabinas is in Mexico. Marilla
finds out about the imposters and gets her ranch foreman
Slim Shelby (Keel) to keep tabs on Cornie and Debbie.
Shelby takes a liking to Debbie and Cornie becomes
interested in Sunshine Jackson (Miller) who is the
sheriff's (Tully) daughter and an oil millionaire.
    Cornie plays poker with cattleman Tex Hodgkins
(Strange) and looses to him in the amount of $17,000.
Hodgkins makes a deal that the winner of a chuckwagon race
would get everything. Cornie beats Hodgkins.
    When Marilla and the real Sabinas show up, Cornie and
Debbie return to the carnival. Shelby and Sunshine follow
and the couples are reunited.

SONGS: "Carnie's Pitch"; "Whoa! Emma" (Keel); "It's
Dynamite" (Miller); "Deep in the Heart of Texas"; "Clap Your
Hands"; "Young Folks Should Get Married" (Keel); "Schnaps."

REVIEWS: New York Times, Bosley Crowther, (October 13, 1951)
Crowther felt that despite the named stars in the film,
TEXAS CARNIVAL was "entirely Red Skelton's show." and that
it would have been nice to let the others do more. Reviewed
at Loew's State in New York.

Variety (September 12, 1951) felt that TEXAS CARNIVAL was an
"excellent" comedy that was "light, easy-to-take entertainment" and that it should do "good biz" at the box office.
It was felt that Keel was "at ease" and that his personality
"gets over" and that he did "high standard vocal work."
Previewed at the Tradeshown in Hollywood on September 6,
1951.

ADDITIONAL REVIEWS: B.F.I./Monthly Film Bulletin (November
1951); Commonweal (November 9, 1951); Film Daily (September
17, 1951); Motion Picture Herald Product Digest (September
15, 1951); Newsweek (October 22, 1951); Time (November 5,
1951).

COMMENTS: Each movie in which Esther Williams appeared

was required to have a swimming sequence. Since her role
in TEXAS CARNIVAL did not require her to swim, director
Charles Walters made up a dream scene. For the scene, a
room was constructed at the bottom of the outside water
tank used for her swimming movies. (See V17)

F 7. ACROSS THE WIDE MISSOURI (MGM, October 1, 1951)
Color. 78 Minutes.

CREDITS: Producer: Robert Sisk. Director: William
Wellman. Based on Story by Talbot Jennings, Frank
Cavett. Screenplay by Talbot Jennings. Cinematographer:
William Mellor (Technicolor). Editor: John Dunn. Music
by David Racksin. Art Directors: Cedric Gibbons, James
Basevi.

CAST: Clark Gable (Flint Mitchell); Ricardo Montalban
(Iron Shirt); John Hodiak (Brecan); Adolphe Menjou
(Pierre); Maria Elena Marques (Kamiah); J. Carrol Naish
(Looking Glass); Jack Holt (Bear Ghost); Alan Napier
(Capt. Humberstone Lyon); George Chandler (Gowie);
Richard Anderson (Dick Richardson); Henri Letondal
(Lucien Chennault); Douglas Fowley (Tin Cup Owens);
Louis Nicoletti (Roy DuNord); Ben Watson (Markhead);
Russell Simpson (Hoback); Frankie Darro (Cadet);
Howard Keel (Narrator).

SYNOPSIS: A Kentucky trapper, Flint Mitchell (Gable), leads
an expedition, in 1829, into Blackfoot land to hunt beavers.
In order to assure safe passage through indian territory,
Flint marries Chief Bear Ghost's (Holt) granddaughter Kamiah
(Marques).
    After surviving an indian attack, Kamiah leads the
trappers on a longer but safer route. The chief declares
peace and the trappers build a winter encampment.
    Flint realizes he has fallen in love with Kamiah and
when they have a son, he decides to lead the trappers out
of the area to safety then return with his family to the
tribe.
    One of the trappers kills the chief and starts trouble
with the indians. In the battle Kamiah is killed. Flint
survives the battle and with his son returns to the tribe.

REVIEWS: New York Times (November 7, 1951) It was felt that
ACROSS THE WIDE MISSOURI was a "disappointment." It was
"halting" and "verbose"..."it rarely captures the imagina-
tion and fleetingly portrays the excitement... or the fear-
less, sturdy men" of the period. Reviewed at Loew's State in
New York on November 6, 1951.

Variety. (September 19, 1951) It was felt that ACROSS THE
WIDE MISSOURI was a "tepid outdoor actioner" that would do
"just fair" at the box office. Reviewed at the Tradeshown
in Hollywood on September 13, 1951.

ADDITIONAL REVIEWS: American Cinematographer (May 1951);
B.F.I./Monthly Film Bulletin (November 1951); Catholic
World (November 1951); Christian Century (November 21,

1951); **Film Daily** (September 24, 1951); **The Hollywood Reporter** (September 18, 1951); **Library Journal** (November 1, 1951); **Motion Picture Herald Product Digest** (September 29, 1951); **Newsweek** (November 19, 1951); **Saturday Review** (October 27, 1951); **Time** (November 19, 1951).

COMMENTS: Two problems with the film included the interruption of the narration in which Keel was speaking as Gable's son and the translation of the indian language. The film was shot in a rugged area of Colorado. Sylvia, Gable's fourth wife, joined Gable on location at their cabin which was separate from the other cast. She tried to make things cozy even putting up fancy curtains and having the cabin area landscaped. Gable felt funny when she brought Minnie, a tiny Terrier, to the meals at the tables shared by cast and crew. Gable spent his free time fishing. Sylvia tried the sport but did not have the skill for it. She was glad when the film was over and she returned home. (See V1)

F 8. CALLAWAY WENT THATAWAY [THE STAR SAID NO-British title] (MGM, November 15, 1951) B&W 81 Minutes.

CREDITS: Producer/Director/Author/Screenplay: Norman Panama, Melvin Frank. Cinematographer: Ray June. Editor: Cotton Warburton. Music by Marlin Skiles. Art Directors: Cedric Gibbons, Eddie Imazu. Set Designers: Edwin Willis, Hugh Hunt. Dorothy McGuire's Costume Designer: Helen Rose. Howard Keel's Costume Designer: Gile Steele. Makeup Artist: William Tuttle. Hair Stylist: Sidney Guilaroff. Recording Supervisor: Douglas Shearer. Special Effects by Arnold Gillespie, Warren Newcombe. Montage Director: Peter Ballbusche.

CAST: Fred MacMurray (Mike Frye); Dorothy McGuire (Deborah Patterson); **Howard Keel** ("Smoky" Callaway/ Stretch Barnes); Jesse White (Georgie Markham); Fay Roope (Tom Lorrison); Natalie Schaefer (Martha Lorrison); Douglas Kennedy (Drunk); Elizabeth Fraser (Marie); Johnny Indrisano (Johnny Terrento); Stan Freberg (Marvin); Don Haggerty (Director); Walk Ons: Esther Williams, Elizabeth Taylor, Clark Gable, June Allyson, and Dick Powell.

SYNOPSIS: Mike Frye (MacMurray) and Deborah Patterson (McGuire) run an advertising agency and have made a deal with television to show thirty of "Smoky" Callaway's western films. The kids go wild over the pictures begging for more. Tom Lorrison (Roope), the owner of North American Corn Company, is willing to put up $2,000,000 for the films. Smoky is a drunk and has been out of the limelight for ten years. Mike and Deborah get his ex-manager to search for him.

In the meantime, Mike and Deborah discover a real cowboy by the name of Stretch Barnes (Keel) which is the spliting image of Smoky. They eventually get him to impersonate Smoky saying its for the good of the children.

While on a personal appearance tour at Niagra Falls, Stretch gives Deborah an engagement ring. Feeling he

could do more for the children, Stretch sets up the Smoky
Callaway Foundation donating most of his income.
     Markham finds the real Smoky Callaway (Keel). Smoky
wants all he can get out of his new found popularity, but
is thwarted when Stretch publicly commits his income to
the foundation. Markham and Smoky head for a tropical
island where they plan to spend their remaining days
getting drunk.
     Deborah realizes her love for Stretch and puts on the
ring he gave her at Niagra Falls. Stretch decides to let
the Callaway legend continue knowing he has made millions
of children happy and that he has Deborah's love.

SONG: "Where the Tumbleweed is Blue" (Keel).

REVIEWS: <u>New York Times</u>, Bosley Crowther, (December 6, 1951)
Crowther felt that the film had a "full head of rowdy humor
and occasional wit" although the pace slowed down a little
when the real Callaway is brought to Hollywood. He felt
that Keel's performance was "surprisingly humorous and
adroit." Reviewed at Loew's State in New York on December
5, 1951.

<u>Variety</u> (November 14, 1951) felt that CALLAWAY WENT THATAWAY
was an "amusing spoof on video cowpokes." The idea is
"interestingly showcased" in a "light, easy style" and
should do "okay" at the box office. It was felt that Keel
"pleases soundly" and comes across "neatly" in his two
parts. Previewed at Tradeshown on October 31, 1951.

ADDITIONAL REVIEWS: <u>Catholic World</u> (December 1951);
<u>Christian Century</u> (January 16, 1952); <u>Film Daily</u> (November
15, 1951); <u>Motion Picture Herald Product Digest</u> (November
17, 1951); <u>The New Yorker</u> (December 15, 1951); <u>Newsweek</u>
(December 17, 1951); <u>Saturday Review</u> (December 1, 1951);
<u>Theatre Arts</u> (January 1952); <u>Time</u> (December 10, 1951).

COMMENTS: Howard Keel went through three weeks of
training for the fight sequences in the picture. When a
fight trainer was needed in the film, Keel's trainer, Johnny
Indrisano was cast.
     El Rio was the name of the pinto that Keel rode. The
horse was the second generation to be in films and is the
son of Dice a stunt horse.
     Keel sang "Where the Tumbleweed is Blue" in the non-
musical motion picture.
     You can see Clark Gable, Elizabeth Taylor, and Esther
Williams in cameo appearances in a night club scene where
they are introduced to the fake Callaway. Taylor appeared
for the only time in a film playing herself.
     The Keel character was drawn from a combination of the
careers of Gene Autry, Roy Rogers, and especially William
Boyd who had bought the rights to Hopalong Cassidy films and
made money when he sold them individually to be shown to
children.

F 9. LOVELY TO LOOK AT (MGM, May 1952) Color. 105 Minutes.

CREDITS: Producer: Jack Cummings. Directors: Mervyn
LeRoy and Vincente Minnelli. Based on the novel by
Alice Duer Miller and on the stage musical ROBERTA by
Otto Harbach. Screenplay by George Wells, Harry Ruby,
Andrew Solt. Cinematographer: George Folsey (Techni-
color). Editor: John McSweeney, Jr. Lyrics and Music by
Jerome Kern, Otto Harbach and Dorothy Fields. Revised
Lyrics by Dorothy Fields. Musical Directors: Carmen
Dragon, Saul Chaplin. Choreographer: Hermes Pan. Art
Directors: Cedric Gibbons, Gabriel Scognamillo. Set
Designers: Edwin Willis, Jack Moore. Costume Designer:
Adrian. Makeup Artist: Sydney Gailaroff. Recording
Supervisor: Douglas Shearer. Special Effects by Arnold
Gillespie. Technical Advisers: Henri Jaffa, James
Gooch. Fashion Show by Tony Duquette.

CAST: Kathryn Grayson (Stephanie); **Howard Keel** (Tony
Naylor); Red Skelton (Al Marsh); Marge Champion
(Clarisse); Gower Champion (Jerry Ralby); Ann Miller
(Bubbles Cassidy); Zsa Zsa Gabor (Zsa Zsa); Kurt
Kasznar (Max Fogelsby); Marcel Dalio (Pierre); Diane
Cassidy (Diane).

SYNOPSIS: Al Marsh (Skelton), Tony Naylor (Keel), and
Jerry Ralby (Gower Champion) are not successful in their
attempts to raise money to back a Broadway show. One of
the show girls, Bubbles Cassidy (Miller), likes Naylor and
is willing to put up her life savings but is turned down.
It is then that Marsh finds out he has inherited half a
Paris dress shop from his Aunt Roberta. He goes to Paris
with friends Ralby and Naylor to claim it in hopes of
selling the store to raise money for the show.
     Upon arrival in Paris, they meet two sisters Stephanie
(Grayson) and Clarisse (Marge Champion) who were adopted
by Aunt Roberta and have inherited the other half of
Roberta's. They inform Marsh that the shop is not doing
well. Naylor gets the idea to spark interest in the shop
by having a musical fashion show and getting American
designer Adrian to create the gowns.
     Naylor gets the creditors to sponsor the fashion show.
He also is in love with Stephanie. When Bubbles arrives on
the scene, she is not happy to learn of Naylor's interest
in Stephanie. Clarisse and Ralby are also in love and Nash
takes an interest in Stephanie.
     While rehearsing the fashion show, one of the models,
Zsa Zsa (Gabor), introduces her boy friend, Max Fogelsby
(Kasznar), to Naylor. He learns that Fogelsby is a
Broadway producer who offers to put up the money for the
show if the group returns to New York. Marsh, Ralby, and
Bubbles do not want to let Stephanie and Clarisse down so
they turn down the offer. Naylor does accept but soon
realizes he made a mistake. He returns to Paris in time to
see that the fashion show is successful. Stephanie
realizes Naylor loves her and Marsh and Bubbles get
together too.

SONGS: "Opening Night" (Keel, Skelton, Gower Champion);
"Lafayette" (Skelton, Keel, Gower Champion); "Smoke Gets

in Your Eyes" (Grayson); "I Won't Dance" (Marge & Gower
Champion); "You're Devastating" (Grayson, Keel);
"Yesterdays" (Grayson); "Lovely to Look At" (Keel); "I'll Be
Hard to Handle" (Miller); "The Touch of Your Hand" (Grayson,
Keel); "Lovely to Look At"-Reprise (Chorus).

REVIEWS: New York Times, Oscar Godbout, (May 30, 1952) Oscar
felt that Kathryn Grayson and Howard Keel were in "fine
voice" and made a "handsome couple." The best parts of
the film were the fashions in the fashion show and the
songs but the plot was a "shade duller" then that of the
original production. Reviewed at Radio City Music Hall in
New York on May 30, 1952.

Variety (May 28, 1952) felt that LOVELY TO LOOK AT was
"entertaining" even though the years have caused much of the
"freshness" to be "worn off." The stars and "overall
production" make it an "above-average musical." The critic
felt that the players "all deliver expertly." It was also
felt that the script made Keel "appear a heel" and nothing
could change that and that Miss Grayson was "lovely" and in
"good voice." Previewed in Hollywood on May 21, 1952.

ADDITIONAL REVIEWS: B.F.I./Monthly Film Bulletin (September
1952); Catholic World (July 1952); Christian Century
(August 13, 1952); Commonweal (June 20, 1952); Film Daily
(May 29, 1952); The Hollywood Reporter (May 27, 1952);
London Times (September 22, 1952); Motion Picture Herald
Product Digest (May 31, 1952); National Parent-Teacher
(September 1952); The New Yorker (June 7, 1952); Saturday
Review (June 21, 1952); Time (June 2, 1952).

COMMENTS: The film was a remake of ROBERTA (based on the
1933 Broadway Production) which was made by RKO in 1935 and
starred Irene Dunne, Fred Astaire, and Ginger Rogers.
Howard Keel also did ROBERTA on TV's "Bob Hope Show" (NBC,
September 19, 1958), on which he played the role of John
Kent.
        For the "I'll Be Hard to Handle" sequence, the male
chorus and dancers wore wolf masks. In the "Lovely to Look
At" number, Keel stood before four mirrors to sing with
himself in four-part harmony.
        In the fashion show sequence wire was placed through
insulated underwear, worn by the male dancers, up to gold
circlets on top of their heads. Each circlet contained
five candles that were lit electrically. (See D35, V11)

F10. DESPERATE SEARCH (MGM, 1952) B&W. 73 Minutes.

CREDITS: Producer: Matthew Rapf. Director: Joseph
Lewis. Based on the novel by Arthur Mayse. Screenplay
by Walter Doniger. Cinematographer: Harold Lipstein.
Editor: Joseph Dervin. Musical Director: Rudolph Kopp.
Art Directors: Cedric Gibbons, Eddie Imazu. Set
Designers: Edwin Willis, Ralph Hurst. Makeup Artist:
William Tuttle. Hair Stylist: Sydney Guilaroff.
Special Effects by Arnold Gillespie, Ralph Hurst.
Sound by Douglas Shearer. Recording Supervisor:

Douglas Shearer.

CAST: **Howard Keel** (Vince Heldon); Jane Greer (Julie Heldon); Patricia Medina (Nora Steed); Keenan Wynn (Brandy); Robert Burton (Wayne Langmuir); Lee Aaker (Don); Linda Lowell (Janet); Michael Dugan (Lou); Elaine Stewart (Stewardess); Jonathan Cott (Detective); Jeff Richards (Ed); Dick Simmons (Communicator); Robert Whitney, Gil Dennis.

SYNOPSIS: Learning that his children were the only survivors of a plane crash in the Canadian Wilderness, Vince Heldon (Keel) heads a search to find them. He is accompanied by his present wife, Julie (Greer), and his ex-wife, Nora Steed (Medina), who happens to be the mother of his children.
    The children spend several days and nights in the wilderness and to make matters worse, they are stalked by a cougar. Vince arrives in the nick of time to save them from the cat.

REVIEW: Variety (November 26, 1952) felt the suspense was "patly contrived" and came across "okay" but as a whole the film was a "routine offering." Previewed on November 19, 1952.

ADDITIONAL REVIEWS: B.F.I./Monthly Film Bulletin (February 1953); Film Daily (December 5, 1952); The Hollywood Reporter (November 24, 1952); Library Journal (January 1, 1953); Motion Picture Herald Product Digest (November 29, 1952).

COMMENT: The film was based on Mayse's 1952 novel.

F11. I LOVE MELVIN (MGM, March 20, 1953) Color. 76 Minutes.

The film starred Debbie Reynolds and Donald O'Connor. Keel's scenes were cut from the final print.

F12. FAST COMPANY (MGM, May 12, 1953) B&W. 67 Minutes.

CREDITS: Producer: Henry Berman. Director: John Sturges. Assistant Director: Al Jennings. Based on the story by Eustace Cockrell. Screenplay by William Roberts, Don Mark Lewicz. Cinematographer: Harold Lipstein. Editor: Joseph Dervin. Music by Alberto Colombo. Art Directors: Cedric Gibbons, Leonid Vasian. Set Designers: Edwin Willis, Ralph Hurst. Recording Supervisor: Douglas Shearer. Special Effects by Arnold Gillespie, Warren Newcombe.

CAST: **Howard Keel** (Rick Grayton); Polly Bergen (Carol Maldon); Marjorie Main (Ma Parkson); Nina Foch (Mercedes Bellway); Robert Burton (Dave Sandring); Carol Nugent (Jigger Parkson); Joaquin Garay (Manuel Monales); Horace McMahon (Two-Pair Butford); Sig Arno (Hungey); Iron Eyes Cody (Ben Iron Mountain); Perez Sheehan, Pat Golding, Jonathan Cott, Benny Burt, Jack

Ksuschen, Paul Brinegar, Jess Kirkpatrick, Lou Smith.

SYNOPSIS: Rick Grayton (Keel) has a run down horse he takes around the country to small tracks. He is also taking care of a horse Carol Malson (Bergen) has inherited. He makes sure that her horse loses so she might be willing to sell it to him cheap.
      Carol arrives on the scene and finds out about Rick's dealings and decides to take charge herself. She is inexperienced and is taken advantage of by others. Rick ends up trying to help her and the two begin to fall in love. Mercedes Bellaway (Foch) comes between them for awhile but in the end Carol and Rick end up together.

REVIEW: <u>VARIETY</u>. (April 8, 1953) felt that the film "had titter here and there" but did not "merit consideration" other than as a supporting booking. It was also felt that Keel and Bergen were "likeable." Previewed on April 2, 1953.

ADDITIONAL REVIEWS: <u>Film Daily</u> (May 4, 1953); <u>National Parent-Teacher</u> (June 1953); <u>Time</u> (May 18, 1953).

F13. RIDE VAQUERO (MGM, July 17, 1953) Color. 90 Minutes.

CREDITS: Producer: Stephen Ames. Director: John Farrow. Assistant Director: Jerry Thorpe. Based on the story by Frank Fenton. Screenplay by Frank Fenton. Cinematographer: Robert Surtees (Lansco Color). Editor: Harold Kress. Music by Bronislau Kaper. Art Directors: Cedric Gibbons, Arthur Lonergan. Set Designers: Edwin Willis, Fred MacLean. Costume Designer: Walter Plunkett. Makeup Artist: William Tuttle. Hair Stylist: Sydney Guilaroff. Recording Supervisor: Douglas Shearer. Special Effects by Arnold Gillespie.

CAST: Robert Taylor (Rio); Ava Gardner (Cordelia Cameron); **Howard Keel** (King Cameron); Anthony Quinn (Jose Esqueda); Kurt Kasznar (Father Antonio); Ted de Corsia (Sheriff Parker); Charlita (Singer); Jack Elam (Barton); Walter Baldwin (Adam Smith); Joe Dominquez (Vincente); Frank McGrath (Pete); Charles Stevens (Vaquero); Rex Lease (Deputy); Tom Greeway (Deputy); Paul Fierro (Valero); Percy Helton (Storekeeper); Norman Leavitt (Dentist); Movita Castenda (Hussy); Almira Sessions (Woman); Monte Blue (Bartender); Philip Van Zandt (Dealer); Stanley Andrews (General Sheridan); Italia DeNubila (Specialty Dancer); Kay English (Woman in Park); Joey Ray (Croupier).

SYNOPSIS: The story takes place after the Civil War and concerns Jose Esqueda (Quinn), who with the help of his right hand man Rio (Taylor), has control of a group of gangs in Brownsville, Texas. King Cameron (Keel) brings settlers with him in order to build a cattle empire. The outlaws do not want settlers around to ruin their control.
      When King arrives with his wife Cordelia (Gardner), he finds his homestead burned. King rebuilds stronger than

before but is unable to get the townspeople united. Jose
attacks King's new place. King and Cordelia fend him off
with the help of Father Antonio (Kasznar) and take Rio
captive but spare his life when Rio agrees to help King
rebuild.
     Jose attacks Brownsville wounding King who tries to
stop Jose alone. Jose and Rio kill each other in a shoot-
out.

REVIEWS: New York Times, Howard Thompson, (July 16, 1953)
felt that Anthony Quinn's performance as the head bad guy
was "vigorous, colorful" and a "pleasure to watch" as was
Keel's "spunky attempt" at playing in a western. It was
felt that at least for awhile the film "promised sensible
muscularity" but the incidents eventually become
"sputtering in a coventional, slow rut." Reviewed at the
Capitol Theatre in New York on July 15, 1953.

Variety (June 24, 1953) felt that Keel "did well" in the
"satisfactory top-of-the bill" film. Previewed, in
Hollywood, on June 10, 1953.

ADDITIONAL REVIEWS: Commonweal (August 7, 1953); Film Daily
(July 1, 1953); National Parent-Teacher (October 1953);
Newsweek (July 27, 1953); Saturday Review (July 18, 1953);
Time (July 27, 1953).

COMMENTS: This was the second time Quinn worked with
director Farrow in a western. RIDE VAQUERO was the first
wide screen production for MGM.

F14. **CALAMITY JANE** (Warner Bros., November 14, 1953) Color.
     101 Minutes.

     CREDITS: Producer: William Jacobs. Director: David
     Butler. Screenplay by James O'Hanlon. Cinematographer:
     Wilfrid Cline (Technicolor). Editor: Irene Morra.
     Original Songs by Sammy Fain, Paul Francis Webster.
     Musical Director: Ray Heindorf. Musical Numbers Staged
     & Directed by Jack Donahue. Orchestrator: Frank
     Comstock. Vocal Arranger: Norman Luboff. Art Director:
     John Beckman. Set Designer: G. W. Bertsen. Costume
     Designer: Howard Shoup. Makeup Artist: Gordon Bau.
     Sound by Stanley Jones, David Forrest. Technicolor
     Consultant: Mitchell Kovaleski.

     CAST: Doris Day (Calamity Jane); **Howard Keel** (Wild
     Bill Hickock); Allyn McLerie (Katie Brown); Philip
     Carey (Lieutenant Gilmartin); Dick Wesson (Francis
     Fryer); Paul Harvey (Henry Miller); Chubby Johnson
     (Rattle Snake); Gale Robbins (Adelaide Adams); Lee
     Shumway (Bartender); Rex Lease (Buck); Francis
     McDonald (Hank); Monte Montague (Pete); Emmett Lynn
     (Artist); Forrest Taylor (MacPherson); Lane Chandler,
     Glenn Strange, Zon Murray, Budd Buster, Terry Frost,
     Tom Landon, Billy Bletcher (Prospectors); Buddy
     Roosevelt, Reed Howes, Stanley Blystone, Lee Morgan,
     Kenne Duncan, Bill Hale, Tom Monroe (Ad Libs).

SYNOPSIS: Calamity Jane (Day) tries to help Henry Miller (Harvey), who owns a dance hall, from going under. Calamity goes to Chicago to get an important show business personality but gets the star's maid Katie Brown (McLerie) by mistake. Wild Bill Hickock (Keel) and Lieutenant Gilmartin (Carey) take a liking to Katie much to Calamity's dislike.
    Katie admits she is not who everyone thinks she is. Calamity gets the townspeople to still give Katie a chance. Katie does fine and takes up residence with Calamity.
    Calamity becomes jealous over Katie and Gilmartin and starts a feud. Wild Bill, who has not seen eye-to-eye with Calamity, stops her from making a fool of herself. Bill and Calamity fall in love, but Katie has left town because she feels responsible for the trouble between Calamity and Gilmartin. Calamity settles things with Katie and convinces her to return to town. A double wedding takes place between Katie and Gilmartin and Calamity and Wild Bill.

SONGS: "The Deadwood Stage" (Day); "Higher Than a Hawk" (Keel); "Tis Harry I'm Plannin' to Marry" (Robbins); "I Can Do Without You" (Day, Keel); "I've Got a Hive Full of Honey" (Wesson); "Keep It Under Your Hat" (McLerie); "Just Blew in From the City" (Day); "A Woman's Touch" (Day, McLerie); "Tis Harry I'm Plannin' to Marry" (McLerie); "Secret Love" (Day); Finale (Day, Keel, McLerie).

REVIEWS: New York Times, Bosley Crowther, (November 5, 1953) Crowther felt that the film resembled ANNIE GET YOUR GUN. He felt the script was "cheerful" and the story and some songs were "silly." He felt that Howard Keel "lost stature and momentum" because of Doris Day's "overpowering violence and stridence." He felt that the part of a tomboy was not Miss Day's strong point. Reviewed at the Paramount Theatre in New York on November 4, 1953.

Variety (October 21, 1953) felt that the film was "unimaginative hokum" and that the staging and music "help provide fair business." It was also felt that Keel played Bill Hickock "with listless amiability." As far as the song "Higher Than a Hawk" the critic felt Keel sang it "with full authority" and that his duet with Day "I Can Do Without You" was handled in "ingratiating fashion." Previewed in New York on October 15, 1953.

ADDITIONAL REVIEWS: America (December 12, 1953); Catholic World (December 1953); Farm Journal (January 1954); Film Daily (October 29, 1953); The Hollywood Reporter (October 28, 1953); Library Journal (December 1, 1953); National Parent-Teacher (December 1953); Newsweek (November 23, 1953); Saturday Review (November 14, 1953); Time (November 23, 1953).

COMMENTS: CALAMITY JANE won an Academy Award for best song "Secret Love" and was nominated for best scoring of a musical. "Secret Love" became a million seller for Doris Day. Jean Arthur played Calamity Jane in THE PLAINSMAN in Paramount's 1936 version co-starring Gary Cooper as Wild

Bill Hickock. In the 1966 Universal remake of THE
PLAINSMAN, Don Murray and Abby Dalton revived the roles.
(See D22, V4)

F15. KISS ME, KATE (MGM, November 26, 1953) Color. 109
Minutes.

CREDITS: Producer: Jack Cummings. Director: George
Sidney. Assistant Director: George Rhein. Based on the
story by Samuel & Bella Spewack and the play produced
on stage by Lemuel Ayers. Screenplay by Dorothy
Kingsley. Cinematographer: Charles Rosher (3-D Ansco
Color). Editor: Ralph Winters. Lyrics & Music by Cole
Porter. Musical Director: Andre Previn. Associate
Musical Director: Saul Chaplin. Choreographer: Hermes
Pan. Vocal Arranger: Robert Tucker. Conductor: Conrad
Salinger. Art Directors: Cedric Gibbons, Urie McCLeary.
Set Designers: Edwin Willis, Richard Pefferle. Costume
Designer: Walter Plunkett. Makeup Artist: William
Tuttle. Hair Stylist: Sydney Guilaroff. Recording:
Supervisor: Douglas Shearer.

CAST: Kathryn Grayson (Lilly Vanessi/Katherine);
Howard Keel (Fred Graham/Petrichio); Ann Miller (Lois
Lane/Bianca); Keenan Wynn (Lippy); Bobby Van (Gremio);
Tommy Rall (Bill Calhoun/Lacentio); James Whitmore
(Slug); Kurt Kasznar (Baptista); Bob Fosse (Hortensio);
Ron Randell (Cole Porter); Willard Parker (Tex
Callaway); Dave O'Brien (Ralph); Claud Allister (Paul);
Ann Codee (Suzanne); Specialty Dancers: Carol Haney,
Jeanne Coyne; Hermes Pan (Specialty Sailor Dance); Ted
Eckelberry (Nathaniel); Mitchell Lewis (Stage
Doorman).

SYNOPSIS: Composer Cole Porter (Randell) and actor-director
Fred Graham (Keel) want Graham's ex-wife Lill Vanessi
(Grayson) to play Katherine, the lead, in KISS ME, KATE, a
musical version of THE TAMING OF THE SHREW.
    Lilli is at Graham's apartment, in order to hear the
show's score, when Lois Lane (Miller), Graham's girlfriend,
arrives and announces that she will be playing Bianca, a
younger sister of Katherine's. Lilli decides she can not
do the show because of her pending marriage. When Lois
volunteers to play Katherine, Lilli has a change of heart.
    Things are not going well at rehearsals because Graham
and Lilli are not getting along and because Bill Calhoun
(Rall), the show's Lucentio and Lois's dancing partner,
arrives late to rehearsal because he has acquired a $2,000
gambling debt and has forged Graham's name on an I.O.U.
    Lippy (Wynn) and Slug (Whitemore) show up on opening
night to collect on the I.O.U. for their boss Mr. Hogan.
Graham says he does not know anything about the I.O.U.
    When Graham learns that his butler Paul (Allister) has
mistakenly given flowers, meant for Lois, to Lilli's maid
Suzanne (Codee) to deliver to Lilli, he tries to retrieve
the note (he had sent to Lois) from Lilli who stuffs it in
her bosom just before show time.
    In the show, a mate must be found for Katherine

before Lucentio, Gemio (Van) and Hortensio (Fosse) can ask
to marry her younger sisters. Lucentio's friend Petruchio
(Keel) comes to town and makes a deal with Katherine's
father, Baptista (Kasznar). During the show, Lilli looks
at the note and becomes furious. She begins straying from
the script and Graham places her across his knee and spanks
her as the curtain comes down on Act I.
     Lilli quits the show and calls Tex Callaway (Parker)
telling him to come get her that she will wed him right
away. Lippy and Slug will not permit her to leave because
if they do there will not be any money to pay the I.O.U.
     Lois realizes Callaway was one of her old boy friends
from Houston. When Lippy reports in to Mr. Morgan, he
discovers Morgan is being killed as they speak. Since
their boss is dead, the debt does not exist any more so the
two gangsters depart.
     As Lilli and Callaway are about to leave, Graham
confesses his love for her and tells her that her place is
with the theatre. Graham announces that Lilli's understudy
will do the finale. Lilli realizes her love for Graham and
decides to finish the show and to stay with Graham.

SONGS: "Why Can't You Behave" (Miller, Rall); "Wunderbar"
(Keel, Grayson); "So In Love" (Keel, Grayson); "We Open in
Venice" (Keel, Grayson, Miller, Rall); "Tom, Dick, or
Harry" (Miller, Rall, Van, Fosse); "I've Come to Wive It
Wealthily in Padua" (Keel); "I Hate Men" (Grayson); "Were
Thine That Special Face" (Keel); "Too Darn Hot" (Miller);
"Where is the Life That Late I Led" (Keel); "Always True to
You in My Fashion" (Miller, Rall); "Brush Up Your
Shakespeare" (Wynn, Whitemore); "From This Moment On"
(Miller, Rall, Van, Fosse, Haney); "Kiss Me, Kate" (Keel).

REVIEWS: New York Times, Bosley Crowther, (November 6,
1953) Crowther said that KISS ME, KATE was "beautifully
staged, adroitly acted and really superbly sung." He
thought that Miss Grayson's and Mr. Keel's voices and
acting were "juicy and uninhibited." The best parts of the
film according to Crowther were Grayson's and Keel's "songs
and cut ups." It was also felt that Keel's solos were done
in "top-notch style." Reviewed at Radio City Music Hall in
New York on November 5, 1953.

Variety (October 28, 1953) felt that KISS ME, KATE was
"great" and that Keel was "dynamic" as the male lead and
that he was in "complete command" while acting and handled
his songs "superbly." Previewed at Loew's State in New
York on October 22, 1953.

ADDITIONAL REVIEWS: America (November 21, 1953);
B.F.I./Monthly Film Bulletin (February 1954); Catholic
World (December 1953); Commonweal (November 20, 1953); Film
Daily (October 27, 1953); Films in Review (December 1953);
The Hollywood Reporter (October 27, 1953); Library Journal
(November 15, 1953); Life (November 30, 1953); Look
(December 1, 1953); National Parent-Teacher (December
1953); Newsweek (November 9, 1953); The New Yorker
(November 14, 1953); Saturday Review (November 14, 1953);

<u>Time</u> (November 16, 1953).

COMMENTS: The 1948 Broadway Production of KISS ME, KATE was Porter's first musical to be filmed intact. The film was the only musical to use the 3-D process. The popularity of 3-D was on its way out by the time the picture was released. Some places showed it in 3-D but it was generally shown in 2-D.
     "Bianca," "Another Opening Another Show" (except instrumentally), and "I Am Ashamed That Women Are So Simple" were deleted from the film. "From This Moment On" dropped from Porter's Broadway production of OUT OF THIS WORLD was used in the film. "Too Darn Hot" was given to Ann Miller instead of the minor male character for which it was intended. This was Grayson's last film for MGM.
     Ann Miller had been invited to the Shah of Iran's palace, for a week, to be his guest. However, Miller was in the middle of filming KISS ME, KATE and director George Sidney would not let her go because it would have cost millions to shoot around her.
     Cummings felt Keel was too heavy and not in good voice and wanted Lawrence Olivier for his lead. He was going to use another singer for Olivier's songs. Keel went on a diet, began working on his voice and proceeded to quit smoking. He eventually got the role.
     KISS ME, KATE received an Academy Award nomination for best scoring of a musical. MGM sent Ann Miller on a three-week tour to publicize KISS ME, KATE but did not allow her to dance. MGM took out a $1,000,000 insurance policy on her legs. (See S10, D33, V10)

F16. ROSE MARIE (MGM, April 1954) Color. 115 Minutes.

     CREDITS: Producer: Mervyn LeRoy. Director: Mervyn LeRoy. Screenplay by Ronald Miller. Cinematographer: Paul Vogel (CinemaScope, Eastman Color). Editor: Harold Kress. Lyrics & Book by Otto Harbach, Oscar Hammerstein II. Music by Rudolph Frimil, Herbert Stothart. Musical Director: George Stoll. Musical Numbers Staged by Bushby Berkeley. Screen Version Lyrics by Paul Francis Webster. Art Directors: Cedric Gibbons, Merrill Pye. Costume Designer: Helen Rose.

     CAST: Ann Blyth (Rose Marie LeMaitre); **Howard Keel** (Mike Malone); Fernando Lamas (James Severn Duval); Bert Lahr (Barney McCorkle); Marjorie Main (Lady Jane Dunstock); Joan Taylor (Wanda); Ray Collins (Inspector Appleby); Chief Yowlachie (Black Eagle); Paul Fierro (Valero); Percy Helton (Storekeeper); Norman Leavitt (Dentist); Movita Castenda (Hussy); Almira Sessions (Woman); Monte Blue (Bartender); Philip Van Zandt (Dealer); Stanley Andrews (General Sheridan); Italia DeNubila (Specialty Dancer); Kay English (Woman in Park); Joey Ray (Croupier); James Logan (Clerk); Thurl Ravenscroft (Indian Medicineman); Abel Fernandez (Indian Warrior); Billy Dix (Mess Waiter); Al Ferguson, Frank Ragney (Woodsmen); Marshall Reed (Mountie); Sheb Wooley (Corporal); Dabbs Greer (Committeeman); John

Pickard, John Damler (Orderlies); Sally Yarnell
(Hostess); Gordon Richards (Attorney); Lumsden Hare
(Judge); Mickey Simpson (Trapper); Pepi Lanzi (Johnny
Lang).

SYNOPSIS: Mike Malone (Keel), a Royal Canadian Mounted
Policeman, is trying to tame Rose Marie (Blyth) but falls
in love with her. She is also interested in trapper James
Duval (Lamas) thus resulting in a love triangle.
An indian girl is in love with Duval and becomes
jealous when Duval falls for Rose Marie. She is beaten by
the chief when he learns she has been with the white man.
She pulls out a knife, she had taken from Duval, and kills
the chief. Malone arrests Duval for the murder but later
learns it was the indian girl who did it and Duval is
cleared of charges.
Rose Marie must make a choice between the two men.
Mike gives her up and she rides away with Duval.

SONGS: "The Right Place For a Girl" (Keel); "Free to Be
Free" (Blyth); "Love and Kisses" (Lahr, Main); "Indian
Love Call" (Blyth); "Rose Marie" (Keel); "I'm a Mountie Who
Never Got His Man" (Lahr); "I Have the Love" (Blyth,
Lamas); "Mounties" (Keel).

REVIEWS: New York Times, Bosley Crowther, (April 2,
1954) Bosley Crowther felt that the songs and scenery were
the film's "salvation" and that the plot was an "antique."
He felt that Keel played his role "robustly." Reviewed at
Radio City Music Hall on April 1, 1954.

Variety (March 3, 1954) felt that ROSE MARIE was "slow-
moving" but that the film had "enough ingredients" to make
it do okay at the box office. Previewed in New York on
March 1, 1954.

ADDITIONAL REVIEWS: America (April 10, 1954);
B.F.I./Monthly Film Bulletin (September 1954); Commonweal
(April 16, 1954); Farm Journal (May 1954); Film Daily
(March 3, 1954); Films & Filming (October 1954); The
Hollywood Reporter (March 3, 1954); Library Journal (May
15, 1954); Life (February 22, 1954); London Times
(September 6, 1954); Motion Picture Herald Product Digest
(March 6, 1954); National Parent-Teacher (May 1954); The
New Yorker (April 17, 1954); Saturday Review (April 10,
1954); Senior Scholastic (April 21, 1954); The Tatler
(September 15, 1954); Time (March 15, 1954).

COMMENTS: ROSE MARIE (based on the 1924 Broadway play) was
filmed two other times by MGM. The first time was in 1928
(Silent) starring Joan Crawford and James Murray and again
in 1936 with Jeanette MacDonald and Nelson Eddy. Even
though it was a remake, it was different than the play or
the two preceding films.
This was the first film musical (but not first to come
out) to be made in CinemaScope. Four of the original songs
were kept and the location of the film was the Canadian
Rockies. Special material was written for Lahr's "The

Mountie Who Never Got His Man" by George Stoll and Herbert Baker.

Keel never complained about his parts, but balked at this film because he did not like the script. He was put on suspension by the studio until the script was rewritten.

One day while Jack Benny was visiting the set, Keel got him to put on a mountie uniform, climb up onto the back of one of the more gentler horses and ride in front of the camera. Director Mervyn LeRoy laughed at the joke and cut the footage. (See D40, V14)

F17. SEVEN BRIDES FOR SEVEN BROTHERS (MGM, August 1954)
Color. 103 Minutes.

CREDITS: Producer: Jack Cummings. Director: Stanley Donen. Assistant Director: Ridgeway Callow. Based on Stephen Vincent Benet's Sobbin' Women. Screenplay by Albert Hackett, Francis Goodrich, Dorothy Kingsley. Cinematographer: George Folsey (CinemaScope, Ansco Color). Editor: Ralph Winters. Songs by Johnny Mercer, Gene DePaul. Musical Director: Adolph Deutsch, Saul Chaplin. Choreographer: Michael Kidd. Art Directors: Cedric Gibbons, Urie McCleary. Set Designer: Edwin Willis, Hugh Hunt. Costume Designer: Walter Plunkett. Sound by Douglas Shearer.

CAST: Jane Powell (Milly); **Howard Keel** (Adam Pontabee); Jeff Richards (Benjamin Pontabee); Russ Tamblyn (Gideon Pontabee); Tommy Rall (Frank Pontabee); Howard Petrie (Pete Perkins); Virginia Gibson (Lisa); Ian Wolfe (Reverend Elcott); Marc Platt (Daniel Pontabee); Matt Mattox (Caleb Pontabee); Jacques d' Amboise (Ephraim Pontabee); Julie Newmeyer (Dorcas); Nancy Kilgas (Alice); Betty Carr (Sarah); Ruth Kilmonis (Ruth); Norma Doggett (Martha); Earl Barton (Harry); Dante Di Paolo (Matt); Kelly Brown (Carl); Matt Moore (Ruth's Uncle); Russell Simpson (Mr. Bixby); Marjorie Wood (Mrs. Bixby); Dick Rich (Dorcas' Father); Anna Nilsson (Mrs. Elcott); Larry Blake (Drunk); Lois Hall (Girl); Jarma Lewis (Lem's Girlfriend); Walter Beaver (Lem); Sheila James (Dorcas' Sister); Phil Rich (Prospector); Russ Saunders, Terry Wilson, George Robotham (Swains); Stan Jolley, Tim Graham (Fathers).

SYNOPSIS: The action takes place in the 1800s at an Oregon farm. Adam Pontabee (Keel) goes to town in order to find a bride. He takes a liking to Milly (Powell), a cafe waitress, and awkwardly proposes. She accepts but does not know the deal includes his six brothers until she arrives at Adam's farm. Milly is mad at first, but decides to teach them some manners and cleanliness.

The brothers are at a barn-raising with the townspeople and take an interest in the girls there but get into a fight with some boys from town who tried to embarrass them.

When the brothers return home, they are still thinking about the girls. Adam convinces them to go to town and kidnap the girls of their choice. They do this and are protected from pursuing townspeople by an avalanche.

Milly is upset by the brothers actions. Adam takes offense
and goes to his hunting cabin where he remains until the
spring thaw. Meanwhile, Milly has a baby.
     With the spring thaw, the boys and girls begin court-
ing. The snow melts and the townspeople come after their
girls. Reverend Elcott (Wolfe) wants to know whom the baby
belongs to. All the girls claim it and at gun point, the
boys marry the girls.

SONGS: "Wonderful, Wonderful Day" (Powell); "Bless Your
Beautiful Hide" (Keel); "When You're in Love" (Keel,
Powell); "Goin' Co'tin'" (Powell, Brothers); "June Bride"
(Platt, Girls); "Barn Raising Ballet" (Boys & Girls);
"Spring, Spring, Spring" (Brothers & Girls); "Lonesome
Polecat" (Mattox, dubbed by Bill Lee).

REVIEWS: New York Times (July 23, 1954) felt that the film
was "engaging, bouncy, tuneful and panchromatic." It was
felt that Keel's baritone was as "big and impressive as his
frame." Reviewed at Radio City Music Hall in New York on
July 22, 1954.

Variety (June 2, 1954) felt that the film was "slick and
entertaining" and that the songs and cast were "good."
Keel's "robust baritone" and Powell's "lilting soprano" make
their songs "extremely listenable" and that the teaming of
Keel and Powell "comes across very satisfactorily" when they
sing and act. Previewed in Hollywood on May 26, 1954.

ADDITIONAL REVIEWS: America (July 31, 1954); B.F.I./Monthly
Film Bulletin (December 1954); Catholic World (August
1954); Commomweal (August 13, 1954); Cue (July 17, 1954);
Dance Magazine (August 1954); Farm Journal (August 1954);
Film Daily (June 1, 1954); Films and Filming (October
1954); Films and Filming (January 1955); Films in Review
(August 9, 1954); The Hollywood Reporter (June 1, 1954);
Library Journal (August 1954); Life (July 26, 1954); Motion
Picture Herald Product Digest (June 5, 1954); National
Parent-Teacher (September 1954); The New Yorker (July 31,
1954); Newsweek (September 20, 1954); New York Times
Magazine (July 4, 1954); Saturday Review (August 7, 1954);
Saturday Review (January 1, 1955); Senior Scholastic
(September 15, 1954); Sight and Sound (January-March 1955);
The Spectator (December 31, 1954); The Tatler (December 22,
1954); Time (July 12, 1954).

COMMENTS: SEVEN BRIDES FOR SEVEN BROTHERS (based on Benet's
mid-1920s The Sobbin' Women) was a trend setter because it
was an original piece during a time when they were filming
Broadway hits. The studio put its money in BRIGADOON and
almost did not make SEVEN BRIDES FOR SEVEN BROTHERS. It was
producer Jack Cummings who persuaded MGM to take on the
project even if it meant a cut in the budget. Joshua Logan
held up the film for five years because he held the rights
and wanted to turn the property into a Broadway show.
Designer Walter Plunkett went to the Salvation Army where he
picked up some old quilts and designed authentic dresses for
the girls. The movie was on the New York Times list of 10

best films of 1954. Ironically, in 1978-1979, Powell and
Keel toured in a stage production which would later star
Debbie Boone in a short-lived Broadway version in 1982.
Even though Jane Powell and Howard Keel were husband and
wife in the picture, they were not in many scenes together.
Their friendship really grew when they co-starred in such
stage shows as SEVEN BRIDES FOR SEVEN BROTHERS, SOUTH
PACIFIC, and I DO! I DO!.
    The film took 34 days to shoot and grossed $6,298,000.
Keel earned $10,000 for his role and the film helped him
get $3,000 a week when he renegotiated his MGM contract.
    SEVEN BRIDES FOR SEVEN BROTHERS received an Academy
Award for best scoring of a musical and received nominations for best picture, screenplay, cinematography, and
film editing. It was also a top moneymaker and inspired
the TV show "Here Come the Brides" which was broadcast by
ABC between 1968-1970. (See S36, D42, V15)

F18. DEEP IN MY HEART (MGM, December 24, 1954) Color. 132
Minutes.

    CREDITS: Producer: Roger Eden. Director: Stanley
    Donen. Assistant Director: Robert Vreeland. Based on
    the book by Elliott Arnold. Screenplay by Leonard
    Spigelgass. Cinematographer: George Folsey (Eastman
    Color). Editor: Adrienne Fazan. Musical Director:
    Adolph Deutsch. Choreographer: Eugene Loring. Vocal
    Arranger: Robert Tucker. Conductors: Hugh Friedhofer,
    Alexander Courage. Art Directors: George Gibbons,
    Edward Cargango. Set Designers: Edwin Willis, Arthur
    Krams. Women's Costume Designer: Helen Rose. Men's
    Costume Designer: Walter Plunkett. Makeup Artist:
    William Tuttle. Hair Stylist: Sydney Guilaroff.
    Recording Supervisor: Wesley Miller. Special Effects
    by Warren Newcombe. Color Consultant: Alvord Eiseman.

    CAST: Jose Ferrer (Sigmund Romberg); Merle Oberson
    (Dorothy Donnelly); Helen Traubel (Anne Mueller); Doe
    Avedon (Lillian Romberg); Walter Pigeon (J. S.
    Shubert); Paul Henreid (Florenz Ziegfeld); Tamara
    Toumanova (Gaby Deslys); Paul Stewart (Bert Townsend);
    Isobel Elsom (Mrs. Harris); Jim Backus (Ben Judson);
    Douglas Fowley (Harold Butterfield); Russ Tamblyn
    (Berrison, Jr.); David Burns (Lazar Berrison, Sr.);
    Also: Rosemary Clooney, Gene & Fred Kelly, Jane
    Powell, Vic Damone, Ann Miller, William Olvis, Cyd
    Charisse, James Mitchell, **Howard Keel**, Tony Martin,
    Joan Weldon.

SYNOPSIS: Sigmund Romberg (Ferrer) and his small band are
playing at New York's Cafe Vienna owned by Anna Mueller
(Traubel), a friend of Romberg's from Vienna. Romberg longs
to write music but it is felt his waltzes are not in
fashion.
    When he writes "Leg of Mutton," Broadway star Gaby
Deslys (Toumanova) wants Romberg to write a song for her
new show and gets J. J. Shubert (Pidgeon) to approach
Romberg. Romberg is paid $200 by Shubert's business

manager, Bert Townsend (Stewart) to compose "Softly, As in a Morning Sunrise" which Gaby delivers as a girly number at the close of Act I.

At the cafe, Anna sings the song properly. Dorothy Donnelly (Oberson) gets Romberg to compose songs for WHIRL OF THE WORLD. When the show is a hit, he does the show MIDNIGHT GIRL and ends up singing "Mr. and Mrs." with the show's star Rosemary Clooney after her leading man cannot do the show. Romberg is becoming famous and in his next show DANCING AROUND, the O'Brien brothers (Gene & Fred Kelly) perform "I Love to Go Swimmin' with Women."

Shubert does not like the MAYTIME songs but the show is a big success with such songs as "Road to Paradise" sung by Vic Damone and the duet "Will You Remember" performed by Jane Powell and Damone.

When MAGIC MELODY is not a success, Romberg decides to stick with composing. He works with Townsend and Ben Judson (Backus) on the show JAZZ-A-DOO. While working on the show at a resort, Lillian Harris (Avedon) tries out for the show much to her mother's (Elsom) surprise.

In the show ARTISTS AND MODELS, Ann Miller sings and dances to the song "It." Dorothy and Romberg work together on THE STUDENT PRINCE in which William Olvis sings "Serenade."

Romberg and Lillian are married and she becomes caught up in the thrill of the theatre and cannot wait for the next two shows to open. The first is THE DESERT SONG in which Cyd Charisse and James Mitchell not only perform "One Alone" but dance to it. The second is MY MARYLAND in which Howard Keel performs "Your Land and My Land."

Dorothy's illness and subsequent death hit Romberg hard but Lillian persuades him to return to work. His new collaborator is Oscar Hammerstein II and together they work on THE NEW MOON in which Tony Martin and Joan Weldon sing "Lover Come Back to Me."

After the passage of time during a symphony concert, Romberg honors Lillian by dedicating the song "When I Grow Too Old to Dream" to her.

SONGS: "Leg of Mutton" (Ferrer, Traubel); "Your Land and My Land" (Keel); "You Will Remember Vienna" (Traubel); "It" (Miller); "Auf Wiedersehn" (Traubel); "I love to Go Swimmin' with Women" (Gene & Fred Kelly); "Softly As in a Morning Sunrise" (Traubel); "The Road to Paradise" (Damone); "When I Grow Too Old to Dream" (Ferrer); "Lover Come Back to Me" (Martin, Weldon); "Serenade" (Olvis); "Mr. & Mrs." (Ferrer, Clooney); "Stouthearted Men" (Traubel); "Will You Remember" (Damone, Powell); "One Alone" (Carol Richards for Charisse, Mitchell).

REVIEWS: New York Times, Bosley Crowther, (December 10, 1954) Bosley Crowther felt that the film was more of a showcase for the better known Romberg tunes than the story of his life and career. The music is considered the high point of the film. The film is "disconnected vaudeville." Mr. Ferrer can make Sigmund Romberg no more than a "mawkish platitude" and the screenplay does not help." Reviewed at Radio City Music Hall in New York on December 9, 1954.

Variety (December 1, 1954) felt that the all-star cast and
the music of Sigmund Romberg are the major assets of the
film that has "generally okay box office prospects."
Previewed in Hollywood on November 24, 1954.

ADDITIONAL REVIEWS: America (December 18, 1954);
B.F.I./Monthly Film Bulletin (April 1955); Catholic World
(January 1955); Collier's (January 7, 1955); Commonweal
(December 24, 1954); Dance Magazine (January 1955); Farm
Journal (January 1955); Film Daily (December 1, 1954);
Films in Review (January 1955); The Hollywood Reporter
(December 1, 1954); Library Journal (January 15, 1955);
Motion Picture Herald Product Digest (December 4, 1954);
National Parent-Teacher (February 1955); Newsweek
(December 20, 1954); The New Yorker (December 18, 1954);
Saturday Review (January 8, 1955); Time (January 17, 1955).

COMMENTS: In 1950, Arthur Freed had planned to film THE
ROMBERG STORY with stars Kurt Kasznar and Lana Turner with
a special appearance by Romberg. By the time the project
was made, in 1954, Romberg had died and Roger Edens became
a first-time producer. Numbers cut from the final print
included "Dance My Darling" sung by Traubel and Powell's
song "One Kiss." Carol Richards dubbed for Cyd Charisse
and Betty Wand for Tamara Toumanova. Esther Williams was to
have appeared in an acqua pageant as an American Beauty Rose
and George Murphy was to have served as a master of ceremony
but the scene was dropped.
     DEEP IN MY HEART started production on May 3, 1954,
and finished on August 3, 1954, at a cost of $2,104,025.23
and grossed $4,075,000. After her appearance in her first
film, Roger Edens launched the night club career of Helen
Traubel.
     Gene Kelly and brother Fred, who was also a dancer,
teamed only this once in the number "I Love to Go Swimmin'
with Women" which had originally been written for LOVE
BIRDS, in 1921, but was cut from the show.
     Romberg was an important writer for four decades and
wrote more than 2,000 songs and 80 plays, revues, and
operettas. Poetic license was taken with history and the
placement of songs with the wrong show. (See D23, V6)

F19. JUPITER'S DARLING (MGM, February 18, 1955) Color. 96
Minutes.

     CREDITS: Producer: George Wells. Director: George
     Sidney. Assistant Director: George Rhein. Based on
     Robert Sherwood's The Road to Rome. Screenplay by
     Dorothy Kingsley. Cinematographers: Paul Vogel, Charles
     Rosher (CinemaScope and Eastman Color); Editor: Ralph
     Winters. Songs by Burton Lane, Harold Adamson. Musical
     Supervisor: Saul Chaplin. Musical Director: David Rose.
     Choreographer: Hermes Pan. Vocal Director: Jeff
     Alexander. Art Directors: Cedric Gibbons, Urie
     McCleary. Set Designers: Edwin Willis, Hugh Hunt.
     Recording Supervisor: Wesley Miller. Special Effects by
     Arnold Gillespie, Warren Newcombe.

CAST: Esther Williams (Amytis); **Howard Keel** (Hannibal);
Marge Champion (Meta); Gower Champion (Varius); George
Sanders (Fabius Maximus); Richard Haydn (Horatio);
William Demarest (Mago); Norma Varden (Fabia); Douglas
Dumbrille (Scripio); Henry Corden (Carthalo); Michael
Ansara (Maharbal); Martha Wentworth (Widow Titus); John
Olszewski (Principal Swimming Statue); Cris Alcaide
(Ballo); Tom Monroe (Outrider); Bruno VeSota
(Bystander); Paul Maxey (Lucullus); William Tanner
(Roman Courier); Albert Morin (Arrow Maker); Richard
Hale (Auctioneer); Frank Jacquet (Senator); Paul Newlan
(Roman Captain); Jack Shea (Drunken Guard); Mitchell
Lowal (Sentry); Frank Radcliffe (Specialty); Mort
Mills, Gene Roth, Michael Dugan (Guards); The
Swimming Cherubs.

SYNOPSIS: JUPITER'S DARLING is a fictional account of
Hannibal's (Keel) crossing the Alps, in 216 B.C., with his
army to take over Rome. Fabius Maximus (Sanders), Rome's
dictator, does not know how to stop Hannibal. His fiancée,
Amytis (Williams), goes to see Hannibal and uses seduction
to try and get his mind off of his goal but is taken
prisoner and is branded a spy. Hannibal sentences her to
be executed. Amytis makes another try to get Hannibal to
forget his conquest. He falls in love with Amytis and Rome
is saved.

SONGS: "I Have a Dream" (Williams); "If This Be Slav'ry"
(Marge & Gower Champion); "The Life of an Elephant" (Marge
& Gower Champion); "I Never Trust a Woman" (Keel); "Don't
Let This Night Get Away" (Keel); "Horatio's Narration"
(Haydn); "Hannibal's Victory March."

REVIEWS: New York Times, Bosley Crowther, (February 18,
1955) Bosley Crowther felt that the film had an "elephantine
style and mood" and that jest was indicated but "barely
perceptible." Reviewed at Radio City Music Hall in New
York on February 17, 1955.

Variety (January 26, 1955) felt the film was satirical and
"fairly entertaining" but would have a "mixed reaction" at
the theatres because the general filmgoer would not react
"favorably" to the satire or understand what was the meaning
behind the satire. Previewed in Hollywood on January 7,
1955.

ADDITIONAL REVIEWS: Film Daily (January 25, 1955); Look
(February 22, 1955); Newsweek (February 21, 1955); Radio
City Music Hall Program (February 17, 1955); Saturday
Review (March 5, 1955); Time (March 7, 1955).

COMMENTS: The film was based on The Road to Rome which was
written in 1926 by Robert Sherwood. The swaying and rocking
motion of the elephant Keel was riding on a hot day while
singing "Hannibal's Victory March" caused him to become
violently sick.
    It took just about 30 years for the play to reach the
screen. Elephants were painted. The film was bad and

resulted in the release of Esther Williams, George Sidney, and the Champions from their MGM contracts.   (See V8)

F20. KISMET (MGM, December 23, 1955) Color. 113 Minutes.

CREDITS: Producer: Arthur Freed. Director: Vincent Minnelli. Assistant Director: William Shanks. Based on the story by Charles Lederer, Luther Davis, Edward Knoblock. Screenplay by Charles Lederer, Luther Davis. Cinematographer: Joseph Ruttenberg (CinemaScope and Eastman Color). Editor: Adrienne Fazan. Lyrics & Music by Robert Wright, George Forrest. Adapted from themes by Alexander Borodin. Musical Director: Andre Previn. Conductor: Jeff Alexander. Musical Numbers & Dances Staged by Jack Cole. Vocal Arranger: Robert Tucker. Orchestrators: Conrad Salinger, Alexander Courage, Arthur Morton. Art Directors: Cedric Gibbons, Preston Ames. Set Designers: Edwin Willis, Keogh Gleason. Costume Designer: Tony Duquette. Makeup Artist: William Tuttle. Hair Stylist: Sidney Guilaroff. Recording Supervisor: Wesley Miller. Special Effects by Warren Newcombe. Color Consultant: Charles Hagedon.

CAST: **Howard Keel** (Haji, a Poet); Ann Blyth (Marsinah); Dolores Gray (LaLume); Vic Damone (Caliph); Monty Woolley (Omar); Sabastian Cabot (Wazir); Jay C. Flippen (Jawan); Mike Mazurki (Chief Policeman); Jack Elam (Hassan-Ben); Ted de Corsia (Police Subaltern); Reiko Sato, Patricia Dunn, Wonci Lui (Princesses of Ababu); Ross Bagdasarian (Fevvol).

SYNOPSIS: The action takes place in old Persia where a beggar, magician and poet by the name of Haji (Keel) out- smarts Jawan (Flippen) out of some gold pieces. The Wazir (Cabot), knowing of Haji's shady dealings, arrests him and threatens to cut off his hands.
Haji tells the Wazir about his magical powers and he is persuaded to use those powers to help the Wazir gain more power. The Wazir brings the princesses (Sabo, Dunn, Lui) as potential wives for Caliph (Damone). He wants Haji's help to keep Caliph from marrying another. For his help, the poet is given free run of the Wazir's harem which includes LaLume (Gray) his first wife.
Haji learns that his daughter, Marsinah (Blyth) loves Caliph. The poet tries to arrange things so his daughter can wed Caliph and ends up killing the Wazir. He is arrested by Caliph who sets him free as long as he leaves Bagdad. He does and takes LaLume with him.

SONGS: "Fate" (Keel); "Not Since Nineveh" (Gray); "Baubles, Bangles, and Beads" (Blyth); "Stranger in Paradise" (Blyth, Damone); "Gesticulate" (Keel); "Night of My Nights" (Damone); "Bored" (Gray); "The Olive Tree" (Keel); "And This is My Beloved" (Keel, Blyth, Damone); "Sands of Time" (Keel); "Rhymes Have I" (Keel); "Bazaar of the Caravans"; "Rahadlakum."

REVIEWS: New York Times, Bosley Crowther, (December 9,

1955) Mr. Crowther felt that the film was "handsome" and the music was "lovely" but that the drama, tension, and spiraling romance that were in the stage production were missing in the film. Reviewed at Radio City Music Hall in New York on December 8, 1955.

Variety (December 7, 1955) felt that KISMET was "fair entertainment." It was felt that Keel was the "big entertainment" and without him and Dolores Gray there would be little to the film. Keel was "robust" both vocally and in appearance and that he played the role with "just the right amount of tongue-in-cheek." Previewed in Hollywood on December 12, 1955.

ADDITIONAL REVIEWS: Film Daily (December 6, 1955); Newsweek (December 19, 1955); The New Yorker (December 17, 1955).

COMMENTS: Freed saw a stage production of KISMET in Los Angeles on August 17, 1953, and liked it so he acquired the rights for $125,000 and paid $16,000 for copyright from Boosey and Hawkes and gave $75,000 to Chappell who had published the music.
    Charles Lederer and Luther Davis, who had written the show's book, were hired to do the screenplay. Despite Vincent Minnell's flat refusal to direct, he was assigned the project by Dore Schary.
    Otis Skinner had filmed the 1920 and 1930 versions. KISMET had been done, in 1944, as a drama starring Marlene Dietrich. Composers Wright and Forrest were MGM alumni who adapted operettas for Jeanette MacDonald and Nelson Eddy. "Was I Wazir" and "He's in Love" were dropped from the film and replaced with "Bored."
    KISMET started production (No. 1676) on May 23, 1955. Minnelli lost his enthusiasm for KISMET and concentrated more on LUST FOR LIFE starring Kirk Douglas and Anthony Quinn. Stanley Donen had to take over the completion of KISMET ten days before its completion as Minnelli went to France to work on LUST FOR LIFE. KISMET finished shooting on July 22, 1955, and cost $2,292,960. It grossed $2,920,000.
    To enhance his dances, Keel worked out in a gym and rehearsed four hours a day with choreographer Jack Cole.
    Andre Previn relates the story of the scene when Vic Damone comes through the garden and a peacock is to spread its feathers. It needed prodding to shake it up enough to spread its feathers. After several takes, the peacock got wise and would move out of camera range. In order to keep it from moving, its legs had to be placed in a harness. (See D31, V9)

F21. FLOODS OF FEAR (Universal, April 1959) B&W. 82 Minutes.

    CREDITS: Executive Producer: Earl St. John. Producer: Sydney Box. Associate Producer: David Deutsch. Production Supervisor: Jack Swinburne. Director: Charles Crichton. Assistant Director: Robert Asher. Based on the story by John & Ward Hawkins. Screenplay by

Charles Crichton. Additional Dialogue by Vivienne
Knight. Cinematographer: Christopher Challis.
Cameraman: Dudley Lovell. Editor: Peter Bezencenet.
Music by Alan Rawathorne. Music Conductor: Muir
Mathieson. Art Director: Cedric Dawe. Set Designer:
Arthur Taksen. Costume Designer: Joan Ellacott. Makeup
Artist: W. T. Partleton. Sound by Donald Sharpe,
Desmond Saunders. Technical Adviser: David Kanter.

CAST: **Howard Keel** (Donavan); Anne Heywood (Elizabeth);
Cyril Cusack (Peebles); Harry Corbett (Sharkey); John
Crawford (Murphy); Eddie Byrne (Sheriff); John
Phillips (Dr. Matthews); Mark Baker (Fatchman); James
Dyrenforth (Major); Jack Lester (Businessman); Peter
Madden (Banker); Guy Kingsley Poynter (Deputy); Gordon
Tanner (Lt. Colonel); Robert MacKenzie (Police
Captain); Vivian Matalon, Gordon Sterne, Bill Edwards,
Graydon Gould, Kevin Scott, Ed Devereaux.

SYNOPSIS: Donavan (Keel) is in prison for murdering the
wife of his ex-business partner Murphy (Crawford). When
storms cause the American river to flood the town of
Humboldt, Donavan escapes in order to prove his innocence.
Along the way, he rescues a girl named Elizabeth (Heywood),
Pebbles (Cusack), one of his fellow convicts, and Sharkey
(Corbett) an injured guard. They take refuge from the
flood in a house half submerged by water. There is where
Elizabeth learns who Donavan is.
    Sharkey runs off to get help and Pebbles escapes when
the remaining three are carried down the swollen river.
Donavan and Elizabeth hide on an island and Elizabeth
learns of Donavan's innocence.
    Donavan wants revenge on Murphy and after making sure
Elizabeth is safe, he rows off in search of his enemy in
order to kill him. Elizabeth follows him in an attempt to
keep him from killing Murphy but is unable to stop the man
she has fallen in love with.
    Donavan finds his enemy and beats him senseless but
the desire to kill Murphy is no longer there. Donavan is
no longer wanted for murder and is free to be with
Elizabeth.

REVIEWS: <u>New York Mirror</u>, Justin Gilbert, (June 4, 1959)
Mr. Gilbert felt that the plot was "weak" and that the film
"loses its dramatic grip" because the characters "seem cut
from cardboard." He thought the acting was "fair-to-mid-
dling because of the melodramatic nature of the story."

<u>New York Post</u>, Archer Winsten, (June 4, 1959) Mr. Winsten
thought the picture was "soggy around the edges and pretty
soggy in the middle" and the result of the picture was a
"total lacking in credibility." He felt that the
"performers can be considered adequate in their roles."

<u>Variety</u>, (November 26, 1958) felt that there was "some
sound acting" and the production quality was "tops." It is
"reasonable entertainment" that was not as good as it
could have been. Keel gave a "robust display combining

virility with a surprising gentleness." Reviewed at
Gaumont Haymarket in London on November 18, 1958.

ADDITIONAL REVIEWS: Commonweal (May 22, 1959); Film Daily
(April 23, 1959); Library Journal (May 15, 1959).

COMMENTS: David Kanter was the technical adviser who drew
on his real life experiences as a medical aide in the 1952
flood at Council Bluffs, Iowa to ensure accuracy.
    Anne Heywood had a fear of water because at the age of
16 she nearly drowned. To help conquer her fear, she took
swimming lessons.
    FLOODS OF FEAR was probably the most powerful of Keel's
performances although not one of his most rewarding.

F22. **THE BIG FISHERMAN** (Buena Vista, 1959) Color. 180
      Minutes.

      CREDITS: Producer: Rowland Lee. Associate Producer:
      Eric Stacey. Director: Frank Borzage. Based on the
      story by Lloyd Douglas. Screenplay by Howard
      Estabrook, Rowland Lee. Cinematographer: Lee Garmes
      (Technicolor). Editor: Paul Weatherway. Music by
      Albert Hay Malotte. Musical Director: Joseph
      Gershenson. Conductor: David Tamkin. Art Director:
      John DeCuir. Technical Adviser: Dr. Lamsa.

      CAST: **Howard Keel** (Simon Peter); Susan Kohner
      (Princess Fara); John Saxon (Prince Voldi); Martha
      Hyer (Herodias); Herbert Lom (Herod Antipas); Ray
      Stricklyn (Prince Deran); Marian Seldes (Princess
      Aron); Alexander Scourby (David Den-Zadok); Beulah
      Bondi (Hannah); Jay Barney (John the Baptist);
      Charlotte Fletcher (Queen Rennah); Mark Dana (King
      Zendi); Rhodes Reason (Andrew); Henry Brandon
      (Menicus); Brian Hutton (John); Thomas Troupe (James);
      Marianne Stewart (Ione); Leonard Mudie (Ilderan);
      James Griffith (Beggar); Peter Adams (Herod Philip);
      Joe Di Reda (Arab Assassin); Stuart Randall (King
      Aretas); Herbert Rudley (Emperor Tiberius); Francis
      McDonald (Scribe Spokesman); Perry Ivins (Pharisee
      Spokesman); Tony Jochim (Aged Spokesman); Don Turner
      (Roman Captain); Jo Gilbert (Deborah); Michael Mark
      (Innkeeper); Ralph Moody.

SYNOPSIS: THE BIG FISHERMAN not only tells the story of
Simon Peter (Keel) but of the love story between Prince
Voldi (Saxon) and Princess Fara (Kohner).
    The princess would like to see the evil Herod Antipas
(Lom) killed because he left her mother for Herodias
(Hyer).
    The prince has his eye on the throne and plans to
marry the princess. This does not happen after they meet
up with Simon Peter.

REVIEWS: New York Times (August 6, 1959) felt that the film
was "honestly reverentian but rarely moving." Keel
manages to "tower above" the limitations of the script.

Reviewed at the Rivoli Theatre in New York on August 5, 1959.

Variety (July 1, 1959) said that THE BIG FISHERMAN was "overlong" but "handsomely done." It was felt that it would fare better in general areas more so than the big cities. Howard Keel was "handsomely pictured" and as an actor "held his own." Previewed at the Fox Wilshire Theatre on June 23, 1959.

ADDITIONAL REVIEWS: Christian Herald (September 1959); Film Daily (June 29, 1959); Good Housekeeping (September 1959); Newsweek (August 10, 1959); Time (August 17, 1959).

COMMENTS: The film was based on Douglas's 1948 story. Some of the technical errors in the film included the microphone boom shadows, Kleig lights, and Martha Hyer's vaccination. Some liberties were taken with the facts.
      Producer Rowland Lee almost did not cast Keel because he felt he was too sophistcated. Lee's family had seen Keel in SEVEN BRIDES FOR SEVEN BROTHERS and persuaded Lee to test Keel.
      Seventy-five sets needed to be built including that of the city of Tiberius which took nearly 200 acres. It cost $400,000 to build the city on a hill in the San Fernando valley. The reservoir there served as the Sea of Galilee. The set included Tetrarch's palace, mansions for the nobles, an amphitheater, temples, and Simon Peter's home.
      The shooting schedule was set for 5 months. The film used more than 6,000 props. Producer Rowland was a personal friend of author Lloyd Douglas. The cast included 23 principals, 86 bit-players, and 500 extras. Lee tested 12 stars before choosing Keel for the role of Simon Peter.
      Other sets included Roman streets, the place of Emperor Tiberius, palaces for the Roman nobles, Jerusalem, Herod's palace, Judean temples, farm houses, markets, and hovels. An Arabian tent city was built in the desert near Palm Springs. Three weeks of filming were done there. Rare silks and brocades came from Damascus. Furniture had to be built or found overseas to represent as close as possible the true items.
      Goats came from Navajo reservations in New Mexico because they came closest to those from the Holy Land. Broad-tail sheep came from a New Mexico ranch as it was the only place in the country where they could be found. Twelve camels and 200 Arabian horses (worth $25,000 each) were used.
      It took seven wig makers 5 weeks to make 500 beards and 750 wigs. An assembly line was used to handle the extras for costumes, makeup, and hairdressing.
      The film was shot in 70mm Panovision and received Academy Award nominations for color, cinematography, art direction/set direction, and costume design for a color film. It also won the Motion Picture Award of the California Federation of Woman's Clubs for 1959. The organization had 90,000 members.

F23. ARMORED COMMAND (Allied Artists, July 1961) B&W. 99
Minutes.

CREDITS: Producer: Ron Alcorn. Director: Byron Haskin.
Assistant Director: Frank Guthke. Screenplay by Ron
Alcorn. Cinematographer: Ernest Haller. Editor: Walter
Hanneman. Assistant Editor: Hanni Ruda. Music by Bert
Grund. Art Director: Hans Berthel. Set Designer: Pia
Arnold. Sound by F. W. Dustmann, J. Rapp. Production
Manager: Lonnie D'Orsa. Special Effects by Augie
Lohman. Technical Adviser: Thomas Ryan in cooperation
with the U.S. Army and Defense Department.

CAST: **Howard Keel** (Col. Mark Devlin); Tina Louise
(Alexandra Bastegar); Earl Holliman (Sergeant Mike);
Burt Reynolds (Skee); Carleton Young (Captain
Macklin); Warner Anderson (Lt. Colonel Wilson); James
Dobson (Arab); Marty Ingels (Pinhead); Clem Harvey
(Tex); Charles Nolte (Captain Swain); Maurice Marsac
(Jean Robert); Thomas Ryan (Major); Peter Capell
(Little General); Brandon Maggart.

SYNOPSIS: The Nazis plan to attack the Vosges Mountains on
New Year's Eve. In order to help their plan, they hand out
cognac in the morning to any G. I. they see. Col. Mark
Devlin (Keel) has the cognac taken away making him
unpopular with the men.
    The Nazis shoot Alexandra Bastegar in the shoulder and
leave her in the snow where she will be found by the
G.I.'s.
    She manages to slip out from under the bed covers once
in awhile so she can report the troop's plans to the Nazis.
However, the colonel manages to outwit the enemy.

REVIEWS: New York Times (October 7, 1961) felt that ARMORED
COMMAND was an "improbable little melodrama." Reviewed
October 6, 1961.

Variety (August 2, 1961) felt that ARMORED COMMAND was a
"bit shopworn, sluggish, and disappointing" but that Howard
Keel was "competent" as the colonel. Previewed at Allied
Artists in Hollywood on July 24, 1961.

ADDITIONAL REVIEW: New York Daily News (September 21,
1961).

COMMENTS: The film opened in Omaha, Nebraska. (See V3)

F24. DAY OF THE TRIFFIDS (Allied Artists, 1963) Color. 93
Minutes.

CREDITS: Producer: George Pitcher. Director: Steve
Sekely, Freddy Francis (uncredited). Assistant
Director: Douglas Hermes. Based on the novel by John
Wyndham. Screenplay by Philip Yordan. Cinematographer:
Ted Moore (CinemaScope). Editor: Spencer Reeve. Music
by Ron Goodwin. Art Director: Cedric Dawe. Special
Effects by Wally Veevers.

CAST: **Howard Keel** (Bill Masen); Nicole Maurey
(Christine Durrant); Janette Scott (Karen Goodwin);
Kieron Moore (Tom Goodwin); Mervyn Johns (Professor
Coker); Janina Faye (Susan); Alison Leggatt (Miss
Coker); Ewan Roberts (Doctor Soames); Colette Wilde
(Nurse Jamieson); Carole Ann Ford (Bettina); Geoffrey
Mathews (Luis); Gilgi Hauser (Teresa); Katya Douglas
(Mary); Victor Brooks (Poiret); Thomas Gallagher
(Burly Man); Sidney Vivian (Ticket Agent); Gary Hope
(Pilot); John Simpson (Blind Man).

SYNOPSIS: After watching meteorites fall to earth, people
end up being blinded by the time they awaken the next
morning. Only a few people have escaped the blindness. The
survivors include a patient under sedation, a seaman (Keel)
recovering from an eye operation, and two married patients
who are found quarreling in a secluded lighthouse.
      The blind are walking about the fires in the streets.
Disease and starvation seem inevitable. To add to the
problems, the meteorites have caused flesh-eating plants
(Triffids) to spring up rapidly. All of this brings out
beast-like characteristics in man. A Marine biologist
(Moore), who is stranded in a lighthouse with his wife
(Scott), comes up with the solution to get rid of the
Triffids with simple sea water. Lab technicians arrive and
take charge of the plants. However, there are still many
who are blind at the pictures end.

REVIEWS: <u>New York Times</u> (May 11, 1963) felt that the film
had an "old-fashioned plot" and was "above par" for this
type of movie. Reviewed May 10, 1963.

<u>Variety</u> (May 1, 1963) thought that despite "script incon-
sistencies and irregularities" the film was a "more than
adequate" film for its type and that the acting was
"generally capable." Previewed at Allied Artists in
Hollywood on April 26, 1963.

ADDITIONAL REVIEWS: <u>Commonwealth</u> (May 31, 1963); <u>Newsweek</u>
(May 13, 1963); <u>New York Daily News</u> (May 2, 1963).

COMMENTS: This was the third use of John Wydham's work
written in 1951. The first was VILLAGE OF THE DAMNED
(1960) and CHILDREN OF THE DAMNED (1963). Keel disliked the
script, so he penned much of his own lines. There was a TV
movie made in Britain in 1981 which starred John Duttine as
Bill and Emma Ralph as Jo. The film served as the inspiration for a science fiction TV series produced in Britain.
It aired between September and October 1982 and lasted for
six episodes starring John Duttine in the Bill Masen role.
(See V5)

F25. MAN FROM BUTTON WILLOW (United Screen Arts, January
      1965) Color. 84 Minutes.

      CREDITS: Producer: Phyllis Bounds Detiege. Director:
David Detiege. Screenplay by David Detiege. Production
Supervisor: Bill Redlin. Production Designer: Ernie

Nordli. Cinematographer: Max Morgan. Editors: Ted
Baker, Sam Horta. Lyrics by Phil Bounds. Music by Dale
Robertson, George Burns, Mel Henke. Conductor: George
Stoll. Original Themes by George Stoll, Robert Van
Eps. Animators: Morris Gollub, Ed Friedman, Walt
Clinton, Ken Hultgren, Ambi Palwoda, Gil Turner, Don
Towsley, Harry Holt, Benny Washam, Don Lusk, Stan
Green, George Rowley, John Sparey, John Dunn.

CAST: (Voices) Dale Robertson (Justin Eagle); **Howard
Keel**; Edgar Buchanan (Sorry); Barbara Jean Wong
(Stormy); Hershel Bernardi, Ross Martin, Cliff
Edwards, Verna Felton, Edward Platt, Clarence Nash,
Buck Buchanan, Pinto Colvig, Thurl Ravenscroft,
Shepherd Menken, John Heistand.

SYNOPSIS: In 1869, the United States government was trying
to get the East and West linked by the railroad.
Montgomery Blaine and his comrade, The Whip, are forcing
land owners along the path of the railroad to sell him
their land and turning around and charging the government
high prices in order to get the right of way through his
land.
    Meanwhile, U.S. Senator Freeman is trying to organize
a movement to bypass Blaine's land. Before a meeting in
San Francisco can be held to finalize Freeman's plan, he is
kidnapped and put aboard a schooner.
    Undercover agent, Justin Eagle (Robertson), is sent to
San Francisco to settle the matter. After causing a
diversionary fight in Shanghai Kelly's saloon, Eagle gets
himself kidnapped and put aboard the same ship as the
senator. He finds Freeman and with the help of a sailor
Andy the Swede, he takes over the ship, turns it around and
returns to San Francisco. After being commended by the
U.S. government, Eagle returns to Button Willow and his
ranch the Eagle's Nest to await his next case.

REVIEW: Variety (January 27, 1965) felt that the film would
appeal to the younger children but was "too naive" for
teenagers and adults. The picture was "nicely" animated the
few songs were "bouncy" but "not memorable" and the color
was "good." Reviewed at the Preview Screening Room in New
York on January 21, 1965.

ADDITIONAL REVIEWS: B.F.I./Monthly Film Bulletin (April
1966); Film Daily (February 1, 1965); The Hollywood
Reporter (February 18, 1965); Motion Picture Herald Product
Digest (February 3, 1965).

COMMENTS: This was the first film for Dale Robertson's
distribution company. He created the idea for the film,
wrote the original story and some of the film's songs. He
served as the physical model for the lead character.
Robertson appeared live on camera to introduce what was
billed as the first full-length animated color western.
May animators felt it was too hard to give natural movement
to horses and thus stayed away from westerns.
    Howard Keel performed the theme song and for the

first time on film you hear Dale Robertson and Edgar
Buchanan sing. The film was Robertson's production. He
invested a million dollars of his own money because he felt
there was a need for more family type pictures. He
contacted theatre owners all over the country and appeared
at their conventions in order to gain their support in his
cause for more family entertainment.

The soundtrack was recorded first and then came the
drawings. The film got its name from the Cephalanthus
Occidentalis Californius which means Button Willow Tree
which was located in the town of Button Willow, California.

Director Dave Detiege, who had worked for Disney
making cartoons, felt that THE MAN FROM BUTTON WILLOW was
his hardest project because he had to match the cartoon
character to a real person. He and his animators matched
mannerisms and habits by watching Robertson's films and TV
show "Tales of Wells Fargo."

The town fathers were planning the Button Willow Museum
of Animated Arts and History to house the art work from the
film and that donated by other animation companies as well
as artifacts from the Tokuts indians who had been the earl-
iest residents of Button Willow.

Musical director, George Stoll and Robertson met in
Italy while Robertson was filming ANNA OF BROOKLYN. They
became friends which resulted in Stoll scoring THE MAN FROM
BUTTON WILLOW.

F26. WACO (Paramount, June 25, 1966) Color. 85 Minutes.

CREDITS: Producer: A. C. Lyles. Director: R. G.
Springsteen. Assistant Director: James Rosenberger.
Based on the story Emoria by Harry Sanford, Max Lamb.
Screenplay by Steve Fisher. Cinematographer: Robert
Pittack (Technicolor). Editor: Bernard Matis. Theme
Song sung by Lorne Greene. Lyrics by Hal Blair. Music
by Jimmy Haskell. Art Directors: Hal Pereira, Al
Roelofs. Set Designers: Robert Benson, Chuck Pierce.
Costume Designer: Edith Head. Sound by Terry Kellum,
John Wilkinson. Production Manager: Howard Roessel.

CAST: **Howard Keel** (Waco); Jane Russell (Jill Stone);
Brian Donlevy (Ace Ross); Wendell Corey (Preacher
Sam); Terry Moore (Dolly); John Smith (Joe Gore); John
Agar (George Gates); Gene Evans (Deputy Sheriff
O'Neill); Richard Arlen (Sheriff Billy Kelly); Ben
Cooper (Scott Moore); Tracy Olsen (Patricia West);
DeForest Kelley (Bill Rile); Anne Seymour (Ma Jenner);
Robert Lowery (Mayor Ned West); Willard Parker (Pete
Jenner); Jeff Richards (Kallen); Reg Parton (Ike
Jenner); Fuzzy Knight (Telegraph Operator); Russ
McCubbin, Dan White, Red Morgan, King Johnson, Barbara
Latell.

SYNOPSIS: When Sheriff Billy Kelly (Arlen) is killed, an
older gunman, Waco (Keel), is given the job of bringing law
and order to Emporia.

When Waco comes to town, he discovers his old girl
friend, Jill Stone (Russell), has married preacher Sam

Stone (Corey). She becomes interested in Waco again.
     People become concerned when it appears Waco is headed
back to his old ways but he makes good his promise to clean
up the town. Preacher Stone is killed when he tries to
prevent a street gun fight.

REVIEW: Variety (August 10, 1966) felt that WACO had a
"first-rate technical production value but actors and
script never seem to be on same footing." Keel "looked like
but didn't have the James Arness appeal." Reviewed at
Paramount Studio in Hollywood on August 1, 1966.

COMMENTS: Lorne Greene, best remembered for his role as Ben
Cartwright on the hit TV series "Bonanza," sang the theme
song "Waco." The film opened in Reno, Nevada.

F27. RED TOMAHAWK (Paramount, January 1967) Color. 82
     Minutes.

     CREDITS: Producer: A. C. Lyles. Director: R. G.
     Springsteen. Assistant Director: James Rosenberger.
     Based on the story by Steve Fisher, Andrew Craddock.
     Screenplay by Steve Fisher. Cinematographer: Wallace
     Kelley. Editor: John Schreyer. Music by Jimmy Haskell.
     Art Directors: Hal Pereira, Al Roelofs. Set Designers:
     Robert Benton, Ray Moyer. Sound by Harold Lewis, John
     Wilkinson. Unit Business Manager: Ted Leonardi.

     CAST: **Howard Keel** (Captain Tom York); Joan Caulfield
     (Dakota Lil); Broderick Crawford (Columbus Smith);
     Scott Brady (Ep Wyatt); Wendell Corey (Elkins);
     Richard Arlen (Telegrapher); Tom Drake (Bill Kane);
     Tracey Olsen (Sal); Ben Cooper (Lt. Drake); Donald
     Barry (Bly); Reg Parton (Third Prospector); Gerald
     Jann (Wu Sing); Ray Jenson (Second Prospector); Dan
     White (First Prospector); Henry Wills (Samuels); Saul
     Gross (Townsman).

SYNOPSIS: After coming upon the aftermath of the Battle of
the Little Big Horn, the massacre of Custer, and the
Seventh Cavalry, Army Captain Tom York (Keel) reports the
news to the folks of Deadwood who become alarmed at the
news.
     York is accused of deserting Custer and is mobbed.
Columbus Smith (Crawford) stops the mob scene and takes on
York single-handed until Ed Wyatt (Brady) informs him York
is a special agent of the Army. York says C & F troops are
going to join the Seventh and have to be warned about what
happened to Custer and that reinforcements need to be sent
from Fort Bastion along with four Gatling guns Custer left
behind. Wyatt tells them Dakota Lil (Caulfield) knows the
whereabouts of two of them that are in Deadwood.
     York finds Lil at her roulette table and asks her
about the guns. She feels they have caused enough trouble
and she is not going to give them to anyone. Elkins
(Corey) and the other roulette players hear the discussion
and try to force her to tell them where the guns are so
they can use them for the town's defense. York, Wyatt,

and Smith step in and stop Elkins and the others from
roughing up Lil.

The guns had been purchased by Lil's husband and a
partner. Her husband refuses to let his partner sell the
guns to the indians and hides them on his ranch. Lil's
husband and son are killed by indians who raid the ranch
after learning about the guns from the partner. Lil has
decided to let the soldiers have the guns.

Wyatt and Smith scout out the location of the indians
and are to join York who has gone to the ranch to assemble
the guns. He is followed and knocked out by Elkins. When
he wakes up, during an evening storm, he finds himself
being tended by Lil. After kissing her, he goes off
looking for the guns. Lil tells Wyatt and Smith where York
has gone. They join him in town where they find the
ammunition. They storm a corral where Elkins is trying to
assemble the Gatlins and shoot him.

The town prepares barricades in preparation for an
indian attack while York assembles the guns and puts them
on a buckboard. Smith, driving the buckboard, follows
York and Wyatt out of town killing a few indians along the
way. When they reach the river, they hide the guns and
head out to bring the soldiers. Smith is killed. York, on
foot, finds C Troop and leads them to where the guns are
hidden.

The calvary are being beaten by the indians until York
and Lt. Drake (Cooper) use the guns to mow down the indians
who scatter.

Lil gives up the roulette business and winds up with
York.

REVIEW: Variety (January 11, 1967) thought that the
technical part of the film was "excellent" but the film's
weaknesses were the "cliche-laden" script and the "less
than inspired" acting. Keel handled himself "beautifully"
in the fight scenes. Reviewed at Paramount in New York on
January 9, 1967.

COMMENTS: Wendell Corey was running for the House
representing the 28th Congressional District--Santa Monica
when he signed for the film. Betty Hutton gave up the role
that went to Joan Caulfield. Miss Caulfield was buying
Birch Trees in a Beverly Hills nursery when she ran into
producer A. C. Lyles who asked her if she would be
interested in the Hutton role.

F28. WAR WAGON (Universal, May 23, 1967) Color. 101
Minutes.

CREDITS: A Batjac-Marvin Schwartz Production.
Producer: Marvin Schwartz. Director: Burt Kennedy.
Assistant Directors: Al Jennings, H. A. Silverman.
Based on Clair Huffaker's novel Badman. Screenplay
by Clair Huffaker. Cinematographer: William Clothier
(Panavision, Technicolor). Editor: Harry Gerstad.
Theme Song Sung by Ed Ames. Lyrics and Music for
"Ballad of the War Wagon" by Ned Washington, Dimitri
Tiomkin. Music by Dimitri Tiomkin, Ned Washington.

Art Director: Alfred Sweeney. Set Designer: Ray Moyer.
Costume Designers: Robert Chinquy, Donald Walz. Makeup
Artists: Donald Roberson, Dave Grayson, Bud Westmore.
Sound by Waldon Watson.

CAST: John Wayne (Taw Jackson); Kirk Douglas (Lomax);
Howard Keel (Levi Walking Bear); Robert Walker (Billy
Hyatt); Keenan Wynn (Wes Catlin); Bruce Cabot (Frank
Pierce); Valora Noland (Kate); Gene Evans (Hoag);
Joanna Barnes (Lola); Bruce Dern (Hammond); Terry
Wilson (Strike); Don Collier (Strack); Sheb Wooley
(Snyder); Ann McCrea (Felicia); Emilio Fernandez
(Calita); Frank McGrath (Bartender); Chuck Roberson
(Brown); Red Morgan (Early); Hal Needham (Hite); Marco
Antonio (Wild Horse); Perla Walter (Rosita); Jose
Trinidad Villa (Townsman at Bar); Miko Mayama Midori,
Margarite Lune.

SYNOPSIS: Frank Pierce (Cabot) stole Taw Jackson's (Wayne)
land that was filled with gold and framed Taw. Taw is
paroled and goes after Pierce by planning to get hold of
Pierce's armor-plated wagon full of gold dust.
   Taw enlists the help of Lomax (Douglas), who used to
work for Pierce, explosion expert Billy Hyatt (Walker), who
drinks, Levi Walking Bear (Keel), who left his tribe, and
Wes Catlin (Wynn) who drives wagons.
   Pierce wants Taw dead and offers $12,000 to Lomax to
do the job. Lomax turns him down because he feels he can
make more by robbing the wagon.
   Lomax shoots Pierce during the robbery and the flour
barrels containing the gold dust are placed in Catlin's
wagon.
   The Kiowa indians, whom Taw had gotten to help him,
kill Catlin and try to take the gold but are stopped by a
nitric explosion. However, other indians appear and start
taking the spillage because they believe it is flour.
   Taw knows Lomax has stashed some of the gold and plans
to surprise Lomax when he goes to claim it.

REVIEWS: New York Times (August 3, 1967) felt that WAR
WAGON was "pretty flabby prairie stuff" but not a "bad"
film but obvious." Reviewed August 2, 1967.

Variety (May 24, 1967) felt that WAR WAGON was an
"excellent oater" with a "powerful John Wayne-Kirk Douglas
teaming." The film had a "lush exterior" production and a
"strong" box office appeal. Keel's portrayal of an indian
was a "good change of pace." Reviewed at the Director's
Guild of America in Los Angeles on May 16, 1967.

ADDITIONAL REVIEWS: Commonweal (June 30, 1967); Life
(August 4, 1967); New York Daily News (August 3, 1967); New
York Post (August 3, 1967); The New Republic (August 5,
1967); Saturday Review (July 15, 1967); New York Sunday
Telegraph (November 26, 1967); Time (June 16, 1967).

COMMENTS: The film was based on Huffaker's novel Badman
written in 1958. WAR WAGON in which Keel plays an indian

Levi Walking Bear was his best assignment in several years.

Kirk Douglas (in his third appearance with Wayne) told Hal Needham he was not needed because he wanted to do his own stunt work. Douglas used a trampoline to jump onto the back of his horse.

Douglas enjoyed westerns. He took off to make an anti-Reagan ad when Reagan was running for governor of California. Wayne (who's company Batjac co-produced the film) got even when he closed down shooting to make a pro-Reagan ad and did not tell Douglas who reported to the desert for shooting. (See V23)

F29. ARIZONA BUSHWHACKERS (Paramount, March 1968) Color. 86 Minutes.

CREDITS: Producer: A. C. Lyles. Director: Lesley Selander. Assistant Director: Dale Hutchinson. Based on story by Steve Fisher, Andrew Craddock. Screenplay by Steve Fisher. Cinematographer: Lester Short (Techni-color). Editor: John Schreyer. Music by Jimmie Haskell. Art Directors: Hal Pereira, Al Roelofs. Set Designers: Robert Benton, Jerry Welch. Hair Stylist: Nellie Manley. Sound by Joe Edmondson, John Wilkinson. Special Effects by Paul Lerpae.

CAST: **Howard Keel** (Lee Travis); Yvonne DeCarlo (Jill Wyler); John Ireland (Dan Shelby); Marilyn Maxwell (Molly); Scott Brady (Tom Rile); Brian Donlevy (Major Joe Smith); Barton MacLane (Sheriff Lloyd Grover); James Craig (Ike Parton); Montie Montana (Stage Driver); Eric Cody (Bushwhacker); James Cagney (Narra-tor); Roy Rogers, Jr. (Roy); Reg Parton (Curly).

SYNOPSIS: Because of the overcrowded military prisons, during the Civil War, Confederate prisoners are allowed to join the Union Army in order to help bring law and order to towns that are lawless. Among the prisoners is riverboat gambler and gunfighter Lee Travis (Keel).

When the town of Cotton, Arizona learns that Travis is going to take over Sheriff Lloyd Grover's (MacLane) place, they are unhappy with the exception of Major Joe Smith (Donlevy). Smith knows that Grover has been taking a bribe from saloon owner Tom Rile (Brady).

Deputy Sheriff Dan Shelby (Ireland) is in love with milliner Jill Wyler (DeCarlo) and does not want Travis in town. Grover skips town before Travis arrives and is ambushed. Travis outwits those who are waiting to ambush him and kills their leader. Ike Clanton (Craig) and one of the men tell Travis that Rile was behind the ambush.

Travis turns out to be a confederate spy who gets the job in Cotton in order to make contact with Jill Wyler. Their job is to get the arms and ammunition, hidden under the floor of a warehouse, to the confederate soldiers waiting for it outside of town.

In order to clean up the town, Travis uses Grover's bribe money to get into a crap game. He wins the saloon and closes it down making it clear he wants Rile to leave Cotton. Saloon girl Molly (Maxwell) takes a liking to

Travis and tells him Rile has been selling arms to renegade
Apaches. Travis goes to the warehouse where Rile has
hidden the guns and ammunition. He finds Rile and his men
loading wagons and when he confronts them is shot. Jill
gets Travis to a doctor.
    Shelby becomes suspicious of Travis and Jill and after
searching her room learns what they are up to. Shelby is
in the process of turning them over to the major when
Grover rides in announcing the end of the war. He also
tells them Rile and the Apaches are headed for town to get
the rest of the guns and ammunition. Grover, Shelby,
Travis, and Smith join forces to stop Rile and the indians.
After the defeat of Rile, Jill goes to Shelby. Before
Travis leaves town, he gives Molly the deed to the saloon.

REVIEW: Variety (February 14, 1968) thought the film was a
"routine" western with "good" technical work, "excellent"
photography, "lively" score, "tight" editing, and "fast-
paced" direction. Keel is "convincing" as Lee Travis.
Reviewed at Paramount Studios on February 6, 1968.

COMMENTS: The film is more interesting because of western
movie veterans Ireland, Brady, Donlevy, and MacLane. This
became Roy Rogers, Jr's. first film. The film also marked
director Lesley Selander's 151st feature. (See V2)

F30. THAT'S ENTERTAINMENT! III (MGM/Turner Entertainment
Co.) Color. 113 Minutes. Rated G.

    CREDITS: Executive Producer: Peter Fitzgerald.
    Producers, Directors: Bud Friedgen, Michael Sheridan.
    Screenplay by Bud Friedgen, Michael Sheridan. Editors:
    Bud Friedgen, Michael Sheridan. Additional Music
    Arranged by Marc Shaiman. Musical Director: Marilee
    Bradford.

    CAST: June Allyson, Cyd Charisse, Lena Horne, **Howard
    Keel**, Gene Kelly, Ann Miller, Debbie Reynolds, Mickey
    Rooney, Esther Williams.

SYNOPSIS: The film features more excerpts from MGM musicals
as well as outtakes, numbers that were never completed, and
a look behind-the-scenes at the musical films.

REVIEWS: New York Post, Michael Medved, (May 6, 1994) "The
filmmakers might have made better use of these great stars
by presenting them in unguarded interview settings--or
altogether avoiding their pointless interruptions of this
otherwise impressive picture." Reviewed at the Ziegfeld in
New York.

The New York Times, Caryn James, (May 6, 1994) THAT'S
ENTERTAINMENT! III "cleaverly focuses on outtakes,
unfinished numbers and behind-the-scenes glimpses of the
old musicals. This results in a lively and funny
compilation of curiosities suggesting what might have
been." Reviewed at the Ziegfeld in New York.

ADDITIONAL REVIEW: <u>Entertainment Weekly</u> (May 6, 1994).

COMMENTS: The host segments began shooting in April 1993 at various spots around the MGM lot (now Sony Columbia Studios) and were not delayed by a fire on the Sony lot. The film opened in New York and California and the proceeds from opening night benefited the American Film Institute. (See D47, V20)

5

BROADCAST

This chapter documents Mr. Keel's U.S. and British Broadcast credits and is divided into two parts--radio followed by television. Each part is arranged chronologically. Where possible, network, air date, time, length, credits, casts, songs (where applicable), comments, and a review are given for each show. Beginning with the mid-1960s, most television shows were broadcast in color. The abbreviation ATV stands for Associated TeleVision. If a recording or video tape exists a cross reference is given.

RADIO

BC 1. HEDDA HOPPER SHOW (NBC, 1951) 8 p.m. 30 Minutes.

> Hostess: Hedda Hopper. Orchestra: Frank Worth.
> Guests: **Howard Keel**, Tony Curtis, Jan Sterling.

COMMENT: This show was a variety show consisting of inter-views, comedy sketches, and commentary.

BC 2. LUX RADIO THEATRE (CBS, February 11, 1952) 9 p.m. 60 Minutes.

> Host: Irving Cummings. Announcer: Ken Carpenter.
> Guests: Kathryn Grayson, **Howard Keel**, Ava Gardner, Marge & Gower Champion, and William Warfield.

COMMENTS: This show was a broadcast of SHOW BOAT. It was an anthology program that adapted both Broadway shows and motion pictures. Its sponsor was Lever Brothers and it served as the forerunner of television's "Lux Video Theatre."

BC 3. 1951 ACADEMY AWARDS (ABC, March 20, 1952) 8 p.m.

> Host: Danny Kaye. Presenters: Sally Forrest, Janice Rule, Constance Smith, Zsa Zsa Gabor, George Murphy, Marge & Gower Champion, Lucille Ball, Cyd Charisse,

Vera-Ellen, Leslie Caron, Charles Booth Lice, Joseph
Mankiewicz, Claire Trevor, George Sanders, Greer
Garson, Ronald Colman, Jessie Lasky.

NOMINATED SONGS: "In the Cool, Cool, Cool of the Evening"*-
Danny Kaye, Jane Wyman; "A Kiss to Build a Dream On"-Kay
Brown; "Never"-Dick Haymes; "Too Late Now"-Jane Powell;
"Wonder Why"-**Howard Keel**. (* indicates winning song)

COMMENT: This show was broadcast from the RKO Pantages
Theatre in Hollywood.

BC 4. SARDI'S RADIO SHOW (1989)

COMMENTS: **Howard Keel** was interviewed at Sardi's restaurant
located on West 44th Street which was the same street in New
York where Keel appeared in the 1945 Broadway productions of
OKLAHOMA! and CAROUSEL.

BC 5. GLORIA HUNNIFORD (British) (BBC Radio 2-April 1994)

COMMENTS: Keel was interviewed by Miss Hunniford and
discussed his career, family, appearances in London
including the 32-date concert series he was about to begin
despite last year's announcement of a farewell concert. He
said his HOWARD KEEL SHOW BOAT THEATRE, in Branson,
Missouri, did not materialize because the backer had
changed his mind. He said hopefully something would still
develop so his theatre would become a reality. Miss
Hunniford played the following Keel recordings: "Oh What a
Beautiful Morning," "Surrey With the Fringe on Top,"
"People Will Say We're in Love," "Oklahoma!," "Ol' Man
River," and "I Won't Send Roses." Miss Hunniford did a
similar interview with Keel in 1993, prior to his starting
his farewell concert series.

TELEVISION

BC 6. TOAST OF THE TOWN-"MGM Salute" (CBS, February 14,
1954) 8 p.m. 60 Minutes.

Host: Ed Sullivan. Co-Host: Dore Zachary. Guests: Gene
Kelly, Fred Astaire, **Howard Keel**, Esther Williams,
Debbie Reynolds, Cyd Charisse, Lana Turner, Ann
Miller, Ann Blyth, Jane Powell, Lionel Barrymore,
Walter Pigdeon, Van Johnson, Piper Angeli, Louis
Calhern, Keenan Wynn, Vera-Ellen, Lucille Ball, Desi
Arnaz.

COMMENTS: The show was a salute to MGM on their 30th
anniversary. It was the first "Toast of the Town" to
originate from the West coast. It advertised THE LONG LONG
TRAILER starring Lucille Ball and Desi Arnaz. Film clips
were also shown from the motion pictures WIZARD OF OZ,
EASTER PARADE, SHOW BOAT, MADAME CURIE, and GONE WITH THE
WIND. (See V22)

BC 7. PRESIDENT EISENHOWER: SIXTY-SIXTH BIRTHDAY (CBS, October 13, 1956) 30 Minutes.

Host: James Stewart. Performers: Irene Dunne, Eddie Fisher, Gordon MacRae, **Howard Keel**, Helen Hayes, Nat Cole, Fred Waring & his orchestra.

COMMENTS: This was a country-wide celebration honoring President Dwight D. Eisenhower's birthday. President Eisenhower spoke concerning the various festivities seen. Also taking part were the first lady and other members of the family. The performers entertained from studio remotes.

BC 8. SUNDAY NIGHT AT THE LONDON PALLADIUM (British) (ATV, May 19, 1957)

Producer: Val Parnell. Emcee: Tommy Trinder. Orchestra: Cyril Ornadel. Guests: The Platters, Leo de Lyon (comic), Rudy Cardinas (Juggler). Special Guest: **Howard Keel**.

REVIEW: Variety (May 29, 1957) said of Keel's appearance, "If the reception he got was any indication of the future, then he's set for a highly successful British vaude stint in coming weeks."

COMMENTS: Keel made a surprise appearance and sang "Bless Your Beautiful Hide."

BC 9. DINAH SHORE CHEVY SHOW (NBC, November 3, 1957) 9 p.m. 60 Minutes.

Hostess: Dinah Shore. Regulars: Skylarks, Tony Charmoli Dancers. Orchestra: Harry Zimmerman Orchestra. Theme: "See the U.S.A. in Your Chevrolet." Guest: **Howard Keel**.

BC10. GENERAL MOTORS FIFTIETH ANNIVERSARY SHOW (NBC, November 17, 1957) 120 Minutes.

Producer: Jess Oppenheimer. Director: Charles S. Dubin. Musical Director: Bernard Green. Writer: Helen Deutsch. Extra Material by Arnie Sultan, Marvin Worthy, Richard Deroy. Narrator: Kirk Douglas, assisted by Ernest Borgnine. Guests: Cyril Ritchard, Claudette Colbert, Helen Hayes, Pat Boone, Dean Martin, Carol Burnett, June Allyson, Steve Lawrence, Dan Dailey, Claudia Crawford, Doretta Morrow, Dinah Shore, **Howard Keel**, Eddie Bracken, Hans Conreid, Jacques d' Amboise (Ballet Dancer), Bambi Linn, Peg Lynch, Chita Rivera, Kent Smith, Don Ameche, Alice Ghostly, Carmen Mathews.

REVIEW: Variety (November 20, 1957) felt the show was "a smooth-running, practically flawless production that combined warmth with rich entertainment values...the topper came in the song and dance department when Dinah Shore, Howard Keel, Doretta Morrow, and Dan Dailey either in solo, duet, or foursome, had themselves a 15-minute ball as their vocals registered to the shows 'love' sequence."

COMMENTS: This was a celebration of the 50th Anniversary of General Motors. The show was broadcast from New York. Keel's sequence centered around songs on the subject of "love" with Doretta Morrow, Dean Martin, Bambi Linn, and Jacques de Amboise. The show cost $750,000.

Howard Keel had appeared earlier that month on the "Dinah Shore Chevy Show." He would later star with Kirk Douglas and John Wayne in the 1967 Universal film WAR WAGON. (See D26)

BC11. **POLLY BERGEN SHOW** (NBC, December 7, 1957) 9 p.m. 30 Minutes.

Hostess: Polly Bergen. Regulars: Peter Gennaro Dancers, Bill Bergen (her father). Orchestra: Luther Henderson, Jr. Theme: "The Party's Over" composed by Jule Styne. Guest: **Howard Keel**.

BC12. **ZANE GREY THEATER**-"Gift From a Gunman" (CBS, December 13, 1957) 8:30 p.m. 30 Minutes.

Host: Dick Powell. Producer: Hal Hudson. Cast: **Howard Keel** (Will Gorman); John Dehner (Col. Overton); Jean Willes (Marcy).

SYNOPSIS: After being wounded in a gun fight, gunman Will Gorman (Keel) decides to reform until a visit to a friend, whose restless wife and gun threaten to force him to go back to his old lifestyle.

COMMENTS: This was a western anthology and Dick Powell occasionally starred in an episode. This segment was shot on RKO's Pathe lot. When the show began Zane Grey's short stories and novels were adapted but stories by other western writers were used when all of Grey's material had been used.

BC13. **BING CROSBY AND FRIENDS** (CBS, January 12, 1958) 90 Minutes.

Producer: Cecil Barker. Director: Seymour Berns, Bob Quinlan. Musical Director: Buddy Cole. Writer: Joe Quillan. Hosts: Bing, Kathryn Crosby. Emcee: John Daily. Commentators: Tom Harmon, Gil Stratton. Golfers: Byron Nelson, Jackie Burke, Dick Mayer, Doug Ford, Lloyd Mangrum, Julius Boros, Marty Furgol, Gene Little, Jimmy Demaret. Celebrity Golfers: Fred Mac-Murray, Fred Waring, Robert Sterling, **Howard Keel**, Dennis Morgan, Forest Tucker, Richard Arlen, Buddy Rogers, Randolph Scott, Guy Madison, Gordon MacRae, Dennis O' Keefe, Johnny Weissmuller, Bob Crosby, Freeman "Amos 'N' Andy" Gosden, Howard Hill, Bob Lemon, Ralph Kiner, Jimmy McLaren, Lefty O' Doul, Jackie Jensen.

COMMENTS: The show was telecast from Pebble Beach during the Bing Crosby National Pro-Amateur Golf Championship. Commentators Harmon and Stratton made their reports on the last two holes of the 3-day 72-hole tournament. The prize was $50,000. Bob Hope and Phil Harris did comedy sketches and Kathryn Crosby reported on women's golf fashions. The proceeds went to charities and songs and sketches were recorded on film.

BC14. **THE BIG RECORD** (CBS, March 12, 1958) 8:00 p.m. 30 Minutes.

Hostess: Patti Page. Orchestra: Vic Schoen. Guests: Pearl Bailey, **Howard Keel**, Florence Henderson, Four Voices, Hawaiian music of Harry Owens Orchestra with Hilo Hattie.

COMMENTS: Singers sang their songs that were on the charts or those associated with them. The show included a wide range of music including show music, standards, as well as Rock 'n' Roll which was in its early stage.

BC15. **SUNDAY NIGHT AT THE LONDON PALLADIUM** (British) (ATV, April 27, 1958)

Emcee: Tommy Tinder. Dancers: George Carden. Orchestra: Cyril Ornadel. Guest Star: **Howard Keel**. Guests: Florian Zabach (Fiddler); Roger Price (Cartoonist); Yana (Songstress).

REVIEW: Variety (May 7, 1958) felt that Keel "hasn't any gimmicks and little patter, but a large share of charm and a fine voice more than compensate for these minor failings."

COMMENTS: Keel performed established hits, a sentimental piece, and did a neat soft-shoe routine.

BC16. **ROBERTA** (NBC, September 19, 1958) 90 Minutes.

Producer: Jack Hope. Director: Dick McDonough, Ed Greenberg. Musical Director: Les Brown. Writers: Mort Lachman, Bill Larkin, Lester White, John Rapp, Charles Lee, Norman Sullivan. Music: Jerome Kern, Otto Harbach. Host: Bob Hope. Cast: **Howard Keel** (John Kent); Anna Maria Alberghetti (Stephanie); Bob Hope (Huckelberry Haines); Janis Page (Scharwenka); Sara Dillon (Sophie Teake); Lilli Valenti (Aunt Minnie/ Roberta).

SYNOPSIS: John Kent (Keel), an all-American halfback, inherits his Aunt Minnie's fashion shop and falls for Stephanie (his aunt's assistant).

SONGS: "Let's Begin" (Hope, Alberghetti); "Hard to Handle" (Hope, Paige); "Smoke Gets in Your Eyes" (Alberghetti); "Touch of Your Hands" (Alberghetti, Keel); "You're Devastating" (Keel); "Lovely to Look At" (Alberghetti);

"Yesterdays" (Alberghetti); "Something Had to Happen" (Paige).

COMMENTS: The show had been done earlier on the NBC "Colgate Comedy Hour" on April 10, 1955 and starred Gordon MacRae as John Kent. The show was done again on NBC on November 6, 1969, and starred John Davidson as John Kent, Michele Lee as Stephanie. Bob Hope and Janis Page repeated their roles.
    Howard Keel had starred in the 1952 MGM film LOVELY TO LOOK AT which was a film version of ROBERTA. (See F9)

BC17. A TOAST TO JEROME KERN (NBC, September 22, 1959) 9 p.m. 90 Minutes.

Producer/Writer: Bob Wells. Orchestra: Paul Weston. Host: Robert Cummings. Guests: **Howard Keel**, Patrice Munsel, Louis Prima, Keely Smith, Carol Channing, Dancers: John Bubbles, Bambi Linn, Kelly Brown.

SONGS BY KEEL: "All the Things You Are" (Keel, Linn, Brown); "They Didn't Believe Me"; "Ol' Man River"; Medley of Kern Songs (All); "Song is You" (All).

COMMENT: Lyricist Otto Harbach recalled his working together with Kern on "Smoke Gets in Your Eyes."

BC18. BELL TELEPHONE HOUR (NBC, March 4, 1959) 8:30 p.m. 60 Minutes.

Executive Producer: Barry Wood. Producer: Roger Englander. Director: Kirk Browning. Set Designers: William & Jean Eckhart. Musical Director: Donald Voorhees. Conductor: Donald Voorhees. Theme: "The Bell Telephone Waltz" (composed by Donald Voorhees) Orchestra: The Bell Telephone Orchestra. Staging by John Butler. Guests: **Howard Keel**, Ann Blyth, Isaac Stern (Violinist), Joe Bushkin (Jazz Pianist), Eileen Farrell (Soprano), Ximenez (Vargas Ballet).

REVIEW: Variety (March 11, 1959) felt the show was "a top sampling of Bell's achievement in musical TV." It was thought that Howard Keel and Ann Blyth appeared "in a fine show-tune segment."

COMMENT: "The Bell Telephone Hour" showcased every type of music except Rock 'n' Roll.

BC19. 1958 ACADEMY AWARDS (NBC, April 6, 1959)

Hosts: Bob Hope, David Niven, Tony Randall, Mort Sahl, Lawrence Olivier, Jerry Lewis. Presenters: Bette Davis, Anthony Quinn, Barbara Rush, Jacques Tati, Janet Leigh, Tony Curtis, Shelley Winters, Red Buttons, June Allyson, Dick Powell, Jane Wyman, Charlton Heston, Wendell Corey, Ernie Kovacs, Jean Simmons, Louis Jourdan, Natalie Wood, Robert Wagner, Sophia Loren, Dean Martin, Shirley MacLaine, Peter

Ustinov, Eva Marie Saint, Anthony Franciosa, Cyd
Charisse, Robert Stack, Doris Day, Rock Hudson,
Rosalind Russell, Vincent Price, Eddie Albert, Buddy
Adler, Millie Perkins, Gary Cooper, Elizabeth Taylor,
Dirk Bogarde, Van Heflin, Kim Novak, James Cagney,
Irene Dunne, John Wayne, Ingrid Bergman.

NOMINATED SONGS: "Almost in Your Arms" (Anna Maria
Alberghetti, Tuesday Weld, Connie Stevens, Nick Adams, Dean
Jones, James Darren); "A Certain Smile" (John Raitt, danced
by Marge & Gower Champion); "Gigi"* (Tony Martin, danced by
Taina Elg); "To Love and Be Loved" (Eddie Fisher); "A Very
Precious Love" (**Howard Keel**, Rhonda Fleming). *-Indicates
winning song.

COMMENT: The show was televised from the RKO Pantages
Theatre in Hollywood and was introduced by William Holden
and John Wayne.

BC20. **BELL TELEPHONE HOUR**-"Main Street U.S.A." (NBC, March
11, 1960) 8:30 p.m. 60 Minutes.

> Executive Producer: Barry Wood. Conductor: Donald
> Voorhees. Orchestra: Bell Telephone Orchestra. Theme:
> "The Bell Telephone Waltz" (composed by Donald
> Voorhees). Host: **Howard Keel**. Guests: Connie Francis,
> American Ballet Theatre, Hi Lo's, Eddie Hodges, Carol
> Lawrence, Roger Williams.

SONGS: "Country Fair," "76 Trombones," "It's a Most Unusual
Day," "Have You Met Miss Jones," "Let's Be Buddies," "Lazy
Afternoon," "Isn't This a Lovely Day," "It's Almost Like
Being in Love," "Time After Time," "Side By Side."

REVIEW: Variety (March 16, 1960) felt the show was "a
joyous musical affair."

COMMENTS: The stars performed in settings representing a
country fair, a concert in the park, a barn and school
dance. The "Graduation Ball" was danced to Johann Strauss
and with choreography by David Lichine.

BC21 **BELL TELEPHONE HOUR**-"Holiday in Music" (NBC, September
30, 1960) 9 p.m. 60 Minutes.

> Executive Producer: Barry Wood. Writer: Gordon Cotler.
> Orchestra: Bell Telephone. Conductor: Donald Voorhees.
> Host: **Howard Keel**. Guests: Sally Ann Howes, Sleeping
> Beauty Ballet with Melissa Hayden, Andre Eglesvsky,
> Francisco Moncion, Michael Hand, Conrad Ledlow, Benny
> Goodman & his Orchestra. Special Guest: Van Cliburn.

SONGS BY HOWES AND KEEL: "We're Off to See the Wizard,"
"Over the Rainbow," "Stout-hearted Men," "Tonight," "A
Bushel and a Peck," "Wunderbar," "What's the Use of
Wonderin'," "Some Enchanted Evening," "I'm Gonna Wash That
Man Right Outa My Hair," "Heart."

REVIEW: <u>Variety</u>, N. W. Ayer, (October 5, 1960) N. W. Ayer
felt the show "was more colorful in sound that in
sight...it was unpretentious and practically pure music.
Ayer said that Miss Howes and Mr. Keel's offerings were
done with "appropriate voicings."

COMMENTS: The show was broadcast from Hollywood and played
opposite "77 Sunset Strip."

BC22. **SATURDAY SPECTACULAR** (British) (ATV, October 8, 1960)

<u>Star</u>: **Howard Keel**. <u>Guests</u>: Adele Leigh, Patricia
Marmont, Maurice Denham.

SONGS BY Keel: "Oh What a Beautiful Morning," Medleys from
SOUTH PACIFIC, WEST SIDE STORY, "Porgy & Bess" (Keel,
Leigh).

SKETCH: "Tea For Three" with Keel, Marmont, Denham. The
sketch was about an American who goes back to England to
see an old girlfriend and learns she has married. They do
not want her husband to know about their old affair. They
learn that he knows when he tells them he spent a night in
New York with the American's wife.

REVIEW: <u>Variety</u> (October 12, 1969) felt that Keel was
"always sure of a sturdy following...and pleased the
receptive customers." Concerning the skit it was felt
that "they all forced the material until it was inclined
to squeak."

BC23. **HERE'S HOLLYWOOD** (NBC, 1961) 4:30 p.m. 30 Minutes.

<u>Co-Hosts</u>: Dean Miller, Jo-ann Jordan. <u>Guest</u>: **Howard
Keel**.

COMMENT: The show consisted of interviews of celebrities.

BC24. **BERNARD DELFONT'S SUNDAY SHOW** (British) (ATV,
September 3, 1961)

<u>Emcee</u>: Billy Dainty. <u>Guests</u>: **Howard Keel**, Alfred
Marks, Pat Coombs.

SONGS BY KEEL: "Welcome Home," "London By Night," "Where is
the life That Late I Led," "What Kind of Fool Am I," "Climb
Every Mountain."

REVIEW: <u>Variety</u> (September 6, 1961) felt that the show was
"curiously lax in its format" that it "lacks shape" and the
"personality of a strong emcee." It was thought that Keel
had "sturdy and stalwart pipes."

COMMENTS: This was the last show for the summer.

BC25. **TALES OF WELLS FARGO**-"Casket 73" (NBC, September 30,
1961) 7:30 p.m. 60 Minutes.

Regular Cast: Dale Robertson (Jim Hardie); Jack Ging
(Assistant, Beau McCloud); William Demarest (Ranch
Forman, Jeb Gaine); Virginia Christine (Neighbor and
Widow, Olvie); Mary Jane Saunders (Olvie's Daughter,
Mary Gee); Lori Patrick (Olvie's Daughter, Tina).
Guest Cast: **Howard Keel** (Justin Brox); Suzanne Lloyd
(Christine); Torin Thatcher (Grey Man); Stephen
Roberts (Wells Fargo Official); Norman Leavitt
(Agent); Eve McVeagh (Woman).

SYNOPSIS: A casket is stolen in New Orleans, by a group of
ex-confederates.

COMMENTS: Robertson was an agent for a transport company.
With this show, the program expanded to one hour.
Robertson not only continues to work for Wells Fargo but
aquires a ranch near San Francisco as well as five new
regulars. Keel would later work with Robertson in the 1965
United Screen Arts (Robertson's distribution company)
animated western film MAN FROM BUTTON WILLOW. (See F25)

BC26. BELL TELEPHONE HOUR-"The Music of Richard Rodgers"
(NBC, November 10, 1961) 9:30 p.m. 60 Minutes.

Host: Ray Bolger. Guests: Richard Rodgers, Helen
Gallagher, **Howard Keel**, Dolores Gray, Anita Darian,
Ron Husman, Martha Wright, Elizabeth Howell.
Orchestra: Bell Telephone. Conductor: Donald
Voorhees.

SONGS BY KEEL: "There is Nothing Like a Dame," "You Always
Love the Same Girl," "People Will Say We're in Love," "Some
Enchanted Evening," "Have You Met Miss Jones," "If I Loved
You," "Most Beautiful Girl in the World."

COMMENT: This was a musical salute to Rodgers and Hart and
Rodgers and Hammerstein II.

BC27. LET FREEDOM RING (CBS, December 31, 1961) 3 p.m. 60
Minutes.

Narrator: Richard Evans. Organists: Frank Asper,
Alexander Schreiner. Choir: Richard P. Condie.
Sponsors: American Motors, Kelvinator. Guests:
Loraine Day, Richard Boone, **Howard Keel**, Dan
O'Herlihy, Mormon Tabernacle Choir.

COMMENTS: The program was a salute to the U.S.A. in words
and music and was taped at the Mormon Tabernacle in Salt
Lake City, Utah. "The Gettysburg Address" was read by
Boone. "The Prologue to Morning" was done by Boone, and
O'Herlihy. "Lincoln's Letter to Mrs. Bixby" was read by
Day and "Founding Fathers" by O'Herlihy.

BC28. VOICE OF FIRESTONE (ABC, December 16, 1962) 10 p.m.
30 Minutes.

Narrator: John Daly. Conductor: Glenn Osser.

Orchestra: Firestone. Theme: "If I Could Tell You,"
"In My Garden" (composed by Mrs. Harvey Firestone).
Guests: **Howard Keel**, Patrice Munsel, New York Ballet
Stars: Melissa Hayden and Jacques d' Amboise.

COMMENTS: The show presented all kinds of music but
primarily classical, semi-classical and better pops. In
the 1962-1963 season, Howard Barlow began conducting
occasionally and among the rotating conductors were Arthur
Fiedler, Winfred Pelletier, and Harry John Brown.

BC29. HOLLYWOOD MELODY (NBC, March 19, 1962) 9 p.m. 60
Minutes.

Executive Producer: Arthur Freed. Musical Director:
David Rose. Sponsor: Chrysler. Host: Donald O'
Connor. Guests: Juliet Prowse, Richard Chamberlain,
Shirley Jones, Nanette Fabray, **Howard Keel**, Yvette
Mimieux.

SONGS BY KEEL: "Broadway Melody," "Lovely to Look At," "You
Were Meant For Me," "Temptation," "Tonight," "Singing in
the Rain" (All), "On With the Show" (All).

COMMENTS: The show was a special tribute to movie musicals
past, present and the future. Film clips included MEET ME
IN ST. LOUIS, AN AMERICAN IN PARIS, GIGI.

BC30. 1961 ACADEMY AWARDS (ABC, April 9, 1962)

Host: Bob Hope.

COMMENTS: The show was broadcast from the Santa Monica
Civic Auditorium. **Howard Keel** accepted Eugene Shufton's
award for black and white cinematography for the film THE
HUSTLER.

BC31. KISS ME, KATE (British, BBC, 1963) 90 Minutes.

COMMENTS: **Howard Keel** appeared in KISS ME, KATE with
Patricia Morison in the roles of Fred Graham/Petrichio and
Lilly Vanessi/Katherine.

BC32. DEATH VALLEY DAYS-"Diamond Jim Brady" (Syndicated,
June 3, 1963) 7 p.m. 30 Minutes.

Creator: Ruth Woodman. Script by Ruth Woodman. Host:
Stanley Andrews. Sponsor: 20 Mule Team Borax
(Commercials done by Rosemary DeCamp). Guest Cast:
Howard Keel (Diamond Jim Brady), Charles Cooper
(Buchanan).

SYNOPSIS: Because he feels certain that he will win
a $50,000 bet, Diamond Jim Brady throws a $20,000 party.
Those opposing him are angry and plan to reveal his scheme.

COMMENTS: The show was a western anthology that presented
mostly human-interest stories. The show was filmed

frequently in Death Valley. Andrews was host from 1952–
1965.

BC33. MATCH GAME (NBC, 1964) 4 p.m. 30 Minutes.

> <u>Producer</u>: Goodson-Todman. <u>Host</u>: Gene Rayburn. <u>Guest</u>:
> **Howard Keel.**

COMMENTS: Two teams with three members (one of which was a
celebrity) competed to complete the sentences read by the
host.

BC34. BELL TELEPHONE HOUR-"Salute to Veteran's Day" (NBC,
     1965) 60 Minutes.

BC35. RUN FOR YOUR LIFE-"The Time of the Sharks" (NBC,
     December 6, 1965) 10 p.m. 60 Minutes.

> <u>Script by</u> Frank Fenton. <u>Star</u>: Ben Gazzara (Paul
> Bryan). <u>Guest Cast</u>: **Howard Keel** (Hardie Rankin),
> Melodie Johnson (Carol), Dolores Dorn-Heft (Elizabeth
> Rankin), Tony Bill (Charlie Carson), Bernie Hamilton
> (J. C.), Steve Carlson (Doc).

SYNOPSIS: A sportsman friend joins Paul on a small
Tahitian Island where they intend to fish for killer
sharks. Some youngsters claim that such fishing will
interfere with their work as photographers.

COMMENTS: The show concerned Paul Bryan, a 35-year-old
lawyer, who learns he has a disease with no cure and has a
two-year life expectancy. He decides to spend his remaining
time traveling and experiencing as much of life as he can.

BC36. HERE'S LUCY-"Safari Man" (CBS, 1968) 8:30 p.m. 30
     Minutes.

> <u>Star</u>: Lucille Ball (Lucy Carter). <u>Regulars</u>: Lucy Arnaz
> (Kim), Desi Arnaz, Jr. (Craig), Gale Gordon (Harrison
> Otis Carter). <u>Guest</u>: **Howard Keel.**

COMMENTS: In this version of the show, Lucy worked for her
brother-in-law Harrison Otis Carter at the Unique Employment
Agency.

BC37. SONNY & CHER COMEDY SHOW (CBS, September 15, 1972) 60
     Minutes.

> <u>Theme</u>: "The Beat Goes On" (by Sonny Bono). <u>Orchestra</u>:
> Jimmy Dale. <u>Stars</u>: Sonny & Cher. <u>Regulars</u>: Tom Solari,
> Clark Carr, Murray Langston, Freeman King, Peter
> Cullen, Tony Mordente Dancers, Earl Brown Singers,
> Steve Martin. <u>Guests</u>: Governor Ronald Reagan, **Howard
> Keel**, Wilfred Hyde-White, Jackson 5, Larry Storch.

COMMENTS: Sonny & Cher ended the show with "I've Got You
Babe." Sketches included an operetta featuring Cher as a
princess with a problem. Cher's vamps (as Sadie Thompson)

included Cleopatra, and Anna of Siam.

BC38. MERV GRIFFIN SHOW-"A Salute to MGM" (Syndicated, November 1, 1973)

> Host: Merv Griffin. Director: Dick Carson. Guests: Kathryn Grayson, **Howard Keel**, Ann Miller, Donald O'Connor, Fernando Lamas.

COMMENTS: Dick Carson previously directed "The Tonight Show" starring his brother Johnny Carson. This version of Merv's show was produced by Metromedia and appeared in many areas in the afternoon.

BC39. THE QUEST-"72 Hours" (NBC, November 3, 1976) 10 p.m. 60 Minutes.

> Creator: Tracey Keenan Wynn. Producer: Mark Rodgers, James Brown. Executive Producer: David Gerber & Columbia Pictures Television. Writer: Anthony Lawrence. Director: Alf Klellin. Stars: Kurt Russell (Morgan "Two Persons" Beaudine); Tim Matheson (Quentin Beaudine). Guests Cast: Cameron Mitchell (Marshall Horne), **Howard Keel** (Shanghai Pierce), Aldo Ray (Chippy), Maria-Elona Cordero (Sweet Woman), Mitch Vogel.

SYNOPSIS: The Baudine's good time in a cattle town comes to an end after their friend is hit by a stray bullet fired from the gun of a drunk.

COMMENTS: As youngsters, Morgan (Russell) and his sister Patricia had been separated when they were captured by Cheyenne. Morgan was raised by Cheyenne while his brother Quentin was raised by whites. Morgan, now grown, returns to the white nation and finds his brother who plans to become a doctor. Together they set out to find their missing sister.

BC40. TOMORROW (NBC, late 1970s/early 1980s)
Host: Tom Snyder. Guest: **Howard Keel**.

BC41. DALLAS (CBS, February 20, 1981-May 3, 1991) 9 p.m. 60 Minutes.

> Creator: David Jacobs for Lorimar Productions. Executive Producers: Phillip Capice, Lee Rich. Producer: Leonard Katzman. Theme: "Dallas" by Jerrold Immel. Regulars: Jim Davis (Jock Ewing); Barbara Bel Geddes (Miss Ellie); Larry Hagman (J. R. Ewing); Patrick Duffy (Bobby Ewing); Linda Gray (Sue Ellen); Victoria Principal (Pam); Ken Kercheval (Cliff Barnes); **Howard Keel** (Clayton Farlow); Donna Reed (Miss Ellie-1984-1985); Steve Kanaly (Ray Krebs).

COMMENTS: "Dallas" was a nighttime soap and aired April 2, 1978, and ran to May 3, 1991. From March to December 1990 it aired at 10 p.m. It concerned the Ewing family who were in the oil business and were wealthy and powerful. Most of the conflict was caused by JR's wheeling and dealing.

In the 1960s, "Peyton Place" became the first night serial to become popular. "Dallas" finished in fifth place in the 1979-1980 season. It became the second dramatic series to become number one in the ratings (1980-1981 season) the first being "Marcus Welby M.D." It would also finish in first place during the 1981-1982 season. It dropped to second place in the 1982-1983 and returned to first place in the 1983-1984 season. In the 1984-1985 seasons it dropped to second place and finished in sixth place in the 1985-1986 season. In the 1986-1987 season, it finished in spot eleven. Between July 1980-December 1980, "Dallas" was ranked number one in the top fifty Neilson ratings for the episode "Who Shot JR?" The series ran 14 seasons and as of 1991 was ranked 10th out of the all-time top 100 series. "Dallas" became a hit in just about every nation but Japan. "Knots Landing" became a spinoff of "Dallas" and premiered on CBS on December 20, 1979. "Dallas" was Howard Keel's first TV series. His role as Clayton Farlow, father of Dusty Farlow (Jared Martin), came about after the death of Jim Davis (Jock Ewing). The producers wanted a strong older character to fill the void created by the death of Davis. The character was only to be for a couple of episodes but became so popular that Keel became a regular (in the 1981-1982 season) and eventually married Miss Ellie (Barbara Bel Geddes). During Miss Bel Geddes heart bypass operation and recovery, Donna Reed was brought in as a replacement for Bel Geddes during the 1984-1985 season. When the producers brought back Miss Bel Geddes, Donna Reed sued for breach of contract and won a seven-figure settlement.

Keel's appearances were only a few in the last season because Miss Bel Geddes left the series and the writers had him traveling with her making an occasional return to Southfork (minus Miss Ellie).

On the show, the Southern Cross, Clayton's ranch, was supposed to be in San Angelo but really was in Forney, Texas just a short distance from Southfork.

In the 1984-1985 season, Clayton and Miss Ellie became engaged in the episode "Barbecue Four."

"Dallas" was in production every week but Christmas week, although the cast was on hiatus from April 1 to June 1. On June 1, they reported to the MGM/Lorimar studio for interior shots and between mid June to mid August exterior shots were done in Dallas. During production, Sundays were the only days off.

Keel's co-star in MAN FROM BUTTON WILLOW, Dale Robertson, courted Miss Ellie but his character was short-lived.

Each season, twelve shows were done with 25 scenes each. A scene may have between 2-2½ pages of dialogue. Writers made about $16,000 per script. A red covered script was prepared for the production people while the cast used a yellow covered script. Colored rewrite pages were added as needed. Each script was confidential and really important ones like cliff-hangers were given to those only who needed them.

The cast did not know what was going to happen until

the script was in their hands. Directors and producers
gave the actors guidance because they were the only ones
who knew where the character was headed. It took seven
days, for the director and production people to prepare the
weeks show and seven days to shoot it. The director could
make $16,800 for the two weeks involved. The budget per
episode was about $1,000,000.

Some locations scenes were shot in Los Angeles.
Lorimar rented the J.M.J. ranch in Hidden Hills, California
which resembled Southfork. The typical day ran from 5:30
a.m. for some makeup. The crew reported at 7:18 a.m. and
shooting ran from 8 a.m. to 6-6:30 p.m. There was usually
one rehearsal and a walk-through for the camera and the
scenes were usually filmed twice.

They used a bank building to represent the Ewing
offices. Sound was usually added later through a process
called looping. A call-sheet was prepared the day before
about 3 p.m. telling the actor's who was needed for the
next day's shooting and which time and set. Actors
received between $5,000-$100,000 for each episode and were
paid only for the episodes they appeared in. If one of the
main characters directed an episode, they were paid an
additional $16,800. The temperature during shooting in
Dallas could go over 100 degrees.

Morgan Brittany was pregnant when her character,
Katherine Wentworth, was to kill Bobby. The hit-and-run
idea was chosen so she would be in the car thus hiding the
pregnancy.

When Victoria Principal underwent back surgery, a
kidnap idea was developed in case she would be out for a
long time. She returned to work quickly and the kidnapping
ended quickly.

When Jim Davis had cancer, the producers kept his
character alive to give him hope that he would return to
the show. They had him on a second honeymoon until they
knew what was going to happen. When he died, they killed
off his character with dignity by having him serving his
country.

The women on "Dallas" were scheduled to have an hour
for makeup, while the men were scheduled for a half-hour.
Victoria Principal decided what hairstyle she would wear.
As the men had the same skin coloring, they wore Blasco
Ruddy Beige #4 and most of the women wore Chanel Tawny
Beige. Between $5,000-$7,000 was spent yearly for makeup
which was purchased from Neiman-Marcus.

Designer Bill Travilla, who won an Emmy in 1984,
designed Marilyn Monroe's white halter dress for the film
THE SEVEN YEAR ITCH. Clothes were purchased at specialty
shops and there was an account with Neman-Marcus. The
average woman's outfit ran $1,000. All clothes, even those
custom made by the stars, remained the studio's property
and were stored in wardrobe housed in MGM's Barrymore
Building. At the end of the season, clothes no longer
needed were sold. Jack Blair handled the wardrobe for the
men. In films, the dressing rooms were on the set but on
"Dallas" they were not because the entire set was taken up
with scenery. All the men on "Dallas" had one dresser.

During the years, "Dallas" received a number of Emmy

Awards and nominations. In the 1978-1979 season, Barbara
Bel Geddes was nominated for Outstanding Lead Actress in a
Drama Series but lost to Mariette Hartly in "The Incredible
Hulk." Fred Berger was also nominated for Outstanding Film
Editing for a Series for the episode, "Dallas Reunion, Part
II" but the winner was Pam Blimenthal for "Taxi." The next
season (1979-1980), "Dallas" was nominated for Outstanding
Drama Series but "Lou Grant" was the winner. Larry Hagman
was also nominated for Outstanding Lead Actor in a Drama
Series but Ed Asner beat him for his character in "Lou
Grant." That year, Barbara Bel Geddes won an Emmy for
Outstanding Lead Actress in a Drama Series. Bruce
Broughton was nominated for Outstanding Music Composition
for a Series (Dramatic Underscore) for the episode "The
Lost Child." The winner was Patrick Williams for "Lou
Grant." In the 1980-1981 season, "Dallas" was nominated for
Outstanding Drama Series but lost to "Hill Street Blues."
Other nominations included Lead Actor in a Drama Series for
Jim Davis who lost to Daniel Travanti of "Hill Street
Blues." Linda Gray was also nominated for Lead Actress in a
Drama Series but Barbara Babcock won for "Hill Street
Blues." Bruce Broughton won an Emmy in the 1982-1983 season
for Outstanding Music Composition for a Drama Series
(Dramatic Underscore). He also won for the same category
during the 1983-1984 season. Bill Travilla won an Emmy for
Outstanding Costume Design for a Series during the 1984-1985
season. (See D54)

BC42. **LOVE BOAT**-"Maid For Each Other" (ABC, May 9, 1981)
9 p.m. 60 Minutes.

Theme: "The Love Boat" by Paul Williams & Charles
Fox. Sung by Jack Jones (1977-1985) and Dionne Warwick
(1985-1986). Regular Cast: Gavin MacLeod (Captain
Merrill Stubing); Bernie Kopell (Dr. Adam Bricker);
Fred Grandy (Burl "Gopher" Smith-Yeoman Purser); Ted
Lange (Isaac Washington-Bartender); Lauren Tewes
(Julie McCoy-Cruise Director); Jill Whelan (Vicki
Stubing). Guest Cast: **Howard Keel** (Daniel Harlow),
Jane Powell (Gopher's aunt).

SYNOPSIS: Although Gopher's aunt has lost her money, she
still pretends she is wealthy. Keel and Powell fall in
love.

COMMENTS: Various kinds of love stories were told weekly in
short comic skits and included guest stars.
       Real passengers were used as extras when filming was
done aboard The Pacific Princess or the Island Princess.
       Jeraldine Saunders wrote a novel The Love Boats based
on her experiences as a cruise hostess and it was this
novel from which the series drew its basis.

BC43. **FANTASY ISLAND**-"Nancy and the Thunderbirds" (ABC, May
1, 1982) 10 p.m. 60 Minutes.

Executive Producer: Aaron Spelling, Leonard Goldberg.
Theme: "Fantasy Island" by Laurence Rosenthal

Regular Cast: Ricardo Montalban (Mr. Roarke); Herve Villechaize (Tattoo); Wendy Schael (Julie). Guest Cast: **Howard Keel** (Colonel Kinross); John James (Corky); Patrick Wayne (Woody); Lydia Cornell (Judy); Tim Rossovich (Ben); Paul Cavonis (Charlie).

SYNOPSIS: One of the fantasies concerns Mary Ann Mobley who plays a skeptical woman who tries to carry out an ancient prophecy. A second fantasy involves a large bet which rides on whether a man can meet up with a centerfold model and how that meeting goes.

COMMENTS: People were brought to Fantasy Island where Mr. Roarke would grant them a life-long dream. Several stories were told each week. The show was filmed twenty-five miles from Los Angeles at Arboretum which was a park open to the public.

BC44. **LOVE BOAT** (ABC, 1983)-"Kiss and Make-Up" 9 p.m. 60 Minutes.

Theme: "The Love Boat" by Paul Williams & Charles Fox. Sung by Jack Jones (1977-1985) and Dionne Warwick (1985-1986). Regular Cast: Gavin MacLeod (Captain Merrill Stubing); Bernie Kopell (Dr. Adam Bricker); Fred Grandy (Burl "Gopher" Smith-Yeoman Purser); Ted Lange (Isaac Washington-Bartender); Lauren Tewes (Julie McCoy-Cruise Director); Jill Whelan (Vicki Stubing). Guest Cast: **Howard Keel** (Hal Cummings).

BC45. **SONG BY SONG BY IRVING BERLIN** (PBS, June 25, 1983)

Performers: David Kernan, Millicent Martin, Sheryl Kennedy, **Howard Keel**.

COMMENTS: This series originally premiered from 1978-1980. It premiered again on June 18, 1983, with "Song By Song By Johnny Mercer."

BC46. **LOVE BOAT**-"Long Time No Sea" (ABC, November 12, 1983) 9 p.m. 60 Minutes.

Theme: "The Love Boat" by Paul Williams & Charles Fox. Sung by Jack Jones (1977-1985) and Dionne Warwick (1985-1986). Regular Cast: Gavin MacLeod (Captain Merrill Stubing); Bernie Kopell (Dr. Adam Bricker); Fred Grandy (Burl "Gopher" Smith-Yeoman Purser); Ted Lange (Isaac Washington-Bartender); Lauren Tewes (Julie McCoy-Cruise Director); Jill Whelan (Vicki Stubing).

SYNOPSIS: A carnival owner (**Howard Keel**) is attracted to a young woman (Jan Smithers) and later discovers she is his daughter.

BC47. **ALL-STAR PARTY FOR FRANK SINATRA** (CBS, December 11, 1983) 8 p.m.

Guests: James Stewart, Carol Burnett, Florence
Henderson, **Howard Keel**, Michelle Lee, Dionne Warwick,
Bob Newhart, Foster Brooks, Ricardo Montalban, Julio
Iglesias, Burt Reynolds, Steve Lawrence, Vic Damone,
Richard Burton, Cary Grant.

COMMENTS: This tribute to Frank Sinatra was a benefit for
Variety Clubs International. Sinatra was honored for his
artistry and humanitarism at a black-tie affair in Burbank,
California. His career was recounted in songs and
speeches. Keel was part of the toasts and roasts.

BC48. 1985 ACADEMY AWARDS (ABC, March 24, 1986)

Hosts: Jane Fonda, Alan Alda, Robin Williams.

COMMENTS: The show was broadcast from the Dorothy Chandler
Pavilion in Los Angeles. Howard performed in a tribute to
MGM musicals and sang "Once a Star, Always a Star." Others
in the tribute included: June Allyson, Leslie Caron, Cyd
Charisse, Marge Champion, Kathryn Grayson, Jane Powell,
Debbie Reynolds, Anne Miller, and Esther Williams. The
production number was choreographed by Ron Field.

BC49. IRVING BERLIN'S AMERICA (1986)

BC50. FROM TAHITI BOB HOPE'S TROPICAL COMEDY SPECIAL (NBC,
February 23, 1987) 8 p.m. 60 Minutes.

Host: Bob Hope. Guests: John Denver, Morgan Brittany,
Howard Keel, Jonathan Winters, Susan Akim (Miss
America 1986), Miss Tahiti. Sponsor: Texaco.

COMMENTS: The show was taped in Tahiti and Moorea. A spoof
"Mutiny & the Bounty" had the following cast: Hope (Captain
Bligh), Denver (Fletcher Christian), Keel (the ship's
tipsy doctor), Brittany (a prim British missionary), and
Winters (a Polynesian king). While paddling on Moorea
Cook's Bay, the cast sing "Far Away Places," "A Slow Boat
to China," and "On Moonlight Bay." Keel also sang "Some
Enchanted Evening."

BC51. HOWARD KEEL AT THE ROYAL ALBERT HALL (British) (PBS,
June 10, 1990) 60 Minutes.

COMMENTS: **Howard Keel** sang "This Nearly Was Mine," "Some
Enchanted Evening," "Ol' Man River," songs from SHOW BOAT,
SEVEN BRIDES FOR SEVEN BROTHERS, MAN OF LA MANCHA, as well
as contemporary songs. The show had been taped in London
in 1987. PBS rebroadcast the show on December 2, 1990.
(See NC22)

BC52. GOOD SPORTS-"Bobby and Gayle Go on a Date" (CBS, June
22, 1991) 30 Minutes.

Creator: Alan Zweibel. Theme Song: "Good Sports" by
Andy Goldmark and sung by Al Green. Stars: Farrah
Fawcett (Gayle Roberts), Ryan O'Neal (Bobby

Tanner). <u>Regulars</u>: Lane Smith (Owner of Rappaport Broadcasting System); Brian Doyle-Murray (John Mac-Kinney); Cleavant Derricks (Jeff Mussberger); Paul Feig (Leash); Christine Dunford (Missy Van Johnson); Lois Smith (Mrs. Tanner, Bobby's mother); William Katt (Nick Calder). <u>Guest Stars</u>: **Howard Keel** (Gayle's father); Terry Pendleton (Himself); Rev. Mark Holsinger (Himself).

SYNOPSIS: After receiving her father's (Keel) approval of Bobby (O'Neal), Gayle (Fawcett) decides to date him.

COMMENTS: The show concerns an ex-model (Fawcett) who becomes a sportscaster on an All-Sports Cable Network run by Rappaport Broadcasting System. She ends up working with an ex-football star (O'Neal) with whom she had spent a romantic weekend (some twenty years before) while they were in college. Terry Pendleton played for the Atlanta Braves, and Rev. Mark Holsinger was from the Los Angeles Mission.

BC53. **HOWARD KEEL: CLOSE TO MY HEART** (PBS, August 9, 1991) 60 Minutes.

<u>Producer</u>: Land Thompham. <u>Director</u>: Gordon Elsby. <u>Star</u>: **Howard Keel**.

SONGS: "Bless Your Beautiful Hide," "Surrey with the Fringe on Top," "Rose Marie," "Secret Love," "There's No Business Like Show Business," "Music of the Night," "Oh What a Beautiful Morning," "So in Love," "Make Believe," "If I Loved You," "Wind Beneath My Wings," "Love Changes Everything," "Bring Him Home," "Colours of My Life."

COMMENTS: This non-stop song-fest by Keel was filmed at his California ranch and surrounding area. With each song there was a scene change. (See D28, V7)

BC54. **MURDER SHE WROTE** (CBS, November 24, 1991) 8 p.m. 60 Minutes.

<u>Creators</u>: Peter S. Fischer, Richard Levinson, William Link. <u>Executive Producers</u>: Peter S. Fischer, Richard Levinson, William Link. <u>Producer</u>: Robert F. O'Neil. <u>Music</u>: John Addison, David Bell. <u>Star</u>: Angela Lansbury (Jessica Beatrice Fletcher). <u>Regular Cast</u>: Tom Bosley (Sheriff Amos Tupper-1984-1988); William Windom (Dr. Seth Hazlitt); Ron Masak (Sheriff Mort Metzger from 1989); Alan Oppenheimer (Dr. Raymond Auerbach from 1991). <u>Guest Cast</u>: David Soul (Wes McSorley); **Howard Keel** (Larry Thorson); Amy O'Neill (Susan Hartley); Jeff Kaake (Eddie Wheaton); Stephen Macht (Frank Stinson); Joan McMurtrey (Alice Baxter); Shelley Smith (Katherine McSorley); Richard Portnow (Lt. Murphy); Bruce Gray (Ted Hartley).

SYNOPSIS: Jessica is at a Las Vegas hotel where she discovers that someone is cashing in the hotel manager's chips.

COMMENTS: The series concerns widow and famed mystery writer Jessica Fletcher (Lansbury) who ends up being a sleuth and helping solve murders. Beginning with the fall 1991 season, Jessica teaches a course in criminology at Manhattan University. She moves into an apartment in the city where she stays during the week and goes back to Cabot Cove on weekends.

This episode was to have aired on October 27, 1991, but was postponed because of the World Series.

BC55. BRUCE'S GUEST NIGHT (British) (BBC1, May 24, 1993)

Producer: John L. Spencer. Director: Kevin Bishop. Host: Bruce Forsyth. Guests: **Howard Keel**, Ronn Lucas (Ventriloquist).

COMMENTS: This British show was Mr. Forsyth's second group of programs that highlighted musical and comedy entertainers.

BC56. HART TO HART-"Home is Where the Hart Is" (NBC, February 18, 1994) 9 p.m. 120 Minutes.

Creator: Sidney Sheldon. Executive Producer: James Veres. Producers: James Polster, Stephanie Powers. Director: Pete Hunt. Writer: Lawrence Hertzog. Musical Director: Arthur Rubinstein. Stars: Robert Wagner (Jonathan Hart), Stephanie Powers (Jennifer Hart). Additional Cast: Lionel Stander (Max), Alan Young (Charley Loomis), **Howard Keel** (Captain Jack-Quintin Jackson), Maureen O'Sullivan (Eleanor Biddlecomb), Roddy McDowall (Jeremy Sennet), Mitchell Ryan (Chief Carson), Jack Kruscher (Major Trout), Tracey Ellis (Claire Stinson).

SYNOPSIS: An old friend of Jennifer Hart's, Eleanor Biddlecomb, owns the town of Kingman's Ferry and is planning to tear down the town museum and rebuild the water front but is killed in an automobile accident.

The Harts return to Kingman's Ferry (Jennifer's home town) to attend her funeral and learn that Eleanor has left Jennifer the town.

While investigating the strange goings-on in the town, with the help of Max and Charlie (a retired F.B.I. agent) the Harts discover that Eleanor and the major were killed by Captain Jack who is trying to prevent the restoration of the town as he is smuggling oil out of the cove and stands to lose millions.

Captain Jack is shot and killed by the Chief of Police while attempting to do away with the Harts and Max. The town is now booming because of the oil and Jennifer sells it back to the people for a dollar.

COMMENTS: This was the second of four "Hart to Hart's" to be aired during the 1993-1994 season as part of the "NBC Friday Night Mystery Movie." "Hart to Hart" originally appeared on ABC-TV between August 25, 1979 and July 31, 1984 and concerned wealthy Jonathan Hart who ran Hart

Industries and his journalist wife, Jennifer, who solved
mysteries with the help of their chauffeur, Max. They also
had a dog named Freeway.

Howard Keel in the 1947 London production of *Oklahoma!* Angus McBean photograph, Harvard Theatre Collection.

Howard Keel, Louis Calhern, and Betty Hutton in *Annie Get Your Gun*, 1950. Photograph courtesy of Milton Moore, Jr.

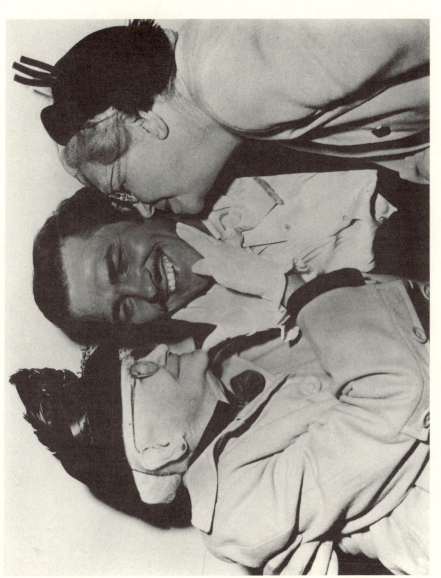

Grandma Osterkamp, Howard Keel, and his mother, Grace, on the set of *Show Boat*, 1951. Photograph courtesy of Milton Moore, Jr.

Kathryn Grayson and Howard Keel in the MGM film *Show Boat*, 1951. Photograph courtesy of Milton Moore, Jr.

Howard Keel in the MGM film *Kiss Me, Kate*, 1953. Photograph courtesy of Milton Moore, Jr.

Howard Keel and Jane Powell in the MGM film *Seven Brides for Seven Brothers*, 1954. Photograph courtesy of Photofest.

Host Ed Sullivan, Ann Miller, Howard Keel, Debbie Reynolds, Van Johnson, and Ann Blyth on CBS-TV's *Toast of the Town* "MGM Salute," February 14, 1954. Photograph courtesy of Photofest.

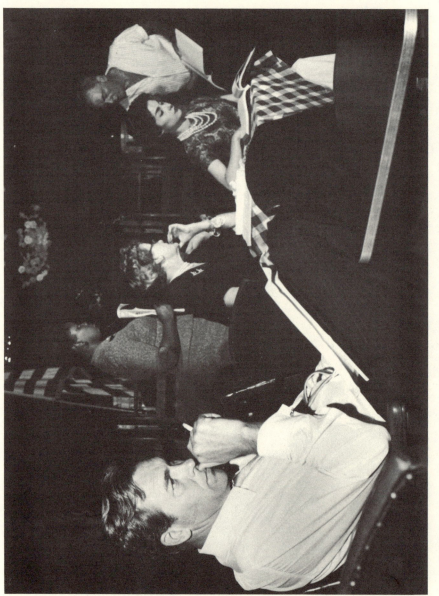

Howard Keel and Carol Lawrence rehearsing the Broadway show *Saratoga*, 1959. Photograph courtesy of Photofest.

Howard Keel and Barbara McNair in *No Strings*, 1963. Photograph courtesy of Milton Moore, Jr.

Linda Gray and Howard Keel in the CBS-TV series *Dallas* circa 1981. Photograph courtesy of Photofest.

6

DISCOGRAPHY

This chapter divides Mr. Keel's recordings into two
parts--45s and album's, cassettes, and CDs. Both parts are
arranged alphabetically. Where possible, for each
recording, the label and number, year, conductor, size,
various versions, songs by side (albums) with singers
performing with Keel are given. Charted and Gold records
are noted. For the charted records, date of charting,
length of charting, and highest position reached are given.
When a soundtrack or cast album is listed a cross reference
is made to the film or show.

45s

D 1. **AMERICAN DREAM**
   Hudson 1007
   March 1956

D 2. **ANNIE GET YOUR GUN**
   MGM K-50 (4-record set)
   1950
   with Betty Hutton

D 3. **I CAN DO WITHOUT YOU**
   Columbia 5-1777
   1953
   with Doris Day
      (From CALAMITY JANE)

D 4. **I'LL STAY WITH YOU FOR A LIFETIME**
   Warner Bros. 7-28827
   Date Unknown

D 5. **LOVELY TO LOOK AT**
   MGM K-150 (4-record set)
   1952
   with Kathryn Grayson

D 6. **LOVELY TO LOOK AT**
   THE MOST EXCITING NIGHT
   MGM 30591 (1952)

D 7. **PAGAN LOVE SONG**
MGM K64 (3-record set)
1950
with Esther Williams

D 8. **THE RIGHT GIRL FOR ME**
MGM 4078
1954

D 9. **ROSE MARIE**
THE RIGHT GIRL FOR ME
MGM 30840
1954

D10. **SEVEN BRIDES FOR SEVEN BROTHERS**
MGM X 244 (2-record set)
1954
with Jane Powell

D11. **SHOW BOAT**
MGM K-84 (4-record set)
1951
with Kathryn Grayson

D12. **THE TOUCH OF YOUR HAND**
YOU'RE DEVASTATING
MGM 30589
1952
with Kathryn Grayson
    (From LOVELY TO LOOK AT)

D13. **WHOA EMMA**
YOUNG FOLKS SHOULD GET MARRIED
MGM 30415
September 1951
    (From TEXAS CARNIVAL)

D14. **THE WORLD IS MINE TONIGHT**
MGM X-1068 (Extended Play)
1951

D15. **THE WORLD IS MINE TONIGHT**
MY MAGIC HEART
MGM 30378
1951
with conductor David Rose

ALBUMS/CASSETTES/CDs

D16. **AMBASSADOR**
RCA SER-5618 (British production)
12"-1971

with Gareth Davies conducting

    LAMBERT'S QUANDARY
    LILAS
    RIGHT TIME, RIGHT PLACE

```
SURPRISE
LILAS/WHAT HAPPENED TO PARIS?
YOUNG WITH HIM
TOO MUCH TO FORGIVE
THAT'S WHAT I NEED TONIGHT
GOSSIP
NOT TOMORROW
ALL MY LIFE
THANK YOU, NO
A MAN YOU CAN SET YOUR WATCH BY
IT'S A WOMAN
CHARMING
WHAT CAN YOU DO WITH A NUDE?
TELL HER
I THOUGHT I KNEW YOU
YOU CAN TELL A LADY BY HER HAT
THIS UTTERLY RIDICULOUS AFFAIR
```

NOTE: (See S27)

D17. AMBASSADOR OF SONG
MGM 2353042 (British)
12"

Howard Keel sings his greatest hits from ROSE MARIE
(1), ANNIE GET YOUR GUN (2), KISS ME, KATE (3), KISMET
(4), SEVEN BRIDES FOR SEVEN BROTHERS (5), and SHOW BOAT
(6).

Side One

```
ROSE MARIE (1)
MY DEFENSES ARE DOWN (2)
WHERE IS THE LIFE THAT LATE I LED (3)
WERE THINE THAT SPECIAL FACE (3)
I'VE COME TO WIVE IT WEALTHILY IN PADUA (3)
THE OLIVE TREE (4)
```

Side Two

```
BLESS YOUR BEAUTIFUL HIDE (5)
MAKE BELIEVE (6) with Kathryn Grayson
SOBBIN' WOMEN (5)
THE GIRL THAT I MARRY (2)
GESTICULATE (4)
SANDS OF TIME (4)
```

D18. AND I LOVE YOU SO
Warwick WW-45137 (British)
12"-1984 (Also on CD)

Side One

```
BLESS YOUR BEAUTIFUL HIDE
SEND IN THE CLOWNS
SO IN LOVE
YESTERDAY WHEN I WAS YOUNG
WHAT 50 SAID
```

```
THIS IS ALL I ASK
ROSEMARIE
MEMORY
SHOW BOAT MEDLEY:
    WHY DO I LOVE YOU
    MAKE BELIEVE
    OL' MAN RIVER
```

Side Two

```
IF
AND I LOVE YOU SO
SOFTLY AS I LEAVE YOU
BORN AGAIN
YOU WERE ALWAYS ON MY MIND
I'VE NEVER BEEN TO ME
ANNIE GET YOUR GUN MEDLEY:
    THE GIRL THAT I MARRY
    FALLING IN LOVE IS WONDERFUL
    MY DEFENSES ARE DOWN
```

NOTES: This album was released in the U.S.A. as WITH LOVE. In Britain it sold 100,000 copies in one week and reached the number 3 position on the British album charts and was right behind Michael Jackson's THRILLER and Lionel Richie's CAN'T SLOW DOWN. It hit the British charts on April 14, 1984, for nineteen weeks eventually going gold. (See D48)

D19. ANNIE GET YOUR GUN
MGM E-509 (10"-1950)
MGM EP-X50 (Extended Playing 45s-1950)
MGM E-3227 (12" Reissue-1955 with EASTER PARADE)
MGM E-3768 (12" Reissue-1960 with THREE LITTLE WORDS)
Metro M/MS-548 (12" Reissue-1965)
MGM 2SES-42ST (12" Reissue-1973 with SHOW BOAT)

with Betty Hutton, Louis Calhern, Keenan Wynn, and conductor Aldoph Deutsch

Side One

```
I'VE GOT THE SUN IN THE MORNING-Hutton
MY DEFENSES ARE DOWN-Keel
YOU CAN'T GET A MAN WITH A GUN-Hutton
THEY SAY IT'S WONDERFUL-Hutton, Keel
```

Side Two

```
THE GIRL THAT I MARRY-Keel
DOIN' WHAT COMES NATURALLY-Hutton
ANYTHING YOU CAN DO-Hutton, Keel
THERE'S NO BUSINESS LIKE SHOW BUSINESS
```

NOTES: MGM 509 appeared on the charts on June 2, 1950, and remained on the charts for twenty-seven weeks peaking at number 3. MGM 2 SES-42 (with SHOW BOAT) reached the charts on September 15, 1973, for a seven week charting and a peak position of one hundred eighty-five. (See F2, D2)

D20. **ANNIE GET YOUR GUN**
Sound/Stage 2302 (12")
Sandy Hook SH-2053 (12"-1981)
Sandy Hook Records C SH-2053 (Cassette-1981)

with Judy Garland, Howard Keel, Keenan Wynn, Benay
Venuta, Frank Morgan, conductor Adolph Deutsch, with
vocal arrangement by Roger Edens

Side One

COLONEL BUFFALO BILL-Wynn, Venuta, Keel
DOIN' WHAT COMES NATUPALLY-Garland
THE GIRL THAT I MARRY-Keel
YOU CAN'T GET A MAN WITH A GUN-Garland
THERE'S NO BUSINESS LIKE SHOW BUSINESS-Wynn,
    Morgan, Keel, Garland
THEY SAY IT'S WONDERFUL-Garland, Keel
THEY SAY IT'S WONDERFUL (Reprise)-Garland

Side Two

THERE'S NO BUSINESS LIKE SHOW BUSINESS (Reprise)-
    Garland
MY DEFENSES ARE DOWN-Keel
I'M AN INDIAN TOO-Garland
THE GIRL THAT I MARRY (Reprise)-Garland
I GOT THE SUN IN THE MORNING-Garland
LET'S GO WEST AGAIN-Garland
ANYTHING YOU CAN DO-Garland, Keel
THERE'S NO BUSINESS LIKE SHOW BUSINESS-Garland,
    Morgan, Keel, Wynn

NOTES: This recording was made before Hutton replaced
Garland and had never previously been released. The song
"Let's Go West Again" was written by Berlin especially for
Garland and was dropped from the film when Garland left.
The Sound/Stage version was a limited release for the
Garland Fan Club. (See F2)

D21. **THE BEST OF HOWARD KEEL**
Success (CD) 16176CD (1993) (British)

HELLO
OH WHAT A BEAUTIFUL MORNING
THE WAY WE WERE
OKLAHOMA!
PEOPLE WILL SAY WE'RE IN LOVE
YESTERDAY WHEN I WAS YOUNG
SOME ENCHANTED EVENING
THE IMPOSSIBLE DREAM
I WON'T LAST A DAY WITHOUT YOU
BLESS YOUR BEAUTIFUL HIDE
THE SURREY WITH THE FRINGE ON TOP
SOMETIMES WHEN WE TOUCH
TO ALL THE GIRLS I'VE LOVED BEFORE
LOVE THE WORLD AWAY
MEMORY

OL' MAN RIVER
SOMEWHERE MY LOVE

D22. CALAMITY JANE
Columbia CL-6273 (10"-1953)
Columbia EP B-347 (Extended Playing 45s-1953)
Columbia Special Products P-19611 (Reissue-February
1987 with I'LL SEE YOU IN MY DREAMS)
Columbia Special Products M/P-19611 (CD version with
I'LL SEE YOU IN MY DREAMS)
CBS 4676102 (with PAJAMA GAME) (British)

with Doris Day, Howard Keel, and conductor Ray
Heindorf

DEADWOOD STAGE-Day
I CAN DO WITHOUT YOU-Day, Keel
THE BLACK HILLS OF DAKOTA-Day
JUST BLEW IN FROM THE WINDY CITY-Day
A WOMAN'S TOUCH-Day
HIGHER THAN A HAWK-Keel
TIS HARRY I'M PLANNIN' TO MARRY-Day
SECRET LOVE-Day

NOTES: Columbia 6273 reached the charts on January 23, 1954
peaking at number three and remaining charted for eighteen
weeks. (See F14, D3, D55)

D23. DEEP IN MY HEART
MGM E-3153 (Boxed set-1954)
MGM EP X-276 (Extended Playing 45s-1954)
MGM 2-SES-54 ST (12"-1973 with WORDS & MUSIC)
MCA Records MCA-5949 (Reissue-February 1987 with WORDS
AND MUSIC)
MCA Records MCAC 5949 (CS-1987)-with WORDS & MUSIC
MCA Records MCAD 5949 (CD-1987)-with WORDS & MUSIC
Sony Music Special Products (CS-1991) AT47703
Sony Music Special Products (CD-1991) AK47703

with Jose Ferrer, Rosemary Clooney, Helen Traubel, Gene
Kelly, Fred Kelly, Jane Powell, Vic Damone, Anne
Miller, Cyd Charisse, Tony Martin, William Olvis,
Howard Keel, James Mitchell and conductor Adolph
Deutsch

Side One

OVERTURE
LEG OF MUTTON-Ferrer, Traubel
YOUR LAND AND MY LAND-Keel
YOU WILL REMEMBER VIENNA-Traubel
IT-Miller
AUF WIEDERSEHN-Traubel
SERENADE-Olvis

Side Two

SOFTLY AS IN A MORNING SUNRISE-Traubel

ROAD TO PARADISE-Damone
WILL YOU REMEMBER-Powell, Damone
MR. AND MRS.-Ferrer, Clooney
I LOVE TO GO SWIMMIN'-Gene & Fred Kelly
LOVER COME BACK TO ME-Martin, Joan Weldon
STOUT HEARTED MEN-Traubel
ONE ALONE-Carol Richards (for Charisse), Mitchell
WHEN I GROW TOO OLD TO DREAM-Ferrer

NOTES: MGM 3153 reached the charts on January 22, 1955, for
fifteen weeks peaking at number four. Songs appearing on
the Sony CD that were not on the LP were "Softly, As in a
Morning Sunrise" (with Betty Wand for Tamara Toumanova);
"Girls Goodbye" (with Ferrer); "Fat Fat Fatima" (Ferrer);
and "Jazza-Dada-Doo" (Ferrer). (See F18)

D24. AN ENCHANTED EVENING WITH HOWARD KEEL
   Music Collection Int. MCCD006 (CD-1991) (British)

   OKLAHOMA! MEDLEY:
      OH WHAT A BEAUTIFUL MORNING
      SURREY WITH THE FRINGE ON TOP
      PEOPLE WILL SAY WE'RE IN LOVE
      OKLAHOMA!
   SOME ENCHANTED EVENING
      (From SOUTH PACIFIC)
   THIS NEARLY WAS MINE
      (From SOUTH PACIFIC)
   I WON'T SEND ROSES
      (From MACK & MABEL)
   IF EVER I WOULD LEAVE YOU
      (From CAMELOT)
   LA MANCHA MEDLEY:
      DON QUIXOTE
      DULCINEA
      THE IMPOSSIBLE DREAM
   YOU NEEDED ME
   LOVE STORY
   COME IN FROM THE RAIN
   YESTERDAY
   SOMETHING
   ONCE UPON A TIME
   WHAT ARE YOU DOING THE REST OF YOUR LIFE
   WAVE
   MacARTHUR PARK
   SEND IN THE CLOWNS
   YOU WERE ALWAYS ON MY MIND
   I'VE NEVER BEEN TO ME
   ANNIE GET YOUR GUN MEDLEY:
      THE GIRL THAT I MARRY
      FALLING IN LOVE IS WONDERFUL
      MY DEFENSES ARE DOWN

NOTE: This CD is also available on cassette.

D25. FILM & MUSICAL FAVORITES
   LaserLight 15 093 (Germany)

```
DALLAS-Instrumental
BLESS YOUR BEAUTIFUL HIDE
SHOW BOAT MEDLEY:
    WHY DO I LOVE YOU
    MAKE BELIEVE
    OLD MAN RIVER
MEMORY
ANNIE GET YOUR GUN MEDLEY:
    THE GIRL THAT I MARRY
    THEY SAY IT'S WONDERFUL
    MY DEFENSES ARE DOWN
ROSE MARIE
OKLAHOMA! MEDLEY:
    OH WHAT A BEAUTIFUL MORNING
    SURREY WITH THE FRINGE ON TOP
    PEOPLE WILL SAY WE'RE IN LOVE
    OKLAHOMA!
SOME ENCHANTED EVENING
THIS NEARLY WAS MINE
IF EVER I WOULD LEAVE YOU
LA MANCHA MEDLEY:
    DON QUIXOTE
    DULCINEA
    THE IMPOSSIBLE DREAM
COME IN FROM THE RAIN
WHAT ARE YOU DOING THE REST OF YOUR LIFE
WAVE
```

NOTE: This CD is also available on cassette.

D26. GENERAL MOTORS FIFTIETH ANNIVERSARY SHOW
RCA LOC-1037 (TV)
12"-1957

with Pat Boone, Steve Lawrence, Dan Dailey, Carol
Burnett, Cyril Richard, Claudia Crawford, Doretta
Morrow, Dinah Shore, Howard Keel, and conductor
Bernard Green

```
HAPPINESS THEME-Orchestra
WHERE ARE YOU-Boone
FAR AWAY PLACES-Lawrence
THE BULL FROG PATROL-Lawrence, Dailey, Burnett
MUTUAL ADMIRATION SOCIETY-Ritchard, Crawford
HI LILI HI LO-Morrow
MEDLEY-Shore, Morrow, Dailey, Keel
THESE FOOLISH THINGS-Shore
MEDLEY-Morrow, Keel
FINALE-Shore, Dailey
```

NOTE: (See BC10)

D27. THE GREAT MGM STARS
MGM/EMI CD 7958582 (CD & Cassette-1991) (British)

```
BLESS YOUR BEAUTIFUL HIDE
SOBBIN' WOMEN-with Brothers
```

WHEN YOU'RE IN LOVE-with Jane Powell
   (From SEVEN BRIDES FOR SEVEN BROTHERS)
YOUR LAND IS MY LAND
   (From DEEP IN MY HEART)
ROSE MARIE
THE RIGHT PLACE FOR A GIRL
MOUNTIES
   (From ROSE MARIE)
MAKE BELIEVE-with Kathryn Grayson
YOU ARE LOVE-with Kathryn Grayson
WHY DO I LOVE YOU-with Kathryn Grayson
   (From SHOW BOAT)
AND THIS IS MY BELOVED-with Ann Blyth, Vic Damone
   (From KISMET)
LOVELY TO LOOK AT
YOU'RE DEVASTATING
LAFAYETTE-with Red Skelton, Gower Champion
   (From LOVELY TO LOOK AT)
PAGAN LOVE SONG
HOUSE OF SINGING BAMBOO
   (From PAGAN LOVE SONG)
SO IN LOVE-with Kathryn Grayson
WE OPEN IN VENICE-with Kathryn Grayson, Ann Miller,
   Tommy Rall
WERE THINE THAT SPECIAL FACE
WUNDERBAR-with Kathryn Grayson
I'VE COME TO WIVE IT WEALTHILY IN PADUA
WHERE IS THE LIFE THAT LATE I LED
KISS ME, KATE
   (From KISS ME, KATE)

D28. HOWARD KEEL: CLOSE TO MY HEART
Music For Pleasure CDM 795486 2 (CD-1990) (British)
Music For Pleasure 795846 4 (CS-1990) (British)

THERE'S NO BUSINESS LIKE SHOW BUSINESS
OH WHAT A BEAUTIFUL MORNING
SECRET LOVE
SURREY WITH THE FRINGE ON TOP
IF I LOVED YOU
BLESS YOUR BEAUTIFUL HIDE
WIND BENEATH MY WINGS
ROSE MARIE
SO IN LOVE
MAKE BELIEVE
LOVE CHANGES EVERYTHING
BRING HIM HOME
MUSIC OF THE NIGHT
COLOURS OF MY LIFE

NOTE: (See BC53, V7)

D29. HOWARD KEEL-A SELECTION OF HIS SCREEN SUCCESSES
MGM D 146
10"

with the MGM Studio Orchestra & Chorus

Side One

ROSE MARIE
(From ROSE MARIE with George Stoll conducting)
MY DEFENSES ARE DOWN
(From ANNIE GET YOUR GUN with Adolph Deutsch
conducting)
WHERE IS THE LIFE THAT LATE I LED?
(From KISS ME, KATE with Andre Previn conducting)
WERE THINE THAT SPECIAL FACE
(From KISS ME, KATE with Andre Previn conducting)
I'VE COME TO WIVE IT WEALTHILY IN PADUA
(From KISS ME, KATE with Andre Previn conducting)

Side Two

BLESS YOUR BEAUTIFUL HIDE
(From SEVEN BRIDES FOR SEVEN BROTHERS with
Adolph Deutsch conducting)
PAGAN LOVE SONG
(From PAGAN LOVE SONG with Adolph Deutsch
conducting)
SOBBIN' WOMEN
(From SEVEN BRIDES FOR SEVEN BROTHERS with
Adolph Deutsch conducting
THE GIRL THAT I MARRY
(From ANNIE GET YOUR GUN with Adolph Deutsch
conducting)
SANDS OF TIME
(From KISMET with Andre Previn conducting)

D30. JUST FOR YOU
Telstar TCD 2318 (British)
(CD-1988)

Produced by James Fitzgerald, Arranger/Conductor:
George Ennis, * Arranged by Gordon Goodwin

HELLO
WHAT I DID FOR LOVE
FEELINGS*
CYCLES
I WON'T LAST A DAY WITHOUT YOU*
BOTH SIDES NOW*
I JUST CALLED TO SAY I LOVE YOU*
WITH YOU I'M BORN AGAIN*
JUST THE WAY YOU ARE*
SOMETIMES WHEN WE TOUCH
THE WAY WE WERE*
TO ALL THE GIRLS I LOVED BEFORE
LOVE THE WORLD AWAY
LADY
TIME IN A BOTTLE
THE LAST FAREWELL

NOTES: It reached the British albumn charts on May 28, 1988
where it stayed for five weeks peaking at 51. This CD is
also available on cassette.

D31. KISMET
MGM E 3281 (10"-1955)
MGM EP X-3281 (Extended Playing 45s-1955)
Metro M/MS 526 (12"-1965)
MCA Records MCA-1424 (Reissue-1986)
MCA Records MCAC-1424 (CS-1986)
MCA Records MCAD-1424 (CD-1986)
CBS Special Products (CS-1990) AT45393
CBS Special Products (CD-1990) AK45393

with Ann Blyth, Dolores Gray, Vic Damone, and
conductor Andre Previn

Side One

FATE-Keel
NOT SINCE NINEVEH-Gray
BAUBLE, BANGLES AND BEADS-Blyth
STRANGER IN PARADISE-Blyth, Damone
GESTICULATE-Keel

Side Two

NIGHT OF MY NIGHTS-Damone
BORED-Gray
THE OLIVE TREE-Keel
AND THIS IS MY BELOVED-Keel, Blyth, Damone
SANDS OF TIME-Keel

NOTES: Songs appearing on the CBS Special Products CD and
cassette but not on the LP were: "Baghdad," "Rhymes Have
I," "Fate"-Reprise, (Keel), "Dance of the Three Princesses
(Not Since Nineveh)," "The Caliph Sees Marsinah," "What
Does a Poet Need?," "Wazir's Palace," "Rahadlakum" (Keel,
Gray), "Dance of the Wifely Aspirants," "Dance in the
Bazaar." (See F20)

D32. KISS ME, KATE
RCA LPM/LSP-1984
12"-1959

with Gogi Grant, Anne Jeffreys, and conductor Henri
Rene

Side One

ANOTHER OPENING, ANOTHER SHOW-Grant, Keel, Jeffreys
WHY CAN'T YOU BEHAVE-Grant
WUNDERBAR-Keel, Jeffreys
SO IN LOVE-Grant, Keel
TOM, DICK, OR HARRY-Grant
WE OPEN IN VENICE-Grant, Keel, Jeffreys

Side Two

TOO DARN HOT-Grant, Keel, Jeffreys
I'VE COME TO WIVE IT WEALTHILY IN PADUA-Keel
ALWAYS TRUE TO YOU IN MY FASHION-Grant

> WERE THINE THAT SPECIAL FACE-Keel
> BRUSH UP YOUR SHAKESPEARE-Grant, Keel, Jeffreys
> I HATE MEN-Jeffreys
> WHERE IS THE LIFE THAT LATE I LED?-Keel

D33. KISS ME, KATE
MGM E-3077 (1953)
Metro M/MS 525 (Reissue 12"-1965)
MGM 2 SES-44ST (12"-1973 with BAND WAGON)
MCA Records MCA-25003 (1987)
MCA Records MCAC-25003 (CS-1987)
MCA Records MCAD-25003 (CD-1987)
CBS Special Products (CS-1990) AT46196
CBS Special Products (CD-1990) AK46196

with Howard Keel, Kathryn Grayson, Ann Miller, Bobby
Van, Tommy Rall, Keenan Wynn, James Whitemore, Carol
Haney, Bob Fosse, Kurt Kasznar, and the MGM Studio
Orchestra with conductor Andre Previn

Side One

> TOO DARN HOT-Miller
> SO IN LOVE-Grayson, Keel
> WE OPEN IN VENICE-Grayson, Keel, Miller, Rall
> WHY CAN'T YOU BEHAVE-Miller, Rall
> WERE THINE THAT SPECIAL FACE-Keel
> TOM, DICK, OR HARRY-Miller, Van, Rall, Fosse
> WUNDERBAR-Grayson, Keel

Side Two

> ALWAYS TRUE TO YOU IN MY FASHION-Miller, Rall
> I HATE MEN-Grayson
> I'VE COME TO WIVE IT WEALTHILY IN PADUA-Keel
> FROM THIS MOMENT ON-Miller, Rall, Van, Fosse, Haney
> WHERE IS THE LIFE THAT LATE I LED?-Keel
> BRUSH UP YOUR SHAKESPEARE-Whitemore, Wynn
> KISS ME KATE-Grayson, Keel

NOTES: Songs on the CBS Special Products CD and cassette but
not on the LP were: "So in Love"-Reprise (Grayson), "Tale
of the Merchant" (Keel, Kasznar, Miller, Fosse, Van, Rall,
Grayson). (See F15)

D34. LIVE IN CONCERT
Pickwick Music-PWKS 860 (CD-1991) (British)
Pickwick Music-HSC 860 (CS-1991) (British)

with Producer: James Fitzgerald, Musical Director:
Richard Holmes and Arrangers: George Annis, Bruce
Miller

> OVERTURE
> DON QUIXOTE
> DULCINEA
> BLESS YOUR BEAUTIFUL HIDE
> WHY DO I LOVE YOU

```
YESTERDAY WHEN I WAS YOUNG
WHEN I WAS 50 (Robert Frost Poem)
THIS IS ALL I ASK
OKLAHOMA! MEDLEY:
    OH WHAT A BEAUTIFUL MORNING
    SURREY WITH THE FRINGE ON TOP
    PEOPLE WILL SAY WE'RE IN LOVE
    OKLAHOMA!
TRIBUTE TO MY LEADING LADIES:
    TO ALL THE GIRLS I'VE LOVED BEFORE
    THEY SAY IT'S WONDERFUL
    MY DEFENSES ARE DOWN
    WHY DO I LOVE YOU
    MAKE BELIEVE
    SO IN LOVE
    BLESS YOUR BEAUTIFUL HIDE
    WHEN YOU'RE IN LOVE
    SOBBIN' WOMEN
MAN OF LA MANCHA MEDLEY:
    DON QUIXOTE
    DULCINEA
    THE IMPOSSIBLE DREAM
I WON'T SEND ROSES
WUNDERBAR
WHERE IS THE LIFE THAT LATE I LED
SOME ENCHANTED EVENING
SEND IN THE CLOWNS
MEMORY
OL' MAN RIVER
SOFTLY AS I LEAVE YOU
MEMORY (Orchestra)
```

NOTES: This album was recorded live at the Theatre Royal in Norwich, England in 1989. Mr. Fitzgerald is Mr. Keel's personal manager. (See NC25)

D35. LOVELY TO LOOK AT
```
MGM E-150 (10'-1952)
MGM E-3230 (12'-1955 with SHOW BOAT)
MGM 2-SES-50ST (12'-1973 with BRIGADOON)
MCA Records MCA-39084 (12' with SUMMER STOCK)
MCA Records MCAC-39084 (CS)
MCA Records MCAD-39084 (CD)
Sony Music Special Products (CS-1991) AT47027
Sony Music Special Products (CD-1991) AK47027
```

with Kathryn Grayson, Red Skelton, Marge and Gower Champion, Ann Miller, and the MGM Studio Orchestra & Chorus under the direction of Carmon Dragon

Side One

```
LAFAYETTE-Skelton, Keel, Gower Champion
SMOKE GETS IN YOUR EYES-Grayson
I WON'T DANCE-Marge & Gower Champion
YOU'RE DEVASTATING-Grayson, Keel
```

Side Two

    YESTERDAYS-Grayson
    LOVELY TO LOOK AT-Keel
    THE MOST EXCITING NIGHT-Keel
    I'LL BE HARD TO HANDLE-Miller
    THE TOUCH OF YOUR HAND-Grayson, Keel

NOTES: MGM E-150 hit the charts on July 4, 1952, and reached
spot number two remaining charted for nineteen weeks. (See
F9, D5, D6)

D36. **OKLAHOMA!/ANNIE GET YOUR GUN/CAROUSEL**
    World Records SH-393 (1947)
    Encore's Box Office ENBO-CD #5/92 (CD-1992)

    Howard Keel is only in OKLAHOMA! with Jane Watson,
    Dorothea MacFarland, Walter Donahue, Mary Marlo, Henry
    Clarke, Mark Windheim, William McCarthy, and conductor
    Reginald Burston

        OH WHAT A BEAUTIFUL MORNING-Keel
        THE SURREY WITH THE FRINGE ON TOP-Keel, Marlo
        KANSAS CITY-Donahue, Marlo
        I CAN'T SAY NO-MacFarland
        MANY A NEW DAY-Watson
        IT'S A SCANDAL! IT'S AN OUTRAGE!-Windheim
        PEOPLE WILL SAY WE'RE IN LOVE-Keel, Watson
        PORE JUD IS DEAD-Keel, Clark
        OUT OF MY DREAMS-Watson
        THE FARMER AND THE COWMAN-McCarthy, Marlo, Keel,
            Watson, MacFarland
        ALL OR NOTHING AT ALL-Donahue, MacFarland
        OKLAHOMA!-Keel, Watson, Marlo

NOTES: The CD is entitled AMERICANS IN LONDON 1947-1951 with
London cast recordings of the three shows plus ZIP GOES A
MILLION. (See S8)

D37. **OKLAHOMA!/ANNIE GET YOUR GUN**
    Stanyan SR-10069
    (1947)

NOTES: Keel appears on the OKLAHOMA! side only. The
recording is the same as the above without "It's a Scandal!,
It's an Outrage!" (See S8, D36)

D38. **PAGAN LOVE SONG**
    MGM E-534 (10"-1950)
    MGM EP K-64 (Extended Playing 45s 3-record set-1950)
    MGM 2 SES-43ST (12"-1973 with THE PIRATE and HIT THE
        DECK)
    MCA Records MCA-39080 (12" with THE PIRATE)
    MCA Records MCAC-39080 (CS-with THE PIRATE)
    MCA Records MCAD-39080 (CD-with THE PIRATE)

    with Esther Williams and conductor Adolph Deutsch

Side One

    PAGAN LOVE SONG-Keel
    SEA OF THE MOON-Williams
    WHY IS LOVE SO CRAZY-Keel

Side Two

    TAHITI-Keel
    SINGING IN THE SUN-Williams, Keel
    HOUSE OF THE SINGING BAMBOO-Keel

NOTE: (See F3, D7)

D39. REMINISCING WITH HOWARD KEEL-HIS STAGE & SCREEN FAVORITES
Telstar Star 2259 (British)
Silver Eagle Records TLS-2259 (2 record set)
Telstar Records TCD 2259 (CD-1985) This CD is also available on cassette.

    OKLAHOMA! MEDLEY:
        OH WHAT A BEAUTIFUL MORNING
        SURREY WITH THE FRINGE ON TOP
        PEOPLE WILL SAY WE'RE IN LOVE
        OKLAHOMA!
    SOME ENCHANTED EVENING
    THIS NEARLY WAS MINE
    I WON'T SEND ROSES
    IF EVER I WOULD LEAVE YOU
    LA MANCHA MEDLEY:
        DON QUIXOTE
        DULCINEA
        IMPOSSIBLE DREAM
    YOU NEEDED ME
    LOVE STORY
    COME IN FROM THE RAIN
    YESTERDAY
    SOMETHING
    ONCE UPON A TIME
    WHAT ARE YOU DOING THE REST OF YOUR LIFE
    WAVE
    MacARTHUR PARK

NOTES: Telstar Star 2259 hit the British Album charts on November 9, 1985, for twelve weeks and a peak position of 20. It sold 250,000 in one week and eventually went gold.

D40. ROSE MARIE
MGM E-229 (10"-1954)
MGM EP K-229 (Extended Playing 45s-1954)
MGM E-3228 (1955 with MERRY WIDOW)
MGM E-3769 1960 with SEVEN BRIDES FOR SEVEN BROTHERS)
Metro M/MS 616 (12"-1967)
MGM 2 SES-42ST (12"-1973 with SEVEN BRIDES FOR SEVEN BOTHERS)
MCA Records MCA-25009 (12" Reissue-December 1987)
MCA Records MCAC-25009 (CS-December 1987)

MCA Records MCAD-25009 (CD-December 1987)

with Howard Keel, Ann Blyth, Bert Lahr, Majorie Main, Fernando Lamas, and conductor George Stoll

Side One (MGM E-229)

    THE RIGHT PLACE FOR A GIRL-Keel
    FREE TO BE FREE-Blyth
    LOVE AND KISSES-Lahr, Main
    INDIAN LOVE CALL-Blyth, Lamas

Side Two (MGM E-229)

    ROSE MARIE-Keel
    I'M A MOUNTIE WHO NEVER GOT HIS MAN-Lahr
    I HAVE THE LOVE-Blyth, Lamas
    MOUNTIES-Keel

NOTES: MGM E-229 became charted on April 17, 1954, for sixteen weeks peaking at number 4. (See F16)

D41. SARATOGA
    RCA LOC/LSO-1051
    12"-1959

with Carol Lawrence, Odette Myrtil, Carol Brice, and conductor Jerry Arlen

Side One

    ONE STEP, TWO STEP-Myrtil
    I'LL BE RESPECTABLE-Lawrence
    GETTIN' A MAN-Brice, Myrtil
    WHY FIGHT THIS-Keel, Lawrence
    PETTICOAT HIGH-Lawrence
    A GAME OF POKER-Keel, Lawrence
    LOVE HELD LIGHTLY/A GAME OF POKER-Myrtil

Side Two

    SARATOGA DUET-Keel, Lawrence
    COUNTIN' OUR CHICKENS-Keel, Lawrence
    YOU OR NO ONE-Keel
    THE CURE
    THE MAN IN MY LIFE-Lawrence
    THE MEN WHO RUN THE COUNTRY-Keel
    GOOSE NEVER BE A PEACOCK-Brice
    DOG EAT DOG/THE RAILROAD FIGHT
    FINALE

NOTE: (See S6)

D42. SEVEN BRIDES FOR SEVEN BROTHERS
    MGM E-244 (10"-1954)
    MGM EP X-244 (Extended Playing 45s-1954)
    MGM E-3235 (1955 with ROYAL WEDDING)
    MGM E-3769 (with ROSE MARIE)

MGM 2 SES-41ST (12"-1973 with ROSE MARIE)
MCA Records MCA-25021
MCA Records MCA-20021 (12"-1986)
MCA Records MCAD-6176 (CD-1986)
MCA Records MCAC-20021 (CS-1986)
MCA Records MCAD-20021 (CD-1986)
Sony Music Special Products (CS-1992) AT52422
Sony Music Special Products (CD-1992) AK52422

with Howard Keel, Jane Powell, Bill Lee, Virginia
Gibson, and conductor Adolph Deutsch

Side One

   BLESS YOUR BEAUTIFUL HIDE-Keel
   WONDERFUL, WONDERFUL DAY-Powell
   GOIN' CO'TIN'-Powell, Brothers
   SOBBIN' WOMEN-Keel, Brothers

Side Two

   SPRING, SPRING, SPRING-Brothers, Girls
   LONESOME POLECAT-Bill Lee, Brothers
   JUNE BRIDE-Gibson, Girls
   WHEN YOU'RE IN LOVE-Powell, Keel

NOTES: MGM E-244 hit the charts on September 4, 1954, for a
peak position of three and a charting of sixteen weeks.
The Sony CD and cassette contained the following songs not
appearing on the LP: "When You're in Love"-Powell, "The
Barn Dance-(Bless Your Beautiful Hide)"-Orchestra, "When
You're in Love"-Keel. (See F17)

D43. **SHOW BOAT**
   MGM E-559 (10"-1951)
   MGM E-3230 (1955 with LOVELY TO LOOK AT)
   MGM E-3767 (1959 with AN AMERICAN IN PARIS)
   Metro M/MS-527 (12"-1965)
   MGM 2 SES-42ST (12"-1973 with ANNIE GET YOUR GUN)
   MCA Records MCA-1439
   MCA Records MCAC-1439 (CS)
   MCA Records MCAD-1439 (CD)
   CBS Special Products (CS-1990) AT45436
   CBS Special Products (CD-1990) AK45436

   with William Warfield, Kathryn Grayson, Marge & Gower
   Champion, Ava Gardner, Annette Warren, and conductor
   Adolph Deutsch

Side One

   OL' MAN RIVER-Warfield
   MAKE BELIEVE-Grayson, Keel
   I MIGHT FALL BACK ON YOU-Marge & Gower Champion
   CAN'T HELP LOVIN' DAT MAN-Gardner

Side Two

WHY DO I LOVE YOU-Grayson, Keel
BILL-Gardner
LIFE UPON THE WICKED STAGE-Marge & Gower Champion
YOU ARE LOVE-Grayson, Keel
OL' MAN RIVER (Reprise)-Warfield

NOTES: The following songs appear on the CBS Special
Products CD and cassette but not on the LP: "Cotton Blossom"
(Orchestra, Chorus), "Frank & Ellie" (Orchestra, Chorus),
"Where's the Mate for Me" (Keel), "Can't Help Lovin' Dat
Man" (Warren), "Can't Help Lovin Dat Man"-Reprise (Grayson,
Gardner), "Bill" (Warren), "After the Ball" (Grayson), "Kim"
(Orchestra), "Buck & Wing" (Orchestra), "Make Believe"-
Reprise (Keel), "Ol' Man River"-Finale (Warfield, Chorus).
MGM E-559 reached the charts on July 13, 1951, hitting the
number one spot and remaining on the charts for sixty-one
weeks. (See F5)

D44. SHOW BOAT
RCA LOP/LSO-1505
(12"-1958)

with Anne Jeffreys, Gogi Grant, and conductor Henri
Rene

Side One

MAKE BELIEVE-Keel, Jeffreys
OL' MAN RIVER-Keel
CAN'T HELP LOVIN'DAT MAN-Grant
I HAVE THE ROOM ABOVE-Keel
NOBODY ELSE BUT ME-Grant

Side Two

WHERE'S THE MATE FOR ME-Keel
TILL GOOD LUCK COMES MY WAY-Keel
YOU ARE LOVE-Keel, Jeffreys
WHY DO I LOVE YOU-Keel, Jeffreys
BILL-Grant
AFTER THE BALL-Jeffreys

D45. THAT'S ENTERTAINMENT!
MCA 2-11002
(12"-1974)

2-record set featuring Selections from MGM Musicals

Song by Keel

MAKE BELIEVE-with Kathryn Grayson

NOTE: (See F5)

D46. THAT'S ENTERTAINMENT, PART 2
MGM MG 1-5301 (12"-1976)

Sony Music Special Products (CS) A 2T46872
Sony Music Special Products (CD) A 2K46872

More selections from MGM Musicals

Song by Keel

> THERE'S NO BUSINESS LIKE SHOW BUSINESS-with Betty
> Hutton, Keenan Wynn, and Louis Calhern

NOTE: (See F2)

D47, THAT'S ENTERTAINMENT! III
Angel CDQ 5 55215 2 1 (CD-1994)

Song by Keel

> ANYTHING YOU CAN DO-with Betty Hutton

NOTES: This CD is the soundtrack from the movie and is
produced by Joel Moss and Marc Shaiman with the Hollywood
Bowl Orchestra under the direction of John Mauceri. (See
F30, V20)

D48. WITH LOVE
Silver Eagle Records SE-1026 (12"-1984)

with arrangers: George Annis (1), Bruce Miller (2),
Wayne Parker (3)

Side One

> SO IN LOVE (1)
> ANNIE GET YOUR GUN MEDLEY:(1)
>> THE GIRL THAT I MARRY
>> THEY SAY IT'S WONDERFUL
>> MY DEFENSES ARE DOWN
> ROSE MARIE (2)
> BLESS YOUR BEAUTIFUL HIDE (1)
> SEND IN THE CLOWNS (2)
> SHOWBOAT MEDLEY:(1)
>> WHY DO I LOVE YOU
>> MAKE BELIEVE
>> OL' MAN RIVER (2)
> MEMORY (1)

Side Two

> YESTERDAY WHEN I WAS YOUNG (2)
> WHAT 50 SAID (Narrative)
> THIS IS ALL I ASK (2)
> AND I LOVE YOU SO (2)
> IF (1)
> YOU WERE ALWAYS ON MY MIND (3)
> I'VE NEVER BEEN TO ME (2)
> BORN AGAIN (1)
> SOFTLY, AS I LEAVE YOU (2)

NOTE: (See D18, D49)

D49. WITH LOVE-HOWARD KEEL
     LaserLight (CS-1990) 79552
     LaserLight (CD-1989) 15105

          I'VE NEVER BEEN TO ME
          BORN AGAIN
          SOFTLY AS I LEAVE YOU
          SO IN LOVE
          SEND IN THE CLOWNS
          YESTERDAY, WHEN I WAS YOUNG
          WHAT 50 SAID
          THIS IS ALL I ASK
          IF
          YOU WERE ALWAYS ON MY MIND
          YESTERDAY
          SOMETHING
          MacARTHUR PARK
          LOVE STORY
          I WON'T SEND ROSES
          YOU NEEDED ME

NOTE: (See D48)

D50. WITH LOVE FROM HOWARD KEEL
     Capitol 4XL-57020
     (Cassette-1988)

     Side One

          SEND IN THE CLOWNS
          BLESS YOUR BEAUTIFUL HIDE
          YOU WERE ALWAYS ON MY MIND
          THIS IS ALL I ASK
          SOFTLY AS I LEAVE YOU

     Side Two

          AND I LOVE YOU SO
          SO IN LOVE
          MEMORY
          IF

D51. YOU NEEDED ME
     Capitol 4 XL 57095
     (Cassette-1989)

     Side One

          LOVE STORY
          YESTERDAY
          SOMETHING
          YOU NEEDED ME
          IF EVER I WOULD LEAVE YOU

Side Two

> WHAT ARE YOU DOING THE REST OF YOUR LIFE
> WAVE
> I'VE NEVER BEEN TO ME
> MacARTHUR PARK

COMPILATION RECORDS

D52. CLASSIC MOVIE MUSICALS OF SAMMY FAIN
JJA-19842

Song by Keel

> HIGHER THAN A HAWK

D53. COLLECTOR'S SHOW BOAT
Victrola AVM1-1741

D54. DALLAS, THE MUSIC STORY
Warner Bros./Lorimar Records
(12"-1985)

Song by Keel

> J. R.! WHO DO YOU THINK YOU ARE?

NOTE: (See BC41)

**D55. DORIS DAY SINGS SONGS FROM THE WARNER BROS.
PICTURES CALAMITY JANE AND PAJAMA GAME**
CBS 32196 (British)
CBS (CD) 4676102 (British)

Songs by Keel

> I CAN DO WITHOUT YOU-with Doris Day
> HIGHER THAN A HAWK

D56. GOLDEN AGE OF MOVIE MUSICALS
MGM S/SQBO-93890   ·
(12"-1972)

NOTES: This is a double LP set with a 12-page guidebook.
Those appearing on the album are Judy Garland, Fred Astaire,
Jane Powell, Ava Gardner, Gene Kelly, George Gaetary, Bert
Lahr, Kathryn Grayson, Debbie Reynolds, Ann Miller, and
Howard Keel.

D57. GREAT DUETS FROM MGM MUSICALS
MGM 2353.116 (British)

D58. GREAT SINGING SCREEN STARS
Sony Music Special Products AK 47018
(CD-1991)

Songs by Keel

> PAGAN LOVE SONG
> AND THIS IS MY BELOVED-with Ann Blyth, Vic Damone
> WUNDERBAR-with Kathryn Grayson

D59. THE GREAT VICTOR DUETS
RCA (CD) 9967-2-R

Song by Keel

> SO IN LOVE-with Gogi Grant

D60. HOLLYWOOD SINGS VOLUME 2-THE MEN
RCA (CS) 19966-4-RG
RCA (CD) 19966-2R11

D61. HOLLYWOOD YEARS OF HARRY WARREN 1930-1957

Songs by Keel

> WHY IS LOVE SO CRAZY
> YOUNG FOLKS SHOULD GET MARRIED-with Esther Williams

D62. INTERNATIONAL STARS OF THE TALK OF THE TOWN
2-EMI DUO-117 (British)

D63. KATHRYN GRAYSON-LET THERE BE MUSIC
Azel Records AZ-102

Song by Keel

> SCARBOROUGH FAIR (1969) with Grayson

D64. MGM YEARS
6-MGM/Columbia Special Products P6S-5878

Songs by Keel

> THERE'S NO BUSINESS LIKE SHOW BUSINESS-with Betty
>   Hutton, Keenan Wynn, Louis Calhern
> MAKE BELIEVE-with Kathryn Grayson
> AND THIS IS MY BELOVED-with Ann Blyth, Vic Damone

D65. ORIGINAL MOVIE SOUNDTRACK HITS
Lion 70122

D66. ORIGINAL SOUNDTRACKS
MGM 2353.042 (British)

D67. THEATRELAND SHOWSTOPPERS 1943-1968
3-EMI SCXSP-652 (British)

**D68. 25 YEARS OF RECORDED SOUND 1945-1970 FROM THE VAULTS
OF MGM RECORDS**
DRG Darc 2-2100

Song by Keel

    YOUNG FOLKS SHOULD GET MARRIED-with Esther Williams

D69. VERY BEST OF COLE PORTER
MGM E/SE-4244
12"-July 1964

Songs by Keel

    SO IN LOVE-with Kathryn Grayson
    WUNDERBAR-with Kathryn Grayson
    (From KISS ME, KATE)

D70. VERY BEST OF IRVING BERLIN
MGM E/SE-4240
12"-July 1964

Songs by Keel

    THE GIRL THAT I MARRY
    THERE'S NO BUSINESS LIKE SHOW BUSINESS-with Betty
      Hutton, Louis Calhern, and Keenan Wynn
      (From ANNIE GET YOUR GUN)

D71. VERY BEST OF JEROME KERN
MGM E/SE-4241
12"-July 1964

Songs by Keel

    WHY DO I LOVE YOU-with Kathryn Grayson
    MAKE BELIEVE-with Kathryn Grayson
    (From SHOW BOAT)

D72. VERY BEST OF MOTION PICTURE MUSICALS
MGM E/SE-4171

D73. VERY BEST OF SIGMUND ROMBERG
MGM E/SE-4239
MGM E-3153 RI
12"-July 1964 (Reissue of DEEP IN MY HEART)

Song by Keel

    YOUR LAND AND MY LAND

NOTES: The source for charted LP's up to 1972 was Joel
Whitburn's Top LP's 1945-1972.

The source for charted LP's after 1972 was Joel
Whitburn's Top Pop Albums 1955-1985.

The source for British charted albums was British Hit
Albums by Paul Gambaccini, Tim Rice, Jonathan Rice.

7

SHEET MUSIC

Most of the sheet music listed below was released in connection with Mr. Keel's films. The dates are those of the film and not necessarily the song's publication date. The names under the song are of those pictured on the cover. Under the names is the film title in which the song appeared. Under the film title is listed the name of the sheet music publisher.

SM 1. ACROSS THE WIDE MISSOURI (1951)
   Clark Gable and movie scene
    (From ACROSS THE WIDE MISSOURI)
    Revere

SM 2. AFTER THE BALL (1951)
   Howard Keel, Kathryn Grayson, Joe E. Brown, Ava Gardner
    (From SHOW BOAT)
    Harms

SM 3. ALL BUT THE REMEMBERING (1966)
   Howard Keel, Jane Russell
    (From WACO)
    Ensign

SM 4. ALWAYS TRUE TO YOU IN MY FASHION (1953)
   Howard Keel, Kathryn Grayson
    (From KISS ME, KATE)
    Harms

SM 5. AND THIS IS MY BELOVED (1955)
   Arabic Designs
    (From KISMET)
    Frank

SM 6. ANYTHING YOU CAN DO (1950)
   Betty Hutton
    (From ANNIE GET YOUR GUN)
    Berlin

SM 7. AUF WIEDERSEHN (1954)
Jose Ferrer, Helen Traubel, Dancers
(From DEEP IN MY HEART)
Harms

SM 8. BALLAD OF THE WAR WAGON (1967)
John Wayne, Kirk Douglas
(From WAR WAGON)
Shamley

SM 9. BAUBLES BANGLES AND BEADS (1955)
Arabic Designs
(From KISMET)
Frank

SM10. BIANCA (1953)
Howard Keel, Kathryn Grayson
(From KISS ME, KATE)
Harms

SM11. BLACK HILLS OF DAKOTA (1953)
Doris Day, Howard Keel
(From CALAMITY JANE)
Remick

SM12. BLESS YOUR BEAUTIFUL HIDE (1954)
Howard Keel, Jane Powell, Six Boys, Six Girls
(From SEVEN BRIDES FOR SEVEN BROTHERS)
Robbins

SM13. BORED (1955)
Arabic Designs
(From KISMET)
Frank

SM14. CAN'T HELP LOVIN' DAT MAN (1951)
Howard Keel, Kathryn Grayson, Joe E. Brown, Ava
Gardner
(From SHOW BOAT)
Harms

SM15. COTTON BLOSSOM (1951)
Howard Keel, Kathryn Grayson, Joe E. Brown, Ava
Gardner
(From SHOW BOAT)
Harms

SM16. DAY OF THE TRIFFIDS (1963)
Green cover with title
(From DAY OF THE TRIFFIDS)
Filmusic

SM17. THE DEADWOOD STAGE (1953)
Doris Day, Howard Keel
(From CALAMITY JANE)
Remick

SM18. **DEEP IN MY HEART** (1954)
        Jose Ferrer, Helen Traubel, Dancers
          (From DEEP IN MY HEART)
          Harms

SM19. **DESERT SONG** (1954)
        Jose Ferrer, Helen Traubel, Dancers
          (From DEEP IN MY HEART)
          Harms

SM20. **DOIN' WHAT COMES NATUR'LLY** (1950)
        Betty Hutton
          (From ANNIE GET YOUR GUN)
          Berlin

SM21. **DON'T LET THIS NIGHT GET AWAY** (1955)
        Esther Williams, Howard Keel
          (From JUPITER'S DARLING)
          Chappell

SM22. **ETIQUETTE** (1950)
        Howard Keel, Esther Williams
          (From PAGAN LOVE SONG)
          Robbins

SM23. **FAITHFULLY YOURS** (1954)
        Jose Ferrer, Helen Traubel, Dancers
          (From DEEP IN MY HEART)
          Harms

SM24. **FROM THIS MOMENT ON** (1953)
        Howard Keel, Kathryn Grayson
          (From KISS ME, KATE)
          Harms

SM25. **THE GIRL THAT I MARRY** (1950)
        Betty Hutton
          (From ANNIE GET YOUR GUN)
          Berlin

SM26. **GOIN' CO'TIN** (1954)
        Howard Keel, Jane Powell, Six Boys, Six Girls
          (From SEVEN BRIDES FOR SEVEN BROTHERS)
          Robbins

SM27. **HE'S IN LOVE** (1955)
        Arabic Designs
          (From KISMET)
          Frank

SM28. **HIGHER THAN A HAWK** (1953)
        Doris Day, Howard Keel
          (From CALAMITY JANE)
          Remick

SM29. **THE HOUSE OF THE SINGING BAMBOO** (1952)
        Howard Keel, Esther Williams

(From PAGAN LOVE SONG)
Robbins

SM30. **I CAN DO WITHOUT YOU** (1953)
Doris Day, Howard Keel
(From CALAMITY JANE)
Remick

SM31. **I HATE MEN** (1953)
Howard Keel, Kathryn Grayson
(From KISS ME, KATE)
Harms

SM32. **I HAVE A DREAM** (1955)
Esther Williams, Howard Keel
(From JUPITER'S DARLING)
Chappell

SM33. **I HAVE THE LOVE** (1954)
Ann Blyth, Howard Keel, Fernando Lamas
(From ROSE MARIE)
Harms

SM34. **I'LL BE HARD TO HANDLE** (1952)
Kathryn Grayson, Red Skelton, Howard Keel, Ann
Miller
(From LOVELY TO LOOK AT)
Harms

SM35. **I'M AN INDIAN TOO** (1950)
Betty Hutton
(From ANNIE GET YOUR GUN)
Berlin

SM36. **I MIGHT FALL BACK ON YOU** (1951)
Howard Keel, Kathryn Grayson, Joe E. Brown, Ava
Gardner
(From SHOW BOAT)
Harms

SM37. **INDIAN LOVE CALL** (1954)
Ann Blyth, Howard Keel, Fernando Lamas
(From ROSE MARIE)
Harms

SM38. **I STILL SUITS ME** (1951)
Howard Keel, Kathryn Grayson, Joe E. Brown, Ava
Gardner
(From SHOW BOAT)
Harms

SM39. **IT'S DYNAMITE** (1951)
Esther Williams, Red Skelton, Howard Keel, Ann
Miller
(From TEXAS CARNIVAL)
Miller

SM40. I WON'T DANCE (1952)
      Kathryn Grayson, Red Skelton, Howard Keel, Ann
      Miller
          (From LOVELY TO LOOK AT)
          Harms

SM41. JUNE BRIDE (1954)
      Howard Keel, Jane Powell, Six Boys, Six Girls
          (From SEVEN BRIDES FOR SEVEN BROTHERS)
          Robbins

SM42. JUST BLEW IN FROM THE WINDY CITY (1953)
      Doris Day, Howard Keel
          (From CALAMITY JANE)
          Remick

SM43. LEG OF MUTTON (1954)
      Jose Ferrer, Helen Traubel, Dancers
          (From DEEP IN MY HEART)
          Harms

SM44. LET'S GO WEST AGAIN (1950)
      No Cover
          (Dropped from ANNIE GET YOUR GUN)
          Berlin

SM45. LIFE UPON THE WICKED STAGE (1951)
      Howard Keel, Kathryn Grayson, Joe E. Brown, Ava
      Gardner
          (From SHOW BOAT)
          Harms

SM46. LONESOME POLECAT (1954)
      Howard Keel, Jane Powell, Six Boys, Six Girls
          (From SEVEN BRIDES FOR SEVEN BROTHERS)
          Robbins

SM47. LOVELY TO LOOK AT (1952)
      Kathryn Grayson, Red Skelton, Howard Keel, Ann
      Miller
          (From LOVELY TO LOOK AT)
          Harms

SM48. LOVER COME BACK TO ME (1954)
      Jose Ferrer, Helen Traubel, Dancers
          (From DEEP IN MY HEART)
          Harms

SM49. MAKE BELIEVE (1951)
      Howard Keel, Kathryn Grayson, Joe E. Brown, Ava
      Gardner
          (From SHOW BOAT)
          Harms

SM50. MOUNTIES (1954)
      Ann Blyth, Howard Keel, Fernando Lamas
          (From ROSE MARIE)
          Harms

SM51. MY DEFENSES ARE DOWN (1950)
        Betty Hutton
        (From ANNIE GET YOUR GUN)
        Berlin

SM52. NIGHT OF MY NIGHTS (1955)
        Arabic Designs
        (From KISMET)
        Frank

SM53. NOT SINCE NINEVEH (1955)
        Arabic Designs
        (From KISMET)
        Frank

SM54. OL' MAN RIVER (1951)
        Howard Keel, Kathryn Grayson, Joe E. Brown, Ava
        Gardner
        (From SHOW BOAT)
        Harms

SM55. PAGAN LOVE SONG (1950)
        Howard Keel, Esther Williams
        (From PAGAN LOVE SONG)
        Robbins

SM56. ROAD TO PARADISE (1954)
        Jose Ferrer, Helen Traubel, Dancers
        (From DEEP IN MY HEART)
        Harms

SM57. ROSE MARIE (1954)
        Ann Blyth, Howard Keel, Fernando Lamas
        (From ROSE MARIE)
        Harms

SM58. SANDS OF TIME (1955)
        Arabic Designs
        (From KISMET)
        Frank

SM59. THE SEA OF THE MOON (1950)
        Howard Keel, Esther Williams
        (From PAGAN LOVE SONG)
        Robbins

SM60. SECRET LOVE (1953)
        Doris Day, Howard Keel
        (From CALAMITY JANE)
        Remick

SM61. SERENADE (1954)
        Jose Ferrer, Helen Traubel, Dancers
        (From DEEP IN MY HEART)
        Harms

SM62. SINGING IN THE SUN (1950)
        Howard Keel, Esther Williams

(From PAGAN LOVE SONG)
Robbins

SM63. **SMOKE GETS IN YOUR EYES** (1952)
Kathryn Grayson, Red Skelton, Howard Keel, Ann
Miller
(From LOVELY TO LOOK AT)
Harms

SM64. **SOBBIN' WOMEN** (1954)
Howard Keel, Jane Powell, Six Boys, Six Girls
(From SEVEN BRIDES FOR SEVEN BROTHERS)
Robbins

SM65. **SOFTLY AS IN A MORNING SUNRISE** (1954)
Jose Ferrer, Helen Traubel, Dancers
(From DEEP IN MY HEART)
Harms

SM66. **SO IN LOVE** (1953)
Howard Keel, Kathryn Grayson
(From KISS ME, KATE)
Harms

SM67. **SPRING, SPRING, SPRING** (1954)
Howard Keel, Jane Powell, Six Boys, Six Girls
(From SEVEN BRIDES FOR SEVEN BROTHERS)
Robbins

SM68. **STOUT HEARTED MEN** (1954)
Jose Ferrer, Helen Traubel, Dancers
(From DEEP IN MY HEART)
Harms

SM69. **STRANGER IN PARADISE** (1955)
Arabic Designs
(From KISMET)
Frank

SM70. **THERE'S NO BUSINESS LIKE SHOW BUSINESS** (1950)
Betty Hutton
(From ANNIE GET YOUR GUN)
Berlin

SM71. **THEY SAY IT'S WONDERFUL** (1950)
Betty Hutton
(From ANNIE GET YOUR GUN)
Berlin

SM72. **TIS HARRY I'M PLANNIN'TO MARRY** (1953)
Doris Day, Howard Keel
(From CALAMITY JANE)
Remick

SM73. **TOTEM TOM TOM** (1954)
Ann Blyth, Howard Keel, Fernando Lamas
(From ROSE MARIE)
Harms

SM74. THE TOUCH OF YOUR HAND (1952)
        Kathryn Grayson, Red Skelton, Howard Keel, Ann
        Miller
            (From LOVELY TO LOOK AT)
            Harms

SM75. WACO (1966)
        Howard Keel, Jane Russell
            (From WACO)
            Ensign

SM76. WERE THINE THAT SPECIAL FACE (1953)
        Howard Keel, Kathryn Grayson
            (From KISS ME, KATE)
            Harms

SM77. WHEN I GROW TOO OLD TO DREAM (1954)
        Jose Ferrer, Helen Traubel, Dancers
            (From DEEP IN MY HEART)
            Harms

SM78. WHEN YOU'RE IN LOVE (1954)
        Howard Keel, Jane Powell, Six Boys, Six Girls
            (From SEVEN BRIDES FOR SEVEN BROTHERS)
            Robbins

SM79. WHERE THE TUMBLEWEED IS BLUE (1951)
        Howard Keel, Dorothy McGuire, Fred MacMurray
            (From CALLAWAY WENT THATAWAY)
            Miller

SM80. WHOA EMMA (1951)
        Esther Williams, Red Skelton, Howard Keel, Ann
        Miller
            (From TEXAS CARNIVAL)
            Miller

SM81. WHY CAN'T YOU BEHAVE (1953)
        Howard Keel, Kathryn Grayson
            (From KISS ME, KATE)
            Harms

SM82. WHY DO I LOVE YOU (1951)
        Howard Keel, Kathryn Grayson, Joe E. Brown, Ava
        Gardner
            (From SHOW BOAT)
            Harms

SM83. WHY IS LOVE SO CRAZY (1950)
        Howard Keel, Esther Williams
            (From PAGAN LOVE SONG)
            Harms

SM84. WILL YOU REMEMBER (1954)
        Jose Ferrer, Helen Traubel, Dancers
            (From DEEP IN MY HEART)
            Harms

SM85. A WOMAN'S TOUCH (1953)
   Doris Day, Howard Keel
    (From CALAMITY JANE)
     Remick

SM86. WONDERFUL WONDERFUL DAY (1954)
   Howard Keel, Jane Powell, Six Boys, Six Girls
    (From SEVEN BRIDES FOR SEVEN BROTHERS)
     Robbins

SM87. THE WORLD IS MINE (TONIGHT) (1951)
   Howard Keel
    Sam Fox

SM88. WUNDERBAR (1953)
   Howard Keel, Kathryn Grayson
    (From KISS ME, KATE)
     Harms

SM89. YESTERDAYS (1952)
   Kathryn Grayson, Red Skelton, Howard Keel, Ann
   Miller
    (From LOVELY TO LOOK AT)
     Harms

SM90. YOU ARE LOVE (1951)
   Howard Keel, Kathryn Grayson, Joe E. Brown, Ava
   Gardner
    (From SHOW BOAT)
     Harms

SM91. YOU CAN'T GET A MAN WITH A GUN (1950)
   Betty Hutton
    (From ANNIE GET YOUR GUN)
     Berlin

SM92. YOUNG FOLKS SHOULD GET MARRIED (1951)
   Esther Williams, Red Skelton, Howard Keel, Ann
   Miller
    (From TEXAS CARNIVAL)
     Miller

SM93. YOU'RE DEVASTATING (1952)
   Kathryn Grayson, Red Skelton. Howard Keel, Ava
   Gardner
    (From LOVELY TO LOOK AT)
     Harms

SM94. YOUR LAND AND MY LAND (1954)
   Jose Ferrer, Helen Traubel, Dancers
    (From DEEP IN MY HEART)
     Harms

SM95. YOU WILL REMEMBER VIENNA (1954)
   Jose Ferrer, Helen Traubel, Dancers
    (From DEEP IN MY HEART)
     Harms

8

VIDEOLOG

The following is an alphabetical list of VHS, Laserdisc,
Beta, and RCA CED versions of Mr. Keel's work released on
video. Often videos are repackaged and released under new
release dates. Where possible, an earlier release date is
given followed by the latest release date (as of this
writing). All are VHS versions except where noted.

V 1. **ACROSS THE WIDE MISSOURI**
MGM/UA 202366 (December 1991)
MGM/UA 202366 (Beta-December 1991)

V 2. **ARIZONA BUSHWHACKERS**
Paramount 6744 (June 1993)

V 3. **ARMORED COMMAND**
CBS Fox Video 7760 (1990)
CBS Fox Video 7760 (June 1991)

V 4. **CALAMITY JANE**
Warner Home Video 11209 (1987)
Warner Home Video 11209 (Laserdisc-October 1991)
Warner Home Video 11209 (April 1992)
Warner Home Video 11209 (Beta-April 1992)

V 5. **DAY OF THE TRIFFIDIS**
Media Home Video M115 (1985)
Goodtimes Home Video VGT-5090 (1985)
Image ID763850 (Laserdisc-April 1991)

V 6. **DEEP IN MY HEART**
MGM/UA 300626 (January 1992)
MGM/UA 300626 (Beta-January 1992)
MGM/UA 100626 (Laserdisc-April 1992)

V 7. **HOWARD KEEL: CLOSE TO MY HEART**
(British release) Music For Pleasure/Picture Music
International MVP 9912733 (1991)

NOTE: This is a video of Keel's PBS-TV special. (See
BC53)

V 8. JUPITER'S DARLING
MGM/UA ML102660 (Laserdisc-March 1992)
MGM/UA 202583 (July 1992)
MGM/UA 202583 (Beta-July 1992)

V 9. KISMET
MGM/UA M700130 (May 1990)
MGM/UA M700130 (Beta-May 1990)
MGM/UA ML102180 (Laserdisc-May 1991)

V10. KISS ME, KATE
MGM/UA M300307 (May 1990)
MGM/UA M300307 (Beta-May 1990)
MGM/UA ML102325 (Laserdisc-November 1991)

V11. LOVELY TO LOOK AT
MGM/UA M201828 (May 1991)
MGM/UA M201828 (Beta-May 1991)
MGM/UA ML101828 (Laserdisc-June 1991)

V12. OLD-FASHIONED CHRISTMAS
TV-55 Minutes
Video Artists International VAI-69087

This is a nostalgic look at Christmas in the U.S.A.
and in Europe through the years. Performers included
Jane Morgan, John Raitt, Lennon Sisters, Florence
Henderson, Mildred Miller, Rosemary Clooney, Thomas
Mitchell, **Howard Keel**, and Phyllis Curtin.

V13. PAGAN LOVE SONG
MGM/UA M300909 (July 1992)
MGM/UA M300909 (Beta, July 1992)

V14. ROSE MARIE
MGM/UA M102324

V15. SEVEN BRIDES FOR SEVEN BROTHERS
MGM/UA Home Video MD100091 (RCA CED-1982)
MGM/UA 700091 (1988)
MGM/UA 100091 (Laserdisc-January 1991)
MGM/UA 700091 (October 1991)
MGM/UA 700091 (Beta-October 1991)

V16. SHOW BOAT
RCA 00209 (CED-1981)
MGM/UA M600167 (1989)
MGM/UA ML102302 (Laserdisc-May 1991)
MGM/UA M600167 (October 1991)
MGM/UA M600167 (Beta-October 1991)

V17. TEXAS CARNIVAL
MGM/UA M202701 (July 1992)
MGM/UA M202701 (Beta, July 1992)

V18. THAT'S ENTERTAINMENT!
MGM M600007 (1988)
MGM/UA M600007 (October 1989)

MGM/UA M600007 (Beta-October 1989)
MGM/UA 102126 (Laserdisc-October 1991)

V19. THAT'S ENTERTAINMENT PART 2
MGM/UA M700076 (March 1989)
MGM/UA M700076 (Beta-March 1989)
MGM/UA 102430 (Laserdisc-May 1992)

V20. THAT'S ENTERTAINMENT! III
MGM/UA M905100 (November 1994)

NOTE: This video was released in regular VHS,
Laserdisc, and a deluxe box-set. The box-set contains
an extended director's cut, a behind the scenes
documentary, a souvenir program, the CD soundtrack,
and eight lobby cards.

V21. TLC WAY TO TRAIN YOUR DOG
Cabin Fever Entertainment CF802 (1989)

V22. TOAST OF THE TOWN: MGM SALUTE
Classic Television

This TV show was broadcast on February 14, 1954 and
saluted MGM's 30th anniversary.

V23. WAR WAGON
MCA/Universal Home Video 80016 (1991)
MCA/Universal Home Video 40016 (Laserdisc-January 1991)
MCA/Universal Home Video 80016 (May 1992)
MCA/Universal Home Video 80016 (Beta-May 1992)

9

NIGHT CLUBS AND CONCERTS

This chapter documents, chronologically, Mr. Keel's known night club and concert credits. Where possible, the place, date, those on the bill, songs by Keel, a review, and comment are given.

NC 1. LAST FRONTIER-Las Vegas, Nevada (March 1954) 4 Weeks.

    with Angel Marlo

SONGS: Medleys from OKLAHOMA!, CAROUSEL, SHOWBOAT, ANNIE GET YOUR GUN, KISS ME, KATE, ROSE MARIE, and SEVEN BRIDES FOR SEVEN BROTHERS.

REVIEW: <u>Variety</u> (March 10, 1954) felt that his delivery and selection of songs "prove a memorable experience."

COMMENT: Keel earned $15,000 a week before expenses.

NC 2. PALLADIUM-London, England (1954)

SONGS: Keel performed a medley from OKLAHOMA!, CAROUSEL, and songs from his films.

COMMENT: This was a command performance.

NC 3. DUNES-Las Vegas, Nevada (September 27, 1955) 4 Weeks.

    with Tri Lads

SONGS: "Lonesome Road," "Autumn Leaves," "Yellow Rose of Texas," "Heaven," "Hooray For Love."

COMMENTS: Keel earned $15,000 a week and retained $4,000 after expenses. He rehearsed for four weeks and played the show for four weeks averaging five hundred dollars a week.

NC 4. TOWN CASINO-Buffalo, New York (November 1955)

SONGS: "Lonesome Roads," "Autumn Leaves," "Yellow Rose of Texas," as well as medleys from OKLAHOMA!, CAROUSEL, and his films.

NC 5. COPACABANA-New York, New York (December 1955)

>   with Tri Lads, Betty and Jane Kean, Mello Larks,
>   Tony Foster, Fran Leslie, Meri Miller & Jimmy Sisco,
>   Mike Durso & Frank Marti Orchestras, George Wyle
>   (Arranger/Conductor), and staging by George Englund

SONGS: "Lonesome Road," "Autumn Leaves," "Yellow Rose of
Texas," "Ol' Man River," "Granada," "September Song."

REVIEWS: <u>New York World-Telegram and Sun</u>, Robert Dana,
(December 7, 1955) Mr. Dana said Keel's voice was "rich and
glorious." He also thought that if Keel would show some of
the "individualistic, hell-for-leather personality" that he
had in SEVEN BRIDES FOR SEVEN BROTHERS "he'd really wow
cafe audiences."

<u>Variety</u> (December 7, 1955) felt that Keel was a "natural"
for clubs and that he had "a strong set of pipes" and used
them well. It was felt that he did not talk or joke with
the audience until his third number was over and that he
should have "broken the ice more quickly" and "with a less
formal opening."

NC 6. EMPIRE-Glasgow, Scotland (April 2, 1956)

>   with Falcons, Billy Dainty, Roger Carne, Harry Allen
>   & Alber Sisters, Aerial Kenways, Peter Dulay, Shane &
>   Lamar, the Bobby Dowds Orchestra and conductor Hank
>   Russell

SONG: "Annie Laurie."

REVIEW: <u>Variety</u> (April 11, 1956) felt that Keel's act had
"all-around entertainment value" and that he had "fine
pipes." It was felt that his confidence was stronger than
his previous appearance.

NC 7. PALLADIUM-London, England (April 9, 1956) 2 Weeks.

>   with Nicholas Bros., Tommy Trinder, Ricardi Jr.,
>   Harry Worth, King Bros., Les Curibas, Evie & Joe
>   Slack, George Carden Dancers, Eric Rogers Orchestra

SONGS: Songs from PORGY & BESS, "Ol' Man River," and other
show tunes.

REVIEW: <u>Variety</u> (April 25, 1956) felt that he did not use
gimmicks and relied on his own "warm personality and a
healthy pair of tuneful pipes...which prove more than
adequate."

NC 8. SANDS (Copa Room)-Las Vegas, Nevada (January 13, 1957)
4 weeks.

>   in HIGH WIDE AND THEN SOME with Louis Jordan and his

Tympany Five, Beachcombers, and Natalie, Will Jordan

SONGS: "Guys & Dolls," "Sit Down You're Rocking the Boat."

IMITATIONS: Elvis Presley, Enzio Pinza, Porgy, Nelson Eddy.

REVIEW: Hollywood Reporter (January 15, 1957) felt that "Keel had put together a great act" and he sings "magnificently."

NC 9. EMPIRE-Glasgow, Scotland (May 22, 1957) 3 Weeks.

with musical director Hank Russell, Group One, Benson Dulay & Co., Dickie Dawson, Vera Cody's Dogs and Horses, Hans Recklin & Inge, Horler Twins, Bobby Dowds Orchestra

SONGS: "As Time Goes By," "Love You As I Never Loved Before."

REVIEW: Variety (May 29, 1957) felt that Keel "scores solidly."

NC10. FREMONT-Las Vegas, Nevada (September 1968)

with Kathryn Grayson

SONGS: "Mr. Bojangles," "Don Qixote," "Port of Amsterdam" (Keel); "Tip Toe Through the Tulips" (Comic take off on Tiny Tim done by Keel and Grayson); "Scarborough Fair," "Wunderbar," "Make Believe," "Change," "You Are Love" (Keel, Grayson); "Hi Lilli," "Smoke Gets in Your Eyes" (Grayson).

REVIEW: Variety (October 2, 1968) felt that Keel and Grayson looked "marvelous" and their singing made them "top flight marquee value."

NC11. HARRAH'S-Reno, Nevada (November 29, 1968)

with Kathryn Grayson, Donna Jean Young, Moro-Landis Dancers, and George Hernandez

SONGS: "Try to Remember," "Where or When," "Tonight," "And This is My Beloved," "What the World Needs Now," "Yesterday," "Mrs. Robinson" (Special Lyrics), "Tip Toe Through the Tulips" [Comic take off on Tiny Tim] (Keel, Grayson); "Mr. Bojangles," "Port of Amstredam" (Keel); "Hi Lilli," "Smoke Gets in Your Eyes" (Grayson).

REVIEW: Variety (December 11, 1968) felt the performance represented "excellent musicianship" and that for Grayson and Keel "the standard touches on perfection."

NC12. COCOANUT GROVE-Los Angeles, California (April 23, 1969)

with Kathryn Grayson and the Freddy Martin Orchestra

SONGS: "Port of Amsterdam," "Mr. Bojangles," MAN OF LA
MANCHA MEDLEY (Keel); "Tip Toe Through the Tulips" (take off
on Tiny Tim), "Wunderbar," "Scarborough Fair," "Softly,"
"You Are Love" (Keel, Grayson); "Un Bel Di," "Both Sides
Now" (Grayson).

REVIEW: Variety (April 30, 1969) felt that when they sang
they "nicely segue better-than-average talents" and knew
what it took to please an audience.

NC13. FREMONT-Las Vegas, Nevada (December 24, 1969)

    with Kathryn Grayson, Jay Lawrence, Al Johns
    Orchestra

SONGS: "Mr. Bojangles," "By the Time I Get to Phoenix"
(Keel); Rock Medley with Grayson; "Un Bel Di," "Both Sides
Now" (Grayson).

REVIEW: Variety (December 31, 1969) felt that Keel and
Grayson "issue a pleasant drone and chirp sound" and many
times their pitch was "questionable."

NC14. TALK OF THE TOWN-London, England (March 25, 1971)

    with Burt Rhodes Orchestra, Philip Phillips Group,
    Bernard Delfont's presentation of Robert Nesbitt's
    Review

SONGS: "Oh What a Beautiful Morning," "Surrey With the
Fringe on Top," "People Will Say We're in Love," "Rose
Marie," "Bless Your Beautiful Hide," "Ol' Man River," MAN
OF LA MANCHA MEDLEY including "Impossible Dream," "Swing
Low Sweet Chariot," "Port of Amsterdam."

REVIEW: Variety (March 31, 1971) felt that Keel had a
"splendid virile voice" and a "strong personality" and that
his act was "strong and clear throughout."

NC15. FREMONT (Fiesta Room) Las Vegas, Nevada (February 25,
    1972)

    with Kathryn Grayson, Jack DeLeon, Al Johns
    Orchestra, Producer Moe Lewis

SONGS: "Mr. Bojangles," "Port of Amsterdam" (Keel); "Tip Toe
Trough the Tulips" (take off on Tiny Tim); "Wunderbar,"
SHOW BOAT MEDLEY (Keel, Grayson); "Un Bel Di," "Both Sides
Now" (Grayson).

REVIEW: Variety (March 8, 1972) felt that it was a good idea
that their act has not changed as it was "no use tampering
with success of previous engagements." It was also felt it
was a good idea "to lean on nostalgia" for the older patrons
as well as doing some contemporary songs for the younger
ones.

COMMENT: The SHOW BOAT MEDLEY brought a standing ovation.

NC16. PALLADIUM-London, England (June 18, 1974) 2 Weeks.

with Louis Benjamin & Leslie Grade, Moira Anderson, Stephane Grappelli, Diz Disley Trio, Arthur Worsley, Nick Martin, Rudy Cardenas, the Second Generation, Staged by Albert J. Knight, Choreography by Douggie Squires, London Palladium Orchestra directed by Gordon Rose

REVIEW: Variety (June 26, 1974) felt Keel's act was "skillfully balanced and paced" and performed with "consummate ease."

NC17. AUSTRALIA TOUR (July and August 1975)

with staging by Miriam Nelson, musical director Richard Pribor (real name Priborsky)

SONG: "The Girl From Ipanema."

COMMENTS: The act was a solo. Author Larry Billman said (in a letter to author) that Miriam Nelson "remembers Keel as being a very nice man-disciplined, a gentleman."

NC18. CARIBBEAN CRUISE (November 26, 1978-December 3, 1978)

COMMENTS: The cruise was sponsored by the American Film Institute and featured Howard Keel, actress Olivia de Havilland, and director King Vidor. On the cruise, the stars discussed their Hollywood careers and there were screenings of some of their best films.
    Keel talked about his stage and film career, Arthur Freed and his MGM years as well as co-stars Jane Powell, Ava Gardner, and Kathryn Grayson. His films SEVEN BRIDES FOR SEVEN BROTHERS, and KISS ME, KATE were shown.

NC19. UNITED KINGDON TOUR (Fall 1980)

COMMENT: This tour included 26 concerts.

NC20. UNITED KINGDON TOUR (Spring 1983)

SONGS: "Why Do I Love You," "Dulcinea."

COMMENT: This was a 15-date, sold-out, tour.

NC21. UNITED KINGDOM TOUR (April 16, 1984-May 20, 1984)

The Forum Theatre, Hatfield	April 16, 1984
The Hehagon, Reading	April 17, 1984
Fairfield Hall, Croydon	April 18, 1984
Blazers Club, Windsor	April 19, 1984
The Guildhall, Portsmouth	April 21, 1984
St. David's Hall, Cardiff	April 22, 1984
Cliffs Pavilion, Southend	April 23, 1984
The Derngate, Northampton	April 25, 1984
Conference Center, Harrogate	April 26, 1984
Empire Theatre, Sunderland	April 27, 1984

Opera House, Blackpool	April 28, 1984
Palace Theatre, Manchester	April 29, 1984
City Hall, Sheffield	April 30, 1984
New Theatre, Southport	May 1, 1984
The Playhouse, Edinburgh	May 3, 1984
His Majesty's Theatre, Aberdeen	May 4, 1984
His Majesty's Theatre, Aberdeen	May 5, 1984
Theatre Royal, Glasgow	May 6, 1984
Royal Spa Hall, Bridlington	May 7, 1984
Winter Garden, Bournemouth	May 9, 1984
Leaz Cliff House, Folkstone	May 10, 1984
The Dome, Brighton	May 11, 1984
Conference Center, Wembley	May 12, 1984
The Spectrum, Warrington	May 13, 1984
Royal Concert Hall, Nottingham	May 15, 1984
The Night Out, Birmingham	May 16, 1984
The Night Out, Birmingham	May 17, 1984
The Night Out, Birmingham	May 18, 1984
The Night Out, Birmingham	May 19, 1984
The Hippodrome, Bristo	May 20, 1984

COMMENTS: The thirty-date tour was put together by promoter Derek Block and grossed over $1,000,000. It played to standing room only audiences. He also toured in 1985, 1986, 1987.

NC22. ROYAL ALBERT HALL-London, England (1987)

SONGS: "This Nearly Was Mine," "Some Enchanted Evening," "Ol' Man River," songs from SEVEN BRIDES FOR SEVEN BROTHERS, MAN OF LA MANCHA, as well as contemporary songs

COMMENTS: This concert was aired on PBS-TV on June 10, 1990, and again on December 2, 1990. (See BC51)

NC23. SOUTH SHORE MUSIC CIRCUS-Cohasset, Massachusetts (July 11, 1987)

COMMENTS: The show was promoted by Rawson Promotions. There were 1,434 tickets sold out of 2,300 at a cost of $18.50 per ticket. The show grossed $23,909.

NC24. BARBICAN-London, England (April 1988)

with orchestra leader Richard Holmes

SONGS: from OKLAHOMA!, KISS ME, KATE, SEVEN BRIDES FOR SEVEN BROTHERS, SHOW BOAT, MAN OF LA MANCHA, MACK AND MABEL, CATS, DOCTOR ZHIVAGO, "Send in the Clowns," "Ol' Man River," "Wunderbar."

REVIEW: Stage and Television Today (April 7, 1988) felt Keel's act was a "good tuneful night of great songs by a supreme professional."

COMMENTS: The show was promoted by Derek Block. He also toured in September 1989.

NC25. THEATRE ROYAL-Norwich, England (1989)

> with tour manager and assistant Don Archel, musical
> director Richard Holmes, orchestra contractor Arthur
> Dakin, arrangers George Annis and Bruce Miller.

COMMENTS: The show, which toured all over the United
Kingdom, was recorded at the Theater Royal in Norwich,
England, in 1989, and released, in 1991, by Pickwick Music
on CD and cassette. The recording was produced by Keel's
personal manager James Fitzgerald. (See D34 for songs)

NC26. GREEK THEATRE-Los Angeles, California (July 15, 1989)

> with a 20-piece orchestra

SONGS: "Memory," Medleys from OKLAHOMA!, MAN OF LA MANCHA,
SHOW BOAT, "Music of the Night," "Wind Beneath My Wings,"
"We Never Learn," "This Nearly Was Mine," "MacArthur Park,"
"Just the Way You Are."

REVIEWS: <u>Los Angeles Times</u> (July 1989) felt Keel handled the
Broadway and film musical medleys easily and that he was at
his best with songs like "Wind Beneath My Wings," "We Never
Learn," and with maturity Keel gave a "creative sensitivity
to match the sunny glow of his voice."

<u>Variety</u> (July 18, 1989) felt that "Keel exercised his
still-strong baritone voice to the delight of the over-50
crowd."

NC27. DOMINION THEATRE-London, England (October 1989)

> with 24-piece orchestra and musical director, Richard
> Holmes

SONGS: From OKLAHOMA!, SHOW BOAT, SEVEN BRIDES FOR SEVEN
BROTHERS, MAN OF LA MANCHA, MACK & MABEL, "MacArthur Park,"
"Ol' Man River," SOUTH PACIFIC, "Send in the Clowns," KISS
ME, KATE, PHANTOM OF THE OPERA, CATS, "Yesterday When I Was
Young."

REVIEW: <u>The Stage & Television Today</u>, James Green, (October
5, 1989) Mr. Green felt that Keel "is an oak sturdy singer
with a rich deep voice that reverberates off the walls."
Green also thought that "Keel can be pleased at the way he
has kept old age at bay even if he is no longer Curly."

COMMENTS: Keel seemed to be suffering from a cold. He
received a standing ovation at the end of the show.

NC28. MANCHESTER, ENGLAND (September 6, 1991)

COMMENTS: After playing in a golf tournament, he performed,
at a celebration, with Johnny Mathis and Vic Damone. He
also did a concert tour in England in 1991.

NC29. GLASGOW ROYAL CONCERT HALL–Glasgow, Scotland (April 5, 1993)

COMMENT: This farewell tour was promoted by Barry Clayman Concerts.

NC30. BARBICAN–London, England (April 12, 13, 1993)

COMMENT: The Barbican was the last stop on Keel's farewell World tour promoted by Barry Clayman Concerts.

NC31. HOWARD KEEL SHOW BOAT THEATRE–Branson, Missouri (April 1994)

COMMENTS: Keel's theatre was scheduled to open in April 1994 at a cost $10,000,000 and 2100 seats. The stage was to be large enough to handle Broadway shows. Howard planned to perform there about six months annually. A hotel was also planned. The deal eventually fell through.

NC32. UNITED KINGDOM COMEBACK TOUR (April 23–May 29, 1994)

St. Davids Hall, Cariff	April 23, 1994
Derngate, Northampton	April 24, 1994
Corn Exchange, Cambridge	April 26, 1994
Southport Theatre, Southport	April 27, 1994
Symphony Hall, Birmingham	April 28, 1994
Cliffs Pavilion, Southend	April 30, 1994
New Theatre, Hull	May 1, 1994
St. George's Hall, Bradford	May 2, 1994
Royal Concert Hall, Glasgow	May 3, 1994
Davenport, Stockport	May 5, 1994
Barbican, York	May 6, 1994
Royal Concert Hall, Nottingham	May 7, 1994
City Hall, Sheffield	May 8, 1994
New Pavilion, Rhyl	May 9, 1994
Empire, Sunderland	May 10, 1994
The Swan, High Wycombe	May 12, 1994
Civic Hall, Guildford	May 13, 1994
The Orchard, Dartford	May 14, 1994
Grand, Swansea	May 15, 1994
Dacorum Pavilion, Hemel Hempstead	May 16, 1994
Assembly Halls, Worthing	May 17, 1994
Fairfield Hall, Croydon	May 19, 1994
Leisure Centre, Brentwood	May 20, 1994
Winter Gardens, Margate	May 21, 1994
Theatre Royal, Norwich	May 22, 1994
The Anvil, Basingstoke	May 23, 1994
The Hawth, Crawley	May 24, 1994
Festival Theatre, Paignton	May 25, 1994
Hippodrome, Bristol	May 26, 1994
Apollo, Oxford	May 27, 1994
Barbican, London	May 28, 1994
Barbican, London	May 29, 1994

SONGS: "Oh What a Beautiful Morning," "If I Loved You," Numbers from ANNIE GET YOUR GUN, SHOW BOAT, KISS ME, KATE, SEVEN BRIDES FOR SEVEN BROTHERS.

COMMENTS: This 32-date tour was promoted by Barry Clayman.
Because of popular demand, Keel scheduled this comeback
tour despite doing a farewell tour in 1993.   Ticket prices
ranged from 10.50-14.50 pounds.   Keel was interviewed on
British radio to promote the concert series.   (See BC5)

10

ANNOTATED BIBLIOGRAPHY

This chapter is divided into two sections. The first is
made up of newspaper and magazine articles and the second
of books that give information on Mr. Keel.

NEWSPAPERS AND MAGAZINES

B 1. "Actor Howard Keel Met His Wife on a Blind Date He
      Almost Vetoed." Midnight. September 16, 1974.

      This is an article on how Keel met his wife Judy on
      a blind date he almost did not make when he found out
      about the difference in their ages. Keel is pictured
      with Judy.

B 2. Adock, Joe. "'I DO! I DO!' Revives Memories." The
      Philadelphia Bulletin. October 22, 1980.

      This is a review of Howard Keel and Jane Powell's
      appearance at the Valley Forge Music Fair in the play
      I DO! I DO!

B 3. Agate, James. London Sunday Times. May 4, 1947.

      A review of the London production of OKLAHOMA!

B 4. "A Man of La Mancha Sued Over Swordplay Incident."
      New York Times. July 28, 1973.

      The article reports that a suit was filed in the
      Manhattan Supreme Court by Rody and Maxine Richman who
      claimed Keel injured them by hitting them with a sword
      during a performance of MAN OF LA MANCHA at the West-
      bury Music Fair.

B 5. America. November 21, 1953.

      A review of the film KISS ME, KATE

B 6. _____. December 12, 1953.2

A review of the film CALAMITY JANE

B 7. _____. April 10, 1954.

A review of the film ROSE MARIE.

B 8. _____. July 31, 1954.

A review of the film SEVEN BRIDES FOR SEVEN BROTHERS.

B 9. _____. December 18, 1954.

A review of the film DEEP IN MY HEART.

B 10. American Cinematographer. May 1951.

A review of the film ACROSS THE WIDE MISSOURI.

B 11. Archerd, Army. Daily Variety. October 6, 1992.

A report on Keel's forthcoming Show Boat Theatre due
in April 1994 in Branson, Missouri.

B 12. Archer, Eugene. "Screen: Nazi Strategem." New York
Times. October 7, 1961.

A review of the film ARMORED COMMAND.

B 13. Armstrong, G. "Howard Keel's Untold Story."
Photoplay. November 1952.

An article on Keel.

B 14. Arnold, M. "Even Keel." Photoplay. October 1950.

An article on Keel.

B 15. "Ask Him No Questions." Movie Stars Parade. January
1952.

Keel discusses his not liking publicity. There are
miscellaneous photos.

B 16. Aston, Frank. "Lavish 'Saratoga' Opens Amid Singing,
Dancing." New York World-Telegram & Sun. December 8,
1959.

Howard Keel and Carol Lawrence are pictured.

B 17. Atkins, Brooks. New York Times. September 12, 1957.

A review of New York City Center production of
CAROUSEL.

B 18. Atkins, Brooks. "Da Costa's Version of Ferber Book
Opens." New York Times. December 8, 1959.

A review of Keel's appearance in SARATOGA.   Keel &

Lawrence are pictured.

B 19. Ayer, N.W. _Variety_. October 5, 1960.

A review of Keel's appearance on TV's "Bell
Telephone Hour"-Holiday in Music.

B 20. Bailey, C. "Keel's Kingdom." _Photoplay_. August 1954.

An article on Keel.

B 21. Baker, Richard. "Howard Keel: Surgery Saved My Life-
But It Could Kill My Role on 'Dallas'." _National
Enquirer_.

A discussion of Keel's deciding not to delay an
operation for two blockages of the heart despite the
chance of losing his role on "Dallas." Keel is
pictured golfing and with Barbara Bel Geddes.

B 22. Ballard, Gary. "On An Even Keel." _Hollywood Drama-
Loque_. September 20, 1984.

A discussion of Keel's career from the beginning, its
ups and downs, to the stardom on "Dallas." Keel is
pictured.

B 23. Balsona, Renee. _ABC Film Review_. September 1954.

An article on the film ROSE MARIE.

B 24. Barnes, Clive. _New York Times_. November 20, 1972.

A review of the Broadway production of AMBASSADOR.

B 25. Beaufort, John. "Keel-Darrieux 'Ambassador' Musical
Comes to Broadway." _Christian Science Monitor_.
November 24, 1972.

A review of the Broadway production of AMBASSADOR.

B 26. Beezer, George. "Same Old 'South Pacific'-But the
Qualities Endure." _The Philadelphia Evening Bulletin_.
June 22, 1965.

A review of Keel's appearance at the Valley Forge
Music Fair in SOUTH PACIFIC.

B 27. _BFI/Monthly Film Bulletin_. July 1950.

A review of the film ANNIE GET YOUR GUN.

B 28. _____. March 1951.

A review of the film THREE GUYS NAMED MIKE.

B 29. _____. May 1951.

A review of the film PAGAN LOVE SONG.

B 30. _____. July 1951.

A review of the film SHOW BOAT.

B 31. _____. November 1951.

A review of the film ACROSS THE WIDE MISSOURI.

B 32. _____. November 1951.

A review of the film TEXAS CARNIVAL.

B 33. _____. September 1952.

A review of the film LOVELY TO LOOK AT.

B 34. _____. February 1953.

A review of the film DESPERATE SEARCH.

B 35. _____. February 1954.

A review of the film KISS ME, KATE.

B 36. _____. September 1954.

A review of the film ROSE MARIE.

B 37. _____. December 1954.

A review of the film SEVEN BRIDES FOR SEVEN BROTHERS.

B 38. _____. April 1955.

A review of the film DEEP IN MY HEART.

B 39. _____. April 1966.

A review of the film MAN FROM BUTTON WILLOW.

B 40. Bilowit, Ira. Show Business. September 16, 1957.

A review of Keel's appearance in the City Center production of CAROUSEL.

B 41. Blair, Duncan. "Howard Keel." Picturegoer. November 20, 1948.

Discussion of how Keel got the role in THE SMALL VOICE. Keel is pictured with Valerie Hobson and with Hobson and James Donald.

B 42. Bolton, Whitney. Morning Telegraph. December 9, 1959.

A review of the Broadway production SARATOGA.

B 43. _____. Morning Telegraph. December 28, 1959.

> The article tells of Keel's knowing what hard physical work is and his years growing up as a son of a coal miner.

B 44. Boxoffice. October 17, 1953.

> A trade ad for KISS ME, KATE with Keel and Kathryn Grayson.

B 45. _____. October 9, 1954.

> A cover and photo review of SEVEN BRIDES FOR SEVEN BROTHERS with Jane Powell.

B 46. _____. December 25, 1954.

> A promotional on DEEP IN MY HEART with a new feature review consisting of title, cast, and running time.

B 47. "Breaks Leg in First Film Role." New York Times. April 8, 1949.

> The article reports on when Keel got a fractured leg when his horse fell on him during the filming of ANNIE GET YOUR GUN.

B 48. Brennan, Phil. "Bringing Howard Back From the Dead Almost Killed Him-Twice!" Examiner. February 3, 1987.

> The article discusses Keel's near retirement from show business and his planned move to Oklahoma to work for an oil company and how "Dallas" resurrected his career. It also discusses his fears of losing the role by having heart surgery. Keel is pictured singing, in his role on "Dallas," and with a horse during his movie days.

B 49. Burton, Alex. "Dog Days of Summer For 'Dallas' Howard Keel." Star. August 1, 1989.

> An article on Keel's video TLC WAY OF TRAINING YOUR DOG. Keel is pictured with dogs.

B 50. "But Can He Sing 'Old Man Ewing?'" TV Guide. August 8, 1983.

> The article talks about Keel's surge of popularity because of "Dallas" and of his sold out concert tour in England. Keel is pictured.

B 51. Calamity Jane. Unknown magazine. 1953.

> Story and pictures on the film.

B 52. "Can Howard Keel Afford a Secret Life?" Movie Stars

Parade. April 1951.

An article on Keel.

B 53. Carroll, Kathleen. "New Wayne Western Gets the OK
Brand." New York Daily News. August 3, 1967.
A review of the film WAR WAGON.

B 54. Catholic World. November 1951.

A review of the film ACROSS THE WIDE MISSOURI.

B 55. _____. December 1951.

A review of the film CALLAWAY WENT THATAWAY.

B 56. _____. July 1952.

A review of the film LOVELY TO LOOK AT.

B 57. _____. December 1953.

A review of the film CALAMITY JANE.

B 58. _____. December 1953.

A review of the film KISS ME, KATE.

B 59. _____. August 1954.

A review of the film SEVEN BRIDES FOR SEVEN BROTHERS.

B 60. _____. January 1955.

A review of the film DEEP IN MY HEART.

B 61. "A Chance to Win Ava Gardner's Blouse or Howard
Keel's Shirt." Picture Show. July 3, 1954.

The magazine's contest to win Gardner's blouse or
Keel's shirt from the film RIDE VAQUERO. Scenes are
shown from the film.

B 62. Chapman, John. "'Saratoga' Has Fabulous Gowns Fine
Cast and Trunkful of Plot." New York Daily News.
December 8, 1959.

A review of the Broadway production of SARATOGA.
Carol Lawrence is pictured.

B 63. Chicago Sun Times. December 26, 1950.

A review of the film PAGAN LOVE SONG.

B 64. Chicago Tribune TV Week. August 14-August 20, 1983.

An article on "Dallas" and its world popularity. Keel
is pictured on the cover.

B 65. Christian Century. July 19, 1950.

A review of the film ANNIE GET YOUR GUN.

B 66. _____. March 28, 1951.

A review of the film THREE GUYS NAMED MIKE.

B 67. _____. August 1, 1951.

A review of the film SHOW BOAT.

B 68. _____. November 21, 1951.

A review of the film ACROSS THE WIDE MISSOURI.

B 69. _____. January 16, 1952.

A review of the film CALLAWAY WENT THATAWAY.

B 70. _____. August 13, 1952.

A review of the film LOVELY TO LOOK AT.

B 71. Christian Herald. September 1959.

A review of the film THE BIG FISHERMAN.   Two scenes
are shown one with Keel.

B 72. Christian Science Monitor. December 9, 1959.

A review of the play SARATOGA.

B 73. _____. November 20, 1972.

A review of the London production of AMBASSADOR.

B 74. Churchill, Reba and Bonnie. "Big Tease." Motion
Picture and Television Magazine. December 1953.

The article claims Keel is a big tease, stubborn,
frank, quiet, noisy, and a big country boy.   There are
several pictures of Keel.

B 75. Cinemonde. December 3, 1954.

A photo story on ROSE MARIE.

B 76. Cine Revue. October 5, 1951.

A 4-page pictorial on the film SHOW BOAT with Kathryn
Grayson, Keel, and Ava Gardner.

B 77. _____. December 24, 1954.

A pictorial on ROSE MARIE with Ann Blyth and Keel.

B 78. _____. April 20, 1978.

A full page color portrait and a 3-page photo story on Keel.

B 79. Cleaves, Henderson. "Working Both Sides of B'way." New York World Telegram. 1959.

A discussion of Keel preferring stage to film. It talks about his having the best of both by starring in THE BIG FISHERMAN on film and SARATOGA on Broadway.

B 80. Colford, Paul. "The Hidden Baritone on 'Dallas'." New York Newsday. June 8, 1989

Keel discusses his career from CAROUSEL to "Dallas" as well as his TV concert and his concert schedule in London.

B 81. Collier, Lionel. "Oh Rose Marie I Still Love You." Picturegoer. September 11, 1954.

A pictorial on ROSE MARIE.

B 82. Collier's. January 7, 1955.

A review of the film DEEP IN MY HEART.

B 83. Collins, William. "'I DO' Doesn't-Although It Tries." The Philadelphia Inquirer. 1980.

A review of Howard Keel and Jane Powell's appearance in I DO! I DO! at the Valley Forge Music Fair.

B 84. Commonwealth. June 29, 1951.

A review of the film SHOW BOAT.

B 85. _____. November 9, 1951.

A review of the film TEXAS CARNIVAL.

B 86. _____. June 20, 1952.

A review of the film LOVELY TO LOOK AT.

B 87. _____. August 7, 1953.

A review of the film RIDE VAQUERO.

B 88. _____. November 20, 1953.

A review of the film KISS ME, KATE.

B 89. _____. April 16, 1954.

A review of the film ROSE MARIE.

B 90. _____. August 13, 1954.2

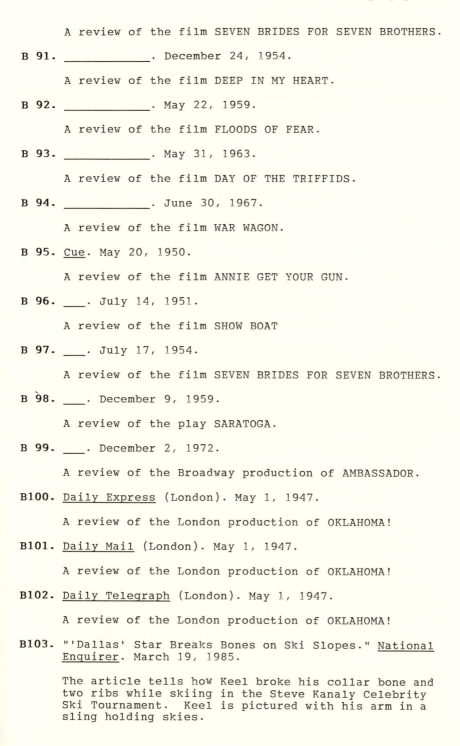

A review of the film SEVEN BRIDES FOR SEVEN BROTHERS.

B 91. _____. December 24, 1954.

A review of the film DEEP IN MY HEART.

B 92. _____. May 22, 1959.

A review of the film FLOODS OF FEAR.

B 93. _____. May 31, 1963.

A review of the film DAY OF THE TRIFFIDS.

B 94. _____. June 30, 1967.

A review of the film WAR WAGON.

B 95. Cue. May 20, 1950.

A review of the film ANNIE GET YOUR GUN.

B 96. ____. July 14, 1951.

A review of the film SHOW BOAT

B 97. ____. July 17, 1954.

A review of the film SEVEN BRIDES FOR SEVEN BROTHERS.

B 98. ____. December 9, 1959.

A review of the play SARATOGA.

B 99. ____. December 2, 1972.

A review of the Broadway production of AMBASSADOR.

B100. Daily Express (London). May 1, 1947.

A review of the London production of OKLAHOMA!

B101. Daily Mail (London). May 1, 1947.

A review of the London production of OKLAHOMA!

B102. Daily Telegraph (London). May 1, 1947.

A review of the London production of OKLAHOMA!

B103. "'Dallas' Star Breaks Bones on Ski Slopes." National
Enquirer. March 19, 1985.

The article tells how Keel broke his collar bone and
two ribs while skiing in the Steve Kanaly Celebrity
Ski Tournament. Keel is pictured with his arm in a
sling holding skies.

B104. "'Dallas' Star Howard Keel: Fans Want Me to Beat Up J. R.-in Real Life!" National Enquirer. October 2, 1984.

A discussion of Keel's role on 'Dallas' and fans' desire for him to beat up J. R. Keel is pictured. with J. R.

B105. Dana, Robert. "Copa Sails Along on Even Keel." New York World Telegram and Sun. December 7, 1955.

A review of Keel's act at the Copacabana.

B106. Dance Magazine. August 1954.

A review of the film SEVEN BRIDES FOR SEVEN BROTHERS.

B107. _____. January 1955.

A review of the film DEEP IN MY HEART.

B108. Dash, Thomas. "'Saratoga' Pretty as a Picture But Old Fashioned." Women's Wear Daily. December 8, 1959.

A review of the Broadway production of SARATOGA.

B109. Dawson, Helen. London Observer. October 24, 1971.

A review of the London production of AMBASSADOR.

B110. Dee, John. "Howard Keel Plays a Saint." Picturegoer. March 21, 1959.

An article on THE BIG FISHERMAN. Keel is pictured on the set of the film.

B111. Devor, Les. The Hollywood Reporter. January 15, 1957.

A review of Keel's show "High Wide and Then Some" at the Sands Hotel.

B112. Downes, Olin. New York Times. June 6, 1943.

A review of the Broadway production of OKLAHOMA!

B113. Druxman, M.B. "Howard Keel." Films in Review. November 1970.

A 13-page article on the life and career of Howard Keel. Keel is pictured in ANNIE GET YOUR GUN, SHOW BOAT, CALLAWAY WENT THATAWAY, RIDE VAQUERO, CALAMITY JANE, KISS ME, KATE, SEVEN BRIDES FOR SEVEN BROTHERS, ARMORED COMMAND, LOVELY TO LOOK AT, with Kathryn Grayson in a night club act, and on stage in MAN OF LA MANCHA.

B114. Eder, Bruce. "'Kiss Me, Kate' in 3-D." Voice Film Special. December 1990.

A discussion of seeing KISS ME, KATE in 3-D at the Film Forum.

B115. Eiga No Tomo. December 1954.

A Japanese import containing pictorials on SEVEN BRIDES FOR SEVEN BROTHERS.

B116. Elliott, Graham. "Passing Parade." Movie Stars Parade. June 1952.

The article discusses the "Lux Radio Theatre" presentation of SHOW BOAT. Keel is pictured with Kathryn Grayson and Ava Gardner.

B117. Ellis, Mollie. "Howard Gimmickless Keel-I Think Not." Unknown paper & date.

A discussion of Keel's use of his talent and not artificial gimmicks. Keel is pictured.

B118. Enge, Charles. "Annie Finds a New Star Who May Start a Trend." Downbeat. July 28, 1950.

The article mentions keeping a watch on Keel who scored strongly in ANNIE GET YOU GUN.

B119. Everett, Todd. "Keel's Newest Kismet." Los Angeles Herald Examiner. July 14, 1989.

A discussion of Keel's rise to stardom, his role on "Dallas," his recording career after getting the part in "Dallas" as well as his appearance at the Greek Theatre in Hollywood.

B120. Farm Journal. January 1954.

A review of the film CALAMITY JANE.

B121. _____. May 1954.

A review of the film ROSE MARIE.

B122. _____. August 1954.

A review of the film SEVEN BRIDES FOR SEVEN BROTHERS.

B123. _____. January 1955.

A review of the film DEEP IN MY HEART.

B124. Film Daily. April 12, 1950.

A review of the film ANNIE GET YOUR GUN.

B125. _____. December 26, 1950.

A review of the film PAGAN LOVE SONG.

B126. _____. February 9, 1951.

A review of the film THREE GUYS NAMED MIKE.

B127. _____. June 5, 1951.

A review of the film SHOW BOAT.

B128. _____. September 17, 1951.

A review of the film TEXAS CARNIVAL.

B129. _____. September 24, 1951.

A review of the film ACROSS THE WIDE MISSOURI

B130. _____. November 15, 1951.

A review of the film CALLAWAY WENT THATAWAY.

B131. _____. May 29, 1952.

A review of the film LOVELY TO LOOK AT.

B132. _____. December 5, 1952.

A review of the film DESPERATE SEARCH.

B133. _____. May 4, 1953.

A review of the film FAST COMPANY.

B134. _____. July 1, 1953.

A review of the film RIDE VAQUERO.

B135. _____. October 27, 1953.

A review of the film KISS ME, KATE.

B136. _____. October 29, 1953.

A review of the film CALAMITY JANE.

B137. _____. March 3, 1954.

A review of the film ROSE MARIE.

B138. _____. June 1, 1954.

A review of the film SEVEN BRIDES FOR SEVEN BROTHERS.

B139. _____. December 1, 1954.

A review of the film DEEP IN MY HEART.

B140. _____. January 25, 1955.

A review of the film JUPITER'S DARLING.

B141. _____. December 6, 1955.

A review of the film KISMET.

B142. _____. April 23, 1959.

A review of the film FLOODS OF FEAR.

B143. _____. June 29, 1959.

A review of the film THE BIG FISHERMAN.

B144. _____. February 1, 1965.

A review of the film MAN FROM BUTTON WILLOW.

B145. Film Review. November 1952.

Kathryn Grayson and Keel are pictured on the cover. They were in LOVELY TO LOOK AT.

B146. _____. April 1954.

A screen story and pictorial on KISS ME, KATE with Kathryn Grayson and Ann Miller.

B147. _____. September 1954.

A full page ad for ROSE MARIE with Ann Blyth and Keel.

B148. _____. July 1955.

A pictorial on JUPITER'S DARLING with Esther Williams.

B149. Films & Filming. October 1954.

A review of the films ROSE MARIE and SEVEN BRIDES FOR SEVEN BROTHERS.

B150. _____. January 1955.

A review of the film SEVEN BRIDES FOR SEVEN BROTHERS.

B151. Film Show Annual. 1958.

A portrait of Keel.

B152. Films in Review. December 1953.

A review and article on the film KISS ME, KATE.

B153. _____. August 9, 1954.

A review of the film SEVEN BRIDES FOR SEVEN BROTHERS.

B154. _____. January 1955.

A review of the film DEEP IN MY HEART.

B155. _____. November 1970.

Howard Keel's career is discussed in 13 pages, with
11 photos, and a filmography.

B156. Flanders, Mark. "He likes 'em Feminine." Screenland.
August 1954.

The article says Keel likes women to be feminine in
looks and behavior. Keel is pictured.

B157. Flett, Scarth. "The Blind Date That Made Howard Keel
a Happy Man." London Sunday Express. June 30, 1974.

The article discusses Keel meeting Judy on a blind
date as well as his early life and career. Keel is
pictured.

B158. Francis, Bob. "Howard Keel Pleasing in N.Y. Nitery
Debut." Billboard. December 10, 1955.

A review of Keel's act at the Copacabana.

B159. Francis, P. and Rudolph, I. "Grapevine." TV Guide.
October 10, 1987.

A discussion of romantic attention on "Dallas." It
also mentions the time Keel sees and becomes obsessed
with a portrait of Laurel Ellis.

B160. Franklin, Frances. "Topics For Gossip." Silver
Screen. June 1951.

The article discusses Kaija cutting her first tooth
and hoping to get away to Florida, where his wife's
family is, to do a concert tour.

B161. Gaver, Jack. "Howard Keel Stays in Rodgers Coterie."
Newark (N.J.) Evening News. July 26, 1963.

The article discusses Keel being in New York for a
Richard Rodgers Alumni Club reunion and about his 18-
month tour in Rodgers' NO STRINGS with Barbara McNair.
His roles in the Broadway and London productions of
OKLAHOMA! and CAROUSEL are mentioned.

B162. "Gene Kelly's Salute to Broadway." Variety. October
8, 1975.

A review of the show GENE KELLY'S SALUTE TO BROADWAY.

B163. Gibbs, Wolcott. New Yorker (The). April 28, 1945.

A review of the Broadway production of CAROUSEL.

B164. Gilbert, Justin. New York Mirror. June 4, 1959.

A review of the film FLOODS OF FEAR.

B165. Gill, Brendan. New Yorker (The). December 2, 1972.

A review of the Broadway production of AMBASSADOR.

B166. Good Housekeeping. September 1959.

A review of the film THE BIG FISHERMAN.

B167. Gould, Jack. "TV: Enjoyable Contrasts-'Bell Telephone Hour' Offers Delightful Sampling of the Concert World." New York Times. March 5, 1959.

A review of "The Bell Telephone Hour."

B168. Graham, Sheila. "Howard Keel-Hauls 'Em." New York Mirror. January 10, 1960.

Keel discusses his not minding constructive criticism but hates critics who get cute with adjectives or complaining cast members. He does not mind doing a role over and over again because you get better at it. He talks about his 9 years at Metro and his now doing Universal's THE BIG FISHERMAN and Broadway's SARATOGA.

B169. Green, James. "Howard's Way." Stage & Television Today. April 7, 1988.

A review of Keel's act at the Barbican. Keel is pictured.

B170. _____. The Stage & Screen Today. October 5, 1989.

A review of Keel's night club act at the Dominion Theatre in London.

B171. Guernsey, Otis. New York Herald Tribune. March 2, 1951.

A review of the film THREE GUYS NAMED MIKE. Jane Wyman is pictured.

B172. Gwynn, Edith. "In Hollywood." Boston Post. August 13, 1953.

The article mentions transporting the cast and equipment to Mammoth Lake, California for the filming of KISS ME, KATE. It also mentions letting the audience decide which process, 3-D or wide screen, that KISS ME, KATE should be released in. Keel is pictured.

B173. Haskell, Harry. The Kansas City Star. July 4, 1978.

A review of Keel's appearance at the Starlight Theatre in the play version of SEVEN BRIDES FOR

SEVEN BROTHERS.

B174. Hawn, Jack. "At 70, Keel to Make L.A. Concert Debut."
<u>Los Angeles Times</u>. July 15, 1989.

The article discusses Keel's first appearance in a
concert at the Greek Theatre even though he had
appeared in plays in Los Angeles. Also discussed is
his British concerts and albumns, his "Dallas" role,
his past roles, love of golf, and his preference for
singing. Keel is pictured.

B175. Herbstman, Mandel. <u>The Film Daily</u>.

A review of the film WAR WAGON.

B176. "He's 64. She's 34, but 'Dallas' Co-star Says; My
Wife Is the Best Thing That Ever Happened to Me."
<u>National Enquirer</u>. February 18, 1982.

A discussion of Keel's meeting his wife Judy and their
happy marriage despite their differences in age. Keel
is pictured with Judy.

B177. Hobson, Harold. <u>London Sunday Times</u>. October 24,
1971.

A review of the London production of AMBASSADOR.

B178. Hobson, Henry. <u>Christian Science Monitor</u>. October 23,
1971.

A review of the London production of AMBASSADOR.

B179. Holland, Jack. "My Hollywood Life." <u>Movieland</u>. May
1951.

A discussion of Keel's rise from doing odd jobs to
Broadway stardom and his Hollywood life making films.
Many photos.

B180. <u>Hollywood Drama-logue</u>. September 20, 1984.

The article discusses how Keel's training at MGM has
helped him continue his durable career.

B181. <u>Hollywood Reporter (The)</u>. April 12, 1950.

A review of the film ANNIE GET YOUR GUN.

B182. _____. December 20, 1950

A review of the film PAGAN LOVE SONG.

B183. _____. February 9, 1951.

A review of the film THREE GUYS NAMED MIKE.

B184. _____. June 5, 1951.

A review of the film SHOW BOAT.

B185. _____. September 18, 1951.

A review of the film ACROSS THE WIDE MISSOURI.

B186. _____. May 27. 1952.

A review of the film LOVELY TO LOOK AT.

B187. _____. November 24, 1952.

A review of the film DESPERATE SEARCH.

B188. _____. October 27, 1953.

A review of the film KISS ME, KATE.

B189. _____. October 28, 1953.

A review of the film CALAMITY JANE.

B190. _____. March 3, 1954.

A review of the film ROSE MARIE.

B191. _____. June 1, 1954.

A review of the film SEVEN BRIDES FOR SEVEN BROTHERS.

B192. _____. December 1, 1954.

A review of the film DEEP IN MY HEART.

B193. _____. January 15, 1957.

A review of Keel's show "High Wide and Then Some" at
the Sands Hotel.

B194. _____. February 18, 1965.

A review of the film MAN FROM BUTTON WILLOW.

B195. Hopper, Hedda. "Hollywood." New York Daily News.
August 3, 1958.

The article mentions how Keel went to England for good
acting roles and his finishing the film FLOODS OF
FEAR.

B196. "Howard Keel Cast in Satire on Singing Cowboys." New
York Herald Tribune. February 28, 1951.

An announcement of Keel being cast as the lead in
the film CALLAWAY WENT THATAWAY.

B197. "Howard Keel Clicks in Palladium Debut." <u>Variety</u>.
April 18, 1956.

A discussion of Keel's appearance at the Palladium in
London.

B198. "Howard Keel Into TV." <u>Variety</u>. October 23, 1957.

An announcement of Keel signing to do a segment of
TV's "Zane Grey Theatre."

B199. "Howard Keel Pacted For 90-Minute Gab Strip!"
<u>Variety</u>. December 23, 1970.

The article discusses the deal with Ralph Edwards
Productions to do a 90-minute variety talk show.

B200. "How Keel Got in Pictures." <u>Morning Telegraph</u>. April
6, 1953.

Keel discusses how a football player for U.C.L.A.
missed a touch down that led to his entry into show
business.

B201. Hyams, Joe. "This is Hollywood." <u>New York Herald
Tribune</u>. September 28, 1955.

A discussion of Keel's second time in Las Vegas, this
time at the Dunes.

B202. "I'll Never Stop Singing." <u>Picturegoer</u>. May 17, 1958.

The article discusses Keel being away from films
since KISMET and his return to Britain to film FLOODS
OF FEAR. It also discusses plans to film PAINT YOUR
WAGON and his popularity in Britain.

B203. Jaffe, Natalie. <u>New York Times</u>. May 11, 1963.

A review of the film DAY OF THE TRIFFIDS.

B204. Jamison, Barbara. "Bonanza in Beards." <u>New York
Times</u>. October 24, 1954.

A discussion of the sudden appearances in films of
stars wearing beards.

B205. Kaufman, Dave. "Keel: From Studio System to
'Dallas'." <u>Variety</u>. October 14, 1985.

Keel discusses getting the role on "Dallas" and the
difference between Hollywood in his musical days
versus today's Hollywood.

B206. "Keel Leads Herald Poll." <u>New York Times</u>. December 8,
1951.

Keel is voted number one on <u>The Motion Picture</u>

<u>Herald's</u> list of "Ten Best Stars of Tomorrow."

B207. "Keel Racks Up on U.K. Comback Tour, Femmes Like Him." <u>Variety</u>. May 16, 1984.

An announcement of Keel's 30-date national tour of the United Kingdom.

B208. Kerr, Walter. "First Night Report." <u>New York Herald Tribune</u>. December 8, 1959.

A review of the Broadway production of SARATOGA. Carol Lawrence is pictured.

B209. _____. <u>New York Herald Tribune</u>. September 12, 1957.

A review of Keel's appearance in the City Center production of CAROUSEL. Keel is pictured as Billy Bigelow.

B210. Kingston, Jeremy. <u>Punch</u>. October 27, 1971.

A review of the London production of AMBASSADOR.

B211. Knox, Collie. "Letter From London." <u>Morning Telegraph</u>. April 7, 1971.

A review of Keel's act at the Talk of the Town.

B212. _____. <u>Morning Telegraph</u>. November 3, 1971.

A review of the London production of AMBASSADOR.

B213. Krutch, Joseph Wood. <u>The Nation</u>. April 17, 1943.

A review of the Broadway production of OKLAHOMA!

B214. Larrabee, Clark. "'Campobello' Is Fine Choice For Political Year." <u>The Philadelphia Inquirer</u>. July 12, 1960.

A review of Keel's appearance in SUNRISE AT CAMPOBELLO at the Playhouse in the Park in Philadelphia.

B215. Lazarus, Charles. "'Show Boats' in Review." <u>New York Times</u>. July 8, 1951.

A discussion of the history and various versions, including Keel's, of SHOW BOAT.

B216. <u>Library Journal</u>. May 1, 1950.

A review of the film ANNIE GET YOUR GUN.

B217. _____. January 15, 1951.

A review of the film PAGAN LOVE SONG.

B218. _____. June 15, 1951.

A review of the film SHOW BOAT

B219. _____. November 1, 1951.

A review of the film ACROSS THE WIDE MISSOURI.

B220. _____. January 1, 1953.

A review of the film DESPERATE SEARCH.

B221. _____. November 15, 1953.

A review of the film KISS ME, KATE.

B222. _____. December 1, 1953

A review of the film CALAMITY JANE.

B223. _____. May 15, 1954.

A review of the film ROSE MARIE.

B224. _____. August 1954.

A review of the film SEVEN BRIDES FOR SEVEN BROTHERS.

B225. _____. January 15, 1955.

A review of the film DEEP IN MY HEART.

B226. _____. May 15, 1959.

A review of the film FLOODS OF FEAR.

B227. Librizzi, Charles. "'South Pacific' at Smithville
Retains It's Failure-Proof Tag." The Philadelphia
Bulletin.

A review of SOUTH PACIFIC at the Smithville Summer
Theatre with Howard Keel and Jane Powell.

B228. "L.I. Couple Sue Howard Keel." July 28, 1973.

Roddy and Maxine Richman were at the September 16,
1972 performance of MAN OF LA MANCHA at the Westbury
Music Fair on Long Island and claimed serious
injuries when a sword slipped from Keel's hand during
the performance.

B229. Life. April 17, 1950.

A review of the film ANNIE GET YOUR GUN.

B230. _____. July 30, 1951.

A review of the film SHOW BOAT.

B231. ____. November 30, 1953.

A review of the film KISS ME, KATE.

B232. ____. February 22, 1954.

A review of the film ROSE MARIE.

B233. ____. July 26, 1954.

A review of the film SEVEN BRIDES FOR SEVEN BROTHERS.

B234. ____. August 4, 1967.

A review of the film WAR WAGON.

B235. London Times. July 3, 1950.

A review of the film ANNIE GET YOUR GUN.

B236. _____. September 22, 1952.

A review of the film LOVELY TO LOOK AT.

B237. _____. September 6, 1954.

A review of the film ROSE MARIE.

B238. Look. December 1, 1953.

A review of the film KISS ME, KATE.

B239. ____. February 22, 1955.

A review of the film JUPITER'S DARLING.

B240. Los Angeles Times. July 17, 1989.

A review of Keel's appearance at the Greek Theatre.

B241. _____. October 6, 1992.

A report on the forthcoming Show Boat Theatre due in April 1994 in Branson, Missouri.

B242. McClain, John. "City Center Stages Best Version Yet." New York Journal-American. September 12, 1957.

A review of Keel's appearance in the City Center production of CAROUSEL.

B243. _____. "A Fine Score Plus Class." New York Journal-American. December 8, 1959.

A review of the Broadway play SARATOGA.

B244. McGuire, John. <u>St. Louis Post-Dispatch</u>. June 20, 1978.

A review of Keel's appearance at the Mundy in the play version of SEVEN BRIDES FOR SEVEN BROTHERS.

B245. McLacklan, Donald. "Howard Keel: A Psychic Predicted My Success." Unknown Paper. 1974.

The article discusses Keel's meeting a psychic in the lobby of a movie theatre who predicted his success in 1944, a slump and then success again in 1945 that would lead him to the top. Keel is pictured.

B246. Manson, Louis. "Howard Keel Gives Up His 12-Room House to Live on a Boat." <u>National Enquirer</u>. August 29, 1971.

The article discusses Keel giving up the hassles of owning a 12-room $150,000 house for the life aboard a cabin cruiser. Keel's home and boat are pictured.

B247. Marriott, R.B. <u>The Stage & Television Today</u>. October 28, 1972.

A review of the London production of AMBASSADOR.

B248. Masters, Dorothy. "Keel Proved He Wasn't Too Slick For a Role." <u>New York Daily News</u>. August 9, 1959.

Keel discusses his role as Simon Peter in THE BIG FISHERMAN. He is pictured as himself and as Simon Peter.

B249. Maxwell, Kenneth. "Too Much Hanging About Says Howard Keel." <u>Stage & Television Today</u>. May 6, 1971.

The article discusses Keel's complaint about the large amount of time waiting between takes just for a TV guest shot.

B250. Mazo, Joseph. <u>Women's Wear Daily</u>. November 21, 1972.

A review of the Broadway production of AMBASSADOR.

B251. Mills, Bart. "Howard Keel Keeping Singing Career Going." <u>Los Angeles Times</u>. January 8, 1972.

A discussion of Keel's London musical AMBASSADOR as a possible vehicle to return him to Broadway and films. He did not feel it a come down to play stock versions of his film successes. Keel is pictured.

B252. _____. "What Happened to Howard?" <u>Motion Picture</u>. 1971.

An article on Keel's career since the movies. It also discusses his appearance in AMBASSADOR in

London.

B253. <u>Modern Screen</u>. July 1951.

A story on Keel.

B254. _____. November 1951.

A photo story on Keel.

B255. _____. May 1955.

Keel discusses his over generousness like when he
took his mother's car for repairs and surprised her
with a new Buick and how such surprises, appearing
spontaneous, were well planned long in advance. He
also remembers visiting Gillespie after his returning
from Europe to visit with his eighty-nine year old
grandmother and another old coal miner. The coal
miner said the town's most famous citizens were John
Dillinger and Howard Keel.

B256. "Morning Report." <u>Los Angeles Times</u>. October 6, 1992.

The article reports on the plans for Howard Keel's
Show Boat Theatre in Branson, Missouri.

B257. <u>Morning Telegraph</u>. December 23, 1959.

A review of the Broadway production of SARATOGA.

B258. Morrison, Hobe. <u>Variety</u>. March 21, 1962.

A review of the Broadway production of NO STRINGS.

B259. Mosby, Aline. "Those Were Good Ol' Days!" <u>Morning
Telegram</u>. December 1, 1952.

Keel says he had less to worry about when he was
earning $9 a week than as a star whose standard of
living has changed. Keel is pictured.

B260. <u>Motion Picture</u>. November 1950.

A photo story on Keel.

B261. _____. August 1951.

A photo story on Keel.

B262. <u>Motion Picture Exhibitor</u>. January 19, 1955.

An ad for JUPITER'S DARLING with Esther Williams &
Keel.

B263. _____. January 26, 1955.

A pictorial of MGM's coming attractions.

B264. <u>Motion Picture Herald</u>. October 17, 1953.

An ad for KISS ME, KATE with Kathryn Grayson & Keel.

B265. <u>Motion Picture Herald Product Digest</u>. April 15, 1950.

A review of the film ANNIE GET YOUR GUN.

B266. _____. December 23, 1950.

A review of the film PAGAN LOVE SONG.

B267. _____. February 10, 1951.

A review of the film THREE GUYS NAMED MIKE.

B268. _____. June 9, 1951.

A review of the film SHOW BOAT.

B269. _____. September 15, 1951.

A review of the film TEXAS CARNIVAL.

B270. _____. September 29, 1951.

A review of the film ACROSS THE WIDE MISSOURI.

B271. _____. November 17, 1951.

A review of the film CALLAWAY WENT THATAWAY.

B272. _____. May 31, 1952.

A review of the film LOVELY TO LOOK AT.

B273. _____. November 29, 1952.

A review of the film DESPERATE SEARCH.

B274. _____. March 6, 1954.

A review of the film ROSE MARIE.

B275. _____. June 5, 1954.

A review of the film SEVEN BRIDES FOR SEVEN BROTHERS.

B276. _____. December 14, 1954.

A review of the film DEEP IN MY HEART.

B277. _____. February 3,
1965.

A review of the film MAN FROM BUTTON WILLOW.

B278. Movie Fan. January/February 1951.

A photo story on Keel.

B279. Movieland. November 1950.

A photo story on Keel.

B280. Movie Life. June 1952.

Keel and Kathryn Grayson are shown after a flight
during a South American tour promoting MGM films.

B281. _____. March 1953.

A photo story on Keel.

B282. Movie Play. January 1954.

A big pictorial on CALAMITY JANE with Doris Day &
Keel.

B283. Movie Stars Parade. October 1951.

Keel is pictured with a wounded soldier at an Air
Force base. There is also an ad for TEXAS CARNIVAL
and a full page photo.

B284. _____. March 1953.

A portrait of Keel.

B285. Movie Story. February 1951.

A photo screen story on PAGAN LOVE SONG.

B286. Movie World. April 1956.

Howard Keel is pictured with his dogs.

B287. Murdock, Henry. "Ferber Story Glitters in Opulent
Musical." The Philadelphia Inquirer. October 27,
1959.

A review of the pre-Broadway tryout of SARATOGA in
Philadelphia.

B288. Nathan, George. New York Journal-American. April 30,
1945.

A review of the Broadway production of CAROUSEL.

B289. The Nation. May 5, 1945.

A review of the Broadway production of CAROUSEL.

B290. _____. April 14, 1962.

A review of the Broadway production of NO STRINGS.

B291. National Parent-Teacher. September 1952.

A review of the film LOVELY TO LOOK AT.

B292. _____. June 1953.

A review of the film FAST COMPANY.

B293. _____. December 1953.

A review of the films CALAMITY JANE and KISS ME, KATE.

B294. _____. May 1954.

A review of the film ROSE MARIE.

B295. _____. September 1954.

A review of the film SEVEN BRIDES FOR SEVEN BROTHERS.

B296. _____. February 1955.

A review of the film DEEP IN MY HEART.

B297. Nepean, Edith. "Round the British Studios." Picture Show & Film Pictorial. 1959.

Scenes from the film FLOODS OF FEAR.

B298. Neville, John. Dallas Morning News. June 7, 1978.

A review of Keel's appearance in the play version of SEVEN BRIDES FOR SEVEN BROTHERS.

B299. Newark Evening News. December 8, 1959.

A review of the Broadway play SARATOGA.

B300. The New Republic. April 19, 1943.

A review of the Broadway production of OKLAHOMA!

B301. _____. May 7, 1945.

A review of the Broadway production of CAROUSEL.

B302. _____. May 29, 1950.

A review of the film ANNIE GET YOUR GUN.

B303. _____. August 5, 1967.

    A review of the film WAR WAGON.

B304. <u>Newsday</u>. December 16, 1959.

    A review of the Broadway production of SARATOGA.

B305. <u>Newsweek</u>. June 5, 1950.

    A review of the film ANNIE GET YOUR GUN.

B306. _____. January 8, 1951.

    A review of the film PAGAN LOVE SONG.

B307. _____. July 2, 1951.

    A review of the film SHOW BOAT.

B308. _____. October 22, 1951.

    A review of the film TEXAS CARNIVAL.

B309. _____. November 19, 1951.

    A review of the film ACROSS THE WIDE MISSOURI.

B310. _____. December 17, 1951.

    A review of the film CALLAWAY WENT THATAWAY.

B311. _____. July 27, 1953.

    A review of the film RIDE VAQUERO.

B312. _____. November 9, 1953.

    A review of the film KISS ME, KATE.

B313. _____. November 23, 1953.

    A review of the film CALAMITY JANE.

B314. _____. September 20, 1954.

    A review of the film SEVEN BRIDES FOR SEVEN BROTHERS.

B315. _____. December 20, 1954.

    A review of the film DEEP IN MY HEART.

B316. _____. February 21, 1955.

    A review of the film JUPITER'S DARLING.

B317. _____. December 19, 1955.

A review of the film KISMET.

B318. _____. August 10, 1959.

A review of the film THE BIG FISHERMAN.

B319. _____. December 16, 1959.

A review of the Broadway play SARATOGA.

B320. _____. May 13, 1963.

A review of the film DAY OF THE TRIFFIDS.

B321. New York Daily News. December 31, 1955.

Keel discusses his nervousness about opening at the Copacabana and his latest film KISMET.

B322. _____. September 21, 1961.

A review of the film ARMORED COMMAND.

B323. _____. May 2, 1963.

A review of the film DAY OF THE TRIFFIDS.

B324. _____. August 3, 1967.

A review of the film WAR WAGON.

B325. The New Yorker. April 10, 1943.

A review of the Broadway production of OKLAHOMA!

B326. _____. May 20, 1950.

A review of the film ANNIE GET YOUR GUN.

B327. _____. March 10, 1951.

A review of the film THREE GUYS NAMED MIKE.

B328. _____. April 17, 1951.

A review of the film ROSE MARIE.

B329. _____. July 28, 1951.

A review of the film SHOW BOAT.

B330. _____. December 15, 1951.

A review of the film CALLAWAY WENT THATAWAY.

B331. _____. June 7, 1952.

A review of the film LOVELY TO LOOK AT.

B332. _____. November 14, 1953.

A review of the film KISS ME, KATE.

B333. _____. July 31, 1954.

A review of the film SEVEN BRIDES FOR SEVEN BROTHERS.

B334. _____. December 18, 1954.

A review of the film DEEP IN MY HEART.

B335. _____. December 17, 1955.

A review of the film KISMET.

B336. _____. December 19, 1959.

A review of the Broadway production of SARATOGA.

B337. New York Mirror. December 8, 1959.

A review of the Broadway production of SARATOGA.

B338. New York News Colorato Magazine. October 4, 1959.

Keel discusses his career briefly and his turning to
drama films including his current film THE BIG
FISHERMAN. Keel is pictured on the cover of the
magazine.

B339. New York Post. December 9, 1955.

A review of the film KISMET.

B340. _____. December 8, 1959.

A review of the Broadway play SARATOGA.

B341. _____. August 3, 1967.

A review of the film WAR WAGON.

B342. New York Times. May 18, 1950.

A review of the film ANNIE GET YOUR GUN.

B343. _____. December 26, 1950.

A review of the film PAGAN LOVE SONG.

B344. _____. March 2, 1951.

A review of the film THREE GUYS NAMED MIKE.

B345. _____. July 20, 1951.

A review of the film SHOW BOAT.

B346. _____. October 13, 1951.

A review of the film TEXAS CARNIVAL.

B347. _____. November 7, 1951.

A review of the film ACROSS THE WIDE MISSOURI.

B348. _____. December 6, 1951.

A review of the film CALLAWAY WENT THATAWAY.

B349. _____. December 8, 1951.

Keel is at the top of the list of Ten Best Stars of Tomorrow in Motion Picture Herald's poll of the nation's theatre owners.

B350. _____. June 7, 1952.

A review of the film LOVELY TO LOOK AT.

B351. _____. July 16, 1953.

A review of the film RIDE VAQUERO.

B352. _____. November 5, 1953.

A review of the film CALAMITY JANE.

B353. _____. December 6, 1953.

A review of the film KISS ME, KATE.

B354. _____. April 2, 1954.

A review of the film ROSE MARIE.

B355. _____. July 23, 1954.

A review of the film SEVEN BRIDES FOR SEVEN BROTHERS.

B356. _____. December 10, 1954.

A review of the film DEEP IN MY HEART.

B357. _____. February 18, 1955.

A review of the film JUPITER'S DARLING.

B358. _____. December 9, 1955.

A review of the film KISMET.

B359. _____. November 16, 1957.

Mention was made of a goodwill tour to the Far East put together by the American National Theatre and

Academy with the cooperation of the United States government.

B360. _____. August 6, 1959.

A review of the film THE BIG FISHERMAN.

B361. _____. October 7, 1961.

A review of the film ARMORED COMMAND.

B362. _____. May 11, 1963.

A review of the film DAY OF THE TRIFFIDS.

B363. _____. July 4, 1954.

A review of the film SEVEN BRIDES FOR SEVEN BROTHERS.

B364. Norbon, Mary Ann. "Howard Keel Settles Down on 'Dallas'." The Philadelphia Inquirer. November 18, 1983.

Keel discusses his getting into "Dallas" because of being tired of traveling. Keel is pictured.

B365. "'Oklahoma!' Wins Hearts of London." New York Times. May 1, 1947.

This article was a special to the New York Times and reports on the reaction by various critics to the London production of OKLAHOMA! starring Harold (Howard) Keel.

B366. Oliver, Edith. The New Yorker. March 31, 1962.

A review of the Broadway production of NO STRINGS.

B367. Osborne, Robert. "'Entertainment III' Filming Stays on Track." The Hollywood Reporter. April 19, 1993.

The article reports on the filming of THAT'S ENTERTAINMENT! III in which Keel hosts a segment. Others hosting segments include Gene Kelly, Ann Miller, Mickey Rooney, Esther Williams, Debbie Reynolds, June Allyson, and Cyd Charisse.

B368. "'Pagan Love Song'"

A 9½ x 12½ French program/pressbook.

B369. The Philadelphia Inquirer. January 4, 1960.

The article discusses Keel's life before stardom. Keel is pictured.

B370. Photoplay. April 1950.

A color photo story and portrait of Keel.

B371. _____. April 1951.

A photo of Keel's appearance on NBC radio's "Hedda Hopper Show." There is also a review of the film THREE GUYS NAMED MIKE. Keel is pictured with Hedda Hopper, Tony Curtis, and Jan Sterling.

B372. _____. August 1951.

A pictorial of SHOW BOAT with Kathryn Grayson and Keel.

B373. _____. November 1952.

A photo story on Keel.

B374. _____. August 1954.

A photo story on Keel.

B375. Pictureqoer. November 20, 1948.

A photo story on Keel.

B376. _____. April 28, 1951.

Keel and Esther Williams are on the cover. There is also a pictorial of the film PAGAN LOVE SONG.

B377. _____. August 4, 1951.

Keel is pictured with Jane Powell, Vic Damone, and Fernando Lamas. There is a discussion of Keel in the films ANNIE GET YOUR GUN and SHOW BOAT.

B378. _____. December 8, 1951.

An article and picture on TEXAS CARNIVAL.

B379. _____. February 6, 1954.

A picture and article on the film CALAMITY JANE.

B380. _____. March 13, 1954.

A double page pictorial and ad for CALAMITY JANE.

B381. _____. May 8, 1954.

A picture of Keel and wife at Ciro's for Peggy Lee's show. Keel had just finished the film ROSE MARIE.

B382. _____. February 19, 1955.

A pictorial and article on the film SEVEN BRIDES FOR SEVEN BROTHERS.

B383. _____. July 16, 1955.

An article on JUPITER'S DARLING.

B384. Picture Show & Film Pictorial. December 11, 1948.

A pictorial on the film THE SMALL VOICE.

B385. _____. October 7, 1950.

An article & pictorial on the film ANNIE GET YOUR
GUN.   Betty Hutton & Keel are on the cover.

B386. _____. September 22, 1951.

A pictorial on the film SHOW BOAT.   Grayson & Keel
are on the cover.

B387. _____. December 1, 1951.

A pictorial on the film TEXAS CARNIVAL.

B388. _____. June 28, 1952.

An article and Pictorial on the film THE STAR SAID NO
(CALLAWAY WENT THATAWAY).   Keel, Dorothy McGuire, and
Fred MacMurray are on the cover.

B389. _____. October 18, 1952.

A pictorial on the film LOVELY TO LOOK AT.   Kathryn
Grayson, Keel, Ann Miller and Marge and Gower
Champion are pictured.

B390. _____. October 2, 1954.

A pictorial on the film ROSE MARIE with portraits of
Ann Blyth, Keel, and Fernando Lamas.

B391. _____. February 26, 1955.

A pictorial on the film SEVEN BRIDES FOR SEVEN
BROTHERS.   Jane Powell and Keel are on the cover.

B392. _____. July 16, 1955.

A pictorial on the film JUPITER'S DARLING.

B393. _____. July 30, 1955.

An article on the life story of Howard Keel.   Keel
is pictured.

B394. _____. May 5, 1956.

A picture and short paragraph on Keel.

B395. _____. March 23, 1957.

A pictorial on the film KISMET.

B396. Platureau, Alan. "Howard Keel Is Riding Out Blows of a Career Storm." <u>Newsday</u>. March 22, 1965.

Keel discusses a low period in his career since SARATOGA flopped. He attributes the low period to the fact that the big baritone voice is out. He has kept busy in stock and concerts. Keel is pictured.

B397. <u>Playbill</u>.

Playbills from such stock productions as I DO! I DO!, MAN OF LA MANCHA, SOUTH PACIFIC, and THE UNSINKABLE MOLLY BROWN.

B398. Porter, Bob. "Brides, Brothers Romp to Open 1978 Musicals." <u>Dallas Times Herald</u>. June 8, 1978.

A review of the play SEVEN BRIDES FOR SEVEN BROTHERS. Keel is pictured in the "Sobbin' Women" sequence.

B399. Powers, James. "Alcorn-Haskin Pic Has Varied Action." <u>The Hollywood Reporter</u>.

A review of the film ARMORED COMMAND.

B400. Pressbooks.

From the films ARIZONA BUSHWHACKERS, CALLAWAY WENT THATAWAY, MAN FROM BUTTON WILLOW, FLOODS OF FEAR, PAGAN LOVE SONG, KISMET, and LOVELY TO LOOK AT.

B401. Programs.

From THE UNSINKABLE MOLLY BROWN, MAN OF LA MANCHA, MOST HAPPY FELLA, CAROUSEL, AMBASSADOR, CAMELOT, MISTER ROBERTS, THE CROSSING, ON A CLEAR DAY YOU CAN SEE FOREVER, PLAZA SUITE, MUSICAL JUBILEE, NO STRINGS, SEVEN BRIDES FOR SEVEN BROTHERS, SUNRISE AT CAMPOBELLO, THE FANTASTICKS.

B402. Quinn, Frank. "Keel Provides His Own Competition." <u>Mirror</u>. December 2, 1955.

Keel was opening at the Copacabana, and in the film KISMET.

B403. <u>Radio City Music Hall Program</u>. August 30, 1951.

Program and review for the appearance of the film SHOW BOAT at Radio City Music Hall.

B404. _____. February 17, 1955.

Program and review of the appearance of the film JUPITER'S DARLING at Radio City Music Hall.

B405. Renfield, Chris. "'Kiss Me'-In 3-D."

A discussion of viewing KISS ME, KATE in 3-D at the Film Forum.

B406. Robinson, Wayne. "Neil Simon's Fun and Games in Room 719 at the Plaza Hotel." <u>Philadelphia Evening Bulletin</u>. January 20, 1970.

A review of the play PLAZA SUITE at the Locust Theatre in Philadelphia.

B407. Rosenfield, John. "Movies Decide Los Angeles Baritone in London Suits Frank Butler Role." <u>Dallas Morning News</u>. July 12, 1950.

A discussion and critique of Keel's role in the film ANNIE GET YOUR GUN. Keel is pictured.

B408. Salmaggi, Bob. "'Armored Command' and 'David and Goliath'." <u>New York Herald Tribune</u>.

A review of the film ARMORED COMMAND and one also of the film DAVID AND GOLIATH.

B409. <u>Saturday Review</u>. June 9, 1951.

A review of the film SHOW BOAT.

B410. _____. October 27, 1951.

A review of the film ACROSS THE WIDE MISSOURI.

B411. _____. December 1, 1951.

A review of the film CALLAWAY WENT THATAWAY.

B412. _____. June 21, 1952.

A review of the film LOVELY TO LOOK AT.

B413. _____. July 18, 1953.

A review of the film RIDE VAQUERO.

B414. _____. November 14, 1953.

A review of the films CALAMITY JANE and KISS ME, KATE.

B415. _____. April 10, 1954.

A review of the film ROSE MARIE.

B416. _____. August 7, 1954.

A review of the film SEVEN BRIDES FOR SEVEN BROTHERS.

B417. _____. January 1, 1955.

A review of the film SEVEN BRIDES FOR SEVEN BROTHERS.

B418. _____. January 8, 1955.

A review of the film DEEP IN MY HEART.

B419. _____. March 5, 1955.

A review of the film JUPITER'S DARLING.

B420. _____. December 26, 1959.

A review of the Broadway production of SARATOGA.

B421. _____. March 31, 1962.

A review of the Broadway production of NO STRINGS.

B422. _____. July 15, 1967.

A review of the film WAR WAGON.

B423. Schickel, Richard. "Duke Packs a Mean Punch." Life. August 4, 1967.

A review of the film WAR WAGON.

B424. Schier, Ernie. "Da Costa's New Musical 'Saratoga' Premiers." Philadelphia Evening Bulletin. October 27, 1959.

A review of the pre-Broadway tryout of SARATOGA at the Shubert Theatre in Philadelphia. Keel and Carol Lawrence are pictured.

B425. _____. Philadelphia Evening Bulletin. July 12, 1960.

A review of Keel's appearance in SUNRISE AT CAMPOBELLO at the Playhouse in the Park in Philadelphia.

B426. Scott, Vernon. "Howard Keel Dislikes Actors Who Act But Can't Sing, Too." New York Morning Telegraph.

Keel discusses his dislike of actors being cast in musicals instead of singers. Keel is pictured.

B427. _____. "Big Guys Out As Crooners?" New York Morning Telegraph. April 29, 1954.

Keel did not feel that a big man could be a crooner and that women like to mother delicate little singers. Keel is pictured.

B428. Screen Guide. September 1950.

A photo story of the filming of PAGAN LOVE SONG with

Keel and Williams.

B429. <u>Screen Stories</u>. August 1950.

An article on the film ANNIE GET YOUR GUN with Keel and Betty Hutton.

B430. _____. February 1951.

A color portrait of Keel.

B431. _____. March 1951.

A pictorial and screen story on the film THREE GUYS NAMED MIKE. Jane Wyman, Van Johnson, and Keel are on the cover.

B432. _____. August 1951.

A screen story on the film SHOW BOAT with Keel and Kathryn Grayson.

B433. _____. November 1951.

A screen story and pictures on the film TEXAS CARNIVAL.

B434. _____. January 1952.

An article on the film CALLAWAY WENT THATAWAY.

B435. _____. August 1952.

A screen story and pictorial on the film LOVELY TO LOOK AT with Kathryn Grayson & Keel.

B436. _____. February 1953.

Coverage of Keel in the film DESPERATE SEARCH.

B437. _____. December 1953.

Photo screen stories on the films KISS ME, KATE and CALAMITY JANE. Keel is pictured with Kathryn Grayson and Doris Day in their respective films.

B438. _____. April 1954.

A pictorial and complete screen story on the film ROSE MARIE.

B439. <u>Senior Scholastic</u>. March 7, 1951.

A review of the film THREE GUYS NAMED MIKE.

B440. _____. April 21, 1954.

A review of the film ROSE MARIE.

B441. _____. September 15, 1954.

    A review of the film SEVEN BRIDES FOR SEVEN
BROTHERS.

B442. "'Seven Brides' at Muny." <u>St. Louis Post-Dispatch</u>.
June 18, 1978.

    An article on the production of SEVEN BRIDES FOR
SEVEN BROTHERS coming to the Muny.

B443. Shipp, C. "Howard's Booming Baritone." <u>Saturday
Evening Post</u>. October 15, 1955.

    A discussion of Keel's rise from poverty to film
stardom.

B444. <u>Showmen's Trade Review</u>. December 22, 1951.

    A full page pictorial and complete credits for the
film SHOW BOAT with Kathryn Grayson and Keel.

B445. _____. November 13, 1954.

    A trade ad for the film DEEP IN MY HEART.

B446. <u>Sight and Sound</u>. January-March 1955.

    A review of the film SEVEN BRIDES FOR SEVEN BROTHERS.

B447. "Singing Swashbuckler." <u>Cue</u>. December 10, 1955.

    A discussion of Keel being at the Copacabana and in
the film KISMET at the same time. It goes on to talk
about his early career on Broadway and his film and
concert work. Keel is pictured in KISMET and in a
western outfit with a horse.

B448. Sloan, Lloyd. "Here and There." <u>Movie Life</u>. April
1951.

    The article discusses the cast of SHOW BOAT going to
Mocambo's after finishing the film.

B449. Smith, Bea. "Keel Lights Up Meadowbrook as the 'Man
of La Mancha'." Unknown Paper.

    A review of Keel's performance in MAN OF LA MANCHA at
the Meadowbrook Theatre Restaurant in Cedar Grove,
New Jersey.

B450. Smith, Stacy. "'Dallas' Co-star Relishes Checkered
Career." <u>Newark (N.J.) Star Ledger</u>. May 25, 1982.

    The article discusses his career from the Golden Era
of Hollywood, ups and downs of his career, to TV's
"Dallas." He talks of his concern about being
accepted by the others on "Dallas" and of his opening

an oil-investment company in Oklahoma City.

B451. Sokolsky, Bob. "Why Some Call Howard Keel Mister
Nasty." Philadelphia Bulletin. October 19, 1980.

A discussion of Keel's discouragement after a long
tour and his thoughts of retirement. Usually his
mood changed at the thought of a new project. Keel
is pictured with Jane Powell dressed in I DO! I DO!
costumes.

B452. "Songsters of the Year." Unknown Magazine. 1953.

A picture and brief biographical paragraph on Keel.

B453. "Space Getter." Hollywood Picture Life. Winter 1955-
1956.

Keel talks about the roles he gets due to his extra
big voice.

B454. The Spectator. June 30, 1950.

A review of the film ANNIE GET YOUR GUN.

B455. _____. December 31, 1954.

A review of the film SEVEN BRIDES FOR SEVEN BROTHERS.

B456. Spero, Bette. "Keel's Lines Are Down Pat as He Steps
Back into the Theatre." Newark (N.J.) Star Ledger.
July 27, 1977.

While appearing at the Smithville in New Jersey with
former co-star Jane Powell, Keel discusses his life
and career. Powell is pictured with a dog and Keel
as he appeared in 1977 and in his early days.

B457. The Stage & Television Today. September 30, 1971.

A review of the play AMBASSADOR at the Palace in
Manchester, England.

B458. _____. April 7, 1988.

A review of Keel's act at the Barbican in London.

B459. "Staging a "'Thoroughly Modern' Party." Chicago's
American. August 10, 1967.

Keel is pictured with Mary Tyler Moore, Carol
Channing, Elliott Reid, and Ross Hunter at the
Ambassador West Hotel at a party celebrating the
opening of the film THOROUGHLY MODERN MILLIE.

B460. Stewart, Jane. "Britain Gets a Water Bale." Picturegoer. August 30, 1958.

A pictorial on the film FLOODS OF FEAR.

B461. Stewart, Perry. Fort Worth Star-Telegram. June 8, 1978.

A review of the play version of SEVEN BRIDES FOR SEVEN BROTHERS.

B462. Stoddard, Sarah. "Have You Seen His Nose?" Picture-goer. August 7, 1954.

A discussion of Keel's change in nose between LOVELY TO LOOK AT and ROSE MARIE. Keel is pictured in both films.

B463. Sykes, Velma West. "'The Big Fisherman' (BV) Voted November Blue Ribbon Award." Boxoffice.

THE BIG FISHERMAN was voted the November Boxoffice Blue Ribbon Award by members of the National Screen Council. Comments are made by members of the National Screen Council. Three scenes from the film are shown.

B464. The Tatler. September 15, 1954.

A review of the film ROSE MARIE.

B465. _____. December 22, 1954.

A review of the film SEVEN BRIDES FOR SEVEN BROTHERS.

B466. Taylor, John Russell. Plays & Players. December 1971.

A review of the London production of AMBASSADOR.

B467. Tempo. November 6, 1953.

A photo story on 3-D movies including the film KISS ME, KATE.

B468. Theatre Arts. January 1952.

A review of the film CALLAWAY WENT THATAWAY.

B469. Thomas, Bob. "Enter Howard Keel on the Scene of 'Dallas'." The Philadelphia Inquirer. August 12, 1981.

A discussion of Keel's return to the MGM stage where he filmed ANNIE GET YOUR GUN to film TV's 'Dallas'."

B470. _____. "Even Keel-Baritone Turns to Biblical Play From Film Musicals." Newark News. December 17, 1958.

A discussion of Keel going from MGM musicals to the film THE BIG FISHERMAN and about his release from his

MGM contract.

B471. Thompson, Howard. <u>New York Times</u>. August 3, 1967.

A review of the film WAR WAGON.

B472. _____. "On the course of Howard Keel Band-wagon." <u>New York Times</u>. May 18, 1952.

Keel discusses his starting out parking cars to his rise to success at MGM where he is likely to become the studio's crown prince of musicals.

B473. <u>Time</u>. April 12, 1943.

A review of the Broadway production of OKLAHOMA!

B474. ____. April 30, 1945.

A review of the Broadway production of CAROUSEL.

B475. ____. April 24, 1950.

A review of the film ANNIE GET YOUR GUN.

B476. ____. January 15, 1951.

A review of the film PAGAN LOVE SONG.

B477. ____. March 19, 1951.

A review of the film THREE GUYS NAMED MIKE.

B478. ____. July 2, 1951.

A review of the film SHOW BOAT.

B479. ____. November 5, 1951.

A review of the film TEXAS CARNIVAL.

B480. ____. November 19, 1951.

A review of the film ACROSS THE WIDE MISSOURI.

B481. ____. December 10, 1951.

A review of the film CALLAWAY WENT THATAWAY.

B482. ____. June 2, 1952.

A review of the film LOVELY TO LOOK AT.

B483. ____. May 18, 1953.

A review of the film FAST COMPANY.

B484. ____. July 27, 1953.

A review of the film RIDE VAQUERO.

B485. ____. November 16, 1953.

A review of the film KISS ME, KATE.

B486. ____. November 23, 1953.

A review of the film CALAMITY JANE.

B487. ____. March 15, 1954.

A review of the film ROSE MARIE.

B488. ____. July 12, 1954.

A review of the film SEVEN BRIDES FOR SEVEN BROTHERS.

B489. ____. January 17, 1955.

A review of the film DEEP IN MY HEART.

B490. ____. March 7, 1955.

A review of the film JUPITER'S DARLING.

B491. ____. December 26, 1955.

A review of the film KISMET.

B492. ____. August 17, 1959.

A review of the film THE BIG FISHERMAN.

B493. ____. December 21, 1959.

A review of the Broadway production of SARATOGA.

B494. ____. March 31, 1962.

A review of the Broadway production of NO STRINGS.

B495. ____. June 16, 1967.

A review of the film WAR WAGON.

B496. Times of London. May 1, 1947.

A review of the London production of OKLAHOMA!

B497. Torre, Marie. "Just a Minor Plunge." New York Herald Tribune. September 24, 1957.

A discussion of Keel's plans to appear on the "Dinah Shore Show" and his feelings about appearing on TV occasionally being okay but not on a long-term basis.

B498. Train, Sylvia. "Brides Rollicking in New Marriage."

Toronto Sun. July 19, 1978.

A review of Keel's appearance in the play version of
SEVEN BRIDES FOR SEVEN BROTHERS at the O'Keefe
Centre in Toronto. Keel is pictured.

B499. "TV Guide Previews." TV Guide. September 13, 1958.

Preview of Bob Hope's TV version of ROBERTA which
included Howard Keel.

B500. "U.S. Film Star's Screen Debut was in England."
Sunday News. February 13, 1955.

A discussion of Keel's success in England before
signing with MGM. The article also talks about his
role in JUPITER'S DARLING. Keel is pictured with
Esther Williams.

B501. Variety. November 24, 1948.

A review of the film THE SMALL VOICE.

B502. _____. April 12, 1950.

A review of the film ANNIE GET YOUR GUN.

B503. _____. December 20, 1950.

A review of the film PAGAN LOVE SONG.

B504. _____. February 14, 1951.

A review of the film THREE GUYS NAMED MIKE.

B505. _____. June 6, 1951.

A review of the film SHOW BOAT.

B506. _____. September 12, 1951.

A review of the film TEXAS CARNIVAL.

B507. _____. November 7, 1951.

A review of the film ACROSS THE WIDE MISSOURI.

B508. _____. November 14, 1951.

A review of the film CALLAWAY WENT THATAWAY.

B509. _____. May 28, 1952.

A review of the film LOVELY TO LOOK AT.

B510. _____. November 26, 1952.

A review of the film DESPERATE SEARCH.

B511. _____. April 8, 1953.

A review of the film FAST COMPANY.

B512. _____. June 24, 1953.

A review of the film RIDE VAQUERO.

B513. _____. October 21, 1953.

A review of the film CALAMITY JANE.

B514. _____. October 28, 1953.

A review of the film KISS ME, KATE.

B515. _____. March 3, 1954.

A review of the film ROSE MARIE.

B516. _____. March 10, 1954.

A review of Keel's act at the Last Frontier in Las Vegas.

B517. _____. June 2, 1954.

A review of the film SEVEN BRIDES FOR SEVEN BROTHERS.

B518. _____. December 1, 1954.

A review of the film DEEP IN MY HEART.

B519. _____. January 26, 1955.

A review of the film JUPITER'S DARLING.

B520. _____. December 7, 1955.

A review of Keel's act at the Copacabana in New York and a second review of the film KISMET.

B521. _____. April 11, 1956.

A review of Keel's act at the Empire in Glasgow.

B522. _____. April 25, 1956.

A review of Keel's act at the Palladium in London.

B523. _____. May 29, 1957.

A review of Keel's appearance on the British TV show "Sunday Night at the London Palladium" on May 19, 1957.

B524. _____. May 29, 1957.

A review of Keel's appearance at the Empire in
Glasgow.

B525. _____. September 18, 1957.

A review of the City Center production of the play
CAROUSEL.

B526. _____. November 20, 1957.

A review of Keel's appearance on TV's "General
Motor's 25th Anniversary."

B527. _____. May 7, 1958.

A review of Keel's appearance on the British TV show
"Sunday Night at the London Palladium" on April 27,
1958.

B528. _____. November 26, 1958.

A review of the film FLOODS OF FEAR.

B529. _____. March 11, 1959.

A review of Keel's appearance on TV's "Bell Telephone
Hour."

B530. _____. July 1, 1959.

A review of the film THE BIG FISHERMAN.

B531. _____. December 9, 1959.

A review of the Broadway play SARATOGA.

B532. _____. March 16, 1960.

A review of Keel's appearance on TV's "Bell Telephone
Hour-Main Street."

B533. _____. October 12, 1960.

A review of Keel's appearance on the British TV show
"Saturday Spectacular" on October 8, 1960.

B534. _____. August 2, 1961.

A review of the film ARMORED COMMAND.

B535. _____. September 6, 1961.

A review of Keel's appearance on the British TV show
"Bernard Delfont's Sunday Show."

B536. _____. May 1, 1963.

A review of the film DAY OF THE TRIFFIDS.

B537. _____. January 27, 1965.

A review of the film THE MAN FROM BUTTON WILLOW.

B538. _____. August 10, 1966.

A review of the film WACO.

B539. _____. January 11, 1967.

A review of the film RED TOMAHAWK.

B540. _____. May 24, 1967.

A review of the film WAR WAGON.

B541. _____. February 14, 1968.

A review of the film ARIZONA BUSHWHACKERS.

B542. _____. October 2, 1968.

A review of Keel and Kathryn Grayson's act at the
Fremont in Las Vegas.

B543. _____. December 11, 1968.

A review of Keel & Kathryn Grayson's act at Harrah's
in Reno.

B544. _____. April 30, 1969.

A review of Keel and Kathryn Grayson's act at the
Cocoanut Grove in Los Angeles.

B545. _____. December 31, 1969.

A review of Keel and Kathryn Grayson's act at the
Fremont in Las Vegas.

B546. _____. March 31, 1971.

A review of Keel's act at London's Talk of the Town.

B547. _____. November 24, 1971.

A review of the London production of AMBASSADOR.

B548. _____. March 8, 1972.

A review of Keel and Kathryn Grayson's act at the
Fremont in Las Vegas.

B549. _____. November 22, 1972.

A review of the Broadway production of AMBASSADOR.

B550. _____. June 26, 1974.

A review of Keel's London Palladium appearance.

B551. _____. July 18, 1989.

A review of Keel's show at the Greek Theatre.

B552. _____. "Howard Keel Into TV." October 23, 1957.

A discussion of Keel being a TV hold out and of his appearance on the TV show "Zane Grey" in the episode "Gift From a Gun Man."

B553. Walker, Derek. "This Film Has Fun With TV." Picturgoer. June 21, 1952.

Pictures and an article on the film THE STAR SAID NO (CALLAWAY WENT THATAWAY).

B554. Wallace, Leonard. "No Business Like Show Business." Picturegoer. October 7, 1950.

An article and pictures on the film ANNIE GET YOUR GUN.

B555. _____. "'Pagan Love Song'." Picturegoer. April 28, 1951.

An article and picture on the film PAGAN LOVE SONG.

B556. Watt, Douglas. "Small World-Coming and Going." New York Daily News. August 10, 1957.

Mention is made of Keel's New York City Center production of CAROUSEL.

B557. _____. "'Ambassador' Lackluster Musical." New York Daily News. November 20, 1972.

A review of the Broadway production of AMBASSADOR. Danielle Darrieux and Keel are pictured.

B558. Watts, Richard. "A Handsome Musical Play Suffers From Book Trouble." New York Post. December 8, 1959.

A review of the Broadway production of SARATOGA.

B559. _____. New York Post. November 20, 1972.

A review of the Broadway production of AMBASSADOR.

B560. Weiler, A. H. "Screen: A Dedicated Story of the Man Simon, Called Peter." New York Times. August 6, 1959.

A review of the film THE BIG FISHERMAN.

B561. Wibman, Hal. "Rosy Promises for Diskers In 'Annie,' 'Rosie' Films"/"MGM's 'Annie' Flick Clicks; Promises

Hypo for Platters."

A review of the film ANNIE GET YOUR GUN as well as a discussion of various artists releasing recordings of songs from the film. The 'Rosie' film is THE DAUGHTER OF ROSIE O'GRADY starring Gordon MacRae.

B562. Widen, Allen. "Coast to Coast." Hartford Times. June 22, 1966.

The article is a discussion of Keel's dislike of people who are indecisive. Also discussed was his tackling the direction of his tour of CAROUSEL and of his taking up flying.

B563. Willard, Bill. "Caught in the Act." Downbeat. April 7, 1954.

A review of Keel's act at the Last Frontier in Vegas.

B564. Winsten, Archer. "'Floods of Fear' at RKO Albee." New York Post. June 4, 1959.

A review of the film FLOODS OF FEAR.

B565. _____. "John Wayne & Kirk Douglas Pack Guns in 'WAR WAGON'." New York Post. August 3, 1967.

A review of the film WAR WAGON.

B566. _____. New York Post. June 4, 1959.

A review of the film FLOODS OF FEAR.

B567. _____. "'Rose Marie' at Music Hall." New York Daily News. December 31, 1955.

A review of the film ROSE MARIE.

B568. Wood, Thomas. "'The Big Fisherman' a Home Product." New York Herald Tribune. June 7, 1959.

An article on the making of the film THE BIG FISHERMAN. Keel is pictured receiving instructions from director Frank Borzage.

B569. Zeitlin, Ida. "Many Brave Hearts." Photoplay. October 1951.

The article discusses for the first time Keel's life story. Miscellaneous photos.

BOOKS

B570. Adams, Les and Rainey, Buck. Shoot-Em-Ups. N.Y.: Arlington House, 1978.

The book covers every western (including musicals) in

chronological order. It includes Keel's westerns.

B571. Amory, Cleveland, editor. International Celebrity
Register. N.Y.: Celebrity Register LTD, 1959.

The book gives a biographical account of Keel
including a picture.

B572. Amory, Cleveland and Blackwell, Earl. Celebrity
Register. N.Y.: Harper & Row, 1963.

The book gives a biographical account of Keel
including a picture.

B573. Aros, Andrew. An Actor Guide to the Talkies
1965-1974. N.J.: Scarecrow Press, 1977.

The book is arranged by film and gives company,
release date, star and character played for films
between 1965-1974.

B574. Aumack, Sheryl. Song & Dance-An Encyclopedia of
Musicals. CA: Sea-Maid Press, 1990.

The book is arranged by title giving company, release
date, credits, running time, cast and character,
songs, a brief synopsis, and soundtracks for musical
films.

B575. Aylesworth, Thomas. Broadway to Hollywood. N.Y.:
Gallery Books, 1985.

The book discusses in words and pictures the Broadway
and Hollywood versions of musicals. It includes
ANNIE GET YOUR GUN, SHOW BOAT, KISS ME, KATE, ROSE
MARIE, KISMET, and the London version of OKLAHOMA!

B576. _____. History of Movie Musicals. CT:
Bison Books, 1984.

As its title suggests, it covers the history of the
movie musical chronologically. It includes a filmography. Keel is included in SHOW BOAT, LOVELY TO
LOOK AT, ROSE MARIE, SEVEN BRIDES FOR SEVEN BROTHERS,
ANNIE GET YOUR GUN, KISS ME, KATE, and KISMET.

B577. Aylesworth, Thomas and Bowman, John. The World
Almanac Who's Who of Film. N.Y.: World Almanac, 1987.

The book gives a brief biographical sketch of Keel
and a selected listing of his films.

B578. _____. World Guide to
Film Stars. N.Y.: Malland Press, 1991.

The book gives a profile of Keel.

B579. Benjamin, Ruth and Rosenblatt, Arthur. Movie Song

Catalog. N.C.: McFarland, 1993.

The book is arranged by film and gives the film's country of origin, year of release, whether the film is in black and white or color, the running time, director, musical director, music score, producer, performer and supporting cast for songs sung in 1,460 musical and non-musical films between 1928-1988.

B580. Badden, David, editor. The Film Dope-Volume 29. England: March 1984.

The book gives a biography and commentary on Keel and includes a filmography.

B581. Bergan, Ronald. Glamorous Musicals. London: Octopus Books Limited, 1984.

The book explores the glamor and glitter of film musicals from the early days to MGM musicals of the 1950s. It includes KISS ME, KATE, ANNIE GET YOUR GUN, SHOW BOAT, SEVEN BRIDES FOR SEVEN BROTHERS, and KISMET.

B582. Bloom, Ken. American Song 1900-1984. N.Y.: Facts on File, 1985.

This two-volume book lists shows, opening date and the number of performances. It also gives cast, credits, and songs including those dropped from the show.

B583. Blum, Daniel. Screen World. N.Y.: Biblio and Tanner.

Reprint of various volumes of Screen World which covers each year's films giving credits, cast, and a picture of each film.

B584. _____. Theatre World 1959-1960. N.Y.: Crown, 1961.

The book covers the entire theatre season including SARATOGA. It includes credits, cast and character, theatre, opening date, and pictures.

B585. Blum, Daniel and Willis, John. A Pictorial History of the American Theatre 1860-1980. N.Y.: Crown, 1981.

This book gives a pictorial history, by year, of the theatre with 6,000 photographs.

B586. Braun, Eric. Doris Day. London: George Weidenfeld and Nicholson, 1991.

This is a biography of Doris Day and includes reference to co-star Keel.

B587. Brooks, Tim. The Complete Directory to Prime Time TV

Stars 1946-Present. N.Y.: Ballantine Books, 1987.

The paperback book is arranged by star and gives a
brief biographical sketch of the star and a listing
of TV series in which the star appeared. Keel is
covered in "Dallas."

B588. Brooks, Tim and Marsh, Earle. The Complete Directory
to Prime Time Network TV Shows. (5th Edition). N.Y.:
Ballantine Books, 1992.

This paperback book gives prime time TV shows with
synopsis, credits, cast, and Emmy winners.

B589. Chamels, Sol and Wolsky, Albert. The Movie Makers.
N.J.: Derbebooks, Inc., 1974.

The book is arranged by star and gives a brief biographical sketch and a sample listing of films.

B590. Clarke, Donald, editor. The Penguin Encyclopedia of
Popular Music. N.Y.: Viking, 1989.

The book gives a profile on Keel.

B591. Connor, Jim. Ann Miller Tops in Taps. N.Y.: Franklin
Watts, 1981.

The book covers the life and career of Ann Miller
including her films with Keel.

B592. Corey, Melinda and Ochoa, George. A Cast of
Thousands. N.Y.: Facts on File, 1992.

This is a three-volume set that lists films with
company, director, cast and characters. Volume 3 is
an index by performer listing their films covered
in the first two volumes.

B593. Cross, Robin. 2000 Movies the 1950s. N.Y.: Arlington
House, 1988.

This is a pictorial book covering, by year, some 2,000
movies of the 1950s by genre. A picture accompanies
each film.

B594. Daniel, John. Ava Gardner. N.Y.: St. Martin's Press,
1982.

This is a biography of Miss Gardner and includes her
films with Keel.

B595. Dimmitt, Richard Bertrand. An Actor Guide to the
Talkies. N.J.: Scarecrow Press, 1967.

The book is arranged by film and gives company,
release date, character and star for some 8,000 films
between January 1949 and December 1964.

B596. Druxman, Michael. <u>The Musical From Broadway to Hollywood</u>. N.J.: A.S. Barnes, 1980.

The book is divided into chronological chapters on shows, discussing both the Broadway and film versions. The author dedicated the book to Keel and his wife Judy.

B597. Eames, John Douglas. <u>The MGM Story</u>. N.Y.: Crown Publishers, 1975.

The book covers, by year, every film made by MGM. Each film is pictured.

B598. <u>Earl Blackwell's Entertainment Celebrity Register</u>. N.Y.: Visible Ink, 1991.

The book gives a profile on Keel.

B599. Essoe, Gabe. <u>The Films of Clark Gable</u>. N.J.: Citadel Press, 1972.

This is a pictorial history of Gable's life and films and gives information on the films ACROSS THE WIDE MISSOURI and CALLAWAY WENT THATAWAY.

B600. Eyles, Allen. <u>John Wayne and the Movies</u>. N.Y.: A.S. Barnes, 1976.

The book covers each of Wayne's movies including the WAR WAGON.

B601. <u>Film Review 1950</u>.

Covers film releases of 1950 with cast, credits, synopsis, and portraits.

B602. Finler, Joel. <u>The Hollywood Story</u>. N.Y.: Crown Publishers, 1988.

The book covers the history of the Hollywood movie industry. Each major studio covered includes their histories, releases, finances, stars, directors, creative personnel, and Academy Awards. It also covers the leading personnel by profession, and studio. Box office hits, and general statistics are also listed.

B603. Fitzgerald, Michael. <u>Universal Pictures</u>. N.Y.: Arlington House, 1977.

This big book covers the history of the studio, and a year by year filmography. It has over 600 photos. The author profiles the top 72 actors and actresses. It lists supporting players, Academy Awards and nominations. Keel is covered in the films FLOODS OF FEAR and WAR WAGON.

B604. Flamini, Roland. _Ava Gardner_. N.Y.: Coward, McCann, and Geohegan, 1983.

This is a biography of Ava Gardner and includes Keel.

B605. Fordin, Hugh. _The World of Entertainment_. N.Y.: Doubleday, 1975.

The book discusses behind the scenes information on the Arthur Freed Unit at MGM including Keel's ANNIE GET YOUR GUN, PAGAN LOVE SONG, SHOW BOAT, and KISMET.

B606. Fowler, Karen. _Ava Gardner: A Bio-Bibliography_. CT: Greenwood Press, 1990.

This book gives credits, cast, synopsis, and reviews on the films SHOW BOAT and RIDE VAQUERO in which Gardner and Keel starred.

B607. Gambaccini, Paul and Rice, Tim and Jonathan. _British Hit Albums_. England: Guinness, 1992.

This paperback book gives a year by year review of albums. It then gives, by artist, the title, label, catalogue number of albums that hit the British charts. For each album it gives the highest position reached and the total weeks charted.

B608. Gammond, Peter. _The Oxford Companion to Popular Music_. N.Y.: Oxford University Press, 1991.

The book gives a profile on Keel.

B609. Ganzl, Kurt. _The Blackwell Guide to the Musical Theatre on Record_. MA: Basil Blackwell Inc., 1990.

The book discusses various versions of recordings of shows and films.

B610. Gardner, Ava. _Ava, My Story_. N.Y.: Bantam Books, 1990.

Autobiography of Ava Gardner with reference to Keel.

B611. Gelb, Alan. _The Doris Day Scrapbook_. N.Y.: Grosset & Dunlap, 1977.

This paperback covers the life and career of Miss Day in words and pictures including Keel and the film CALAMITY JANE.

B612. Gianakos, Larry James. _Television Drama Series Programming: A Comprehensive Chronicle 1959-1975_. N.J.: Scarecrow Press, 1978.

This is a part of a series of books covering each drama series with an episode by episode listing. It includes Keel's appearances between the years given.

B613. _____. Television Drama Series
Programming: A Comprehensive Chronicle 1975-1980.
N.J.: Scarecrow Press, 1981.

This volume covers the drama series by episode for
the years covered including Keel's appearances.

B614. Green, Stanley. Encyclopedia of the Musical Film.
N.Y.: Oxford University Press, 1981.

The author gives a brief biographical sketch of
persons related to the musical film and a
chronological listing of their musical films
including character played.

B615. _____. Encyclopedia of the Musical Theatre.
N.Y.: Dodd, Mead & Co., 1976.

The author gives a profile of stars related to the
musical theatre and a chronological listing of their
musical shows including character played. The book
also lists important shows and songs.

B616. _____. Hollywood Musicals Year By Year. WI:
Hal Leonard Publishing Corp., 1990.

The book covers film musicals by year and includes
credits, cast, songs, release date, a critical
commentary, recordings and video. Keel's films ANNIE
GET YOUR GUN, SHOW BOAT, LOVELY TO LOOK AT, KISS ME,
KATE, ROSE MARIE, SEVEN BRIDES FOR SEVEN BROTHERS,
DEEP IN MY HEART, and KISMET are covered.

B617. _____. Rodgers and Hammerstein Fact Book.
N.Y.: Lynn Farnol Group, 1980.

This paperback gives detailed facts about the
productions of Rodgers & Hammerstein. It covers
Broadway, touring, selected revivals, and films.

B618. _____. The World of Musical Comedy. N.Y.:
A.S. Barnes, 1980.

The book discusses, by chapter, the shows and music
of composers. An appendix gives each composers shows
with cast, credits, songs, and sample recordings.

B619. Guernsey, Otis, editor. The Best Plays of 1967-1968.
N.Y.: Dodd, Mead & Co., 1968.

The book gives the season's shows both on Broadway
and in touring productions.

B620. _____. The Best Plays of 1969-1970.
N.Y.: Dodd, Mead & Co., 1970.

The book covers the season both on Broadway and in
touring productions.

B621. _____. The Best Plays of 1971-1972.
N.Y.: Dodd, Mead & Co., 1972.

The Broadway and touring productions, for the season,
are covered by this book.

B622. _____. The Best Plays of 1972-1973.
N.Y.: Dodd, Mead & Co., 1973.

The book chronicles the theatre season for both
Broadway and touring productions.

B623. _____. The Best Plays of 1975-1976.
N.Y.: Dodd, Mead & Co., 1976.

The book chronicles the theatre season for both
Broadway and touring productions.

B624. _____. The Best Plays of 1977-1978.
N.Y.: Dodd, Mead & Co., 1978.

The book chronicles the theatre season for both
Broadway and touring productions.

B625. Halliwell, Leslie. Halliwell's Film and Video Guide.
N.Y.: Charles Scribner's Sons, 1987.

For each entry, Halliwell gives cast, short credit
list, small summary and critique, Academy Awards, and
availability on video.

B626. _____. Halliwell's Filmgoer's Companion.
N.Y.: Charles Scribner's Sons. 1988.

For each star, Halliwell gives a brief biographical
sketch and a listing of films.

B627. Hardy, Phil. The Western. N.Y.: William Morrow and
Company, Inc., 1983.

The book covers every film western in chronological
order. It includes Keel's musical and non-musical
westerns.

B628. Hardy, Phil and Laing, Dave. The Faber Companion to
20th Century Popular Music. London: Faber and Faber,
1990.

The book gives a profile on Keel.

B629. Hay, Peter. MGM: When the Lion Roars. GA: Turner
Publishing, 1991.

The book gives the history of MGM. Many pictures.

B630. Hewes, Henry. Best Plays 1963-1964. N.Y.: Dodd, Mead
& Co., 1964.

Hewes chronicles the theatre season, covering the Broadway and touring productions.

B631. Hirschorn, Clive. The Hollywood Musical. N.Y.: Crown Publishers, 1981.

Every film musical, by year, is covered from 1927 to the present. Each film is illustrated. For each year, Academy Award winners and nominees are given as well as the top moneymaking films for that year.

B632. _____ . The Warner Bros. Story. N.Y.: Crown Publishers, 1979.

The book covers every Warner Bros. film by year. Each film is pictured. Keel is covered under CALAMITY JANE.

B633. Hodgins, Gordon. The Broadway Musical-A Complete LP Discography. N.J.: Scarecrow Press, 1980.

The book gives various recordings of Broadway shows with record label, year, cast, credits, and songs. It has a book and lyric writer, performer, song and label indexes.

B634. Hotchner, A. E. Doris Day Her Own Story. N.Y.: William Morrow & Co., 1976.

Miss Day's autobiography in which CALAMITY JANE is covered.

B635. Houseman, Victoria. Made in Heaven. IL: Bonus Books, Inc., 1991.

This paperback discusses the marriages and children of more than 700 Hollywood stars.

B636. Hummel, David. The Collector's Guide to the American Musical Theatre. N.J.: Scarecrow Press, 1984.

Volume one of this two-volume set gives detailed information on the different recordings of shows and volume two is an index.

B637. Inman, David. The TV Encyclopedia. N.Y.: Perigee Books, 1991.

This paperback gives birth (deaths where applicable) dates of stars and lists shows they appeared on regularly as well as guest appearances and TV movies.

B638. Jackson, Arthur. The Best Musicals. N.Y.: Crown Publishers, 1977.

The author gives a history of Broadway and film musicals.

B639. Kaplan, Mike, editor. <u>Variety Who's Who in Show Business</u>. N.Y.: Garland, 1983.

There is a small profile on Keel.

B640. Kaplan, Philip. <u>The Best, Worst, & Most Unusual Hollywood Musicals</u>. N.Y.: Beekman House, 1983.

The book discusses, as its title suggests, the best, worst, and most unusual film musicals. Keel's films SHOW BOAT and SEVEN BRIDES FOR SEVEN BROTHERS are covered.

B641. Karney, Robyn, editor. <u>The Movie Star Story</u>. N.Y.: Crescent Books, 1984.

The book gives a listing, by decade, of stars with a biographical and career study, including a picture.

B642. Kass, Judith. <u>Ava Gardner</u>. N.Y.: Jove Publications, 1977.

A biography of Miss Gardner with reference to co-star Howard Keel.

B643. Katler, Susy. <u>The Complete Book of Dallas</u>. N.Y.: Harry N. Abrams, Inc., 1986.

This is a big picture and word book giving behind the scenes information on TV's "Dallas."

B644. Katz, Ephraim. <u>The Film Encyclopedia</u>. N.Y.: Thomas Y. Crowell, 1979.

The book gives film terms, biographical sketches and film credits for persons identified with film.

B645. Kinkle, Roger. <u>The Complete Encyclopedia of Popular Music and Jazz 1900-1950</u>. N.Y.: Arlington House, 1974.

This is a massive four-volume set. The second volume has a biographical sketch on Keel with a chronological film listing and sample recordings.

B646. Kobal, John. <u>Gotta Sing Gotta Dance</u>. N.Y.: Exeter Books, 1983.

The book covers the history of the musical film. It includes Keel's SHOW BOAT, SEVEN BRIDES FOR SEVEN BROTHERS, and KISS ME, KATE.

B647. Kreuger, Miles. <u>Show Boat-The Story of a Classic American Musical</u>. N.Y.: DaCapo Press, 1977.

The book gives a complete history of SHOW BOAT and various productions of the show. It includes a chapter on Keel's film version.

B648. Kronenberger, Louis, editor. <u>Best Plays</u>. N.Y.: Dodd
Mead, 1960.

Keel's version of SARATOGA is covered.

B649. Leiby, Bruce R. <u>Gordon MacRae: A Bio-Bibliography</u>. CT:
Greenwood Press, 1991.

Howard Keel was among the many considered for the
leads in the film versions of both OKLAHOMA! and
CAROUSEL but lost out to Gordon MacRae because he
was still under contract to MGM.

B650. Leonard, William Torbert. <u>Theatre: Stage to Screen to
Television</u>. N.J.: Scarecrow Press, 1981.

This two-volume set discusses shows that were done on
stage and were made into films and were done on
television.

B651. Lloyd, Anne and Fuller, Graham. <u>The Illustrated Who's
Who of the Cinema</u>. N.Y.: Macmillian Co., 1983.

An alphabetical listing of persons connected to the
cinema with a biographical sketch and a sampling of
their films. Keel is pictured with Betty Hutton in
ANNIE GET YOUR GUN.

B652. Lynch, Richard Chigley, compiler. <u>Movie Musicals on
Record</u>. CT: Greenwood Press, 1989.

For each film musical the composer, cast, and songs
(with performer) are given.

B653. _____. <u>TV and Studio Cast Musicals
on Record</u>. CT: Greenwood Press, 1990.

For each TV, stage, or film musical, the TV or studio
cast recording is given along with composer, cast,
and songs (with performer).

B654. McNeil, Alex. <u>Total Television 1948 to Present</u>.
N.Y.: Penguin Books, 1984.

This paperback, arranged by title, gives a synopsis
of the show with cast as well as a listing of
selected specials and a chronological listing of Emmy
winners.

B655. Maltin, Leonard. <u>Leonard Maltin's TV Movies and Video
Guide</u>. N.Y.: Signet, 1992.

This thick paperback covers 19,000 films with cast,
credits, a short summary and review. It gives a star
rating and indicates which films are available on
video.

B656. Mandelbaum, Ken. 40 Years of Broadway Musical Flops.
N.Y.: St. Martin's Press, 1991.

The book discusses musical flops including Keel's
AMBASSADOR and SARATOGA.

B657. Martin, Mick and Porter, Marsha. Video Movie Guide
1993. N.Y.: Ballantine Books, 1992.

This thick paperback lists over 12,000 films with
credits, cast, brief summary, star rating of films
available on video. It includes a director and star
index.

B658. Marx, Kenneth. Star Stats. CA: Price/Stern/Sloan,
1979.

This paperback gives a computerized print out on
important statistics on various stars including Keel.

B659. Mawhinney, Paul. Music Master-the 45 rpm Record
Directory. PA: Record-Rama, 1983.

This is a two-volume set the size of telephone books.
Volume one lists, by artist, their 45 recordings.
The second volume is arranged by title and lists
various artists versions.

B660. Michael, Paul, editor. The American Movies Reference
Book: The Sound Era. N.J.: Prentice Hall, 1969.

The book is divided into chapters on the history of
the film, players, films, films directors, producers,
and awards of films. There is a profile and film listing
on Keel. He is pictured with Ava Gardner in RIDE
VAQUERO.

B661. Mordden, Ethan. The Hollywood Musical. N.Y.: St.
Martin's Press, 1981.

Mordden gives a history of the film musical.

B662. _____. Rodgers & Hammerstein. N.Y.: Harry N.
Abrams, 1992.

The book gives a history, by show, of the Broadway
and film productions of Rodgers & Hammerstein shows.

B663. Morino, Marianne. The Hollywood Walk of Fame. CA:
Ten Speed Press, 1987.

This paperback gives every performer with a star on
the Walk of Fame and for what category. It gives a
brief statement on each person and the location of
the star.

B664. Morris, George. Doris Day. N.Y.: Pyramid Communications, Inc., 1976.

The paperback discusses the life and career of Miss Day including the film CALAMITY JANE and co-star Howard Keel.

B665. Nash, Jay Robert and Ross, Stanley Ralph. <u>The Motion Picture Guide</u>. IL: Cinebooks, Inc., 1985.

This is a twelve-volume set that covers films alphabetically from 1927-1983 giving cast, credits, synopsis, and critical commentary on each film.

B666. <u>New York Times Directory of the Film</u>. N.Y.: Arno/ Random House, 1971.

This huge book gives sample reviews, and a listing, by artist, of films reviewed in the <u>New York Times</u>.

B667. <u>New York Times Directory of the Theatre</u>. N.Y.: Arno/ Quadrangle, 1973.

This huge book gives sample reviews, and a listing, by artist, of plays reviewed by the <u>New York Times</u>.

B668. <u>1991 Arnold Talking Yellow Pages</u> (Sherman Oaks & Studio City Edition).

Keel is pictured on the cover and he is the subject of the cover story. Keel is pictured in the story.

B669. O'Donnell, Monica, editor. <u>Contemporary Theatre, Film and TV</u>. MI: Gale Research.

A profile is given on Keel.

B670. Oliviero, Jeffrey. <u>Motion Picture Players' Credits</u>. NC: McFarland, 1991.

This big volume gives a brief statement on some 150,000 worldwide stars who made films between 1967-1980. It also lists their film credits for that period as well as those between 1905-1983.

B671. Osborne, Jerry. <u>Official Price Guide-Movie/TV/Sound-Tracks and Original Cast Albums</u>. N.Y.: House of Collectibles, 1991.

This big paperback lists, by show, various recorded versions and the range of value.

B672. Osborne, Jerry and Hamilton, Bruce. <u>Movie, TV Soundtrack and Original Cast Albums Price Guide</u>. AZ: O'Sullivan, Woodside & Co., 1981.

This paperback lists alphabetically various show recordings with composer, cast, year, record number, and price range.

B673. Osborne, Robert. <u>50 Golden Years of Oscar</u>. CA: ESC California, 1979.

This paperback gives the official history of the Academy of Motion Picture Arts and Sciences and a yearly record of the nominations and winners of the Oscar.

B674. Parish, James Robert and Bowers, Ronald. <u>The MGM Stock Company</u>. N.Y.: Arlington House, 1973.

The book gives a career study of MGM's stock players with a listing of the person's films. Keel is pictured in ANNIE GET YOUR GUN, ROSE MARIE, and KISMET.

B675. Parish, James Robert and Mark, Gregory. <u>The Best of MGM-The Golden Years: 1928-1959</u>. N.Y.: Arlington House, 1981.

The book gives cast, credits, synopsis, and background information on selected MGM films. There are many illustrations.

B676. Parish, James Robert and Pitts, Michael. <u>The Great Hollywood Musical Pictures</u>. N.J.: Scarecrow Press, 1992.

The book gives an alphabetical listing of musical films and includes credits, songs, cast and character, synopsis, and a critical commentary.

B677. _____. <u>The Great Western Pictures</u>. N.J.: Scarecrow Press, 1976.

The book is arranged alphabetically by film and includes credits, cast and character, synopsis, and commentary.

B678. _____. <u>Hollywood Songsters</u>. N.Y.: Garland, 1991.

This book profiles the lives and careers of 100 musical stars, in mini chapters, and includes their movies, TV series, Broadway shows, radio series, and LP credits. A picture is provided of each star.

B679. Parish, James Robert and Terrace, Vincent. <u>The Complete Actors' Television Credits 1948-1988</u>. N.J.: Scarecrow Press, 1989.

This is a two-volume set. Volume one covers the television credits for film actors and volume two does the same for film actresses.

B680. Pickard, Roy. <u>A Companion to the Movies 1903 to Present</u>. N.Y.: Hippocrene Books, 1972.

The book covers each film genre with sample films and a brief sketch of persons associated with that genre.

B681. _____. The Oscar Movies. N.Y.: Taplinger Publishing Co., 1977.

Each film that has won an Oscar is listed alphabetically giving the Oscars won, production company, director, cast, and a brief synopsis.

B682. Picturegoer Film Annual 1955-1956.

Keel is among the stars featured.

B683. Pierce, David. The Film Daily Yearbook Guide to the Fifties. MD: 1987.

The book lists all of the films reviewed by Film Daily during the fifties giving cast, credits, release date, and date reviewed.

B684. Pitts, Michael. Western Movies-A TV and Video Guide to 4200 Genre Films. N.C.: McFarland, 1986.

The book is arranged alphabetically by film. Credits, cast, synopsis, and a critical comment are given for each film.

B685. Pitts, Michael and Harrison, Louis. Hollywood on Record: The Film Stars' Discography. N.J.: Scarecrow Press, 1978.

The book is arranged alphabetically by star, and for each LPs, compilation records and a sampling of 45s are given.

B686. Powell, Jane. The Girl Next Door...and How She Grew. N.Y.: William Morrow & Co., 1988.

Miss Powell's autobiography in which she discusses SEVEN BRIDES FOR SEVEN BROTHERS and working with Keel.

B687. Preview Annual 1951. London: Harrison Sons Ltd.

The book discusses stars and previews films coming in 1951. Keel and Hutton are pictured on the cover in ANNIE GET YOUR GUN.

B688. Preview: 1951.

A British book containing a photobiography, the year's awards, and items on pictures including SEVEN BRIDES FOR SEVEN BROTHERS.

B689. Quinlan, David. Quinlan's Illustrated Directory of Film Stars. N.Y.: Hippocrene, 1986.

Quinlan gives a brief biographical sketch on some
1,700 stars with 1,660 pictures as well as screen
credits including film shorts.

B690. Ragan, David. <u>Who's Who in Hollywood 1900-1976</u>. N.Y.:
Arlington House, 1976.

Ragan gives a biographical profile on stars, character
actors, and bit players. In the front half of the
book, he updates the person's life and career and in
the second part of the book he profiles deceased
persons. The book was updated by Ragan, in 1992, and
was expanded into two volumes and published by Facts
On File.

B691. Raymond, Jack. <u>Show Music on Record</u>. N.Y.: Frederick
Ungar, 1982.

The book lists the various recordings of shows under
the original year of production with performer, and
record number. It was revised, in 1992, and
published by the Smithsonian Institution Press.

B692. Ricci, Mark and Zmijewsky, Boris and Steve. <u>The Films
of John Wayne</u>. N.Y.: Citadel Press, 1970.

Wayne's life and career are covered in words and many
pictures with detailed coverage of each of his films
including WAR WAGON.

B693. Sackett, Susan. <u>The Hollywood Reporter Book of Box
Office Hits</u>. N.Y.: Billboard Books, 1990.

This paperback takes a year by year, behind the
scenes look at Hollywood's successful movies. Keel
is covered under SHOW BOAT.

B694. _____. <u>Prime Time Hits</u>. N.Y.: Billboard
Books, 1993.

The paperback covers, by decade, the TV hits from
1950 to the present and includes a chapter on
"Dallas."

B695. Scheuer, Steven, editor. <u>Movies on TV and Video-
cassette</u>. N.Y.: Bantam Books, 1992.

This thick paperback lists films with credits,
stars, short review, star rating, and brief summary.

B696. Schuster, Mel. <u>Motion Picture Performers: A
Bibliography of Magazine and Periodical Articles
1900-1969</u>. N.J.: Scarecrow Press, 1971.

The book lists articles on motion picture stars.

B697. Sennett, Ted. <u>Hollywood Musicals</u>. N.Y.: Harry N.
Abrams, 1981.

This is a big picture and word book on the history of
the Hollywood musical. It includes Keel's SEVEN
BRIDES FOR SEVEN BROTHERS, CALAMITY JANE, ANNIE GET
YOUR GUN, SHOW BOAT, KISS ME, KATE, KISMET, and ROSE
MARIE.

B698. Shipman, David. The Great Movie Stars the International Years. N.Y.: Hill and Wang, 1980.

Shipman profiles over 230 stars from the postwar
period. Keel is one of the profiles and is pictured
in PAGAN LOVE SONG (under his profile), in SEVEN
BRIDES FOR SEVEN BROTHERS (under Jane Powell), in
SHOW BOAT (under Kathryn Grayson), and in CALAMITY
JANE (under Doris Day).

B699. _____. Judy Garland: The Secret Life of an
American Legend. N.Y.: Hyperion, 1993.

Shipman discusses Keel being chosen for the film
ANNIE GET YOUR GUN and of Garland's concern about his
overshadowing her. He also mentions that Keel and
Hutton were considered for MGM's BILLY ROSE'S JUMBO.
Shipman states that Hutton's film career was cut
short because of her quarrel with Paramount. He said
that Keel felt that Hutton was so concerned with her
being successful in ANNIE GET YOUR GUN that she did
not consider her fellow players. It is stated that
Keel also thought that MGM made a mistake by letting
Garland go.

B700. Simas, Rick. The Musicals No One Came to See. N.Y.:
Garland, 1987.

The book lists musicals that flopped on Broadway,
Off-Broadway, and during out-of-town tryouts between
1943-1983. Keel is covered under AMBASSADOR, and
SARATOGA.

B701. Springer, John. All Talking! All Singing! All
Dancing!. N.Y.: Cadillac Publishing, 1966.

This is a pictorial history of the film musical.
Keel is included in KISS ME, KATE, SEVEN BRIDES FOR
SEVEN BROTHERS, and KISMET.

B702. Stubblebine, Donald. Cinema Sheet Music. N.C.
McFarland, 1991.

The book is arranged by film and lists the sheet music
for that film. Also included is the song publisher,
and who appears on the cover.

B703. Suskin, Steven. Opening Night on Broadway. N.Y.:
Schirmer Books, 1990.

The book gives some credits, cast, opening date,
theatre, reviews, Tony Awards, number of

performances, and a scorecard of reviews. SARATOGA
is covered.

B704. Taylor, John Russell and Jackson, Arthur. <u>The
Hollywood Musical</u>. N.Y.: McGraw-Hill, 1971.

One section of the book gives an overview of musical
films, another section gives a filmography, and a
third section profiles on musical performers.

B705. Terrace, Vincent. <u>Encyclopedia of Television Series</u>,
<u>Pilots, and Specials</u>. N.Y.: New York Zeotrope, 1986.

One volume covers in detail TV series, pilots, and
specials for the years 1937-1973, another volume
1974-1984. A third volume is an index to the other
volumes.

B706. Thomas, Tony. <u>The Films of Kirk Douglas</u>. N.J.:
Citadel Press, 1972.

This is a pictorial account of the life and career of
Kirk Douglas and includes the film WAR WAGON.

B707. Thompson, Howard, editor. <u>The New York Times Guide to</u>
<u>Movies on TV</u>. IL: Quadrangle Books, 1970.

This paperback gives credits, cast, plots, one-line
and capsule reviews of over 2,000 films with a picture
of each.

B708. Tornabene, Lyn. <u>Long Live the King</u>. N.Y.: Putnam's
Sons, 1976.

This is a biography on Clark Gable. The book
includes background information on the filming of
ACROSS THE WIDE MISSOURI.

B709. Vallance, Tom. <u>The American Musical</u>. N.Y.: A. S.
Barnes, 1970.

This paperback lists persons who were in film
musicals and their musical credits.

B710. <u>Variety Film Reviews 1949-1953</u> (Volume 8). N.Y.:
Garland, 1983.

This is one volume in a set and gives reprints of
reviews appearing in <u>Variety</u>.

B711. <u>Variety Film Reviews 1954-1958</u> (Volume 9). N.Y.:
Garland, 1983.

This volume also gives reprints of film reviews
appearing in <u>Variety</u>.

B712. Warren, John. <u>Warren's Movie Poster Price Guide</u>.
TN: Overstreet Publications, 1986.

This paperback gives the prices for various size posters of films between 1930-1969.

B713. Weaver, John. Forty Years of Screen Credits 1929-1969. N.J.: Scarecrow Press, 1970.

This two-volume book lists stars alphabetically and gives their film credits chronologically.

B714. Whitburn, Joel. Top LP's 1945-1972. WI: Record Research, 1973.

The book gives, by artist, the date a record reached the charts, the top position reached, and how long the record was charted. It also does the same for cast and soundtrack albums.

B715. _____. Top Pop Albums 1955-1985. WI: Record Research, 1985.

This book gives, by artist, the date the record reached the charts, the top position reached, and how long the record remained on the charts. It also does the same for cast and soundtrack albums.

B716. Who's Who in America. IL: Marquis Who's Who, 1977.

The 39th edition is in two volumes and profiles persons from all walks of life. It profiles Keel.

B717. Wiley, Mason and Bona, Damien. Inside Oscar. N.Y.: Ballantine Books, 1986.

The book gives a season by season history of the Oscar including presenters, and singers of nominated songs.

B718. Willis, John. Theatre World 1967-1968. N.Y.: Crown, 1968.

Volume 24 covers the theatre productions for the 1967-1968 season and includes a picture of each Broadway, off-Broadway and touring production. Keel is covered in the touring production of ON A CLEAR DAY YOU CAN SEE FOREVER.

B719. _____. Theatre World 1972-1973. N.Y.: Crown, 1974.

This volume covers the 1972-1973 theatre season and covers Keel in AMBASSADOR.

B720. Woll, Allen. Songs From Hollywood Musical Comedies, 1927 to the present: A Dictionary. N.Y.: Garland, 1976.

The first part of the book lists songs alphabetically and the second half by film with star,
director, and recording.

B721. Young, Christopher. <u>The Films of Doris Day</u>. N.J.:
Citadel Press, 1977.

This is a pictorial history of Miss Day's life and
career. It covers each of her films in detail and
includes Keel in the film CALAMITY JANE.

SONG INDEX

The songs in this index are arranged in a letter-by-letter
format. Numbers without letters preceding them refer to
page numbers. Those preceded by a letter correspond to the
section and entry number: S (Stage), F (Film), BC (Broadcast), D (Discography), SM (Sheet Music), NC (Night Clubs
and Concerts).

TITLE INDEX

Titles for stage, film, recording, broadcasting credits are listed in this index in a letter-by-letter format. Numbers without letters preceding them refer to page numbers. Those preceded by a letter correspond to the section and entry number: S (Stage), F (Film), BC (Broadcast), D (Discography), SM (Sheet Music), V (Videolog), NC (Night Clubs and Concerts), B (Annotated Bibliography).

GENERAL INDEX

Names, literary titles, theatres, companies and organiza-
tions are listed in this index in a letter-by-letter format.
Numbers without letters preceding them refer to page
numbers. Those preceded by a letter correspond to the
section and entry number: S (Stage), F (Film), BC (Broadcast), D (Discography), SM (Sheet Music), V (Videolog), NC
(Night Clubs and Concerts), B (Annotated Bibliography).

About the Author

BRUCE R. LEIBY is a freelance writer. His previous publications include *Gordon MacRae: A Bio-Bibliography* (Greenwood Press, 1991).

Titles in
Bio-Bibliographies in the Performing Arts

ISBN 0-313-28456-3

90000>

EAN

9 780313 284564

HARDCOVER BAR CODE